THE HOUSE OF JAIPUR

JOHN ZUBRZYCKI

The House of Jaipur

*The Inside Story of India's Most
Glamorous Royal Family*

HURST & COMPANY, LONDON

First published by Juggernaut Books 2020.

First published in the United Kingdom in 2021 by
C. Hurst & Co. (Publishers) Ltd.
This paperback edition first published by
C. Hurst & Co. (Publishers) Ltd.,
New Wing, Somerset House,
Strand, London WC2R 1LA
Printed in the United Kingdom

A Cataloguing-in-Publication data record for this book
is available from the British Library.

ISBN: 9781787389595

This book is printed using paper from registered sustainable
and managed sources.

www.hurstpublishers.com

To my late mother, Aleksandra Zubrzycka

CONTENTS

IMAGE CREDITS

Cover image: Alamy Stock Photo

Gayatri Devi and Sawai Man Singh ll of Jaipur, shortly after their wedding. Alamy Stock Photo.

Gayatri Devi and Man Singh found that many of the promises made to the princes at the time of Independence in 1947 were soon broken. Alamy Stock Photo.

Maharani Gayatri Devi on her wedding day with Sawai Man Singh II Bahadur, May 1940. Alamy Stock Photo.

Gayatri Devi, described in Vogue as one of the most beautiful women in the world, at the Rambagh Palace. Portrait by Cecil Beaton. Wikimedia Commons

Portrait of Maharani Indira Devi of Cooch Behar (Gayatri Devi's mother) by Philip de Laszlo, c. 1928. 'There is a delicate, studied, almost insolent self-assurance about her pose.' Wikimedia Commons

Gayatri Devi and Man Singh ll with Queen Elizabeth and Prince Philip in Jaipur, 1961. The nine-foot, eight-inch tiger was shot by Prince Philip. This photo op was followed by a champagne lunch in the jungle. Alamy Stock Photo

US First Lady Jackie Kennedy with Gayatri Devi and Man Singh ll at a polo exhibition match in Jaipur, 1962. Man Singh ll would die on the polo field in 1970, aged fifty-seven. Alamy Stock Photo

Jagat, the only child of Gayatri Devi and Man Singh ll. Photo courtesy of Princess Rajawongse Priyanandana Rangsit of Thailand

Top: Gayatri Devi campaigning as a Swatantra Party candidate during the Lok Sabha elections in 1962. Dinodia Photos RM/Alamy Stock Photo

IMAGE CREDITS

Gayatri Devi and her stepson Bhawani Singh (Bubbles) in 1998. The India Today Group/Getty Images

Jaipur's last maharaja, Bhawani Singh. The India Today Group, Getty Images.

A view of the Maharani Gayatri Devi Girls's High School, Jaipur. Matteo Omied/Alamy Stock Photo

Maharani Gayatri Devi at the Polo Ground, during the Maharaj Prithi Singh Foundation Polo Cup in Jaipur. Pandit Vivek/Alamy Stock Photo

Diya Kumari and her mother, Padmini, during Holi celebrations at the City Palace, 2018. Padmini proved to be a formidable fighter for her family's interests. Nur Photo/Getty Images

Padmanabh Singh during his eighteenth birthday celebrations in 2016 when he became 'titular maharaja' of Jaipur, succeeding his grandfather Bhawani Singh. Hindustan Times/Getty Images

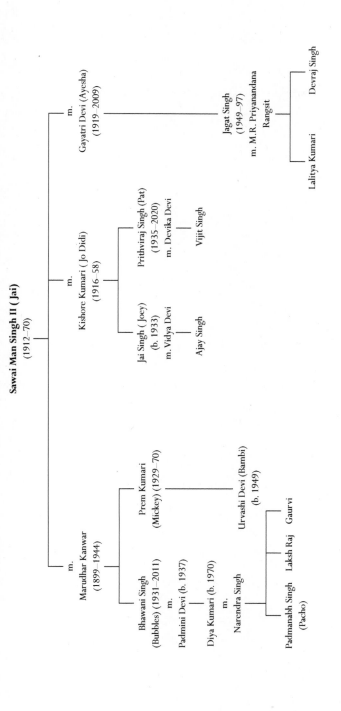

INTRODUCTION

Every year on the full moon night of Sharad Purnima, the harvest festival that coincides with the end of the monsoon, Gayatri Devi would hold a party on the rooftop terrace of her residence, Lily Pool. In Hindu tradition the festival commemorates Krishna's amorous dance of divine love with the female goatherds, or gopis. To reflect the light of the moonbeams, idols of the god are adorned with silver and dressed in white silk. Bowls of a heavenly rice pudding, kheer, absorb the moon's cosmic rays and are distributed as prasad, a food offered to the gods, the following morning. When Gayatri Devi celebrated the festival, there were no electric lights, just the glow of the celestial body. The table service was silver but the dress code and decorations were strictly pale pink—as was the colour of her city. She was, after all, the Queen of Jaipur.

There have been no parties here for well over a decade. Lily Pool's art deco facade is showing its age. Plaster used to repair the walls has cracked and mould from the monsoon rains has stained the paintwork. Lily Pool was once part of the sprawling Rambagh Palace complex, the home of Gayatri Devi and her husband, Sawai Man Singh II, the Maharaja of Jaipur, before it was turned into a five-star hotel.

For years, the only boundary separating Rambagh from Lily Pool was a fringe of bushes and tall ashoka trees. Now a wire fence and a locked gate bar access to the hotel. The locks were put on by the hotel staff in the days after Gayatri Devi's death in July 2009, ostensibly over non-payment of rent. Overnight a brick wall came up, sealing off access to the swimming pool—another symbol of the litigation that sullies the otherwise idyllic surroundings. Across the road from Lily Pool, grounds that once housed horse stables have been turned into a mothballed sports facility, part of a land acquisition drive by the Jaipur Development Authority (JDA).

1

Guests once described Lily Pool as 'heaven on earth'. In the gathering darkness it feels more like an entombed reliquary of distant dreams and arrested glamour.

I am meeting Ayub Khan, whose father once worked at the Rambagh Palace. Khan used to earn a few rupees a day as Gayatri Devi's ballboy on Lily Pool's now abandoned tennis courts. After he completed his college degree, she offered him a job as a typist and bought him a trusty Godrej manual typewriter. It was a trajectory that ultimately saw him become her principal private secretary and a close confidant, often accompanying his employer on her annual visits to Britain. For three decades Khan typed all her correspondence—responses to constituents seeking help for their daughters' dowries, invitations to heads of state to visit her in the Indian winter, complaints to politicians who were neglecting Jaipur's heritage. 'Every year she would send Prince Philip a box of Alphonso mangoes for his birthday,' recalls Khan, who regularly met the British royal at polo matches in England. I imagine Khan's humbleness appealed to Gayatri Devi, who championed those she liked but could be ruthless towards those she didn't.

It is only a decade since Gayatri Devi died, but such was her stature it could have been a few weeks ago. Her memory is revered, her portrait found in many Jaipur homes—though strangely enough not in the City Palace Museum. She was the woman who took on Indira Gandhi, winning three straight elections despite neither speaking nor understanding the language of her constituents, then paid for her success with a lengthy incarceration in Delhi's notorious Tihar Jail. Her ghost-written memoir, *A Princess Remembers*, is still a bestseller, though as a historian I found it more valuable as a resource for what she omitted than what she left in. *Life* and *Vogue* magazines ranked Gayatri Devi with her doe-like eyes, flawless complexion and jetblack hair that fell on her shoulders in perfectly cascading waves, one of the world's most beautiful women—'a dream in sari and jewels'.[1]

Gayatri Devi and Man Singh, or Ayesha and Jai as they were known to their friends—are central to the story of Jaipur over the past century. But the predominantly hagiographic accounts of their lives mask a complex, often tragic and sometimes dark tapestry. Despite being brought up in Cooch Behar, in Bengal, one of India's most progressive princely states where polygamy was frowned upon, Ayesha agreed to be the Maharaja's third wife, knowing she would have to surrender to the norms of the ultra-conservative warrior ethos of Hindu Rajput society. Jai was also an ambiguous character. His duties as a ruler often came a distant second to indulging in the distractions that Western society had to offer—polo, parties and beautiful women. The British accused him of doing too little for the people of his state. Following Independence, stripped of all his powers as a ruler by the Indian government, it became almost impossible for him to do anything meaningful for those very same people.

Today, Jaipur is synonymous with the romance and valour of princely India. The city's romanticized mythology owes much to its First Family. Jai set the sporting world ablaze as captain of the most successful polo team of its day. In the 1950s and 1960s, Jai and Ayesha were India's golden couple, its answer to John and Jackie Kennedy, Queen Elizabeth and Prince Philip. They were the only Indians invited to Truman Capote's Black & White Ball in 1966 at New York's Plaza Hotel—and Ayesha was the only woman who was allowed to break the dress code, arriving in a gold sari and a necklace of emeralds. Frank Sinatra, Rose Kennedy and the Duke and Duchess of Windsor were there too. All were friends of the Jaipurs.

Handsome, personable, athletic and urbane, Jai was the quintessential modern-day maharaja, with a portfolio of gleaming palaces bursting with taxidermied tigers and sporting trophies, garages full of collectible cars and stables full of polo ponies and caparisoned elephants. Ayesha, like her mother, Indira Devi of Cooch Behar, was unique among Indian maharanis, breaking the stereotype of Indian princesses demurely hidden behind their veils. Born into a small eastern princedom, she grew to be a woman who was an international social celebrity, in a class apart from the maharanis of bigger, twenty-one-gun-salute princely states such as Gwalior or Kashmir. She combined the exotic allure of the East with the sophistication of Western aristocracy. Schooled in England and Switzerland, she spoke French better than she spoke Hindi, danced with the grace of a professional and rode horses as if she had been bred for the sport. She wore her trademark chiffon saris with the same stylish elan as she wore trousers, while sipping cocktails and smoking her fashionably long cigarettes. As a couple, Jai and Ayesha entertained their Western friends as royally and lavishly in London, New York and Paris as in their magnificent palaces, forts and hunting lodges in Rajasthan. In the hierarchy of India's princely states, Jaipur was not the most important, but it was the most evocative, the most romantic, the most glamorous. 'Everyone who can possibly contrive it goes to Jaipur. There is no other place quite like it,' wrote Rosita Forbes in the 1930s.[2]

* * *

Jai bequeathed a complicated legacy when he died suddenly in 1970 at the age of fifty-seven while playing polo in Cirencester. He had married three wives, fathered five children, added to his ancestral properties and established a network of trusts to manage the family's wealth. He was a disciplinarian with his family. For as long as he was alive, a certain level of harmony and probity was observed. And then the cracks slowly widened. The dispute over who should inherit his estate now spans three generations. The litigation involves property, shares, tax liabilities, trusts and moveable wealth such as gold and jewellery. As one set of litigants dies, their children inherit a poisoned chalice of complex court proceedings that range from the comical to the tragic. Allegations of forged wills, doctored share certificates, non-disclosure of assets, of treasures gone missing, of sick or senile members being made to sign away their fortunes, lead all the way up to India's Supreme Court.

Royal disputes are nothing new in India. Udaipur, Gwalior and Hyderabad grabbed the headlines for decades with their very public spats over eye-watering amounts of wealth. But in terms of complexity, the House of Jaipur is in a league of its own. Mother versus stepson, half-brother versus half-brother, mother-in-law versus daughter-in-law, uncle versus nephew—the list goes on, cutting across what were once close familial ties.

Not all the animosity relates to legal disputes. Personalities and politics pervade many aspects of this saga. When Ayesha and her stepson Bhawani Singh were imprisoned in Tihar Jail by Indira Gandhi during the Emergency, the rest of the family came together and lobbied politicians and heads of state for their release. A decade later,

Ayesha and Bhawani Singh were shunning each other's company. When Bhawani Singh ran for the Congress party in 1989, Ayesha actively campaigned for his Bharatiya Janata Party (BJP) opponent.

Centuries-old traditions colliding head-on with rapid societal change are bound to cause instability. Laws of primogeniture that once governed successions in princely families no longer apply, but their descendants cling to them nevertheless. A ruler's wealth was once measured in the extent of his landholdings and the strength of his fortifications. Today it is hidden in trusts and offshore bank accounts. Throw in trophy ancestral properties, Persian carpets dating to the Mughal period, precious miniatures and priceless jewels brought back as war bounty from the sacking of Kabul, and one has all the ingredients for a long, complex and bitter confluence of disputes.

* * *

It is impossible to write about the House of Jaipur from the final decades of the British Raj until now without mentioning the years of litigation and antagonism that have torn the family apart. But that was not my intention when embarking on this book. As anyone who has stood by Maota Lake and looked up at the crenellated outline of Amber Fort or sat spellbound in the mirrored Shobha Niwas inside the City Palace can attest, the Kachchwaha Rajputs, Jaipur's rulers, were an extraordinary dynasty. The Kachchwahas trace their lineage to Kush, the son of Lord Ram, the mythical king of Ayodhya, whose reign is immortalized in the *Ramayana*. It is a legacy that the BJP politician Diya Kumari, the mother of the current 'maharaja', Padmanabh Singh,[3] wastes no time in reminding her constituents. As confirmed by palace genealogists, the polo-playing, catwalk-modelling royal who in 2019 made the cover of *Brides* magazine is the 311th descendant of Lord Ram and a potential claimant to what was until recently India's most disputed holy site, Ayodhya.[4]

The Kachchwahas originated in Gwalior in central India, before being driven westwards. The first ruler of the current dynasty, Dhula Rai, conquered a territory known as Dhundar from rival Rajput clans and Mina tribals in the eleventh century. His son Kakildeva captured Amber Fort, which remained the capital for the next six centuries. In the chaos that followed the death of the Mughal Emperor Aurangzeb in 1707, the dynasty's thirtieth ruler, Jai Singh II, decided to build a new capital laid out on a plan that combined the ancient Hindu treatise on architecture, the Shilpa Shastra, with the layout of Europe's greatest cities and his own ideas. His aim, writes the historian Giles Tillotson, was 'to assert himself and his kingdom as an alternative power base to rival the Mughals'.[5] In 1699, when he was eight years old, Jai Singh met Aurangzeb at his camp near Agra. In a famous exchange the Mughal Emperor took the child's hand and asked him: 'Now what will you do?' to which Jai Singh replied: 'Nothing, I am in secure hands.' Impressed by his intelligence, Aurangzeb called him 'Sawai' or as good as 'one-and-a-quarter' men. Ever since the title was formalized as per an edict granted by the Mughal emperor Farrukhsiyar in 1713, it has been used by all Jaipur's rulers, together with the practice of flying two flags, one full and one quarter-sized, from the top of the City Palace, whenever the head of the family is in residence. As the city grew, Jaipur began to attract some of India's most talented artists and ateliers, whose descendants are still producing fine paintings, exquisite textiles, high quality jewellery, marble statuary and other crafts.

In folklore, the Rajputs had a reputation for being a meat-eating, opium-imbibing and alcohol-guzzling martial race. 'A Rajput who reads will never ride a horse' goes an old Marwari proverb. But even a cursory examination of their history reveals that the opposite is true. Once invited into a Rajput family's home, I often began by asking my hosts to explain the stories behind photographs hanging on the walls or displayed on cabinets and side tables. Births, coronations, weddings, elephant processions, polo matches, the odd British Viceroy and the inevitable group shot of nobles standing over the corpse of a tiger told of a long and glorious legacy. Badges pinned on khaki uniforms were a reminder of the role their ancestors played in foreign fields of war. Over cups of tea and glasses of whisky, I was regaled with tales from history and offered lessons on etiquette and ritual. I started to appreciate the sophistication of Rajput society, the importance of close familial ties, the respect for elders and the legacy of their ancestors—something far from unique in India but taken more seriously than I had encountered elsewhere.

The forebears of these stately families called themselves Rajputs to differentiate themselves from other Kshatriyas. The word comes from the Sanskrit rajaputra meaning 'son of kings' and implies a royal ancestry—though that was not always the case. The origin of the Rajputs is the subject of fierce debate, with some historians claiming they were descendants of the Scythians. Others classify them as a caste rather than an ethnic grouping. What is clear is that they ruled over much of northern and western India from the eighth century until they were pushed back to their desert domains by the coming of Arab and Turkic invaders from Central Asia from the twelfth century onward. Their strong military ethos won them admiration and notoriety. The reliance of Rajput warriors on intoxicants before riding into battle, the seventeenth-century English traveller John Fryer noted, 'makes them run upon any Enterprize with a ringing Resolution to die or be victorious. Before Engaging, it is usual for them to embrace one another, as if parting for another World.'[6] During his travels, the East India Company envoy William Finch heard of a Rajput captain who thrust his arm into the mouth of a lion to save his king.

The temptation to overplay the valour and chivalry of the Rajputs is largely the legacy of the early-nineteenth-century English historian James Tod, who almost single-handedly cast them as warrior heroes in the European imagination. Referred to as 'the Herodotus of the history of Rajasthan', it was Tod who helped construct the martial race theory, according to which only certain Indian communities were suitable for recruitment into the Indian army. 'The poorest Rajput of this day retains all the pride of ancestry, often his sole inheritance; he scorns to hold the plough, or to use his lance but on horseback. In these aristocratic ideas he is supported by his reception amongst his superiors and the respect paid to him by his inferiors,' Tod wrote in his two-volume *Annals and Antiquities of Rajasthan* published in 1829.[7] And it was Tod who argued in favour of non-interference in the affairs of the Rajput states and that Indian rulers be treated as loyal vassals, rather than being subjected to direct rule as advocated by Utilitarians such as James Mill. Tod's reputation for favouring Rajput rulers over the British prompted Sir David Ochterlony, the Resident of Rajputana and his direct superior, to characterize him as 'too much of a Rajpoot himself to deal with the Rajpoots'.[8]

Jaipur was one of the 562 princely states that covered two-fifths of India's land mass and one-third of India's population at the time of Independence. Nominally independent, these states recognized the paramountcy of the British Crown. In return for the protection of the Crown against internal and external threats, they ceded their autonomy in areas such as foreign relations and communications. The British had the final say in matters of marriage and succession and could unseat a ruler for maladministration. The perfidy of the Raj in interfering in every aspect of their internal and external relations reached its zenith in states such as Jaipur and Hyderabad.

* * *

After 1947, the feudal order on which princely India was built broke down, forcing erstwhile royals to redefine themselves. But as the story of the House of Jaipur shows, abandoning their antediluvian mindset was not always easy. Traditions die hard and going against ancient codes relating to the role of women, marriage, adoption and one's place in the social hierarchy would lead to schisms within families. When Jai and Ayesha found their relevance as royals slipping, they began to dabble in politics and spent increasing amounts of time orbiting the world of Western aristocracy where deference to blueblooded lineages remains strong.

The transition to modernity was not helped by a government bent on hastening the end of the princely order. For the princes, the ultimate betrayal would come in 1971 with the abolition of the privy purses by Prime Minister Indira Gandhi. Already feeling cast adrift because of the rapid changes going on around them, the loss of privileges came as a further blow to their prestige. Some found new roles for themselves as hoteliers, army officers and diplomats, or as patrons of the arts and upholders of their culture and traditions. Others joined politics, often in opposition to the Congress party that had consigned them to oblivion. Although they earned the wrath of Jawaharlal Nehru and his daughter, Indira Gandhi, they became a powerful political force, proof of their continuing popularity.

In the space of just a couple of generations, India's royalty underwent changes that evolved over hundreds of years in Britain and Europe, leaving some stranded between two worlds. The

INTRODUCTION

House of Jaipur serves as a prism for viewing these momentous changes, as democracy evolved and defined the shape of post-Independence India and the lives of its citizenry. The days when Jaipur's rulers enjoyed the kind of wealth that funded jewellery-buying sprees at Cartier's in Paris, when they could slaughter dozens of tigers and leopards during their hunting parties and break speed limits with impunity while driving their Bentleys, are long gone. Legally and constitutionally, members of erstwhile royal families have no more rights than any other citizen of India. Though many of them still retain a glamour and mystique that helps them win parliamentary and state elections, the power and glory that was once their birthright is no more. Like any other political candidate, they must go from house to house, from village to village to canvass for support. And in today's India their prestige and relevance depends more on their entrepreneurial and managerial ingenuity than on their inheritance.

* * *

So much has been written about the opulence and glamour of the princely states, it is easy to overlook the feuds, calamities and tragedies that afflicted these families. Whether through alcoholism or accidents, too many lives were cut short. Many of the stories in this book are deeply personal and reveal for the first time how these events and tragedies shaped the lives of members of the Jaipur royal family and their closest relations. In assembling this account, I have spoken to all three branches of the family and as wide a range of individuals as possible. I have also consulted thousands of pages of court records and archival material to gain a better understanding of the roots of the current conflicts and the personalities involved. Unfortunately, objectivity is a rare commodity in the Pink City. Apart from a few exceptions, what goes on behind the walls of the City Palace has mostly been off limits to journalists and writers. Stories of intrigues and indiscretions, mostly unverifiable, of 'wheels within wheels', as one source puts it, would fill many a reporter's notebook. In the course of a single day, a person can be deified by one interviewee and vilified by the next, always with a level of certainty that leaves the uninitiated baffled and bemused.

Based on the sheer volume of litigation alone, it would be easy to characterize Jaipur as just another example of a royal family riven by disputes over property and wealth—an aristocratic soap opera where the princely protagonists alternate between waging wars and entering into temporary truces, with a final resolution always just out of reach. The saga of the House of Jaipur is much deeper than that. Behind their carefully curated reputations are complex individuals whose lives were touched by many of the great events of India's history over the last century. The Kachchwaha dynasty has a rich and proud past. Rulers such as Jai Singh I and Ram Singh II managed to put internecine struggles to one side and keep outside interference to a minimum, devoting their energies to creating dreamlike palaces, forts and extraordinary cityscapes, and patronizing the arts. It is perhaps these rulers that the present generation increasingly looks to as role models, as they create new roles for themselves, finding new ways to take their legacy forward while retaining the best attributes of Jaipur's glorious past.

Rajput valour, once tested on the battlefield, is now being played out in the political domain, in corporate boardrooms and on the sporting field. And, as this book also shows, it is in these arenas that the House of Jaipur's fighting spirit is now beginning to shine through.

A BOY NAMED MORMUKUT

Along the route from Jaipur to Kota, the modern clashes with the medieval. It is the Hindu month of Bhadra and traffic on the six-lane highway often slows to a crawl as long processions of pilgrims making their way on foot to the shrine of the folk deity Devnarayan at Newai spill on to the road. Instead of bhajans, Bollywood music bursts from giant speakers mounted on tractors decorated with tinsel. The most devout of all will perform dandapranama, lying prostrate on the ground, then walking two steps and repeating the ritual until they reach the shrine.

Ninety kilometres from Jaipur there is a turn-off for Natwar and for a while the slender strip of bitumen points towards some distant hills. The monsoon rains have been abundant this year. The fields are waterlogged; the dams and reservoirs are full. The road snakes past fields of corn so tall they block out the surrounding landscape. Most of the time it seems to meander without purpose, bypassing an abandoned sugar mill before skirting the town of Siwar, its bulbous fort giving credence to an otherwise innocuous thikana, or noble's estate. Teflon-skinned buffalo saunter lazily down the middle of the road and pigs rut in the mud. As we detour past a lake with a pleasure pavilion that appears to float on its waters, a black cobra slithers across the road—a sign of good luck, my driver assures me.

My destination is Isarda, the birthplace of Mormukut Singh, the village boy who was rechristened Sawai Man Singh II and became the most recognizable face of Indian royalty as the Maharaja of Jaipur. Most people can be forgiven for believing that India's maharajas and rajas, nawabs and nizams knew nothing but opulence. Stories of princes being weighed on their birthdays in silver and precious jewels and showered with rose petals every time they entered their palace gates as their numerous wives and concubines peered through latticed windows of the zenana (women's quarters), are often apocryphal. Jaipur's most famous ruler had a much humbler beginning.

Isarda was once a small thikana, one of hundreds scattered around the erstwhile princely state of Jaipur. Thakurs or nobles were originally granted jagirs or land by the Jaipur durbar. In addition to paying a proportion of the rent they received from their jagirs, they had to provide men, horses and elephants for the maharaja in times of war. Snug inside their fortified palaces, the thakurs patronized artists and musicians, while bards celebrated their family's lineage and deeds.

Isarda is so insignificant that once off the main highway my driver has to stop every few kilometres to ask directions. The town first announces itself as a signpost at a level crossing followed by a row of disused shops outside a railway station. Just when it appears there is nothing more and the road narrows further, a sharp left turn reveals an ancient archway topped by a crenellated wall overgrown with vegetation. The fortifications that once protected Isarda from marauding bands of Marathas, Hindu warrior clans from Western India, have also served to keep it in a kind of time warp. Only one road wide enough for a car loops through the town before exiting another gateway that older residents can still recall being locked every night. Most working-age men are engaged in playing cards.

On the slightest of rises is Isarda Fort, its thick walls hiding a network of durbar halls and pavilions, courtyards, kitchens, storerooms, elephant and horse stables and zenana quarters. Before many of the surrounding houses added a second storey, the fort would have been a prominent landmark, a reminder of the power its thakur once wielded over the surrounding villages. Today it wears an abandoned look—its heavy wooden doors clamped shut with two rusty padlocks and a length of steel cable for added security. Through a chink in the gate I can make out a guardhouse and an open area overgrown with vegetation almost blocking out a low set of buildings in the background. What lies beyond, and the condition of those buildings, is impossible to ascertain. By standing on the roof of a temple at the back of the fort I see domed pavilions swallowed by trees. Wooden beams dislodged by the rain and wind hang precariously like giant scabs.

The fort has been sealed by an order of the Rajasthan High Court since 1996, leaving its once exquisitely painted interiors at the mercy of monkeys, peacocks, parrots and bats. I already knew that every significant property linked to the Jaipur royal family was the subject of litigation, some of it dating back more than three decades, but I never expected that this innocuous fort, not much larger in area than a cricket field, would also be contested. During his travels through Rajputana in the early nineteenth century, James Tod encountered many such contested fiefdoms that had succumbed to the ravages of time. 'The tiger and the wild boar had already become inmates of the capital and the bats flitted undisturbed in the palaces of her princes. The ante courts where the chieftains and their followers assembled to grace their prince's cavalcade were overgrown with dank shrubs and grass through which a mere footpath conducted the descendant of a hundred kings to the ruins of his capital.'[1]

Mormukut Singh was born behind these walls on 21 August 1912. He was the second son of Sawai Singh, the thakur of Isarda. Sawai Singh had inherited the family's jagir consisting of around sixty-five villages at the time of the Mughals. A man of little education, he was nevertheless a great marksman who boasted of killing more than 400 four hundred tigers in his lifetime. He was also fond of wrestling. Mormukut's mother lived in purdah and had her own jagir consisting of several villages, in return for which she had to pay for the wedding clothes and funeral expenses of their inhabitants.

The thakur of Isarda belongs to one of the six branches of the ruling Kachchwaha family of Jaipur, known as the Rajawats, from which a ruler can be adopted. The rise to prominence of the Kachchwaha Rajputs owed much to their marital and political alliances with the Mughals. Raja Bharmal was the first ruler of Amber to offer one of his daughters to the Mughal emperor Akbar, a shrewd move that ensured the longevity of the clan and the prosperity of his kingdom. The Amber rulers were prevented from expanding their territories, but their alliance with the Mughals protected them from internal and external threats. Bharmal and his sons were incorporated into the Mughal hierarchy as amirs in the imperial service. His grandson Man Singh I became the commander-in-chief of the Emperor Akbar's army. Other alliances with Rajput rulers followed, their steadfast loyalty providing crucial support for the expansion of the empire. In return, Akbar treated them on a par with his Mughal lieutenants, allowing them a measure of autonomy, freedom of religion and the right to follow their own traditions. Notes the historian John F. Richards: 'In accepting Akbar's service Rajput thakurs thereby accepted him as a Muslim Rajput who possessed far greater power and sovereignty than even the greatest of Rajput masters.'[2] Bardic tradition from this time equated Akbar with their great ancestor and cultural hero Ram, the righteous divine king. Two of his successors, Jahangir and Shah Jahan, were the sons of Rajput princesses. Many Rajput clans supplied wives for the Mughal emperors, the notable exception being the Sisodias of Mewar who viewed such alliances as disgraceful, leading to a schism among Rajputs that continued until well into the twentieth century.

Stories of Indian princes siring dozens of children from multiple wives and mistresses are often exaggerated, particularly when it came to the Rajputs who frequently had no legitimate male heirs. Adoption became the lynchpin of the inheritance system and on some estimates accounted for at least half of all successions among nobles and ruling princes. When it worked, it ensured continuity. The choice of a successor could be controlled and the adoption usually took place before the death of the ruler. There would then be a 'son' to light the funeral pyre. But if the strict rules governing the selection of an heir were broken, it could lead to bitter jealousies, feuds and even the threat of murder. Rajput history is replete with cases of legitimate heirs being set aside, illegitimate sons being adopted and the deceased ruler's senior widow deciding who would replace her husband on the gaddi.[3]

The authority on Rajput adoption, James Tod, wrote: 'Adoption is the preservative of honours and titles; the great fiefs of Rajasthan can never become extinct.'[4] For Tod the problem lay in the way adoptions were executed—too much consultation with too many vested interests over a long period of time being a sure recipe for internecine conflict.

> The chief and his wife first agitate the subject in private; it is then confided to the little council of the fief, and when propinquity and merit unite, they at once petition the prince to confirm their wishes, which are generally acceded to. So many interests are to be consulted on this occasion, that the blind partiality of the chief

to any particular object is always counterpoised by the elders of
the clan, who must have a pride in seeing a proper Thakur at their
head, and who prefer the nearest of kin, to prevent the disputes
which would be attendant on neglect in this point.[5]

Mormukut became Sawai Man Singh II after his adoption by his
uncle Maharaja Madho Singh II, who himself was adopted from
Isarda by Ram Singh II in 1880. The fort's locked entrance relates
to a third adoption. Its last occupant was Man Singh's elder brother
Bahadur Singh, who had three wives but no children—a potentially
fatal combination when valuable ancestral property with multiple
claimants is up for grabs. Following Rajput tradition, Bahadur ceremonially adopted his nephew and Man Singh's only son, Jagat, by
his third wife Gayatri Devi. The first sign of trouble came when
Bahadur died in 1970 and his widows began fighting over his possessions, leading to most of the rooms in the palace being sealed. By
the early 1980s, when Man Singh's biographer Quentin Crewe
ventured into the fort, the elephant houses were falling down and
many of the stairways were unsafe.

With a penchant for flared denim, leather jackets and bright floral
shirts, Jagat was cut from a different cloth to the average Rajput
thakur. I struggle to imagine what his close friend Mick Jagger thought
of Isarda when Jagat brought him here in 1985 or, for that matter,
what the locals would have thought of the lanky, long-haired rock
star. In those days, reaching Isarda by road required a sturdy four-
wheel drive. Priyanandana Rangsit, Jagat's Thai ex-wife, remembers
the inside of the fort being buried in bat shit and having to sleep in
windowless mosquito-infested rooms. After showing Jagger and
Priyanandana around the interior of his ancestral home, he took them
to the kothi, or bungalow, his father had built close to the Banas river,
which in those days had yet to be stripped of all its fittings.

For once there is no court order barring entry to the kothi, but
the dwelling is empty, traces of gold paint around a fireplace that is
now a Hindu shrine the only hint of its former opulence. From the
rooftop I can see the Banas River in all its monsoonal magnificence.
The seventy-year-old watchman who lives in a stone cottage next
to the kothi recalls dance parties that went on all night, with guests
consuming crates of champagne brought by plane from Jaipur to a
nearby private airstrip that Jai had built back in the 1930s. Groggy

and hung over, patrons would pile into jeeps for the bumpy ride to Sawai Madhopur and what is now the Ranthambore National Park for some shikar, bagging a few unfortunate tigers brought into range by beaters, before another night of partying at the royal hunting lodge.

When not entertaining his celebrity friends, Jagat was also expected to look after his uncle, something that Bahadur's second wife, Phanindra Raj Laxmi, claimed never happened. Allegedly fulfilling that role was Jagmohan, the son of Phanindra's lady-in-waiting. Regardless of his status, Jagmohan claims the fort was bequeathed to him in a will Phanindra made in 1985. Jagat and Priyanandana's son, Devraj Singh, the Raja of Isarda, insists he is the fort's rightful owner and has filed a suit challenging the will's validity. The likelihood of the litigation coming to a conclusion before what is left of the structure falls into an irreparable state seems remote.

* * *

The centrality of Isarda to the story of Jaipur goes back to 1880 when Maharaja Ram Singh II lay on his deathbed. Born in 1833 and invested with full powers when he turned eighteen, his reign coincided with a greater involvement in Jaipur affairs by the British. He learned to speak and write English fluently and took steps to modernize his state, adding a waterworks and a cotton mill, and championing education—at least for the elite—by opening the Noble College for boys and the Maharaja's School for girls. He was also responsible for the construction of the Albert Hall Museum, one of India's first. Not all the changes were welcomed unanimously. His commissioning of wrought-iron gas lamps and carriage drives of hewn stone inscribed with a royal crest that imitated Queen Victoria's had, according to Rudyard Kipling, converted Jai Singh's city 'into a big bewildering practical joke'.[6]

The French traveller Louis Rousselet, who met Ram Singh in the late 1860s, described him as handsome in dress but with an indifference to ornament. 'He wore scarcely any jewels, and no sword or dagger, but an immense revolver was thrust into his belt from which hung a bunch of keys.'[7] Rousselet also noted the maharaja's interest in photography, perhaps the most striking legacy of his reign. He was the first Indian photographer to make portraits of the women of the zenana. None of them are veiled, nor are their poses sexually suggestive. Equally remarkable are his self-portraits. For the first time in the history of the Rajputs, a ruler is portrayed not as a warrior but as a frail man wearing thick glasses, sitting next to a table piled with books. When not posing as an ascetic, he is frequently shown wearing a Rajput turban and English trousers. It was said that the exposure time for photographs taken at his studio was measured not with a clock but by chanting mantras, Hindu devotional hymns.

Ram Singh's principal failure, if it can be termed that, was the lack of a male heir, prompting a succession crisis. To restrict the circle of claimants, laws were established in every state limiting this right to the issue of a certain family in each principality. In Jaipur, the senior branch of the ruling Rajawat family for the purpose of adoption was traditionally recognized as Jhalai, a thikana approximately twenty kilometres north of Isarda. As Ram Singh lay dying, the British Resident asked if he wanted to follow tradition and adopt a successor. He replied that he would but asked the British government to make the choice for him. When pressed a second time, just moments before his death, he named Kaim Singh, the younger son of the thakur of Isarda, as his heir.

Though tradition had been broken, the British were quietly relieved. The thakur of Jhalai at the time was paralysed and a drunkard. Kaim Singh was serving as a commander in the cavalry of the Nawab of Tonk, having been exiled from his home town by his elder brother because of a succession dispute. Barely literate, his upbringing in Isarda consisted mainly of wrestling lessons. It left him with an impressive physique, but not what it took to rule a state of Jaipur's stature and importance. After Kaim Singh was placed on the throne in 1880 as Madho Singh II, the British insisted that the Resident act as a 'joint president' of Jaipur's royal council for two years. The Resident's initial assessment of the new maharaja was unflattering to say the least. Though bright, he was seen as 'indolent, easily flattered, obstinate and fond of inappropriate company'.[8] With the British reluctant to hand over the reins of power, the period of joint regency was extended from two to five years.

The British underestimated the young ruler. Madho Singh turned out to be tough, shrewd and assertive, particularly when it came to dealing with the perennial problem of recalcitrant thakurs. As the historian Robert Stern points out, instead of integrating them into the workings of the durbar, he used his ruling powers to crush them.[9] Known for being an extremely orthodox Hindu, his devotion to his household deity, Gopalji, was such that every morning when he got up he would cover his eyes and grope his way to the special room where the statue resided so that it would be the first object that he saw.[10] Whereas Ram Singh adopted Western hobbies such as photography and wore spectacles, Madho Singh was, in the words of his court biographer Hanuman Sharma, of an 'old nature', preferring 'deshi' (indigenous) customs and 'swadeshi' (homespun) garb over 'videshi' (foreign) ways and clothes. But he also credits the maharaja with 'tending and watering the garden his predecessor had planted'.[11] Dams and canals added thousands of acres of land under cultivation; roads and railways were extended.

His relationship with the British was complicated. Though he was considered among the most loyal to them of all the princes, contributing funds to Britain's war effort against the Boers and its campaign in Chitral and Tirah on the north-west frontier, he was ostentatiously unenthusiastic about English society. He discouraged his nobles from interacting with the British and refused to ride in a motor car until the end of his life. The *Times* praised him for being a ruler who accepted 'all the scientific, economic and political advantages of Western enlightenment', while maintaining all the customs of his forefathers. He had set an example of 'how to become an enlightened and progressive ruler and yet remain an orthodox and pious Hindu'.[12] 'No crowned head in all Asia is surrounded by a more passionately attached people than Madho Singh Bahadur,' enthused another newspaper. 'Native civilization in India is its very best in Jaipur.'[13]

In 1901, Madho Singh was one of the few princes to receive an invitation to attend the coronation of Edward VII. This presented a dilemma. Crossing the kala pani, or black water, would entail flouting the rules of orthodox Hinduism. Just a few years previously he had used this excuse to prevent one of his nobles travelling by ship to England for medical treatment. Madho Singh's quandary was solved by a conclave of Jaipur pandits who ruled that he could go provided he only ate prasad. That meant travelling with his favourite deity Gopalji and that in turn meant finding a vessel on which cows had never been slaughtered or alcohol served.

Thomas Cook, which had its own 'Eastern Princes' Department' that specialized in catering to potentates travelling to Europe with 200 servants, ten elephants and thirty-three tame tigers, came up with a solution: the SS *Olympia*. The passenger liner had just been commissioned. Six special kitchens were constructed, including one for the deity Gopalji, one for the maharaja and one for the accompanying Brahmin priests. Flour, ghee, rice, sugar, lentils, dried vegetables and other necessities made up a large part of the 75,000 kilos of luggage that went from Jaipur to Bombay in eight railway carriages. On board the ship were three huge silver jars filled with enough Ganges water for the four-month-long return journey. A herd of cows provided milk for drinking and dung for purifying the kitchens and dining room. Before the ship's departure from Bombay, Varuna, god of the sea and winds, was propitiated by throwing gold and silver vessels, strings of pearls and precious silks into the water. Assembled on the pier to watch the spectacle were the wealthy merchants of Bombay, many of whom were Marwaris from Rajasthan. As the *Olympia* was being battered by a storm in the Arabian Sea, one of the silver jars was thrown overboard to placate the gods. After sailing through the Suez Canal, the ship berthed at Marseilles, where Madho Singh and his sizeable entourage boarded a train for Calais. On their arrival in Southampton, they were taken to More Lodge in Campden Hill, where a well was dug to provide purified water.

The spectacle of dozens of bejewelled Indian feudatories attending King Edward's coronation at Westminster Abbey sent the press into a frenzy. 'Ranged against the screen in the places of highest canonical honour, were a row of Indian feudatories, whose jewels rivalled in splendour those of the regalia which they had come to see assumed by their Imperial Suzerain. In the stall of the canon residentiary sat the Maharajah of Jaipur, the lord of the coral city where he presides over the solemn worship of the Hindu Sun god.'[14] The *Boston Globe* described Madho Singh as enlightened, distinguished and 'one of the handsomest men in all India ... [a] true Oriental'. The paper also noted his loyalty, faith and duty to the king-emperor.[15]

* * *

Madho Singh might have been a loyal servant of the empire, but Rajput tradition would dictate the choice of his successor. His lack of a male heir had nothing to do with any physical inadequacy. He had dozens of concubines who enjoyed their own zenana quarters in specially constructed apartments in Nahargarh Fort, where he could visit them surreptitiously without earning the ire of his two official wives. His decision not to have children with either of his wives derived from a prophecy that if one of them produced a son he would die within six months. Though he fathered upwards of fifty children with his concubines, he had only one daughter with his senior wife.

Madho Singh's selection of his successor was the culmination of years of secret manoeuvring and palace intrigues. Following Ram Singh's decision to go against tradition and adopt an heir from Isarda, there had been unproven but persistent rumours of a secret undertaking that Jhalai would not be overlooked again. Isarda's claim was further undermined by the fact that its thakur, Sawai Singh, was himself adopted from some minor thikana with only distant ties to the ruling family, rather than a closer branch with a prior claim. But Jaipur's monarch saw things differently. He was afraid that if the eldest son of Jhalai's thakur Goverdhan Singh came to the throne he would not look after his mothers, widows and family after his death. His other reason was that Goverdhan Singh held a 'jagir' (feudal landholding) in Bikaner, from where he had been adopted. His late wife was the niece of the Maharaja of Bikaner and Madho Singh felt that such a close connection with a rival state would not be in Jaipur's interests. Colonel R.A.E. Benn, the Agent to the Governor General of Rajputana, summed up the situation in a memo to the India Office: 'Intrigue and bribery were playing a very prominent part in the Palace at the present moment.'[16]

In 1916, Madho Singh left instructions for the succession in a sealed envelope that was to be opened on his death by the viceroy, Lord Hardinge. The instructions were never revealed but the British believed his preference was for Gopal Singh, the favourite of his two morganatic sons, to inherit the gaddi. When Gopal died of smallpox in 1920, the maharaja asked for the sealed envelope to be returned. A few months later, he took the unusual measure of appointing two Englishmen to his royal council. They were Sir James Roberts, his physician, and Sir Charles Cleveland, an intelligence officer who had just retired as director of the Criminal Investigation Department. Both were 'old friends' of the maharaja but it was Cleveland who dominated the cabinet, becoming his de facto chief minister. His function was to gain British support for his choice of an official heir and stave off the inevitable opposition from the nobles of those Kachchwaha clans that missed out on getting their nominee in the top job. Once the new maharaja had been chosen, Cleveland was expected to block British interference in Jaipur's affairs until the boy achieved majority.[17]

In May 1920, Benn was told by a thakur from Jhalai that Madho Singh was preparing to adopt from Isarda and that if the plan went through there would be trouble. Benn's informant proved reliable. A few weeks later, the maharaja requested photographs of Sawai Singh's sons, Bahadur and Mormukut, who were then summoned to the City Palace. When they entered the durbar hall accompanied by their father, Madho Singh was sitting on a carpet with some courtiers. He asked the three to sit. Bahadur and his father obliged but Mormukut remained standing because he could not find a place, prompting the maharaja to ask the eight-year-old to sit on his lap. The act would later be seen as prophetic. A second incident that might have tipped the scales in Mormukut's favour occurred as the brothers were waiting to pay their respects to Madho Singh. When Mormukut got bored of waiting for the maharaja to accept his tribute, he dropped his hand to the side and pocketed the gold coin. This was interpreted as a sign of independence and character appropriate to a prince. A less prosaic reason for choosing Mormukut may have been Madho Singh's belief that the eldest son of a jagirdar (member of the landed aristocracy) should not be adopted as it would deprive his father of an heir. The Jaipur ruler might have also heard the story that when eight or nine years old, Mormukut had teased an elephant until it was so enraged that it charged at him. But instead of shouting for help the boy stood his ground until a mahout who saw what was happening brought the elephant under control. The British had a more sanguine explanation. Bahadur, they had heard from palace spies, was already showing a weakness for the bottle.

Madho Singh's plan to keep his choice a secret had little hope of succeeding, especially now that years of pent-up anger over his contemptuous treatment of the nobility was finally coming to a head. In September 1921, Jhalai staked its claim to the throne by bringing a petition to the Government of India stating that Goverdhan Singh was the rightful heir and that his claim was supported by the thakurs of Khetri, Samode, Diggi and Chomu as well as the Maharaja of Bikaner, Ganga Singh. The petition warned that violence could erupt if Rajput custom and Hindu law were overturned and cited instances where the British had backed the claims of the nearest relations over the preferences of a dying ruler. To concede to Madho Singh's request would put a question mark over all rightful claimants to princely thrones, the petition concluded.[18]

A crude attempt by the British to evade the issue by claiming they had no knowledge of who had been selected prompted a long letter from Maharaja Ganga Singh of Bikaner to the viceroy. The letter described Jaipur as a hotbed of intrigue and made sinister references to its ruler being manipulated by certain interests in the court. He then referred to a report that said large sums of money were being drained from the treasury 'for the marriage in heaven [!] of the two morganatic sons of His Highness the Maharaja of Jaipur, one of whom died recently'.[19]

The astonishing claim had some basis. The maharaja had been lavishing money on one of his favourite concubines, Roop Rai, whom British intelligence referred to as a 'female Rasputin'.[20] She was rumoured to possess hypnotic power and allegedly had three girls from the zenana beaten to death by eunuchs and had their bodies burned. Her modus operandi was to eavesdrop on Madho Singh whenever he was with his favourite queen. After the queen died, Roop Rai told the maharaja that his wife had appeared to her and asked for certain tasks to be carried out. Because she had overheard their conversations, she was able to persuade him she was telling the truth. She even convinced him that she could send the departed queen a message by meeting her in her dreams and asked him for money to arrange the heavenly marriage of his two morganatic sons, who had died before they reached their twenties. Speaking on behalf of one of them, she demanded money to treat him in the other world.[21]

Roop Rai had firmly entrenched herself as the dominant force in the zenana with the support of Kwasji Bala Bux. As the keeper of the ruler's wardrobe, Bala Bux controlled all access to the maharaja and was said to provide him with women to supplement the services of his wives and concubines. Despite warnings from the British and many of Jaipur's nobles that Bux was corrupt, he was promoted from being a valet to the rank of a noble and put in charge of five forts as well as the kapadwara, or treasury. By the end of Madho Singh's reign, Bala Bux had acquired so much power that the British felt that 'no administration can afford to disregard him'.[22] Their greatest fears, however, were that the dying maharaja was losing his control over Jaipur's durbar and falling deeper and deeper into the clutches of the zenana, just as they were trying to avert a political crisis over the succession. They were also terrified of the influence Roop Rai and Bala Bux would exert on his chosen successor.

Whether it was Roop Rai's vice-like grip or his fear of invoking the curse of his forefathers, Madho Singh continued to ignore the viceroy's insistence that he should make his choice public. Meanwhile, Jhalai kept piling on the pressure by presenting two more petitions endorsing Goverdhan Singh as the rightful heir. Madho Singh responded by accusing the Jhalai thakurs and their supporters of 'disloyalty and sedition' and barred them from the royal council and the palace. To reassert his authority, he convened an open durbar starting on 12 March 1921 to announce that he had chosen his successor but then stopped short of naming who that would be. Over the next three days, thousands of people came forward to sign a document that confirmed his power to adopt anyone of his choosing. Once again, the outliers were the thakurs of Jhalai, Khetri, Samode, Chomu and Diggi. For his part, Madho Singh refused to be swayed by the recalcitrant thakurs, sticking to his policy 'to reward and show special favour to those who are loyal' and 'punish the disloyal'.[23]

Believing that such absolutist behaviour might lead to open conflict and thereby derail an orderly succession, the British finally cajoled him into making a public announcement that Mormukut Singh would be the next maharaja. The worst-kept secret in Jaipur was finally out in the open and the last person to hear the news was Mormukut himself. He was too busy mucking around with his school friends in Kota and dreaming about shooting his first tiger, and not about becoming the thirty-ninth ruler of the Kachchwaha dynasty.

2

'THE LYING COURT'

To be 'reared in an Eastern palace' makes it impossible 'to think straightly or speak freely', an astute Rudyard Kipling observed after visiting Jaipur in the 1880s. Wandering through the great citadel of Amber, the *Civil and Military Gazette* reporter described 'cramped and darkened rooms, the narrow smooth-walled passages with recesses where a man might wait for his enemy unseen, the maze of ascending and descending stairs leading nowhither, the ever present screen of marble tracery that may hide or reveal so much'.[1] Kipling was not alone in his assessment. So infamous was Jaipur for its vortex of intrigues, it was referred to as the jhutha durbar, or lying court, by the British, who never knew when they were falling victim to an internecine power play. 'The purest intentions, the highest talents, will scarcely avail to counteract this systematic vice, and with one party at least, but eventually with all, the reputation of his government will be compromised,' wrote Anil Chandra Banerjee in his study of the Rajput states.[2]

For much of his rule, Madho Singh had been admired by his British overlords for showing 'great shrewdness and sagacity', but with his withdrawal to the zenana in his final years, Jaipur's affairs 'had lapsed into disorder'.[3] By 1920, as Mormukut Singh was being vetted as his heir, the maharaja had become so beguiled by his courtesan Roop Rai and his corrupt valet Bala Bux that Jaipur was demoted from jhutha durbar to the rank of randi ka raj, or a harlot's kingdom.[4]

On a chilly morning in March 1921, Mormukut and his friend Bhim Singh, the son of Maharao Umed Singh of Kota, stood in the courtyard of the Nobles' School waiting for the carriage that was to take them to the Chambal River for a day of shikar. Since there were no schools in Isarda, their father had sent Mormukut and Bahadur to Kota. One of their aunts was the wife of the state's ruler Umed Singh, while the other was married to Major General Onkar Singh of Palaitha. For Mormukut and his friends these were halcyon days with plenty of spare time for swimming, playing football, fishing, birdwatching, bullock cart rides—and crashing the first car ever driven in the state. Tutors taught them horsemanship and polo. But it was the shikars on the Chambal that Mormukut looked forward to most of all. Carriages would take them to the riverbank where they boarded the maharao's Scottish-built steamboat that chugged rather noisily through the gorges. Tigers emerging from the jungles for a drink and crocodiles basking on the shore could be shot from the comfort of the boat—if the sound of its engine did not scare them away.

Having packed their belongings the night before, the two boys were getting impatient for the carriage to arrive. It never did. Instead they were driven to Raj Bhawan, where Maharao Umed Singh, the British political Agent, Colonel McConaghey, and Bhim Singh's English guardian, Captain T.R. Livesey, were waiting. Mormukut couldn't help noticing that the two Englishmen were armed with revolvers. A few minutes later a Rolls-Royce drove through the palace gates and Mormukut, Bahadur and the two Englishmen were ushered inside. As the car was about to drive away, Onkar Singh leaned in through the window and told Mormukut that he was going to Jaipur for his formal adoption by Madho Singh. It was the first he heard that he had been chosen as Jaipur's maharaja. The revolvers, he later learned, were for his own protection. Determined to get their candidate on the gaddi, the thakurs of Jhalai had threatened to kill all other aspirants.[5]

When they were about thirty kilometres from Jaipur, the group had a rendezvous with Charles Cleveland, one of the two Englishmen on Madho Singh's royal council, and switched cars to maintain secrecy. Dusk had fallen by the time they reached the City Palace. Waiting to meet them were Madho Singh, his home minister, Sir Purohit Gopinath, and Bala Bux. What transpired between the maharaja and his heir at that meeting is unknown, but the earlier lapses of etiquette on Mormukut's part would have made way for solemnity. From there he was taken to the zenana quarters, where he was placed under the care of the late ruler Ram Singh II's first wife, Maji Sahiba Rathore Ji. His meals were served on special poison-detecting plates. For good measure food tasters were brought in.

* * *

On 24 March 1921, Mormukut was formally adopted by Madho Singh in a ceremony attended by Sir Robert E. Holland, Agent to the Governor General in Rajputana, and leading nobles in the state. Tributes were presented to the ageing maharaja and the new maharajkumar (son of the maharaja), who was now known as Sawai Man Singh II. The function had all the pomp and pageantry of a royal celebration. Gun salutes were fired and sweets were distributed to the public. Crowds poured into the City Palace, specially illuminated for the occasion. Celebratory parties went on for weeks.

The formal adoption was just the first step. The succession still had to be recognized by the imperial government. Nor were Madho Singh's opponents prepared to give up their fight to get their protégé on the gaddi. Still smarting from having his own preferences ignored, the Maharaja of Bikaner threatened to take the matter up directly with the Secretary of State for India in London. Jaipur's ruler countered by leaking the secret papers on the case to other princes. Cleveland, for his part, accused the thakurs of Chomu and Diggi of plotting to murder the maharaja. Their supporters retaliated by spreading rumours that Madho Singh had paid Cleveland and other British officials massive bribes for securing their government's approval of Mormukut's adoption.[6]

Determined to settle the succession dispute once and for all, the Viceroy, Lord Chelmsford, set up a committee headed by Cleveland to investigate the legality of the maharaja's actions. The committee dismissed counterclaims by Jhalai as being 'utterly false' and urged the viceroy to waste no time in supporting Madho Singh's choice. Despite the legal facade, there were more practical matters at play. Jaipur's ruler did not have long to live and it suited the British to have a lengthy minority before his heir took full control of the state. Regencies were an opportunity for reforming the administrations of princely states as well as for intelligence gathering. They also made it possible to mould the new ruler's character according to British ideals.

After a delay caused by the change of viceroys, the new viceroy, Lord Reading, confirmed the adoption on 21 April 1921, declaring that it had been done according to Hindu law and 'as is the custom of the race'. Six weeks later Reading travelled to Jaipur for the official adoption durbar; the decaying splendour of the court and the demeanour of the bejewelled Sawai Man Singh, were poignantly described by his wife, Alice.

> Imagine a very dirty gilded room, the walls covered with oleo-graphs, conspicuous among them a coloured one of the old Empress William, Königin Louise. Big pieces of furniture swathed in dust sheets, dozens of early Victorian gas chandeliers the colour of dust and only one beautiful thing in the room, another priceless century carpet; and on it you came upon, as if by chance, a figure seated cross-legged, no cushions, leaning against a bolster—the Maharajah! A splendid man with magnificent head and straight features, olive-skinned with a mane of grey hair and dark, flashing eyes. He looked every inch a Rajput chief, but a dying one. The heir sat drowsing cross-legged as H.E. [His Excellency] and the Maharajah had an interesting little talk (interpreted). The boy was hung with emeralds and pearls, and half-a-dozen little sons all about the same age, with kohl-darkened eyes, stared at us as hard as they could stare.[7]

In his speech at the adoption durbar, Holland declared that the event marked the culmination of Madho Singh's 'long and benevolent rule, since by it you have grafted upon the ancient tree of Jaipur a young and vigorous shoot'. The Rajputana Agent then called on the maharaja to impart to his heir 'from your own wisdom and experience, the knowledge and training which will enable him to discharge successfully the duties of his magnificent inheritance'.[8] Looking pale and a little nervous, Mormukut watched his adopted father rise to thank Holland for recognizing and confirming the adoption of his son and successor. He concurred with the Agent's wishes that his adopted son's education should lead him to become 'a truly religious, loyal and wise Ruler of his State who will count the prosperity and happiness of his subjects as the most cherished ambition of his life'. He then took a veiled swipe at the nobles who had opposed the adoption. 'Avoid factions and parties and let self-interest and the dissensions it brings melt and disappear in the fire of true Rajput patriotism.' He finished by announcing several measures in honour of the auspicious day, including distributing sweets to children in state and private schools, releasing prisoners and doubling expenditure on food at Mayo Hospital.[9]

How much the nine-year-old understood the implications of his formal adoption is pure speculation. Protocols had been breached, vast inheritances were at stake and the all-important questions of who would be his formal guardian and who would act as regent until he came of age had the potential to create more meddling. Things could have been worse. Madho Singh confounded the prophecy and lived for another eighteen months after the adoption date, allowing some semblance of order to be restored. But even the short time between Man Singh's arrival in Jaipur and the adoption durbar had taken their toll. 'Long confinement in the zenana has told on his health and he is no longer the cheery light-hearted boy who I saw at Kotah a few months ago,' one English observer wrote.[10]

Jai would later admit that his confinement in the zenana quarters of the City Palace was the most miserable period of his life. He was allowed only occasional visits from his family and these took place in an atmosphere of stifling formality with the women of the zenana hovering in the background, veiled and protective. Compared with the freedom he had enjoyed in Kota, the atmosphere was oppressive. Guards accompanied him everywhere. They had to. Another clan had claimed the right to succeed to the throne. 'The zenana ladies spoiled him, fed him too many sweets, petted him, watched over him and tried to be kind to him,' Gayatri Devi would later recall in her memoir, *A Princess Remembers*. 'But for a young, athletic and fun-loving boy it was naturally lonely and disagreeable, and he got fatter and fatter and sadder and sadder.'[11]

This was putting it mildly. The zenana had been Madho Singh's downfall and the British now feared it would do the same to his young and impressionable heir. Robert Stern in his masterly study of Jaipur under the Raj describes the zenana as 'that indestructible demoness who led Rajput princes to ruin and British plans to nought'. It was more than merely the women's quarters. It was the 'synonym for debilitating and corrupting vice'.[12] Madho Singh had succumbed to the power of the zenana only briefly and at the end of his rule. His successor had a lifetime ahead of him.

* * *

Viewed from the upper storeys of the Chandra Mahal in the City Palace, the zenana deorhi is a sprawling and labyrinthine complex of verandas, balconies, courtyards, chhatris and rawalas, or apartments, linked by avenues, passages and corridors. It stretches almost a kilometre from the south-west corner of the City Palace complex to the Hawa Mahal, where women, concealed by elaborate latticework, could observe the passing parade of street life without being seen. It was home to the maharaja's wives and concubines, each with their ladies-in-waiting, cooks, tailors, beauticians, singers, dancers and musicians as well as relatives. It also functioned as a parallel seat of power. The skill required of chiefs to manage 'the government of the kingdom is but an amusement', wrote James Tod, 'for it is within the Rawala [zenana], that intrigue is enthroned'.[13]

The complex was designed so that women living in adjacent apartments had no knowledge of what was happening to their neighbour, enabling the ruler to visit one of his wives or concubines without the others knowing. Aside from the maharaja, the only males allowed into the zenana were purohits, or priests, and princes. At the end of the long corridors were doors locked and guarded by a retinue of eunuchs known as nazirs or khojas, who kept a vigilant eye on everything that took place in the zenana and vetted the entry of outsiders. They were appointed in much the same way as a ruler appointed nobles to various positions—as a sign of prestige. 'They mediated between the palace, court, barracks and women's apartments to carry out the orders of the king,' writes the historian Manisha Choudhary. 'They served in different capacities as spiritual hooks, administrators, governors, political mediators, envoys, spies, news collectors, guards, superintendents, personal attendants and carried out the imperial civil and military commands.'[14]

At the apex of this medieval microcosm was the maji sahib, or queen mother, followed by the lesser queens and concubines. Women passed their time playing chess and the dice game chauser, drinking wine and being entertained by singers and dancers.

Marriages, births, birthdays and religious festivals were celebrated. Everyone competed for the king's recognition. If a maidservant could attract his attention with her beautiful voice or graceful dance, she might be promoted to the position of a pardayat, or concubine, and granted her own jagir. Giving birth to a male child might see a concubine elevated to the position of a rani (princess) with greater rewards. According to one estimate, one-third of the state treasury went towards maintaining the zenana. Aman Nath, historian and author of *Jaipur: The Last Destination*, recalls visiting the zenana with Gayatri Devi in the late 1970s: 'As we walked through strange corridors we saw a few wrinkled old ladies lying on the floor. They all seemed ninety years old. "These are the concubines of Madho Singh," she said. He had passed away in 1922, so I began to calculate and see the possibility. Yes, they could have been even younger but looked like beggars we see on the Indian streets. To think they once evoked lust in a maharaja!'[15]

One of the few times the young heir apparent was allowed out of the zenana was in June 1922, when his adoptive father took him on a pilgrimage to the Mataji temple at Indergarh. Travelling with him was Roop Rai, who made the ailing Madho Singh stop and roll in the ashes of a cremated sadhu on the way to the shrine. Unfortunately, the act failed to cure the maharaja, who the British believed was at high risk of succumbing to pneumonia as the monsoon had broken and the party was living in tents. A delegation of nobles convinced Cleveland to bring the trio back, pointing out the affront to the state's honour if the ruler died away from his capital. The new Resident, Lieutenant Colonel S.B.A. Patterson, was sent to Indergarh to ascertain the maharaja's health. A tense stand-off occurred at the Indergarh railway station, where Madho Singh arrived accompanied by two hefty eunuchs. Patterson later described feeling sorry for the Jaipur ruler, who looked very ill. 'He is dominated by the female Rasputin, whose creatures the eunuchs are, and he knew he was in the wrong.' When Patterson sent his agent to the camp he found it 'deplorably filthy'. 'Twelve hundred people and 150 animals are in it and no attempt at sanitation.'[16] Patterson reported that aside from the hostile reception from Roop Rai and her cohorts, his visit generated 'open rejoicing'. In the end, Madho Singh was lucky to make it out alive. His car sank up to its axle in mud, and had they postponed their departure by another day, heavy rain would have delayed it for weeks. Patterson wrote to his superiors that there was a strong belief in Jaipur that Roop Rai never wanted the maharaja to return. 'She had a large amount of jewellery with her and hoped to escape with it.'[17]

When Madho Singh died on 7 September 1922 of pneumonia brought on by his ordeal at Indergarh, Sawai Man Singh II was proclaimed the Maharaja of Jaipur, though he would have to wait until he turned eighteen to be invested with full ruling powers. In the meantime, a minority administration headed by Cleveland was established. An able administrator long associated with the Jaipur durbar and unconnected to the Rajputana Agency, Cleveland was Madho Singh's personal choice. His neutrality, Madho Singh believed, would serve the young Man Singh well. What he hadn't bargained for was the hostility the appointment generated among the Foreign and Political Department of the Government of British India and Cleveland's cabinet colleagues.

Madho Singh's death saw the breakout of years of pent-up hostilities. His senior wife, Jhali, filed cases against Roop Rai and Bala Bux, accusing them of embezzlement and breach of trust. She was supported by Patterson who believed Roop Rai had stolen at least a million rupees in cash from the dead king's private treasury and jewels of an even greater value. But instead of absconding, Roop Rai remained at the palace, swindling another 80,000 rupees out of the maharaja's funeral expenses. By now even Cleveland, who as president of the minority council had almost dictatorial power, was feeling that he had 'met his Moscow' in the Jaipur palace, especially in the zenana 'with its swarms of ladies, women and eunuchs'. He felt he could never tackle it, and that 'no Englishman could or should'.[18]

At the same time Cleveland was anxious to protect the ruler-in-waiting from Roop Rai's influence, particularly as his spies were reporting that 'attempts have already been made in the zenana to debauch the young Maharaja by means of girls'.[19] But when the eunuchs tried to expel her from the zenana, Roop Rai and her supporters attacked them with bamboo staves and broomsticks. When her quarters were eventually searched, police found considerable sums in cash, thirty-five swords, numerous bottles of poison and cases of spirits.[20]

Behind Cleveland's exasperation was a secret he had been trying to keep from the durbar. Aided by Bux, the former intelligence officer had been amassing a huge fortune through various speculative enterprises, including trading in gold coins. These dealings were in clear violation of the pledge he had taken before his appointment to the late maharaja's service—that he would 'not take part directly or indirectly in any commercial or industrial transactions in the state'.[21] News of Cleveland's indiscretions led to the resignation of most cabinet members and mass protests on the streets of Jaipur calling for his removal. More worrying for the British were stirrings in the zenana for an alternative regency administration headed by relatives of various ranis. To avoid further embarrassment, the British spun the line that Cleveland had been 'indiscreet' but not 'dishonest'. In early 1923, Patterson was appointed as the regent, a move that prompted Cleveland's immediate resignation. His replacement as president of the minority council was G.I. Glancy. How much tension this caused in the Jaipur durbar and the zenana is unclear from British cables, but it was considered prudent to send Man Singh to Mount Abu for his own safety.

Madho Singh had left instructions in his will that Sir James Roberts, who had been his personal physician, should be Man Singh's guardian. His naming of Roberts marked a turnaround in his attitude to the upbringing of his future heir. Ten years earlier he had argued against the appointment of a European guardian on the grounds that 'the constant companionship of a European officer … engenders in him [the young Prince] not only loss of faith in religious practices of his ancestors but makes him sceptical of the very doctrines of his religion—a deplorable result in the extreme'.[22] The British welcomed this change. Any opportunity to instil Western values and ideas in Indian potentates was seen as creating a class of loyal leaders, particularly at a time when growing demands for independence were gaining a hold in much of India.

On taking up his position, Roberts immediately recommended a strict regime of physical education to counteract Man Singh's 'too intimate association with the zenana'. Roberts also suggested he be warned of 'unmanly' influences. 'From his position and surroundings, the young Prince is destined for much sexual experience, but it is important to remember it is better to guide this after puberty rather than to repress it, the latter means the introduction of intrigues and depravities of the worst description and opens the door to the machinations of unscrupulous blackguards. We must trust to counteract these by the healthy life of exercise and sport he will lead.' Adding his weight as a medical practitioner to the memorandum, he noted that he had seen many young princes 'ruined by the early infection of venereal disease' and recommended that from the age of about fifteen, Man Singh should associate 'with a healthy young girl, and that in moderation'.[23]

Roberts seems to have been curiously unaware of Rajput tradition, where princes were frequently married off at a much younger age—and that was exactly what Madho Singh had in mind for his adopted heir. As early as August 1921 he had sent an emissary to Jodhpur's regent, Sir Pratap Singh, to arrange Man Singh's marriage to the Jodhpur maharaja's sister and her niece. Rajput marriages were not arrangements between individuals but between two houses. They were used to form political alliances with other clans and expand their territorial influence and military strength. Jodhpur state was always the first choice of Jaipur's rulers. Maharaja Umaid Singh's sister Marudhar Kanwar was twenty-two, or thirteen years older than Man Singh, while her niece Kishore Kumari was only five at the time. That Man Singh was still just nine did not matter as much in palace circles as the fact that Marudhar was fast approaching what was considered retirement age by Rajput standards when it came to marriage. The alliance with Jodhpur had another, as yet unrealized, advantage. As he grew older, Man Singh would have access to the best polo players in India, if not in the world. 'It was a package deal,' says the current Maharaja of Jodhpur, Gaj Singh. 'It was an alliance that was political as well as sporting.'[24]

Man Singh was betrothed to both aunt and niece on 31 December 1921. British prudishness now kicked in, with Holland, the Rajputana Agent to the Governor General, expressing alarm at the prospect of the young boy having to consummate the marriage when he had barely reached puberty. In the end a compromise was reached. The wedding was to be held as soon as was convenient, but the part of the ceremony known as the muklawa, without which consummation could not take place, would be left out. Holland consulted Man Singh about the arrangement and after giving what the Agent thought was surprisingly mature consideration, he agreed.

And so, on 20 January 1924 at the age of just eleven, Man Singh was married in Jodhpur to Marudhar Kanwar, who was almost twice his age. The arrival of his train on the morning of the wedding was greeted by a nineteen-gun salute fired from Mehrangarh Fort. Waiting for him at the station were twenty-five cavalrymen from Jaipur in chain armour, fifty camel riders, hundreds of horses and several elephants. As dictated by tradition, the young maharajkumar exchanged the sum of 101 rupees with his counterpart, Maharaja Umaid Singh. He was then taken to the Mediwala Palace for rose-water and betel nut ceremonies. At 3.30 p.m., the bridegroom's procession arrived, taking two hours to cover the short distance to the fort. Another gun salute was fired and for the first time Man Singh set eyes on his twenty-four-year-old bride. Watching the ceremony was Marudhar's niece Kishore Kumari, who was being teased unmercifully by her cousins for not knowing what the concept of a husband meant despite already being officially engaged. Marudhar remained in Jodhpur while Man Singh returned to Jaipur. British fears that his wife's urgency to bear his first son would lead him 'to indulge his sexual appetites to excess' and also keep him a prisoner of the zenana, meant it would be several years before they were allowed to cohabit.[25]

Having dispensed with the tricky issue of marriage, Man Singh's mentors now set about preparing him for the responsibilities of being a ruler in his own right. Jaipur was a seventeen-gun-salute state covering an area of 40,000 square kilometres with a population of around 2.5 million. Although he saw little of it during his first few years in the zenana, he was the overlord of one of the world's most beautiful cities. The capital's foundation stone had been laid by Maharaja Jai Singh II in 1727. According to James Tod, Jai Singh's skills 'as a statesman, legislator and man of science' were so great and worthy of delineation 'they would correct our opinion of the genius and capacity of the princes of Rajpootana'.[26] Though he was first and foremost a warrior, he was also an intellectual, finding time to read and think deeply, to amass a vast library and, most famously, to become an astronomer of 'European reputation'.[27] Rudyard Kipling called him the 'Solomon of Rajputana'. 'He led armies and when fighting was over, turned to literature; he intrigued desperately and successfully, but found time to gain a deep insight into astronomy and by what remains above ground now we can tell that whatsoever his eyes desired, he kept not from him.'[28]

Amidst the crumbling of the Mughal empire, Jai Singh flaunted his independence by moving from Amber to an unprotected site on a plain ten kilometres to the south. It was an unprecedented move. As Kipling would put it so eloquently: 'East of Suez men do not build towers on the tops of hills for the sake of the view, nor do they stripe the mountain sides with bastioned stone walls to keep cattle.'[29] When it came to building forts, the Rajputs excelled. Their impregnable bastions were the preferred redoubts against their many enemies—the Mughals, Marathas and Jats, to name a few. Jai Singh's new capital would have no such protection.

The Jaipur that Kipling described when he visited the city early in the reign of Madho Singh had changed little by the time Man Singh had become his heir. Here was a 'pink city set on the border of a blue lake, and surrounded by the low, red spurs of the Aravalis—a city to see and puzzle over'. Kipling was immensely impressed with its 'huge streets straight as an arrow, sixty yards broad, and cross streets broad and safe'. Jai Singh 'built himself everything that pleased him, palaces and gardens and temples, and then died, and was buried under a white marble tomb on a hill overlooking the city'.[30]

Other travellers were similarly impressed. Edwin Arnold called the Hawa Mahal, the city's most famous landmark, 'a vision of daring and dainty loveliness, nine stories of rosy masonry and delicate overhanging balconies, and latticed windows, soaring with tier after tier of fanciful architecture in a pyramidal form, a very mountain of airy and audacious beauty … Aladdin's magician could have called into existence no more marvellous abode, nor was the pearl and silver palace of the Peri Banou more delicately charming.'[31] Exploring the city in the 1930s, Rosita Forbes found the general pace of the bazaars to be one and a half miles an hour. 'Without exceeding this stately limit, elephants, their tusks ringed with metal and their foreheads painted black, tread with caution lest they crush some particle of the crowd which must seem to them an animated carpet. Camels roped head-to-tail, with immense bells swinging under their chins, pad through the dust with their peculiar soft and swaying gait.'[32] She compared Jaipur's rose-red-tinted buildings to

Petra in Jordan, the rock-hewn churches of Lalibela among the mountains of Abyssinia and to Bamyan in Afghanistan. 'But all these, in reality, are the dusky, purplish reds of hewn rocks stained by centuries of storm and dust. Only Jaipur is the clear pink of oleanders and sugar-cakes, and, I regret to say, flannelette.'[33]

* * *

Behind the wall of the City Palace, the pace of life was even slower. Before Man Singh could take on full powers he had to learn the intricacies of court ritual. 'The court was a space where every activity was enacted on a scale that would appear theatrical to an outsider,' writes Manisha Choudhary in her study of Jaipur society. 'The vision of social order is clearly visible from the day-to-day happenings in the court. Through enactment of these acts, the aim was of distancing the king from the mass of his subjects. The court being the microcosm of society as well as its apex, it reflected and regulated social order by regulating itself.'[34] Gifts presented to visitors depended on their rank with the highest receiving robes of honour, titles (khitabs or padvis), turban bands and turban ornaments, pashmina shawls and so on. Depending on their importance, the ruler either walked to the door of the durbar to meet visitors or all the way to the outer courtyard of the palace. The status of visiting dignitaries determined whether they would be escorted to the palace by a royal guard, the type of embrace they received, and whether they would sit on the left or the right side of the king's seat, the latter being the highest honour as it was in the Mughal court. Similarly, the number of salaams visitors were expected to give varied according to their rank.[35]

Court ritual was one area the British dared not intervene in. But elsewhere they made sure they kept a firm grip on the administration of the state. British officers served as the state's chief ministers, headed the departments of revenue and public works, commanded its army, managed its railways and directed its educational and medical services. As one observer later commented, 'there is perhaps no place in India where the chain of European control is more complete' than in Jaipur.[36] On the ground, however, the state of affairs was somewhat chaotic. In his first report published in 1923,

Jaipur's new Resident found: 'No real accounts or systems of account. No public offices, even members of the cabinet have not their own offices. Law courts squalid beyond conception, and in no way courts of justice. An army which, with the exception of the transport corps, is an extensive, ill-armed and non-disciplined rabble. A police force which is on par with the army. A revenue system which is only systematic in robbery. A customs system that is on the same lines as revenue.'[37]

Within a month of Madho Singh's death, the young maharaja's guardian, James Roberts, established a school at the Rambagh Palace, three kilometres from the old city and at the time surrounded by jungle. Twenty-three boys from noble families were selected to attend the school. 'Although far more bloated than a boy of his age ought to be and a sad contrast to his slim elder brother, he is already a different person to the pallid, sheepish rough who I saw a month ago, and there is good hope of his regaining his normal shape under the present regime,' Holland reported, describing the young maharaja.[38] The experiment, however, proved short-lived, largely because the British feared for his safety if he remained in Jaipur. With the likelihood that it would be years before the administration was no longer 'torn by factions, plots or dissensions', the decision was made to send Man Singh to Mayo College. The only other course of action would have been to 'keep him a prisoner in the palace', something that would certainly interfere with his education.[39]

Located on the outskirts of Ajmer, Mayo College was the brain-child of Lord Mayo, the then viceroy and Governor General, who wanted to set up a college 'devoted exclusively to the education of the sons of Chiefs, Princes and leading Thakurs'. It opened in 1875 with just one student, Maharaja Mangal Singh of Alwar. To make them partners in empire, schools like Mayo and Rajkumar College, Mayo's equivalent in Rajkot, Gujarat, emphasized the study of the English language, the customs and mores of British society as well as sports such as cricket and polo. At Mayo turbans had to be worn to all classes and achkans had to be buttoned right up to the neck, except during examination week. Of the dozen or so princes who comprised the initial enrolment, about half deserted the classroom for the more comfortable surroundings of their zenanas. Those who remained, including the princes of Bhavnagar and Junagadh, were always accompanied to their lessons by 'bands of armed retainers, strange, wild-looking creatures who might have come out of the middle ages'.[40] Some noble families viewed the idea of educating princely youths as inconsistent with their rank and position. Maharajkumars were born 'not to drive the quill', but 'to wield the sword, to command others, to rule and to live in clover on the properties of their ancestors', noted Nasrullah Khan, a graduate of Rajkumar College.[41] 'When it comes to educating the princes, it is the soft love of ease and luxury, rather than the fierce spirit of war and love for dangerous sports, which has to be contended with,' Reverend James Johnson of the Indian Education Commission complained. 'Early marriage with its hindrances and distractions ... [and] in some case hereditary instinct leads him to regard education as scarcely better than a disgrace.'[42]

When Man Singh arrived at Mayo there were ten houses organized to accommodate boys from the states that had endowed the individual buildings. Each house was supervised by prefects, who were responsible for matters such as tidiness and general behaviour. The Maharaja of Kota had 200 servants for whom a special village was built, while Alwar's ruler-in-waiting had a stable of over twenty polo ponies and four carriage horses.[43] Though his retinue was more modest, Man Singh lived in considerable style with a small army of servants and nine grooms. Coryton Mayne, his tutor, was an Englishman who went on to become the headmaster at Rajkumar College. His Indian guardian, Dhonkal Singh from Jodhpur, was considered one of India's finest polo players. It was under him that Man Singh developed the skills that would later make him one of the best players in the world. Mayne, meanwhile, grew so fond of his young charge that in 1926 he suggested that he go to England to stay with his family. This was opposed by the British Resident, who wrote to the Secretary of State expressing concern that a young prince should remain in touch with the religion of his state and his people. A year later Patterson changed his mind and recommended that when he turned sixteen Man Singh should be sent to England for private tuition with a family for a period of eighteen months. Somehow the contents of the letter reached the ears of Marudhar, who wrote to the Resident objecting to the plan, pointing out that the late maharaja had stipulated that her husband be educated in

Jaipur. Other family members, the public and the Maharaja of Jodhpur would also object. In the end Patterson's proposal was overruled by Leonard W. Reynolds, Agent to the Governor General of Rajputana, who feared that: 'Education in England among all classes of Indians tends to develop anti-British feelings.' Moreover, this would be seen by the public as a part of a 'deliberate design to Anglicise the Maharajah'.[44]

In 1927, disturbing news reached the Residency that Marudhar had given her fifteen-year-old husband wine to drink, slept with him and was now expecting a baby, although the real father was a kamdar, or land agent, of the Maharaja of Jodhpur. Patterson discounted the rumours. Every time Man Singh had visited his wife he had been accompanied by a female English chaperone. He did note, however, that there had been two occasions when the couple were together in the zenana without their watchdog and that anything could have happened in that time. Reynolds, the Rajputana Agent, was also sceptical. The rumours—they were just that, for Marudhar wasn't pregnant—emanated from relatives of Kishore, his now eleven-year-old fiancée. The objective was to discredit the maharani in order for Kishore to claim that her baby, when she produced one and assuming it was a boy, would be the heir to the throne. The paternalistic attitude of the British to Man Singh's sexuality reached a peak in the summer of 1927, when Reynolds wrote to the political secretary recommending that the young maharaja not sleep with his wife until he was seventeen. The maharani's propensity to drink was the main reason, though he wished this was not the case as the 'young Maharaja was showing a regrettable interest in boys'.[45]

In April 1929, just a few months short of his seventeenth birthday, Man Singh graduated from Mayo, earning praise from the principal, who wrote: 'His development from a fat little boy to a big athletic young man is as much a testimony to his inherent good qualities as to the system under which he has been brought up.'[46] Though he was not brilliant at schoolwork, he was a gifted horseman and excelled at other sports. The principal's main criticism was that he was too susceptible to the influence of others.

During Man Singh's final year at Mayo, the British had relaxed their prudishness and allowed conjugal visits once a fortnight. On 13 June 1929, Marudhar gave birth to a girl, Prem Kumari, who was nicknamed Mickey by her English nanny. A month later, Mickey's seventeen-year-old father sailed for England to begin a year's training at the Royal Military Academy at Woolwich. According to his biographer Quentin Crewe, Man Singh was happier at Woolwich than he had ever been in his life. 'The military uniforms, parades, medals, everything to do with the army, fascinated [Man Singh]. He always maintained that had he not been a Maharaja, he would have joined the army.'[47] In addition, he was discovering the amusements of London. 'Released from the formalities and intrigues of Jaipur, Man Singh was discovering "fun" ... Life from now was to be divided into two separate existences—responsibilities in India; "fun" abroad.'[48]

When Man Singh asked to extend his time in England to join a cavalry regiment for more training, his request was rejected by Reynolds, who questioned what value it would have. 'The object is to produce a good ruler not a cavalry officer and it is more likely that association with a wealthy cavalry regiment in England will develop tastes not altogether consistent with the qualities required for the ruler of a state like Jaipur,' the Rajputana Agent wrote.[49] The other reason for Reynolds's hesitation was that the maharaja's formal investiture was planned for the spring of 1931 and any delay would be detrimental to the smooth transfer of power.

Man Singh returned to Jaipur in early October 1930 to be greeted by the booming of guns and a guard of honour provided by the imperial service infantry. Thousands of people, including villagers who had trekked to Jaipur through the night, lined up along the road from the city's railway station to the Rambagh Palace. Over the next six months, he went through an intensive programme, learning about the work of each of the main departments in the administration and getting to know the people he was to rule over. He was also apprised of the broader political picture. Mahatma Gandhi and the Congress had largely ignored the Rajput states, but that was changing under the direction of Jamnalal Bajaj, one of Gandhi's closest lieutenants. There was also restlessness among the Jats, the most politically conscious peasant caste in Shekhawati to the north-west of Jaipur.

On 14 March 1931, the Viceroy, Lord Irwin, presided over the investiture of nineteen-year-old Sawai Man Singh on the Jaipur throne with full powers. Assembled in the throne room of the City

Palace were more than 300 nobles bedecked in glittering diamonds, emeralds, rubies and priceless strings of gleaming pearls. Irwin was carried into the hall on a palanquin borne by four bearers, before taking his place to the right of the maharaja on a throne covered by a canopy embroidered in silk and gold. His political officers and members of the state council as well as high-ranking state officials sat to the left. Irwin's message was blunt. The strength of the Jaipur durbar would depend on: 'Promptness in the dispatch of business, impartial justice as between man and man, selection of competent officials, ungrudging support of them as long as they prove worthy of your trust ... moderation in personal expenditure ... [and] development of all agencies for the public benefit such as schools, hospitals, roads and irrigation works.' Referring to growing demands for self-determination, he also warned that ominous developments in British India would affect Jaipur unless high standards of administration were observed. The new ruler responded by expressing his sense of heavy responsibility and pledging his loyalty to the king-emperor.[50]

Following the investiture, Man Singh drove through the city where thousands of people lined the roads. Leading the procession was an elephant bearing the panchranga, the five-coloured flag of the state, followed by more elephants, a bullock-drawn artillery battery and a string of camels with riders carrying swords. Another elephant, this time in full war armour, came next, followed by horses from the royal stables. Red-turbaned halkaras, or men-in-waiting, wearing yellow robes with sashes around their waists, preceded Man Singh, who rode an elephant in a howdah of silver and gold. Escorting him on their elephants were senior thakurs followed by other nobles, a contingent of bodyguards and four squadrons of the imperial service cavalry. When he finally reached the Ajmer Gate, Man Singh alighted from his elephant and got into a car that took him to the Rambagh Palace, where a lavish banquet was held. He told the gathering that Irwin would go down in history as the 'staunchest and most unfaltering friend India had known'. He then listed the reforms and improvements he wanted to make in the future.[51]

In reality, the last thing the British wanted was constitutional reform. The ominous developments Irwin had hinted at were the stirrings of Indian nationalism. Irwin was right that unquestioning acceptance of autocratic rule was gradually disappearing. The answer, however, was not representative forms of government but what the historian Sir Alfred Lyall called 'a more polished and reasonable despotism'.[52]

Man Singh was not showing any inclination of being a ruler who would give the Raj any trouble. Throughout his minority, Jaipur had been administered almost entirely by British officials. After he was removed from the zenana his upbringing and education had also been led by British guardians, tutors and teachers. His early years in the durbar, when the threat of death at the hands of his enemies was a constant companion, had engendered in him a dislike of plotting and intrigue. Now that he was maharaja, he saw no point in changing things. If anything, the structure he had inherited in Jaipur gave him the freedom to indulge his passions—the primary ones being polo and the pursuit of beautiful women.

3

WHITE SATIN PYJAMAS AND A TRIPLE ROW
OF PEARLS

Dominating the dining room in Lily Pool, Ayesha's Jaipur residence, is a full-length portrait of her mother, Indira Devi, painted by the Hungarian portraitist Philip de László. There is a delicate, studied and almost insolent preternatural self-assurance about her pose. She reclines on a divan supported by velvet cushions. Her left foot is tucked underneath her while her right one rests on a Ferragamo slipper. The other slipper lies carelessly discarded. A three-stringed pearl necklace follows the contours of her neck and a similarly designed pearl bracelet graces her right hand. Her svelte figure is draped in an almost transparent white chiffon sari with a gold embroidered border that is drawn over her head like a halo. She dares you to keep on staring, knowing she will always remain impervious.

Her friends called her Ma, short for maharani. To this day her love affairs are spoken of in whispers. Her continental escapades remain the stuff of legend. She was the first person to use chiffon for her saris, which was cooler than silk and more formal than cotton. Of the more than 100 pairs of shoes she ordered from Salvatore Ferragamo, one was decorated with pearls and diamonds from the Cooch Behar treasury and another, called Nymphia, was adorned with white canvas water-lily leaves impregnated with phosphorous to make them glow in the dark.

Never understated, she stood out among the glittering smart sets of Europe with her pearls and her poise. Her friend the author Evelyn Waugh described her as 'the daughter of a rajah, so emancipated as to be déclassée—but still preserving tenuous links with minor royalty. Women sometimes resorted to fisticuffs in her house.'[1] Another author mesmerized by Indira was Daphne Fielding, who described the maharani in her memoir *Mercury Presides*:

> As we entered her Hill Street house we used to be met by the heavy scent of incense; lights were shaded and spirals of joss-stick smoke hung in the air. Indira Cooch Behar looked like a romantic princess out of *The Arabian Nights*. She had a lovely, husky voice and an imperious manner and was always surrounded by a small court; her lady-in-waiting, Lilla Soakhi, who looked like a beautiful venomous snake; a gay little ADC [aide-de-camp] called Jackie, who was always on the crest of a high cocktail wave; and a sad-faced Persian called Captain Mahbou, who worshipped her. Indira had chests full of wonderful embroidered saris, and the first thing we did as we entered her house was to discard the dull cocoon of our own clothes and emerge like jewel-coloured butterflies draped in hers, and then drink champagne laced, to suit Indira's taste, with *creme de menthe*.[2]

Indira Devi was born in Baroda in 1892. Her father, Sayajirao Gaekwad, was the Maharaja of Baroda, one of India's most important princely states. Like Man Singh, he was adopted into the royal lineage. His predecessor, Malharrao, was deposed for maladministration after a failed attempt to force him to abdicate on suspicion of trying to poison the British Resident by putting ground diamonds in his morning sherbet. Sayajirao was an illiterate twelve-year-old village boy when he was brought to Baroda and vetted by Jamnabai, the dowager maharani. He appeared before her with his brother and cousin. According to the most commonly recounted story, the eldest of the trio, when asked why he had come to Baroda replied: 'To see the sights.' The middle one was unsure, but Sayajirao unhesitatingly replied, 'I have come to rule.'[3] A few months later, on 25 May 1875, he was made the chief of one of India's five twenty-one-gun-salute states.

Sayajirao's first marriage to a Tanjore princess ended tragically after just three years when she died of tuberculosis. His advisers urged the heartbroken young ruler to marry again. This time he chose Garabai, the fourteen-year-old daughter of a noble from Dewas. After their marriage her name was changed to Chimnabai. She learned to read and write, paid only lip service to the tradition of purdah, travelled abroad extensively and became an advocate for women's rights. She was her husband's only wife. Sayajirao was one of the few Indian rulers who believed in monogamy.

Under Sayajirao, Baroda became one of India's most progressive states—child marriages and bigamy were outlawed and widows could remarry. In 1904, education was made free and compulsory for all school-age children. He introduced legislation to ban untouchability in his state, years before Mahatma Gandhi took up the cause. Under pressure from his wife he also banned purdah in 1913, becoming one of the first states in India to do so. He also refused to meekly toe the line on what the British expected from the ruler of a princely state. Taking a leaf out of Machiavelli's *The Prince*, he argued that his state was politically equal with the British government. The Raj, he insisted, had 'no more right to interfere with Baroda affairs than it has to interfere in the affairs of Denmark or Portugal'.[4] Offended by such insolence, the viceroy, Lord Curzon, hit back, describing Sayajirao as 'the most disagreeable, contumacious and cantankerous of the whole of our Chiefs ... The man, as you know, was the son of a cow-herd and his humble origin and antecedents are constantly, in spite of his considerable ability, coming out in his words and deeds.'[5] Relations took another dive when in 1900 Sayajirao took his family to Europe without informing Curzon, prompting a dressing-down from the Viceroy for being 'punctilious' about his rights and showing 'questionable loyalty' to the empire.[6]

The Baroda ruler's greatest sin was his sympathies for anti-British nationalists. His administration employed several well-known agitators, including K.G. Deshpande who ran a school and printing press that published anti-British propaganda. Several students from Deshpande's school were linked to the attempted assassination of Viceroy Minto in 1909. Every time Sayajirao and his wife visited England and Europe they were tailed by British agents. In the summer of 1910, Chimnabai met the fiery Madame Cama, whose Paris-based revolutionary cell was calling for the violent overthrow of the British Raj.

When Indira was fifteen, the family moved into the sprawling Laxmi Vilas palace designed by Major Charles Mant, the principal exponent of late-nineteenth-century Indo-Saracenic style. Palace life had a strongly cosmopolitan flavour. The maharaja was attended by an English major-domo, meals were prepared by a French chef, an Irish sergeant major was placed in charge of the stables and in later years Italian chauffeurs drove the family through Baroda's narrow streets.[7] Chimnabai had an English companion and a Swiss lady's maid.[8]

In December 1911, more than a hundred Indian princes, some with retinues numbering in the thousands, descended on Delhi to celebrate the coronation of King George V. It was the first time that a ruling British monarch had visited the jewel in the imperial crown and the British were determined the event pass off as a grand display of pageantry and loyalty. Sayajirao was among the first of the ruling princes to pay homage to the king-emperor on 12 December, the day of the durbar. But instead of bowing deeply and taking two steps back while facing the monarch, he performed an abrupt about-turn and went back to his seat. To turn one's back on the future Emperor of India was decried as bordering on sedition and prompted a wave of demands for his removal. Whether his actions were an intentional snub and proof of his disloyalty or a fit of nerves would be debated long after the incident.

Sayajirao could be forgiven for being distracted. In six weeks, his daughter Indira was due to marry the ruler of Gwalior, Madho Rao Scindia, who at forty-six was nearly three times her age and already married. The union would seal a grand alliance between two of India's most important princely states, but to outsiders it went against everything Sayajirao stood for. In July 1911, the *Times of India* had republished an editorial from the *Oriental Review* rebuking the maharaja. A champion of social reform and enemy of polygamy was 'about to contract a polygamous marriage' for his daughter, it thundered. 'What will be then the effects of such a secession on the minds of the Indian people, and specially the subjects of Baroda State, which look up to His Highness for guidance,' the editorial speculated. 'We fear that such a step of retreat from the fighting ranks will mean the greatest blow to the Social Reform campaign. Alas for India and Indians!'[9]

Scindia had first broached the subject of marrying Indira with Sayajirao two years earlier. After astrologers compared horoscopes and probed auspicious dates, the proposal was finally accepted and preparations for the wedding in Baroda began in earnest. Chimnabai ordered her daughter's trousseau and linen inscribed with the letters IS, standing for Indira Scindia. Welcoming arches spanned the streets and invitations were sent to hundreds of Baroda and Gwalior family members and friends.

Indira, who was known as 'the stormy petrel of the family', had other ideas. She had been brought up very much in the manner of a well-bred English girl and would have regarded life in Gwalior in strict purdah with horror. Just a few days before the durbar, she met twenty-five-year-old Prince Jitendra (or Jit to his friends) of Cooch Behar. She had attended a finishing school in Eastbourne with his sisters, Prativa (Pretty) and Sudhira (Baby), who invited her to visit their camp. By reputation Jit was 'a fairy-tale prince, splendid-looking and full of charm, impulsive, generous and amusing company'.[10] When the two met for the first time, Jit asked Indira why she looked so gloomy when she was about to marry one of India's wealthiest princes. She responded: 'I'm miserable because I'm getting married,' to which Jit replied: 'Well, why don't you marry me?'[11] Whether Jit meant it or not, the throwaway line was the trigger for a full-blown romance. Over the next few days, the young couple took every opportunity they could to meet privately—a challenge in the crowded temporary tented city that had sprung up for the durbar.

The first that Sayajirao knew of the romance was five days after the durbar, when he and his wife boarded their train to Baroda. A few hours into their journey he received a telegram from Scindia asking: 'WHAT DOES SHE MEAN BY HER LETTER?' Without informing her parents, Indira had written to her intended husband before leaving Delhi that the marriage was off. When they questioned her she said she had fallen in love with Jit.

Not only had Indira defied her parents' wishes, she had her heart set on marrying the second-in-line to a thirteen-gun-salute princely state in eastern India. Rumours flew that Gwalior had broken off the engagement because of Sayajirao's conduct at the durbar. Pointing out that betrothals among ruling families were rarely broken, the *Chicago Daily Tribune* speculated that it had more to do with Indira's 'intimacy with English and American customs and life'.[12] 'It occasioned baffled speculation in Baroda and Gwalior,' Gayatri Devi would later write of her mother's decision. 'But beyond that, the scandalised gossip throughout all the Indian princely states focused on the astonishing fact that an alliance between the two most important Maratha families was broken by the casual whim of a girl. Such a thing was unheard of. And for some nonsense about love at first sight? Impossible.'[13]

Despite her parents' attempts to end the romance, Indira and Jit managed to exchange letters, many of them addressed using noms de plume such as 'Mrs Miele Brooke, Poste Restante, Fernhill, Ootacamund' or 'Mrs Sylvia Workman'. In them Jit described the enticing aspects of life in Cooch Behar, the winter season's festivities in Calcutta, the joys of spring in Darjeeling, balls and fancy-dress parties, polo and cricket matches and the big-game shoots.[14] The steadfast opposition of Indira's parents to the marriage only began to give ground because of their fear that she would elope with Jit on their next trip to England, something that would cause an even greater scandal. In the spring of 1913, they finally relented and allowed the pair to marry, but refused to have anything to do with the ceremony.

Jit's parents belonged to the Brahmo Samaj, a monotheistic reform movement that forbade idol worship and meaningless rituals. Before the marriage could take place, Indira had to be initiated into the Brahmo faith. She spent the morning of her wedding day, 24 August 1913, reading passages from the Brahmo scriptures. The diksha, or initiation ceremony, which involved a simple pledge to follow the tenets of Brahmoism, took place in a room at London's Buckingham Palace Hotel where Jit's mother, Sunity Devi, was present. Indira was dressed in a white silk robe bordered with gold, with her head draped with a sheer gauze scarf. Jit wore a tweed suit. At noon a civil ceremony took place at the registrar's office in Paddington. Indira had changed into a European dress of rose pink crêpe de Chine. Her only jewellery was a long platinum and gold chain. Half an hour later the couple returned to the hotel and changed into Indian clothes for the Brahmo blessing during which their hands were wreathed with white flowers. The couple then drove to Sunity Devi's London residence for a celebratory breakfast attended by about thirty guests. Jit cut the wedding cake using the state sword of Cooch Behar. The only acknowledgement of their marriage from Indira's parents, who were in St Moritz, was a telegram from her father wishing her 'all happiness and a steady good life full of usefulness'. In the evening the couple drove to Maidenhead to begin their honeymoon.[15]

Their stay in Maidenhead was short-lived. Less than a week after their wedding, news arrived that Jit's elder brother, Raj Rajendra Narayan Bhup Bahadur, the Maharaja of Cooch Behar, had died. Rajey, as he was called by the family, had been seriously ill in a nursing home at Cromer for weeks. Two years earlier, he had sworn he would drink himself to death, exclusively on champagne, if his parents did not allow him to marry the actress Edna May. They refused. He kept his promise and died of pleurisy caused by alcoholism. Shortly after the funeral, the newly-weds sailed for India with Rajey's ashes, arriving in Cooch Behar in November 1913 not as prince and princess but as maharaja and maharani.

Rajey's alcoholism was to prove the rule rather than the exception not just in Cooch Behar, but also in Baroda, Jaipur and numerous other princely states—and often with the same deadly consequences. Sayajirao's eldest son, Jaisinhrao, had become an alcoholic while at Harvard and would later be treated in England for insanity caused by delirium tremens. His younger brother Shivajirao died of pneumonia brought on by alcoholism in the same year. Jit would succumb to the same vice and so would his sons.

For much of Rajey's reign Cooch Behar had been a well-managed state with several colleges, hospitals and elegant public buildings. Its Italianate renaissance-style palace, completed in 1887, was seen as a symbol of the state's progressive modernity. By far the larger and more important of Bengal's two princely states, Cooch Behar had a population of around 600,000 people spread out over an area of 3,385 square kilometres. Large tracts were covered in jungle, swamps and elephant grass. On clear days, the snow-covered peaks of the Himalayan ranges were visible to the north. Towards the end of Rajey's rule, the state's economy had started to deteriorate. On assuming power in 1911, Rajey had found himself saddled with his father's debts totalling some £37,000 to a host of businesses, ranging from Rolls-Royce to the perfumery firm Penhaligon's. By the time he died, the state's financial situation had further deteriorated and the list of creditors waiting to be paid had lengthened considerably. Having inherited an economic basket case, there was simply no way Jit could meet his father-in-law's expectation that he would pay Indira an allowance of 100,000 rupees a month. Even her pocket money was not forthcoming at first.[16]

In October 1914, less than a year after their arrival in Cooch Behar, the couple's first child, Ila Devi, was born. Just over a year later Indira gave birth to a boy, Jagaddipendra, known as Bhaiya, who would be next in line to the throne. Indira and Jit would have three more children: Indrajit, born in 1918, Gayatri Devi, born in London in May 1919, and Menaka, born in 1920. Gayatri was nick-named Ayesha, not after the wife of the Prophet Muhammad but because her mother was reading Rider Haggard's *She* at the time of her birth. Ayesha in the book is the 'she-who-must-be-obeyed', an ageless and immortal sorceress who waits two thousand years for the reincarnation of her lover.

Absent from Cooch Behar during these years was Sunity Devi, who spent most of her time in Calcutta and London. In her book, *The Autobiography of an Indian Princess*, she praises Indira for giving up 'riches and caste to follow her husband, for love of him' and declares that she had been wanting such a daughter-in-law for years.[17] But aside from these brief mentions, Indira is invisible in the autobiography and relations between the two headstrong women would remain strained. Years later, in 1929 when Sunity Devi was on her deathbed in London and pawning her own jewellery to meet her rent arrears, Indira ignored her mother-in-law's plight and refused to help clear her debts.

Despite their state's dire financial situation, Jit and Indira made frequent trips to England and Europe. James Jupp, who ran the stage door at the Gaiety theatre, recalled Jit's generosity in his 1923 memoir of life in London's West End:

> The Maharaja of Cooch Behar thought as little of presenting a lady with a Rolls-Royce, a diamond tiara, or even a furnished villa in the country or up the river as I should of standing a pal a cup of tea. I mention Cooch Behar's name because on each of his visits to London someone would be the richer, and his generosity was not confined to ladies. This fabulously wealthy Indian Prince was one of the most generous men I have come across, and those people who know nothing of theatrical life and always imagine that there

must be an ulterior motive behind every gift, would but need to know Cooch Behar for a short time to realize that his presents were only the outcome of a generous nature.[18]

Jit's horoscope predicted that if he passed the age of thirty-six he would achieve greatness. By 1918, however, he was succumbing to the effects of alcoholism and in the same year he went to England with Indira and their children for treatment. He never returned to Cooch Behar, dying in London on 20 December 1922, his thirty-sixth birthday. His cremation at Golders Green was a solemn occasion softened only by the bittersweet reunion of Indira with her parents for the first time since her marriage. Also present was the man whose hand she had refused, Madho Rao Scindia of Gwalior, now married to Gajaraju from the Rane family of Goa. At the age of thirty, Indira was a widow with five children to look after. Ayesha recalls her mother on the voyage back to India as 'dressed entirely in white, crying a lot and shutting herself in her cabin'.[19] Jit's ashes were scattered in the Ganges.

Jit's death triggered a political crisis. Bhaiya was now the Maharaja of Cooch Behar, but because he was just six years old, a regent needed to be appointed until he could rule in his own right. As happened when Madho Singh died in Jaipur, the India Office's preference was for a ruling council headed by an Englishman. Female regents were rare, notable exceptions being the four successive begums who ruled Bhopal for more than a century after the death of Nawab Nazar Mohammad Khan in 1820. Strong-willed like her father, educated abroad and out of purdah, Indira was adamant that she would rule in her husband's wake until Bhaiya turned eighteen. Despite relentless pressure and prejudice from the British who dismissed her as irresponsible and incapable of succeeding, she won every important battle ranging from the education of her children to her choice of advisers—and left the state in a better financial position than when her husband died.

That Indira was not prepared to compromise on her core values was evident from the start. When a group of Brahmin priests came to the palace wearing 'tattered robes and ashes to smear [her] with the filth of disgrace' for being a widow, Indira's response was: 'Ashes for me? Absurd you fools. Get out of here. Go back to your ignorant rabble in the temples. You with your drums and charms and witchcraft. Out of my sight, I say, and stay out. I rule this state and if there is trouble I'll smash your temples to dust.'[20]

Another example of her independence was her choice as chief adviser—V.N. Mehta, a Marathi rather than a Bengali. Her defence was that Bengalis were not trusted by Cooch Beharis. Lord Lytton, the Governor General of Bengal, wrote to Viceroy Reading pointing out that such attitudes reflected her Baroda upbringing but should be resisted. 'You will find her a very intelligent woman and easy to talk to. You will not, however, convince her by argument. She is certain to fight to the last to get her way, but she will accept your decision as soon as she finds you are not to be moved,' Lytton explained.[21] Her prejudice against locals in senior positions also extended to Englishmen, whom she tried to exclude from her ruling council. She moved quickly to demonstrate that as regent, she was all-powerful and could get rid of any official, no matter how important their position. 'This is not uncommon among Indian chiefs when they first succeed to ruling powers,' one bureaucrat noted.[22] In Indira's case, however, her taste for power only grew, prompting Lytton to complain that she thought that being a regent gave her the same powers as a ruling chief.

For Indira's children, growing up in Cooch Behar was like a fairy tale. Their home was a massive palace that stood on 1,400 acres with vast stables of ponies to ride and sixty elephants. There were more than 400 staff, including twenty gardeners, twelve mechanics, almost a hundred mahouts and elephant keepers, a professional tennis coach and his assistant, as well as twelve ballboys. Three cooks were employed to prepare English-, Bengali- and Marathi-style foods, each with his separate kitchen, scullery and assistant. Ayesha and her sisters had their individual maids, governesses and tutors. Bhaiya had four servants, while Indira's entourage included a secretary (who, in turn, controlled another secretary and typist), ladies-in-waiting and a number of personal maids.

Ayesha became known as pagli rajkumari, or the mad princess, for taking an intense interest in the lives of the mahouts and the rest of the palace servants. She was allowed the same privileges as her brothers, such as horse riding, duck shooting and shikar. Brought up like a tomboy, she killed her first panther at the age of twelve. Indrajit teasingly called her 'the broomstick' because she was skinny, had straight hair and enjoyed sports. Although her mother approved of these innocent diversions, she wanted her daughters to retain the traditional skills of Indian girls such as cooking.

* * *

In 1919, Indira and Jit had attended a Masonic banquet at one of London's most prestigious dining venues, the Princes' Restaurant in Piccadilly, to honour the contribution of Indian soldiers in World War I. The guest list included Khusru Jung, the dashing twenty-seven-year-old son of the commander-in-chief of the Hyderabad army, Afsar-ul-Mulk. Jung was a cavalry lieutenant, a brilliant polo player and married to the daughter of a Hyderabadi nobleman with whom he had a daughter. Tall and dignified with a carefully manicured moustache, somewhere between a pencil and a toothbrush style, high cheekbones and a receding hairline, he was also the private secretary of the crown prince of Kashmir, Hari Singh. Four years after meeting Indira in London and following the death of his wife and daughter from typhoid, he arrived in Cooch Behar and was appointed her private secretary and controller of the royal household. He went on to be Bhaiya's guardian and would travel with the family whenever they went abroad.

As a Muslim in a position of considerable power in a Hindu state, Jung's appointment was controversial. In June 1925, the leader of Cooch Behar's indigenous Rajbanshi community, Panchanan Varma, submitted a petition to the governor of Bengal objecting to a Muslim being appointed the guardian of a Hindu minor or controlling the affairs of a Hindu royal family. The petition also asked why five Hindus serving on the household staff had been forcibly retrenched to make way for his appointment. Varma alleged that Jung had no educational or other qualifications that would entitle him to 'even half his emoluments'. 'Bad rumours pierce through the ears and tears the Cooch-Beharee's hearts, and the poor Cooch-Beharees are in a very awkward position, as they can neither express nor suppress their feelings.'[23] Varma was later found to have forged the signatures on the petition and was exiled from the state for five years. But its publication in the widely read journal *Modern Review* damaged Indira's standing.

The 'bad rumours' and allegations of nepotism almost certainly related to the widowed maharani's intimate relationship with Jung, something that crossed both moral and communal boundaries. Jung's reputation had already been tarnished over his involvement in attempting to cover up a blackmail attempt against Hari Singh when he was caught in bed in a Paris hotel room with an eighteen-year-old shapely blonde divorcee by an enraged Englishman who claimed to be her husband. Though the sexual tryst happened in 1919, the identity of the unnamed and unwitting 'Eastern potentate' described in court proceedings as only 'Mr A.' was only leaked to the press in 1924. Hari Singh had paid out £150,000 to his blackmailers, prompting *The Times* to call it one of the boldest and most daring cases of its kind in history. Jung was referred to in the report as Hari Singh's private secretary.

The relationship between Indira and Jung is still spoken of in whispered tones. In *A Princess Remembers*, Ayesha refers to him as a Hyderabadi noble who came to look after Cooch Behar's financial affairs. 'He happened also to be a superb horseman and soon began to supervise the care and training of Ma's [Indira's] string of hunters as well as all our ponies. He gave us riding lessons and inspired the boys to try to reach his own mastery.'[24] According to Ayesha, Jung's second daughter, Kamala, who everyone called Baby, was 'adopted' by her mother and 'became so much a part of our family that she lived and travelled with us almost as much as with her father'.[25]

Omitted from official family histories was the fact that Baby was the biological daughter of Indira and Jung and therefore Ayesha's unacknowledged half-sister. 'My father never said much, but all I knew was, yes, that they were very fond of each other and they had a child. And I met her a lot,' admits Ali Khusru Jung, Khusru Jung's son by his third wife. 'It's only human, she being a beautiful woman and he being such a handsome man and being there the whole time looking after the family,' he explains, while urging me to have another lukhmi samosa as we sit talking in his villa overlooking Hussein Sagar in Hyderabad.[26] In photographs taken in the late 1920s and early 1930s, Baby bears a striking resemblance to Ayesha, Ila and Menaka, while retaining some of her father's distinctive features. In the book *From Hyderabad to Hollywood*, the film director Ahmed Lateef, Khusru Jung's grand-nephew, refers to Kamal Apa, another of Baby's nicknames, as Indira's daughter and his grand-uncle as her father.[27]

Since it was never acknowledged officially or by the family, the nature of Indira and Khusru Jung's relationship is difficult to ascertain, but it continued in one form or another until he married a Parsi, Lulu Talyarkhan, in 1941. Photographs and brief mentions of his official role in India Office files provide some clues. An undated photograph taken in Kashmir in 1938, and published in Lateef's book, shows Jung in a pinstriped suit with one hand on Ayesha's shoulder and one on Baby's, with Indira standing just behind him, suggesting a high level of intimacy among the four of them. Another photograph in the possession of a relative shows Jung, Ayesha and Baby speaking to Vivien Leigh on the set of *Gone With the Wind* in 1938. Indira's close and possibly intimate relationship with Douglas Fairbanks ensured that a steady stream of Hollywood actors and directors visited Cooch Behar.

The final separation between Indira and Khusru Jung probably occurred in the late 1930s. According to Indira Dhanrajgir, who was close to the Cooch Behars and knew Jung personally, the pair had parted ways when Indira refused to move to Hyderabad where he had renovated his family home in Somajiguda for her.[28] When he died in 1971, he left nothing for Baby, 'who went back to live with her mother, the Maharani of Cooch Behar', writes Lateef.[29]

What is clear is that the sisterly bond between Ayesha and Baby was a lifelong one. Possibly the last photograph of them together was taken at Lily Pool on Ayesha's seventy-fifth birthday in which Baby bears an uncanny resemblance to Indira in her later years. 'They were friendly and very supportive of each other,' says Prithviraj Singh, Man Singh's son by his second wife, Kishore. Nicknamed Pat, he describes Baby's relationship with the other members of the family as very close. 'She used to call Gayatri, Menaka and Ila didi, or sister.' Pat says that Baby and his deceased wife, Devika, who was Indira's granddaughter, were particularly attached to each other. 'Baby looked after [Devika and her two brothers] because my wife's mother died at a young age.'[30] When pressed on parentage, members of the Jaipur family remain circumspect. 'Baby didn't face up to the reality of what was what ... I mean it's hardly a subject she would discuss,' says a family member who asked to remain anonymous.[31] Baby later married Bijai Singh, the son of the polo great Hanut Singh. The couple had a daughter, Harsh Kumari, and a son, Kunwar Lakshman Singh (usually known as Bunny).

Khusru Jung's presence protected Indira from increasingly hostile attacks from the British over her management of the state. In 1927, she notified the India Office that she was travelling to England to enrol Bhaiya in a boarding school and was taking Jung and her children with her. The trip was a complex undertaking. Guardians and governesses were needed and suitable accommodation for those children attending day school had to be found. And, as always, the India Office had to be informed of every arrangement being planned. But for Indira it was a necessity. The children's privileged upbringing in Cooch Behar was spoiling them, particularly Bhaiya, who was fast approaching the age when he would take over the duties of ruler. He was already insisting that he be addressed as Yuvraj or Crown Prince. 'No one dared to cross him and he got his way in just about everything,' Ayesha recalled.[32] For Indira the last straw was noticing that whenever he played cricket with local boys, they were too afraid to call out 'how's that!' when he was clearly out. Even the umpire would be silent.

In November 1927, Indira joined England's aristocracy for the opening of the hunting season at Melton Mowbray in Leicestershire. In hunting circles royal patronage had secured Melton Mowbray's position as the place to be seen and ensured its reputation for raffish behaviour. The Prince of Wales, who first met Wallis Simpson at Melton Mowbray, recalled the hunting fields around the town: 'Intermixed with the local landed gentry ... was a lively sampling of dashing figures, noblemen and their ladies; wealthy people who had discovered that the stable door was a quick if expensive short-cut into society ... [and] ladies whose pursuit of a fox was only a phase of an even more intense pursuit of romance.'[33]

Indira stayed at the Spinnies in Thorpe Road during the season of 1927–28 and then at Staveley Lodge for the 1928–29 hunt. 'She is a familiar sight in this exclusive district, flying over hill and down dale with her long veil streaming behind her,' the *Springfield Leader and Press* reported. Unfortunately, her habit of riding side-saddle because of her sari, the paper observed, led to a number of severe falls.[34] The presence of her children also attracted attention, with one newspaper describing them as 'attractive little olive-skinned people, who seemed to be quite at home on horseback'.[35] Stories of Indira's regal elegance spread as far as the US Midwest, with the *Arizona Star* informing its readers: 'If one were seeking an up-to-date heroine for an Indian novel, she could be found in this lithe, bobbed-hair enchantress, who has defied all the rules of the Orient for the repression of women.'[36]

Being considered one of the greatest beauties of her time was not the only factor that helped Indira win so many hearts and earn such admiration. She was well educated, well read and had great style. Her boudoir in Cooch Behar was laid out with a rug stitched together from the skins of fourteen leopards shot by Ila.[37] 'The more orthodox maharajas affect to deprecate her Europeanisation; but in actual fact consult her in their affairs and invite her to smarten up their wives, mentally and socially, by her example. To the womanhood of India, she stands for social progress. She is, in their eyes, a heroine,' noted her friend, the novelist and playwright William Gerhardi.[38]

Indira also challenged prevailing social norms in India, where widows were expected to follow a life of inner reflection and asceticism. In his book *Fields Elysian*, Simon Blow claimed that Indira came all the way from India to Melton Mowbray specifically to woo Hugh Molyneux, the 'Adonis of Oakham', who was 'followed everywhere by admiring female eyes'.[39] Molyneux would later become among the first of Edwina Mountbatten's many lovers. It was there that she met the Duke of Kent and the Prince of Wales. Rumours that the prince was one of her paramours are supported by an ambiguously worded secret cable sent from the Secretary of State to the Viceroy on 12 March 1929, stating that the 'maharani's notoriety' was not just the creation of newspapers but relied on facts 'brought to notice by the King and the Prince of Wales by their own personal knowledge'.[40]

What started off as an eight-month-long stay in England and the continent kept getting extended, much to the annoyance of the India Office, which demanded that Indira return to resume her official duties. Her ADC, N. Gupta, defended her absence saying that she was 'in constant contact with her state officials and is not aware of any urgent matters of state awaiting discussion with her'. In any case, she planned to return by autumn.[41] Gupta's excuse failed to appease the Secretary of State for India Lord Birkenhead, who refused to extend permission for Indira to stay beyond September. Indira's response was to get her London-based lawyers to consult the original 1816 kharita, or agreement, between Lord Moira, the Governor General of India, and the ruler of Cooch Behar. As she triumphantly pointed out, the British had 'agreed to abstain from all interference, except in the form of advice and representation, in the unlimited management of the affairs of the State'.[42]

*　*　*

In January 1929, the political secretary to the Government of India, C.C. Watson, wrote to Sir Stanley Jackson, the governor of Bengal, saying it was time to confront the maharani with evidence of her misconduct. Not only had she overstayed her time in England and Europe and run up enormous debts, 'her relations with the opposite sex at Melton Mowbray had attracted unfavourable notice'. The letter ended by noting that 'The King has considerable concern and pressed the Secretary of State for her recall to India'.[43] Once she returned she would be given two options: attending to her duties for at least a year or resigning her post as regent. If she refused both, she would be formally removed as regent, her son's allowances cut and a guardian appointed to look after the boy. If she did return to England, the maharaja and his tutor-guardian must have a separate establishment so that the boy 'may not throughout his holidays be exposed to undesirable influences'. The confidential telegram also stated that Bhaiya had inherited 'an undesirable taint from which two Maharajas have in recent years succumbed and he should there-fore be removed and kept, as far as possible, from the conditions likely to develop this taint in him'.[44] While not spelled out specifi-cally, the taint referred to was almost certainly an excessive con-sumption of alcohol.

A month later, Indira met with Watson at Bikaner House in Delhi and told him she wanted a new comptroller. 'While quite compe-tent for Indian conditions [Khusru Jung] was entirely at sea in England,' she explained to Watson. The large excesses in expenditure that occurred during her first two years in England 'were largely due to his lack of knowledge of English values'. There would not be similar excesses in the future, she assured Watson.[45]

Jung's deficit when it came to 'English values' was unlikely to have been the cause of the rift between Indira and her lover. A more likely explanation is that Indira had found another paramour or that her relationship with Jung was attracting too much attention. In 1933, when he had moved to Kashmir to take up the post of special minister of state, the outspoken newspaper *Guru Ghantal* railed against the appointment of a Muslim to such an important position in Maharaja Hari Singh's administration. 'He is a Minister in a Hindu state, secondly he is too intimate with a Hindu Raja and thirdly he has love connections in a very respectable and noble family of Kooch Behar. All these considerations forced us to acquaint the said family of Kooch Behar with these said affairs, to show to Khusru Jung's sweetheart, name Vassota [presumably one of Indira's pet names], her love letters, and to point out to Hari Singh ... that he is keeping company with a man who is not worth of his confidence.'[46] The maharaja responded by banning *Guru Ghantal*'s circulation in his state. Outraged by the ban, one disgruntled reader published leaked love letters between Khusru Jung and Indira as pamphlets and cir-culated them in Punjab, Jammu and Kashmir, Cooch Behar and Baroda. 'The race course [at Lahore] was full of these booklets. Everybody in the hotel where Raja Hari Singh and his party were staying received a copy,' a confidential India Office memo noted.[47]

The Bikaner House meeting also addressed what Watson described as the 'unfavourable impressions regarding her conduct, which appeared to have gained credence in certain quarters'.[48] He declined to put the contents of the conversation on the record, pre-ferring to share them with the viceroy verbally. 'When she asked my advice, I told her that it was desirable in her own interests that she should be most careful to do nothing that might give grounds for a recrudescence of the stories and I gravely doubted the wisdom of her decision to return to England during the summer.' If she did so, she should keep 'a distance from the milieu with which she had to some extent identified herself while in Melton'. Indira told Watson she intended to do just that once the children were settled in their respective schools and arrangements for tutors and guardians had been made. The conversation ended on a delicate note, with Indira remarking that she had seldom been at a nightclub without meeting Lord Birkenhead there, including one club that was raided by the police. Concluded Watson: 'I felt this was a pretty unanswerable point.'[49]

A few months after the meeting, a secret India Office memo was prepared listing her alleged misdemeanours. It noted that she was appointed regent to administer the state on behalf of her minor son, but instead she went straight to London, making it her headquarters with brief occasional visits to Cooch Behar. 'She bought a place in Melton Mowbray where she maintains a stud of hunters and staff of servants and which she rarely visits. She became very unpopular in Melton with the farmers and tradesmen as she rarely paid her bills.' Despite Lord Birkenhead's insistence that she return to India, she came up with one excuse after another to prolong her stay. Her activities would be of no concern to the India Office except that she was the regent of Cooch Behar, the memo continued. 'She has got into a bad gambling and drinking set and preferred the ministrations of Mrs Maywick in the Soho night clubs to the less stimulating salon in Bloomsbury of the Countess of Oxford and Asquith. She demoralized the youth of the town and the young officers of the Household Cavalry to such an extent that the Royal Horse Guards (Blue) became known as the "the Blacks",' the memo stated. Scribbled in the margin was a notation in pencil stating: 'THIS IS TOO LURID!' with the initials L.T.M. scrawled beside it. The memo went on to add that the thirteen-year-old maharaja was showing plenty of promise 'and it would be a thousand pities if he were not now taken in hand and brought up in a way which will give him a chance of turning out a success. The last two Maharajas have died at an early age of dissipation and drink and the surviving brother of the last one is a genial and undischarged bankrupt.'[50]

Indira's reputation among the British political establishment plunged to unprecedented lows when the *Sunday Times* published details of a party she threw at Cannes in September 1929. The centrepiece of the party was a glittering fountain filled with fifty cases of champagne. 'White-clad guests dined at tables set round a small walled garden which was decorated with tall white pillars entwined with lilies and scattered about with white sofas and chairs,' the paper reported in its society pages. 'In between supping and dancing one could step straight into the baccarat rooms of the new summer casino, which is called Palm Beach, and from the outside resembles nothing so much as a pale pink ice pudding. In the early hours of the morning the Ranee herself came into the rooms wearing white satin pyjamas, with her triple row of marvellous pearls, and laughingly declared she was going to "banco" everyone dressed in white, as they had deserted her party too soon.' Her winnings that night, the paper continued, were considerable.[51] The article was pasted in a secret India Office file on Indira's regency. Handwritten notes by S.B.A. Patterson, the ADC to the secretary of state for India, cautioned that 'this is bound to get into the Indian papers' and referred to Indira as a 'disreputable woman'.[52]

The publication of the article led to renewed calls that Indira be divested of her title of regent. 'If she is to be stripped of this title it should be on the grounds of continuous bad behaviour without too much emphasis on a single report from the *Sunday Times* story as it is part of a cumulative indictment and perhaps not so bad on its own. An option is to consult the Viceroy on the question that on her next return to India she should not politely be given the choice of resigning the Regency or of remaining in India,' recommended the vice president of the council of regency in Cooch Behar, Lieutenant Colonel W.G. Hutchison.[53]

Fortunately for Indira, the one important ally she had in the India Office was the Viceroy, Lord Irwin. 'Until we decide to take a stronger line with Princes like Jamnagar, Kapurthala, Baroda and Rajpipla, I feel that action proposed in the case of the Maharani will be considered oppressive and unjust,' he wrote in response to Hutchison's recommendation.[54] An unsigned note on Whitehall stationary expresses the frustrations of those lower down the chain. 'I do not think we can squabble with the Viceroy about this miserable woman.' Only the King and Queen, the note says, can overrule the Viceroy. 'Of course, the Maharani will make no difficulty about spending a large portion of the summer on the continent, which for her means gambling at Deauville.'[55]

Outside the India Office building at Whitehall, Indira had no shortage of admirers. Her friend the American heiress and socialite Evalyn Walsh McLean described her as 'the embodiment of charm and grace, the Princess of the *One Thousand and One Nights'*. Recalling the first time she saw her at the casino in Le Touquet, she wrote:

> The most fabulously beautiful young Indian lady, holding the longest cigarette holder I had ever seen, wearing a brilliant silk sari and covered with pearls, emeralds, and rubies. She was quite poker-faced but had a pile of chips in front of her to testify to her success and to top it all she had a little live turtle, whose back was laden with three strips of emeralds, diamonds, and rubies and which she was apparently using as a talisman. Every now and then the creature would crawl away across the table but every time she caught it back. The crowd was totally mesmerized by her.[56]

The scandals over Indira's alleged behaviour at Cannes, her intimate relationship with Khusru Jung and her numerous alleged lovers are left out of Ayesha's memoir. In it she merely describes her mother's social life as 'very active'. She recalls often meeting her in the entrance hall of their house on South Audley Street in London, coming home from an all-night party just as she and her sisters were leaving for school.[57] Ayesha would later portray her mother as her role model, but there is little evidence that she inherited much of her liberated spirit. Whereas Indira was not afraid to take on the British establishment and never compromised when it came to asserting herself as a woman, Ayesha tolerated, initially at least, the strictures of purdah and was prepared to accept others sharing her future husband's bed, in return for being the trophy wife of the Maharaja of Jaipur.

* * *

In November 1929, Indira was travelling in an Imperial Airlines seaplane from London to India when it crashed while trying to take-off from Alexandria. The plane hit a reef inside the harbour, tearing a large hole in the hull, which immediately started to fill with water. As the pilot attempted to steer the plane towards shallower water, the eight passengers climbed on top of the fuselage. Indira's coat got caught in the propeller and she narrowly avoided being cut to pieces. William Gerhardi was not so lucky, his foot being cut to the bone by the propeller. After returning to their rooms at Hillier's

Guest House another male passenger unsuccessfully attempted to iron her pyjamas. 'As he had soaked himself up to the neck in an effort to rescue my powder-case, it did not lower him in my estimation,' Indira told reporters.[58]

Just before she left England on that ill-fated plane journey, Indira had met Man Singh, who by now was universally referred to by his friends both in Jaipur and abroad as 'Jai'. They had first become acquainted at Ootacamund when he was a shy, plump thirteen-year-old who turned up at the Cooch Behars unannounced, begging for good Indian food for lunch rather than the bland English fare he had to put up with. It was inevitable that Jai and Indira would meet again. Both loved horses and polo, both moved in similar social circles and shared the same friends, including Noel Coward and the Mountbattens. Quentin Crewe describes the Jaipur Maharaja as being 'very fond' of the glamorous maharani and says that they became 'close friends'. For her part, she found the handsome and gentle young man 'extremely attractive'. Notes Crewe: 'Jai's friendship with her, and later with her children, was to be the most important thing in his private life.'[59] Ann Morrow speculates that they had a passionate and long-running affair, but provides no evidence for it.[60] What is certain is that their liaison was widely known even if it was not met with universal approval. After seeing Jai buying expensive gifts for Indira while in Delhi, the Kanota diarist and head of Jaipur's state forces, Amar Singh, noted: 'This lady is going to ruin him, as I hear she has done to a good many before.'[61]

In October 1930, Jai was back in Jaipur preparing for his coronation. A year later, Marudhar gave birth to a baby boy, Bhawani Singh. When asked more than sixty years later why friends always referred to him as Bubbles, Bhawani told Derek Brown of the *Guardian* that it had to do with a curse. 'Some time ago a holy man came to the palace gates for alms, but he was turned away. So he cursed the family, saying there would be no male heirs for two generations. And do you know, he was right. My grandfather was adopted and so was my father.' His birth, by breaking the curse, prompted so much champagne being drunk, his English nurse nicknamed him Bubbles. 'And so I have been ever since.'[62] *The Jaipur Album*, a gazetteer of important events and personalities, reported that the auspicious news of the first male heir to be born in more than a century 'turned people wild with joy and expressions of their happiness were most earnest and spontaneous. The whole city wore a fairy appearance at night, the highways, palaces and gates were dazzling with electric bulbs of various hues … A special Durbar was held in the City Palace in which His Highness most graciously accepted the congratulations of the subjects and announced certain generous measures for the welfare of his people.'[63]

Two months after the birth celebrations were over, Jai found himself in Woodlands, Indira's family home in the Calcutta suburb of Alipore. It was Christmas season in Calcutta and that meant endless rounds of parties, society balls and polo matches. Full of anticipation for his arrival was Indira's headstrong twelve-year-old daughter, Ayesha.

4

POLO AND PINK CHAMPAGNE

Today nothing remains of one of Calcutta's most glamorous residences. Built in classical East India Company style, with Ionic columns and encircled by deep verandas, Woodlands was used as a prison for the descendants of the great warrior king Tipu Sultan before it was taken over by the British in the early nineteenth century. When Nripendra Narayan, Ayesha's paternal grandfather, purchased it as his Calcutta estate in the 1880s, it was eclipsed in grandeur only by Belvedere, the Governor General's residence located across the road.

Entered through large iron gates emblazoned with the Cooch Behar crest, Woodlands had its own cricket ground, two tennis courts, a riding track and a polo field. Weekly tennis parties attracted up to 200 guests. When the band played 'God Save Our Gracious Queen', a young Jitendra, the future ruler of Cooch Behar, used to sing the words of the anthem from the upstairs porch much to the delight of the assembled guests. Under Indira's guidance the residence received a complete facelift. Every room was decorated in a unique theme. The drawing room featured a wooden Chinese screen encrusted with jade and rose quartz. Her own room was Oriental in style, filled with divans and Persian carpets, carved rosewood side tables and gilded mirrors. She slept on a carved ivory bed, with great elephant tusks sticking dangerously out of the legs. Her bathroom was built in marble with the steam bath disguised as a chaise longue.

In the winter of 1931–32, the guests who came to party and stay included Hari Singh, the Maharaja of Kashmir, Prince Aly Khan, the son of the Aga Khan, and the Hollywood star Douglas Fairbanks, Sr, who arrived minus the buttons on his suit. They had been torn off by souvenir hunters who mobbed him as he tried to cross Howrah Bridge. The most anticipated guest, however, was the eighteen-year-old newly invested Maharaja of Jaipur. A few days later, Jai drove through the gates in an open-topped green Rolls-Royce. Ayesha would later recall her excitement at the sight of sixty polo ponies, each with its own uniformed groom with a flowing orange turban, that preceded his arrival. Despite being almost seven years younger she was clearly enamoured of the handsome prince. 'Calcutta found him charming and relaxed, and yet he generated an air of graceful confidence that was most compelling. He laughed and joked with everyone in his low drawling voice, and was very flirtatious, which made him all the more attractive. It was his humour and the sympathy he added to it that drew me so forcefully to him,' she would later write.[1]

Jai played tennis with Ayesha and her older sister Menaka, inviting his ADC or another member of his staff to make a foursome and then deliberately letting the girls win. Later, when he challenged Ayesha to a bicycle race, she lost decisively, despite considering herself a swift and reckless rider. 'He took to the family and they to him. It was as if they became the family he'd never had after his removal from Isarda,' writes Quentin Crewe.[2] Ayesha couldn't bring herself to address Jai as anything other than Your Highness. He was, in her own words, 'quite outside my orbit'.[3]

After the polo season ended, Jai was back in Jaipur where arrangements were in full swing for his second marriage, this time to fifteen-year-old Kishore Kumari, a decade after they had been betrothed. The marriage made headlines around the world, with the *Washington Post* describing the wedding procession as a 'pageant of Oriental splendour. The maharaja's strings of pearls, priceless diamonds and rubies glistened in the light of the full moon as he passed under arches of multicoloured lamps festooned across the streets.'[4] The *Times of India* piled on the superlatives calling it 'a brilliant and most distinguished gathering, the best of Rajputana and therefore the cream of India'.[5]

Though she was still in her mid-teens, Kishore was no pushover. Plans to make their devotions at various shrines and temples a day after the wedding were delayed by several hours because of her insistence that either her uncle, the Maharaja of Jodhpur, or her brother accompany them. She also broke protocol by demanding a gun salute when she left the palace and again when she arrived at Amber Fort. For his part Jai was disappointed by the twenty-eight 'rather shoddy' horses that came as part of her dowry.[6]

Relations between Kishore—who was now officially Second Her Highness and nicknamed 'Jo Didi' (a reference to Jodhpur)—and First Her Highness, her aunt Marudhar, were bound to be difficult. At first, Jo never touched food brought from outside the zenana and ate only those dishes that were prepared by her own servants for fear of poisoning. Rumours that First Her Highness disliked Second Her Highness because she was much younger and prettier found plenty of takers in the febrile atmosphere of rivalry and intrigue that permeated the women's quarters. When news of Jai's second marriage reached Cooch Behar, Indira described Jo as being 'pretty and petite' as well as 'bright and lively'. Ayesha recalls listening to the news 'with intense interest'.[7]

Jai was back in Calcutta in December 1932 for another season of polo. Fresh from winning the India Polo Championship, he asked Indira if Ayesha could join him for a celebration dinner at Firpo's on Chowringhee Road, famous for its turtle soup and lobster thermidor, and the favourite meeting place for the city's tea planters, jute-wallahs and aspiring gentry. When Indira agreed, Ayesha and her maid went shopping for a special dress and shoes. During the dinner, Ayesha chose to sit next to one of Jai's young ADCs. The group dined on partridges which Jai helped cut for her and after dinner she was driven home by his chauffeur, the experience leaving her 'dizzy and unbelieving'.[8]

Indira's readiness to acquiesce to Jai's request reflected her unconventionality which extended to the upbringing of her children. Even at thirteen Ayesha was better at conversing with Jai than most other Indian girls. Indira was also impressed with Jai's kindness and loyalty. 'He had become a member of the family and would never have betrayed that trust,' Crewe asserts.[9]

By now Ayesha's infatuation had turned into a full-blown teenage crush. Shortly after the dinner at Firpo's, Jai invited her and Menaka to his house for supper. When their governess arrived to take them home at nine, Jai lied, telling her that Indira had given them permis-

sion to stay up late. He then offered Ayesha and her sister champagne. 'After that I began having more ambitious daydreams—that
the floor of his room which was immediately above the one that
Menaka and I shared would fall through in the middle of the night,
land him (miraculously uninjured) in our room to spend the rest of
the night with us. I even began wishing for something that seemed
to me even more unlikely—that I would be beautiful and that Jai
would actually kiss me.'[10]

In early 1933, Indira announced that instead of going straight to
Baroda for one of their periodic visits, the family would take a
detour to Ajmer, where Indrajit, Ayesha's brother, was attending
Mayo College. Hearing that the family was going to Ajmer, Jai
invited them to visit Jaipur first. Ayesha recounts Jai greeting them
dressed in his military uniform, surrounded by immaculately
turned-out ADCs, when their train arrived in the early morning.
She describes Jaipur as having 'an extraordinary pastel, fairy-tale
quality, something quite different from anything I had ever seen
before'. The family was taken to the Rambagh Palace—a series of
pleasure pavilions a couple of miles from the city, which he had
turned into his residence. 'All the servants wore gold cummerbunds
and beautifully tied turbans with dashing great fans of starched cloth
on one side, while the ADCs wore jodhpurs and buttoned-up jackets or military uniforms.'[11] Later he took the family to Amber where
he narrated his entire ancestral history to Ayesha.

In the afternoon, Indira, together with Ayesha and her sisters,
visited the zenana quarters at the Rambagh Palace where they met
Jai's two wives for the first time. Ayesha found Jo to be as pretty
and petite as her mother had described her. What she didn't expect
was a woman wearing make-up, with her hair in a fashionable bob
and speaking excellent English, her manner 'alive and gay and full
of chatter'. Her apartment was appointed with modern furniture
and would not have looked out of place in England, Europe or
Calcutta. First Her Highness was the opposite. She wore no make-
up and made no pretence to modernity, but her manners were
'regal and impeccable'.[12]

Jo was already pregnant with her first child when Ayesha met
her, a fact that she was either unaware of or chose not to mention
in her memoir. She gave birth to a baby boy named Jai Singh on

5 May 1933 at Staines, a town just outside London, while accompanying Jai on his second polo season in England. In late December 1935, the couple had another boy named Prithviraj. The brothers would forever be known as Joey and Pat. Both would complete their schooling at Harrow, the preferred institution for the sons of Indian and Middle Eastern potentates, with Joey attending the same classes as the future kings of Jordan and Iraq and the future Nizam of Hyderabad. After their education both would be sent to work in Calcutta to hone their business skills. Pat recalls the halcyon days of growing up in the Rambagh Palace, riding bicycles up and down its marble corridors and spotting wild panthers drinking at the fountain in the courtyard every day. 'I wouldn't say we had an intimate family relationship, but we had a good relationship,' says Pat referring to his father. 'Maybe a little formal by European standards, but a good relationship.' As for his mother, he scoffs at suggestions that she spent her days confined to the zenana. 'There was a zenana [in Rambagh] but it was a zenana only in name and we were certainly not raised in the zenana.' Jo Didi used purdah only as an escape 'when she wanted to avoid doing something like going to a dinner party'.[13]

The prospect of purdah and the potential intricacies of being part of a polygamous family were far from Ayesha's mind on her second day at Jaipur as she and Jai rode for kilometres through his private nature reserve, spotting blackbuck and peacocks. A few days after this excursion, Jai told Indira he wanted to marry her fifteen-year-old daughter. Indira's response, which she related to Ayesha soon after, was: 'I never heard such sentimental rubbish.'[14]

Jai's formal proposal of marriage came two years later in 1936 when the pair found themselves together in London. Indira had gone back to Cooch Behar with Ila, who had shocked her mother by secretly marrying Romendra Kishore Deb Burman, a cousin of the ruler of the small eastern kingdom of Tripura. Ayesha remained in London with her siblings, in the care of her Baroda grandmother, Chimnabai, who was staying at her usual suite at the Dorchester Hotel. Ayesha had just spent a year attending school at Santiniketan in Bengal and was about to start finishing school at Lausanne. On impulse, she had gone to a fortune teller who told her that her fate 'was inextricably linked with a young man who was going to fly away in an aeroplane and that I must get in touch with him before I left'.[15] Ayesha rang Jai, who picked her up in his Bentley and took her for a drive around Hyde Park. Turning to her he asked her if she remembered that he had told her mother he wanted to marry her when she grew up. Without taking his eyes off the road, he went on to say that although she was only sixteen and still at school he needed to plan ahead. 'Before I ask Ma and go through all the proper formalities, I'd like to know what you feel. Remember I play polo and ride and fly and I may have a horrible accident, still, will you marry me?' Ayesha immediately answered yes.[16]

Over the remainder of the spring of 1936, the couple continued to meet secretly, sometimes on the pretence of Ayesha going to a movie with friends or needing to go to the bank. Arrangements were made using a phone booth in Pont Street as all calls to her room at the Dorchester were monitored by Chimnabai or Ayesha's governess. She would later look back at those heady months with nostalgia. '[It] was more fun than an ordinary approved courtship would have been. There was the challenge of outwitting our elders, of arranging secret meetings, of working out how to have letters posted without the knowledge of the ADCs, governesses, or clerks who usually handled this chore. And every now and again there was the marvellous, unheard-of liberty of going for a drive in the country with Jai, of a stolen dinner at Bray, or of an outing on the river in a boat. Altogether, it was a lovely and intoxicating time.'[17]

The couple sealed their courtship by buying gold rings for each other with their names engraved inside. First Jai and then Ayesha finally wrote to Indira disclosing their plans. Indira's response was non-committal, merely saying that they should wait and see how they felt after a couple of years. Her reticence was understandable. Jai already had two wives and going to Jaipur would mean a life in purdah for her daughter. She also wanted to avoid hurting Jo Didi. And, there may have been an element of jealousy now that Indira was no longer Jai's primary object of desire—even if their 'affair' amounted to nothing more than a reciprocal flirtation. According to Ayesha, what Indira feared most of all was that her daughter would simply become 'the latest addition to the Jaipur nursery'.[18]

When plans for the wedding were announced in early 1940, it was Ayesha's brother Jagaddipendra, known as Bhaiya, by then the ruler of Cooch Behar, who was most concerned. The two men had been each other's closest friends for the best part of a decade—sharing adventures during their London summers that went far beyond attending polo matches and socializing at parties. Bhaiya came straight to the point, warning his sister that if she married Jai she could not expect him to give up seeing other women. 'Jai isn't going to stop liking girls or taking them out just because he's married to you,' he said. 'And really, you mustn't mind.' Ayesha responded by saying that she would mind, adding, 'If he marries me, why does he need all those other girls?'[19] Anne Wright, who was close to the Cooch Behar family, recalls Indira reminding Ayesha: 'You are marrying a Krishna and you may not be very happy. But she was so crazy about him that she didn't care.'[20]

While Ayesha knew her brother might behave in such a way, she was convinced that Jai was different and if they were apart he would mope around rather than have affairs. When she explained this to Bhaiya, he said: 'But men don't do that. Please understand Jai may love you and want to marry you, but that has nothing to do with his being attracted to other girls. Men are like that. It doesn't mean anything.' His sister's response was: 'To me it would mean a lot. I'd hate it.' The conversation ended with Bhaiya saying in a despairing voice: 'Don't say I didn't warn you.'[21]

* * *

On a warm evening in the summer of 1935 in London, heads turned and pedestrians scrambled for cover as two brand-new Bentley saloons raced each other down Piccadilly in London. Even if the police could have stopped the powerful sports cars before they disappeared in the direction of Knightsbridge Barracks, there was little they could have done. The drivers were Indian royalty with diplomatic immunity and had friends in the highest of places.

Released from the tradition-bound strictures that governed their behaviour back in India, Jai and Bhaiya were determined to live on the wild side whenever they were together. 'Jai and myself used to race about Calcutta and Jai once missed a bullock cart by literally six inches while travelling at eighty miles an hour,' Bhaiya recalled. 'I call Jai dangerous, and Jai calls me dangerous, so I expect we both are.'[22]

Each summer, from 1933 onward, Jai and Bhaiya were permanent fixtures on England's polo and party scenes. Jai's routine was
to leave Jaipur in the first week of May and return in late September
or early October, spending most of his time in England and the
continent. The English socialite and aristocrat Ursula d'Abo was one
of many women enamoured by Jaipur's young maharaja when she
met him in 1933 as a seventeen-year-old at the Court Ball in
Buckingham Palace. 'He was dressed in an Afghan safa with a turban
covered in the most dazzling jewels you could ever imagine to see.
I was totally mesmerized by the jewels and his looks because he was
breathtakingly handsome. He had no wife in tow and was very
young and never left my side.'[23] If Jai's ADCs were ever asked what
he did in England they would say: 'Oh, parties, of course.'[24] New
friendships were made as each year Jai and Bhaiya invited their
English compatriots to visit their princely states for more parties,
more polo and the thrill of big-game shooting.

One such friend was Joan Eyres Monsell, the wealthy twenty-
one-year-old daughter of Bolton Eyres Monsell, the First Lord of
the Admiralty. Beautiful and tall and credited with setting a fashion
trend by wearing Grecian curls at the back of her long neck, she was
a semi-professional photographer who moved in the musical and
artistic circles of London and Paris. Among her many admirers was
Alan Pryce-Jones, who later became the editor of the *Times Literary
Supplement*, but in 1932 was an Oxford dropout. Her family discouraged the relationship.[25]

In November 1933, Joan sailed for India and Australia with her
mother and some cousins. The intention was to forget about her
infatuation with Alan. The plan worked, but not as intended. One
infatuation led to another. In February 1934, the *Bystander* reported
that Joan was enjoying her stay in India, 'but in a different way to
what she does in this country. She rides every morning (the ponies
belonging to the Maharajah of Jaipur); she drives in a large and fast
car, also belonging to the Maharajah, and she watches polo.'[26]

There are no details on what transpired between them in the
weeks that Joan spent in Jaipur, but Jai's heart was clearly broken
when she sailed for England on 10 March 1934. In a letter to his best
friend, Man Singh, the Raja of Barwara, Jai wrote: 'My pretty girl
sailed for England on the 10th. Oh Rabbit [Jai's nickname for Man

Singh], I am heartbroken she has gone. I do love her so much and she was so marvellous. Have you found any girl? ... Yours ever, Jai.'[27] Four days later he wrote again: 'You lucky devil finding a girl so soon. I have not been able to look at any since Joan. Anyhow I have got two American girls coming to stay with me today. Will let you know what they are like.'[28] Ayesha, whose mother had been approached by Jai for her daughter's hand in marriage, gets no mention in the correspondence.

Jai and Joan continued to be friends, though not necessarily lovers. In 1935 they were pictured together in London's society pages dancing at a charity ball in aid of the Artists General Benevolent Fund. Jai gave her a piece of jewellery comprising precious stones inlaid in gold. When she sold her jewellery to build a house many years later, it was the only piece she kept. Scribbled on the back of one of her notebooks from 1936 was a piece of doggerel verse that included the lines:

one to marry, black as ink
Maharajah[29]

As Joan's biographer Simon Fenwick notes, she never revealed the full story of her relationship with her Indian admirer. In 1944, while working as a cypher clerk in Cairo, she met the travel writer Patrick Leigh Fermor, who at the time was attached to the Special Operations Executive. They eventually married in 1968.

* * *

Jai's attraction to beautiful women and expensive cars was only eclipsed by his love of polo. His obsession with the game began when he was a student at Mayo College. His tutor remembers how at the age of ten or eleven he would roll up his mattress to make a 'horse'. Sitting astride it he would take an ordinary stick in his hand and practise his backhand and forehand swings. His coach at Mayo, Dhonkal Singh, was a member of the crack team of Jodhpur's three-time regent and later of the Maharaja of Idar, Sir Pratap Singh's team. In 1893, the team comprising Sir Pratap, Major Stuart Beatson, Hari Singh (or Hurjee as he was usually known) and Dhonkal Singh defeated the British regimental teams to win the

Indian Polo Championship in Poona. Now that he was linked to Jodhpur by marriage, Jai had access to India's finest polo players.

In 1932, Jai assembled a team comprising himself, Hanut Singh, who was considered the finest player in the world, Hanut's younger brother Abhey Singh, who had married into the Jaipur royal family, and Prithvi Singh, a nephew of the Maharaja of Baria. Jai and Hanut had handicaps of eight. Abhey and Prithvi had handicaps of seven. In 1933, they sailed to England with thirty-nine horses, most of them from Australia and Argentina, fifty-one syces (grooms) and a polo stick maker. The team was virtually unknown. At first they had mixed success, winning against a side from the west of England but losing to another team, Osmaston. Then their luck changed. In June, Jai's players stunned the polo world by beating Osmaston at the Ranelagh Open Cup. A few days later they won the Ranelagh Challenge and then beat Osmaston again to take the Hurlingham Champion Cup. When they were victorious in the Roehampton Open they became the first side to win all four open championships in the same year. Newspapers lauded them as 'the best polo team ever seen in the West'. Each syce was dressed in green livery with a crimson turban, while the players arrived on the field wearing turbans of the finest silk muslin. 'This is magnificent polo: in tactics, in stick work, in hitting ... and it looks as if Jaipur will carry all before them in London this season.'[30] Their winning spree continued until the end of the season in September, with the Indians taking another five cups back home with them. They went on to win every Indian Polo Association Championship Cup from 1933 to 1939 and most of their tournaments abroad. Before every match, Jai prayed to the goddess Durga, his head bowed in front of his pony. His rivals were starting to wish they had a god of their own.

An unbeatable line-up headed by a prince whose fortune was estimated to be half a billion dollars at the time sent the American press into a frenzy ahead of a possible visit in the late summer of 1934. There was speculation that Jai would bring his two wives, described as having 'panther-like slimness and grace, and the dusky attractions of the most vaunted houri who ever stalked across the pages of "The Arabian Nights" and gladdened the hearts of the ancient rulers of Baghdad'.[31] Jai's team never crossed the Atlantic, though several American players competed with Jai in matches in the UK.

The elitist nature of polo gave Jai a perfect entrée into the world of British high society with its slothful opulence, loose morals and fashionable depravity. The exotic bejewelled maharaja who cut a dashing figure on the polo field became a much sought-after prize. Between matches Jai could be found dining at Veeraswamy's—the favourite restaurant of Eastern potentates, calling on King George at Buckingham Palace, or having afternoon tea with the Labour Prime Minister Ramsay MacDonald at 10 Downing Street in the company of Kashmir's ruler Hari Singh. In June 1935, he was spotted at the Court Ball at St James's Palace dressed in gold brocade and 'draped in countless necklaces composed of outsize rubies, emeralds, sapphires and diamonds. What could be seen of his turban was red and white, but it was hidden by waterfalls of diamonds,' *Tatler* magazine reported.[32] In the same week he attended a party hosted by Vijaysinhji, the Maharaja of Rajpipla, at the Savoy, which was 'notable for the number of pretty women present' and still going strong at 4 a.m.[33] The following month, an elephant greeted guests at an 'Indo-Chinese' themed party hosted by the American-born German baroness Vivienne Woolley-Hart. Jai was photographed dancing with one of Cecil Beaton's favourite models, the debutante socialite Bridget Poulett.

The endless rounds of parties, pink champagne and polo matches that lasted the length of the English summer offered Jai a break from the unending intrigues and stifling atmosphere of sycophancy in the attar-scented palaces of Jaipur. Leading figures of the polo-playing and horse-owning elite included Louis (Dickie) Mountbatten, who had fallen in love with the game when he visited India in 1921, and who became one of Jai's closest friends. Jai was also a frequent visitor at the home of Dickie's older brother George Milford Haven and his wife, Nada. The smarter of the two Mountbattens—he had been a maths and engineering genius since childhood—George is also remembered for his vast collection of pornography. Lovingly bound into volumes emblazoned with the family crest, the collection specialized in images of incestuous orgies, Marquis de Sade–style sadism and bestiality. The volumes, together with an array of artificial sex organs, were thoughtfully left to the British Museum. Russian-born Nada was a lesbian whose longest relationship was with the mother of the socialite Gloria Vanderbilt. She was also close to Edwina and their extensive travels together to obscure parts of the world fuelled rumours of Lady Mountbatten's bisexuality. Jai, the Mountbattens and the Milford Havens became part of what was known as the 'Palace Gang'.

* * *

In the spring of 1935, the Palace Gang welcomed a new member. Virginia Cherrill was the daughter of an Illinois rancher, whose life would change forever when Charlie Chaplin noticed her on a beach in California. Having never acted before, she starred opposite the silent-era star as the blind flower girl in the 1931 classic *City Lights*. The film critic James Agee would later describe the final scene—in which Virginia encounters Chaplin's Tramp at her flower stand—as 'the greatest single piece of acting ever committed to celluloid'.[34] Suddenly the previously unknown twenty-one-year-old was the most talked about actress in Hollywood.

After a brief marriage to a Chicago lawyer, she met the suave actor Cary Grant at a film premiere. He soon became her second husband. Grant declared Virginia to be 'the most beautiful woman I had ever seen'[35] and told his friend Douglas Fairbanks that she was the 'best lover he'd ever had'.[36] Their marriage, however, proved short-lived. After just seven months he tried to throttle her, leaving her 'bruised and croaking like a bullfrog'. Grant then staged a fake suicide attempt. His jealousy coupled with sexual insecurity was at the root of the couple's marital problems, Virginia told her mother.[37]

After the very public failure of her marriage, Virginia moved to England where she was an instant hit on the party scene. When a gossip columnist drew up a list of England's ten most eligible bachelors, the unifying link was that all but one were regularly seen in Virginia's company. London of the mid-1930s was a world of 'rigid etiquette, discreet affairs, and the observation of class boundaries across the limits of which only a favoured few might be permitted to leap', observes Virginia's biographer Miranda Seymour. For the city's smart set, 'life's goal was entertainment supported by shrewdly conserved private fortunes'.[38]

One of Virginia's first introductions to the local social scene was a reception given by the Milford Havens and attended by Jai, Bhaiya and Vijaysinhji of Rajpipla. At what point Virginia replaced Joan as the primary object of Jai's affection is not clear but by the end of 1935, her photograph occupied the place of honour on his desk and he wrote her a letter begging that she come to Jaipur for Christmas. He signed off with the words, 'Longing to be with you, Jai.'[39]

Competing for Virginia's affections was Bhaiya, who also wrote her heartfelt appeals to visit his state. Just nineteen years of age, rotund and bespectacled, Bhaiya was no match for the handsome and athletic Jai. He was completing his first year at Trinity College in Cambridge and had yet to be invested as the Maharaja of Cooch Behar. Jai was four years his senior, the ruler of one of India's richest and most romantic states, a champion polo player and a consummate Casanova. 'Jai was handsome, so amusing, so fearless: there wasn't anything at which he didn't excel. He treated Bhaiya like a younger brother, but that didn't help. Bhaiya wanted to be Jai. And, of course, he wasn't,' said Virginia.[40] In the end, Virginia rebuffed both Jai's and Bhaiya's invitations and spent part of the winter performing in a provincial theatre play called *Uneasily to Bed*, which flopped so badly that it closed after one month. Stung by her refusal to visit India, Bhaiya wrote her a letter in which he stated that from the first light touch of her hand upon his he had felt that they were destined to be friends. 'And we were friends,' Virginia insisted. 'Only Jai and I were all wrapped up in one another, from the very moment we met. I didn't have much time to think about Bhaiya.'[41]

Virginia would later recall that she fell for Jai almost as soon as they met and she knew that the feeling was mutual. 'I think the first time Jai slept with me, he knew the truth. I adored him, no question, but he wasn't Cary. And the divorce papers weren't even finalized.'[42] The couple spent much of the summer of 1935 together. When in London they would dine at the Savoy or at Ciro's, a branch of the famous Paris restaurant, then wander through the streets of Mayfair and Piccadilly until after dawn. Their travels took them from Le Touquet to Paris, from Biarritz to Budapest. Though she described the summer as one of the happiest of her life, their personal lives were complicated. She was still married to Grant while Jai had two wives and was about to propose to Ayesha. It's doubtful that he revealed either of these facts to Virginia. Yet this did not stop him from asking her to marry him.

Instead of following Ayesha's lead and immediately saying yes, Virginia decided to consult Bhaiya, who seized the opportunity to enlighten her on realities of life in India and more importantly on some facts about Jai he had been withholding from her, namely, the existence of First and Second Her Highnesses. He also explained the system of purdah that awaited the wife of a maharaja. 'I didn't even know what the word meant until Bhaiya spelled it all out,' she conceded. 'I thought purdah was something you ate.'[43]

Bhaiya tried to further sabotage the romance by telling his mother, Indira, that the relationship between Jai and his 'American gold-digger' was not serious. He also warned Virginia about the pitfalls of marrying Jai. 'You see, Jai's life is laid out for him and he must stick to the schedule, yet it would be inhuman not to be natural, even though very occasionally,' he wrote in an oblique reference to Jai's propensity for having affairs. He concluded his letter by stating that Virginia should reconcile herself to becoming just another of Jai's pleasant memories. 'He is too nice a gentleman to forget.'[44] Three years later Bhaiya would caution Ayesha using almost exactly the same wording and logic. Her refusal to believe him suggests she too was ignorant of his affairs with women like Joan and Virginia, or was very good at pretending such things were the exception rather than the rule.

Bhaiya's sniping paid off. When Jai returned to England in May 1936, Virginia's social diary was full of engagements and her most regular escort was George Child Villiers, nicknamed 'Grandy'. He was the Earl of Jersey and belonged to one of England's most illustrious families. He had just publicly announced his separation from Pat, his Australian-born wife of ten years, and spent most of May and June escorting Virginia and her mother around his family estates and introducing them to his relatives. Virginia described Grandy as 'a cold fish. The absolute opposite of Jai. You can't imagine two men more different.'[45] By the first week of July she had resumed her affair with Jai and the two of them were once again almost inseparable.

This time Virginia decided she needed to see Jai on his home turf. A group of friends were planning a visit to India in December and she was determined to go with them 'to case the joint'. When Grandy found out she was going to Jaipur, he added himself to the party. Grandy's presence hardly perturbed Jai. When they arrived by steamer in Bombay, Jai's personal bearer greeted Virginia and announced he would conduct her wherever she wanted to go and protect her. Jai lavished her with jewellery—bracelets, toe rings and anklets—until she was 'laden down like a dancing girl'.[46] He arranged for beautiful silk saris to be made for her and then one evening took her to Amber Fort where he regaled her with stories of hidden treasures that a ruler was allowed to touch only once in his lifetime. To Virginia, being in Jaipur was like something out of an Oriental fairytale. 'When we arrived, there were elephants to carry us up to the front of the palace, and flaming torches and fireworks, and guards in the most beautiful uniforms, with turquoise and gold turbans standing to attention all along the facade.'[47] Gazing at the pink city of Jaipur from the ramparts above Amber she found it strange that all the people of the state should be ruled by just one person.

While most members of her group were satisfied with the daily round of sightseeing, shopping and eating, Virginia grew increasingly frustrated at not meeting Jai's wives or children. Finally, after stubbornly resisting for two weeks, Jai gave in and took her to the zenana quarters at the Rambagh Palace. There to greet her was Second Her Highness. Virginia took an instant liking to Jo, whom she described as 'a darling, so pretty and such fun!' First Her Highness by contrast was 'pretty tiring ... Always stuffing herself full of medicines and grumbling about her health.'[48] One of Jo's first questions to Virginia was whether she was going to come and live in the zenana after marrying Jai.

The two women developed a close relationship, so close in fact that rumours flew within the corridors of the Rambagh Palace that they were having an affair. That doesn't seem likely as there is no evidence to substantiate the rumours, but they continued to exchange confidences through letters for years. Virginia offered Jo tips on how to satisfy her husband sexually so that he would visit her more often. A year later, Jo confided to becoming so 'sexy' she could 'hardly wait for the night to come'. For her part, Virginia confessed that she wished she had never left Cary Grant.

Jo not only liked Virginia, she saw her as a passport to escape the tradition-bound confines of the zenana. If Virginia became Jai's third wife, the three of them could travel together and have fun.

Jo couldn't understand why, if Virginia loved Jai enough to sleep with him, she wouldn't marry him. But as Virginia later revealed, she couldn't cope with the gossip swirling around her affair. She hated the caste system, the tradition of keeping women behind purdah and the cruelty inflicted on animals. 'And the way everything had to be shot! Pure butchery! Tigers, elephants, leopards: It was awful, awful.'[49]

Despite her disenchantment with the realities of life in Jaipur, she elected to stay on after Grandy and the rest of the party returned to England. Photographs contained in an album Miranda Seymour found at the back of a drawer in Virginia's home reveal that the couple travelled together through Karachi, up the Euphrates to Basra, then across to Palestine, Athens and finally Vienna, where they parted ways. When she arrived back in England, she wrote to Jo saying that she wouldn't marry Jai but wanted the relationship to continue in its present form. Jo wrote back voicing her approval and declared that the two people she loved most in the world were Virginia and Jai. 'I am ready to do anything for you, even give up my life if that is necessary.'[50]

If Grandy knew about Virginia and Jai's sojourn, he clearly didn't care. His first question to her when they met in March 1937 was whether she was going to marry her Indian lover. When she replied no, he handed her a diamond engagement ring. The fact that Virginia didn't love Grandy—something that she would constantly remind him of—had little effect on their marriage plans. The impending coronation of King George VI following the abdication of his brother Edward VIII was a welcome distraction, because it meant that Jo would soon be arriving to join her husband on what was only her second overseas trip.

Jo's ship, the *Tuscania*, docked in Liverpool in early April 1937. Her thirty-strong entourage included servants, a doctor and English nurses 'to calm her excited children with dolls and other toys', and a private detective to guard the £200,000 worth of jewels she had brought with her to wear on state occasions. As her ADC told excited journalists after the ship berthed, customs had changed since Madho Singh had embarked on the *Olympia* thirty-five years earlier for Edward VII's coronation. Religious ceremonies to prepare the ship had been scrapped, there were no special preparations for worship and the 'Maharanee was most anxious to mix freely with the other passengers'. Though she did not dance herself, she watched the other passengers dancing.[51] Once Jo reached London, Virginia took her shopping to the jewellers Aspreys and together they went to watch Jai's polo team play at Cowdray Park. Accompanied by friends, the three of them went boating on the Thames and hosted parties at his Mayfair flat.

Jai was only one of dozens of Indian potentates who had descended on London for the coronation. Bhaiya, now officially the Maharaja of Cooch Behar, was one of the attendees, along with his mother and his siblings, including Ayesha. In her memoir, Ayesha writes affectionately about Jo's presence in London. But there is no mention of Virginia. Together with other pupils from her school, she had been given twelve days' holiday for the coronation but with Jo and Jai's children in London, there were few opportunities for the couple to meet alone. Jo sometimes visited the Cooch Behar family at their flat on Connaught Square and became particularly friendly with Ayesha's brother Indrajit, who often took her to the theatre and the cinema. 'It could have been an awkward situation for me, but Jai, with his usual tact, handled all these relationships perfectly,' Ayesha concluded somewhat naively, in what was just one of many examples of her airbrushing inconvenient truths in her memoir.[52] The only hint that she was aware of what was happening would come decades later, and well after Jai's death, when she told Elisabeth Bumiller of the *Washington Post*: 'I think it's much easier to get on with your husband's other wife, who has an official position, and a status, than his mistress, who's usurping you.'[53]

Looming over this complicated love triangle was Indira, who was coming around to the fact that Jai would marry Ayesha. In her memoir Ayesha would attribute her mother's opposition to fears about her daughter going into purdah, when in fact Indira was more concerned about her potential future son-in-law conducting a well-publicized romance with an American actress and his penchant for having affairs. The tension was somewhat defused at the beginning of July when Virginia and Grandy officially announced their engagement. Grandy's divorce was finalized towards the end of July and a week later the couple were married at the Chelsea Register Office. The formal wedding ceremony on 11 August was attended by Jai and Jo.

From the beginning there was nothing conventional about the marriage. 'Sex was never part of it,' Virginia would later insist. Following the pattern set by the Mountbattens, she summed up the relationship as follows: 'I could do just as I wished, so long as I was discreet—and so could he.'[54] That liberality, though not necessarily the discretion, was evident within a month of their wedding when Jai and Virginia flew down to Biarritz without their respective spouses. Jo was distraught, not about her husband's continuation of his affair with Virginia, but at having to say goodbye to her best friend. 'Do talk to Jai about my coming there every year,' she pleaded in a letter to Virginia on 3 September 1937. 'I do want to be with you for four or five months a year at least,' she added.[55] But her hope that Virginia might persuade Jai to allow her that freedom was misplaced. Shortly afterwards, Jo was back in purdah with 'people coming to see me every day and every time of day that suits them, but not to welcome me but to gaze'.[56]

As their correspondence continued, Jo wrote to Virginia expressing displeasure at the fact that Indira was becoming a frequent visitor to Jaipur and was in secret communication with Jai about undisclosed matters. Jo's letters do not elaborate on what these matters were, but it is hard to imagine she was not aware of rumours of her husband's affair with Indira. On 22 November 1937, she wrote again to Virginia saying, 'there are lots of muddles here', and added that she suspected the British were trying to corrupt Jai. 'All the people here are giving cocktail parties, with the idea of getting Jai into wine and women.' Jaipur's prime minister, Sir Henry Beauchamp St John, she said, was trying to turn Jai into a playboy so they could 'keep him under their thumb and then kick him out'.[57]

In December 1937, Virginia made her second trip to India accompanied by Grandy. After a few days in Jaipur, they travelled by train to Delhi. Jo went with them but was forced to sit in a special purdah carriage. In Delhi, Virginia visited Bhaiya, who was recovering from a polo accident that had left him with a broken collarbone. Around the same time Jai had almost broken his back falling off his horse and was bedridden in the Rambagh Palace. This did not stop him from giving Jo and Virginia two matching Bentleys for them to drive around Jaipur state. For two women to enjoy such freedom was too much for the tradition-bound durbar, where gossipmongers again started hinting at an illicit relationship. The road trip was the last time the two women were together. For Jo, lonely and clearly starved of love, saying goodbye to her friend was heart-breaking. 'I wish we could always be together. Think how marvellous that would be,' she wrote to Virginia just before the latter returned to England. 'However, darling, it doesn't matter where you are. I'll always be thinking about you.'[58]

When Jai travelled alone to England in May 1938, Virginia gave him the cold shoulder, offering up a variety of flimsy excuses for being too busy to see him. Jai returned to India in July where he penned a quick note remonstrating with her for her 'stupidity'. The rest of the letter was more affectionate, ending with the words: 'My only moments of happiness were when I said goodbye to you ... wish every moment had been like that. All my love, darling.'[59]

* * *

The reason for Jai's early return to Jaipur had nothing to do with being rejected by Virginia. One hundred kilometres to the north-west of Jaipur, a revolt was brewing, which threatened the integrity of his state and presented Jai with his first real challenge as a ruler. In what one Western correspondent likened to a scene from a 'comic opera', the recalcitrant thakur of Sikar, Rao Raja Kalyan Singh, had assembled a force of thousands of fierce Rajput warriors armed mostly with spears, staves and ancient muzzle loaders in a direct challenge to the authority of the Jaipur durbar.

Covering an area of 4,000 square kilometres, Sikar was the largest thikana in the state. It was located in a region known as Shekhawati, a roughly triangular area bounded by Jaipur in the south, Bikaner in the north and Khetri in the east. The area had enjoyed a long period of autonomy until the eighteenth century, when Sawai Jai Singh managed to reassert control over it with the help of Mughal troops. Under the terms of Jaipur's 1818 treaty with the Crown, the British promised that as the colonizing power they would endorse and enforce the right of the Jaipur durbar over the region.[60] The thikanedars of Shekhawati saw things differently and took every opportunity they could to assert their independence. Kalyan Singh, who became the ruler of Sikar by adoption in 1922, was uneducated, illiterate even in his own dialect, prone to drinking and had several gripes with the Jaipur durbar. In 1933, Jai wanted to fine him Rs 500 for shooting a tiger. Under a rule set down by Maharaja Ram Singh II, the right to hunt tigers, bears or sambhar deer was limited to the ruler of Jaipur and the rajas of Sikar and Khetri. Jai, however, wanted to annul those exceptions, an action guaranteed to provoke their anger, particularly as they had previously questioned his right to sit on the throne. It was left to the head of the Jaipur State Forces, Amar Singh, to tell Jai not to 'behave like a child' and point out that he should have told the Rao Raja of the exclusion before, rather than after, the act had been committed.[61] Jai eventually reneged but insisted that Sikar accept an Englishman as the senior member of his council. Kalyan Singh managed to thwart Jai's plans by paying off the first appointee and making life miserable for the second.

The third appointee in three years was A.W.T. Webb, a tough army officer who had fought in the Boer War. Webb moved quickly to assert his position, removing the Rao Raja's chief personal adviser and then depriving the ruler of the keys to his treasury. His progressive reforms in areas such as taxation, education, economic development and agriculture were welcomed in Jaipur but despised in Sikar. When Kalyan Singh tried to sack Webb, Beauchamp St John issued an order on 12 April 1937 effectively deposing him and placing the administration of Sikar directly under the control of a senior officer to be appointed by the Jaipur durbar. That officer was Webb, whose three-year contract was renewed. But this time he took his orders directly from Jaipur's ruling council.

The immediate spark for what became known as the 'Sikar Revolt' by the India Office and the 'Arabian Nights War' by the tabloid press was the question of what to do about the education of Kalyan Singh's heir, Hardayal Singh. Born in 1921, he was betrothed at the age of twelve to the daughter of the Maharaja of Dhrangadhra, a thirteen-gun-salute state in Gujarat. The wedding was to take place in 1938. Hardayal had been attending Mayo College but was removed when Webb suspected he was coming under 'sodomistic influences'.[62] The decision on what to do next fell on Jai's shoulders. His preference was to send Hardayal to study at an English university such as Cambridge. But this was opposed by Webb and

Beauchamp St John. Sending him abroad would also mean a post-ponement of his marriage, which, if Webb's suspicions about his sexuality were correct, was also undesirable. The strongest opposition to the move came from the Rao Raja himself, who doted on his son and spoilt him outrageously, on one occasion bribing his instructor at Mayo to prevent him from doing any physical training. Sikar's ruler was irked by the fact that Jai hadn't bothered to consult him on the matter of his son's marriage or travel. He was also fearful that once in England, he might marry a foreigner, be seduced by European society and never return.

Sensing his options were closing, Kalyan Singh urged his wife, the Rao Rani, to write letters to Jai's wives as well as to the wives of Beauchamp St John and Sir Arthur Lothian, the Resident for Rajputana, opposing the marriage plans. He also met with Jai to try to persuade him to change his mind, but he refused to budge. Meanwhile, the mood in Sikar was growing increasingly restless. An unusually large number of Rajput soldiers were detected arriving in the town. In April 1938, Jai ordered Webb and F.S. Young, the Jaipur police chief, to go to Sikar and bring the Rao Raja back to Jaipur. But the Rao Raja refused and dismissed the delegation saying he had to attend to his sick wife. At this point, Young put his hand on Kalyan Singh's shoulder, a gesture that his followers interpreted as an attempt to arrest their leader. Young was knocked to the ground while the ruler's supporters ushered him into his car and drove at breakneck speed to the fort where they declared a hartal, or strike.

The actions of the 'mad Rajah', as the Western press was labelling the Sikar ruler, were the last straw for Young and Webb, who telegraphed Jaipur for a large detachment of troops, arguing that only a show of force would resolve the crisis. Beauchamp St John, however, urged restraint and instead sent Amar Singh with a new set of conditions to try to negotiate an end to the stand-off. Kalyan Singh and his son would be allowed to travel by boat to England and return after just four months. Hardayal's marriage to the Dhrangadhra princess would be arranged at a mutually agreed time. It soon became clear to Amar Singh that the Rao Raja was not interested in a negotiated settlement and was gathering his forces for a final stand with hundreds of armed Rajput warriors now taking up position inside the fort. Then unexpectedly on 16 April, the Rao Raja agreed to travel to Jaipur the following day—but only at the auspicious hour of noon. By now, however, he had lost control of the situation. The assembled Rajputs would not let him leave the fort, despite Amar Singh's assurances that nothing would happen to their ruler. Decked out in Scottish kilts and playing bagpipes to alarm Sikar's defenders, Jai's troops marched on Sikar.

Jai's response to this unravelling crisis can be gleaned from Amar Singh's diary. While he was too tactful to openly criticize the Jaipur ruler even in his private writings, his frustrations are easy to discern. While Sikar seethed, Jai was often seen playing bridge or dining with his wives in the zenana. He procrastinated about how to end the stand-off—at times believing the best course of action would be to send for enough artillery pieces to blow down Sikar's gates, despite Amar Singh's warning that this would 'create a great noise in the papers'.[63]

Jai now sought Arthur Lothian's advice, who urged him to permit Hardayal to get married before going to England. The Rajputana Resident also persuaded Jai to send Beauchamp St John and a senior nobleman to Sikar to attempt a compromise. After two days in the rebel stronghold, Jaipur's prime minister told the press that the situation was grave, but that no attempt would be made to storm the fort. The present state of affairs was 'engaging serious attention in the Durbar', Beauchamp St John added.[64]

Despite offers of a general amnesty for all his followers and an early wedding for his son, the Raja Rao continued to prevaricate. By now the number of Rajputs involved in the rebellion had grown to 30,000. The balance of forces, however, was still in Jaipur's favour. Against Jaipur's two units of infantry, a squadron of Jaipur lancers, four cannons and numerous machine guns, Raja Rao's forces possessed only two ancient muzzle-loading cannons—relics of the Crimean War—mounted on the walls of the fort. Otherwise they were mostly armed with swords, sticks, stones and a couple of old rifles found in a local museum. 'The cannon was fired off but it sounded more like a toy pistol and its discharge was mostly rust and dust,' reported a correspondent at the scene.[65] 'There is a comic opera air about the situation, for one burst of machine-gun fire would easily breach the mud-wall which the defenders of Sikar have erected near the main gate. The fort walls themselves are reminiscent of medieval sword warfare and are easily scalable in many places.'[66]

Complicating things was the involvement in the Sikar revolt of the Praja Mandal (People's Conference) of Jaipur. Comprising the educated urban elite and mercantile classes, the Praja Mandal was closely allied with the Indian National Congress, which saw the dismissal of Webb and restoration of the Rao Raja's rule as an opportunity for Sikar to gain its independence from Jaipur and set up a representative government. The only problem with this scenario, as Barnett Rubin points out in his book *Feudal Revolt and State-Building*, was that the Rao Raja 'could neither read English nor Hindi, and he had never left India. Hence he had never read about nor seen democratic political systems.'[67]

Keen to prevent the Praja Mandal from exploiting the unrest, Lothian convinced Jai to drop his demand for Hardayal to go to England for his education and to reiterate his offer of a general amnesty. To their relief, Kalyan Singh agreed to the new terms, ordered the strike over and the city gates to be thrown open. On 1 May, he left Sikar to formalize the end of the rebellion by paying obeisance to the Jaipur maharaja. As part of the agreement the Rao Raja was formally exiled from Jaipur state until Sikar was stabilized. He would spend the next few months in the hill station of Mount Abu. For his part, Jai agreed with Lothian's recommendation to set up a commission of enquiry to look into the question of Sikar's administration. Believing the situation was back to normal, Jai departed for his annual summer trip to Europe on 7 May 1938. A letter intercepted by the British revealed just how desperate he was to go. 'It's pretty hot here ... God help if I am held back because of this [Sikar] trouble. I am looking forward to my holiday.'[68]

The situation, however, was anything but normal. The day after Jai's departure, the Jaipur council declared the Rao Raja incapable of managing his own property on account of 'mental infirmity' and placed the thikana of Sikar under the Jaipur Court of Wards. The Sikar ruler's reaction was swift. He insisted that the council's declaration violated the agreement and his reputation. A citizens' committee in Sikar lodged a protest, declaring that their ruler was 'endowed with a pure, serene and sober mind and is held in high esteem and awe for his character and refined manners'.[69] It also called for Webb's removal. When a second round of negotiations failed, the Sikar rebels, this time without the Rao Raja to lead them, barricaded the city gates and prepared for the Jaipur troops to attack.

The Indian government was growing increasingly alarmed by the unrest, with newspapers quoting unnamed sources in Simla complaining that 'the administration of Jaipur was sadly unprogressive and was making itself unpopular by tactless actions. It was necessary for the Prime Minister to get into more intimate touch with the people of the State and also for the Maharaja to remain in the state, when critical problems arise.'[70] Jai's absence and the fact that Beauchamp St John was now calling the shots only heightened the perception that the Sikar revolt was no longer about feudal rights but was about the autocracy of the British-controlled durbar versus the demand for responsible government under the Rao Raja who had promised to turn his administration over to the people in line with the Congress's demands.

Meanwhile, the stand-off in Sikar took a violent turn. On 4 July 1938, several people were killed when British-led troops surrounded a train carrying Rajput reinforcements. Refusing to return to their villages, they attacked the troops with ancient pistols and swords. Official reports said five people were killed and the rest taken prisoner. The firings prompted a mass exodus of townspeople from Sikar. There were reports that Rajputs were rising in their thousands to come to the city's defence, motivated not so much by the issues involved in the dispute as by 'the spirit of old Rajput warriors who were prepared to follow their leaders anywhere'.[71] When Kalyan Singh's political adviser, R.L. Chudgar, appealed to the Rajputs to lay down their arms and surrender, their response was: 'We were born with arms and will die with arms. Our arms are our lives. If we give up our arms we will lose our self-respect. Our very life will disappear.'[72]

If Jai was troubled by the Sikar revolt he did not show it. He was in England. In June 1938, he was photographed at Ranelagh for the Buenos Aires Cup final, wearing a striped tie and Savile Row suit. Even Lothian was starting to complain that Sikar had been 'badly managed' and that 'Jaipur had become the laughing stock of the whole world'.[73] The Indian National Congress was quick to exploit the agitation, pointing out the ineptitude with which British officials had handled the situation. The only way forward, one senior Congress leader said, 'was for the Maharaja of Jaipur to rise to the occasion and not only get defined the political rights of Sikar Rao Raja, but also declare his intention to grant all political and civil rights to his people'.[74]

Such statements only heightened the nervousness among the British, who didn't want the revolt to be used to bring about radical democratic changes in the princely states. What was clear, however, was that Jai's continued preference for spending time playing polo and partying in England could only have a negative effect on the outcome of the crisis. Shortly after the firings, Lothian suggested to Beauchamp St John that he ask Jai to cut short his vacation and return to India. Jai duly obliged, leaving London on 13 July, but not before giving a party to some friends and an interview to Reuters. 'This business is a very great trouble for me,' Jai told the reporter while sitting in bed wearing apple-green silk pyjamas in his London flat. 'I am going back on the first available plane to see what can be done.'[75] Jai's attempt to appear serious about tackling the crisis without bothering to get out of bed did little to alter perceptions about his association with Britain's dissolute aristocracy. It was an image that would come back to haunt him time and time again.

Immediately after arriving in Jaipur, Jai met with Lothian, who urged him to go to Sikar as soon as possible. Jai was finally beginning to grasp the urgency of the situation. He told Lothian he had lost faith in the actions of Beauchamp St John and wanted his revenue minister, Abdul Aziz, to present the rebels with an ultimatum—an immediate surrender in return for an amnesty for all except the ringleaders, who would be brought to trial. On July 20, Jai and Beauchamp St John met with Jamnalal Bajaj, the leader of the Praja Mandal, who told Jai that only his personal intervention would prevent more bloodshed.[76] Three days later, after receiving the all-clear from Young that it was safe to do so, Jai travelled to Sikar accompanied by Hardayal Singh. On arriving in the city, Hardayal went straight to see his mother, who had remained in the fort throughout the rebellion, acting as a conduit for her husband while he was in exile. But it was Jai's presence that tipped the scales. The last Rajput rebellion in pre-Independence India melted away almost the moment Jai set foot in Sikar. He inspected a guard of honour, held a durbar, received nazars from Sikar officials and was given the key to the fort by one of the Rao Raja's kinsmen.

The peaceful resolution of the Sikar rebellion was a turning point for Jai. For well over a century India's princes had had little incentive to involve themselves in the affairs of their states. The British guaranteed their position by protecting them from external aggression and internal revolts. Their mishandling of the Sikar rebellion was a wake-up call, instilling in Jai a certain political instinct about the direction future India might take—a direction where Indians would have a greater say in their affairs and become more Indian and less British. 'This change in no way affected his loyalty to the King-emperor, but it altered radically his dealings with officialdom,' Crewe observed.[77]

In April 1939, Jai sacked Beauchamp St John, whose handling of the rebellion was widely seen as incompetent. Despite opposition from the viceroy, Jai also reached out to the Praja Mandal, which had been banned under the Public Societies Regulation Act. When Jamnalal Bajaj was arrested after numerous attempts to enter the state, Jai defiantly met him in jail. Confidential India Office files suggest that the British had little time for Jai, whom they referred to as a 'veritable prince charming'.[78] When he left for England for his annual vacation at the end of May 1939, the viceroy wrote to London saying, 'I doubt that the young man has any interest in the running of his state or in its problems.'[79] Jai's response was that Sikar had been pacified so there was no urgency to remain in the state. The British did nothing to stop him.

5

'WHO THE HELL DO YOU THINK YOU ARE? QUEEN MARY?'

The story of Ayesha and Jai's courtship, their engagement and ulti-mately their wedding occupies more than sixty pages of *A Princess Remembers*. Much of it reads like a fairy tale, complete with a dashing Prince Charming, designed to elicit breathless wonder from the reader: stolen moments in Budapest and Bombay, picnics in private corners of the vast grounds of the palace in Cooch Behar, a marriage proposal while driving in Jai's Bentley. As Ayesha's schoolgirl crush turns into a teenage fantasy and then a full-blown romance, she weathers Ma's misgivings, Bhaiya's warnings, Indrajit's regret that Jai, his hero, had stooped to an alliance with the 'broomstick', and Ila's accusations that she was too 'spineless' in Jai's presence and would never cope with his philandering. Missing from her memoir, like so much else that might have contradicted the over-romanticized life story she projects, is the opposition to the marriage from the British, who considered scuttling the whole arrangement, fearing it would lead to unrest between Jaipur and other states in Rajputana. Then there was the hostility of the Jaipur nobility, the broader Rajput establishment and, finally, the reaction of Jai's two Jodhpur-born wives.

While Marudhar, who took a traditional view of her role, accepted Jai taking a third wife, Jo had tasted freedom, albeit briefly, through her friendship with Virginia and her two visits abroad. What little we know about Jo's reaction to the news of Ayesha's engagement to Jai comes from a letter she wrote to Virginia just before Christmas 1938. 'I bet she is happy now that she is hoping to get what she wanted all the time. Hope this hasn't worried you too much, but I had to tell you. I haven't got anyone except you, Anita and Grandy, whom I can call my friends.'[1] It is doubtful that Jai recognized the depth of affection between Jo and Virginia or ever realized that Jo saw her American friend as an escape route from the tradition-bound life she felt so trapped in. With Ayesha about to become Third Her Highness, Jo was to assume a very secondary role. Moreover, she knew almost nothing about Ayesha, who would be coming into the royal household as a complete outsider.

Jai's attempts to console Jo about his engagement were clumsy to say the least. Throwing a party on the night he told her was probably the least considerate thing he could have done. Nor did his engagement mean the end of his affair with Virginia. In March 1939, he wrote her a letter expressing his pining for her. 'I wish to God that you were here. There is nothing I long for more than to have a real friend by me and, darling, you know how I feel towards you ... Please, darling, write to me. You can understand the conditions I live in here. I need you in every way ... all my love, forever, Jai.'[2] Two months later he was back in England, where Virginia was busy helping Grandy prepare for the public opening of the family home, Osterley. Notwithstanding the fact that Grandy and his wife seemed closer together than ever, Jai and Virginia spent their last London summer dining at Ciro's or the Coq d'Or and watching plays in the West End. Jo wrote to Virginia urging her friend not to mention Ayesha. Virginia heeded the advice. Meanwhile Bhaiya, probably thinking that Jai's imminent marriage meant that Virginia had got over her infatuation with his soon-to-be brother-in-law, wrote to her in July 1939 saying that he was 'still crazy' about her 'and always will be'.[3] Jai never quite let go of his feelings for Virginia. According to Bubbles, his father kept an inscribed photo of her on his desk until his death in 1970.[4]

The threat of war meant that Jai had to cut short his European holiday and return to his military duties in Jaipur. But he managed to spend a short time in Kashmir, where Indira had rented Moon House in Srinagar for the family. Chimnabai and several of her grandchildren from Baroda took a house nearby. Khusru Jung, who was now the commerce minister in Hari Singh's government, turned up with some relatives and the Nizam of Hyderabad's brother and wife. The families spent their days together picnicking, going on boat rides on Dal Lake, playing card games and rounds of tennis, cricket and hockey. 'I was living in the clouds because every morning we rode together, and with Baby and Menaka as chaperones we went on bear hunts or picnics or for shikara trips. I remember it all as the last idyll of my girlhood,' Ayesha writes.[5]

Also present in Kashmir was Sher Ali Khan, the uncle of the cricketer Tiger Pataudi and a close friend of Bhaiya's. As is clear from his memoir, *The Elite Minority, The Princes of India*, the twenty-six-year-old was infatuated with the young Ayesha—and it is possible that she reciprocated at least some of his cloddish attempts at affection. His description of summer in Kashmir is full of silent walks and horse rides and of hands occasionally touching. Sher Ali confesses to lying awake at night 'producing thoughts that kept sleep away' about the time they spent together alone in a grove of pine trees.[6] At one point he overhears Ayesha telling Baby: 'Just my luck he had to be married.'[7] While reading her palm he predicts: 'You will get what you want, but there is no limit to what you want. Eventually you will get your wealth, but at the expense of real wealth. You will live long—[a] very long life, still trying to find what's real life.'[8]

Sher Ali and Ayesha remained close friends despite his move to Pakistan after Partition. He describes her as an 'enigma, entangled in her own thoughts, even from childhood, quite happy in her own company and sometimes more relaxed with strangers than in her own crowd', an observation that is borne out by many of her closest friends.[9] His recollections about their time spent in Kashmir, just a year out from her wedding with Jai, are particularly prescient. 'For Ayesha to be in love with Jai was like an illness. She wasn't certain where it began. It had come without much awareness, without symptoms, unless one could call symptoms the joking that had gone on between them from the very beginning, more from him than from her.'[10] From the moment he had arrived in his Rolls-Royce convertible at Woodlands back in 1930 as the 'Maharaja ... from Rajputana and on top of that from Jaipur', Ayesha had fallen in love 'not so much perhaps with the man himself, but with the idea of him'.[11] Sher Ali puzzled (perhaps out of jealousy) over her motivations to be Jai's third wife. 'How could she compromise on her background, her mother being such a sophisticated person and both her grandmothers, paternal and maternal, so enlightened on such subjects—of child marriage and dual marriages, and what they couldn't understand they attributed to other motives.'[12] Did the promise of glamour turn puppy love into real love, he wondered. Or was it a chance to swap Cooch Behar with its mud houses and thatched roofs for the fortresses of Rajputana with their legendary treasuries full of jewels?

According to Sher Ali, the thought of emulating Indira and creating another scandal appealed to the headstrong Ayesha, even though the controversy over her being neither a Jodhpuri nor a Rajput paled into insignificance when compared with Indira's dumping of Scindia of Gwalior for the second-in-line to the throne of a minor state. Jai, he believed, took a more practical approach to the whole matter. 'Marriage was a necessity and to produce children a duty, to the state and to the House.'[13] One more wife made no difference. Ayesha could ride well and she loved hunting and sport. He could take her to polo matches and parties when he was abroad; she could dine and dance with him at clubs and restaurants.

Ayesha's initial crush had evolved into a full-blown infatuation, a blind adulation that was highly addictive. Jai was the supreme Lothario and his storybook kingdom was the ultimate aphrodisiac. Seduced by the glamour that Cooch Behar could never provide, Ayesha was prepared to become the dutiful wife of a man she naively believed would always support her even if it meant going against the strictures of Jaipur's conservatism. Accepting her role reveals the extent to which Jai and Ayesha viewed their relationship as a means to fulfilling each other's aspirations.

* * *

Back at the Residency in Jaipur, practical matters were occupying the minds of British officials who toyed with vetoing the marriage—something that was within their powers. Jai's decision to choose as his third wife someone the India Office puzzlingly described as a 'non-Aryan' would deliver a 'serious blow to Rajput pride of race'.[14] Although the rulers of Cooch Behar were Kshatriyas, they were seen as inferior to the Rajputs. Jai's argument that 350 years earlier one of his ancestors had married a Cooch Behar princess didn't cut much ice, given that the state's rulers had been tainted by intermarriage with princesses from neighbouring, mostly tribal, hill states. 'It is for the Rajputs themselves to maintain their prestige and traditions in such matters and all we can do is to point out to them, as has been done in this case, the consequences of departing from their customs,' B.J. Glancy, the political adviser to the Viceroy, wrote to Lord Linlithgow.[15] Then there were the apparently undeniable reports that Jai's finance minister, Pandit Amarnath Atal, was illegally channelling funds from the state's public works budget to build the ultimate in palatial accommodation for Ayesha.[16] Finally, the British feared that the marriage would be an affront to the other wives, particularly now that both of them had produced sons. Alarmed by the possible consequences of the marriage, Linlithgow sent for Jai. According to his ADC, Major Parbat Singh, Jai told the Viceroy that while he had the power to depose him, he had no control over his private life. He was going to marry Ayesha whatever the consequences. Seeing his determination, Linlithgow shook Jai's hand and wished him luck.

While it stopped short of vetoing the marriage, the India Office refused to give the union its official endorsement. An edict from Linlithgow stated: 'No officer of my Government should attend, whether from Cooch Behar or from Jaipur, or anywhere else, and no congratulations or good wishes should be offered unless with the preface that the offerer stands in his private capacity only.'[17] Jai's long-term mentor and the commander of the Jaipur State Forces, Amar Singh, also joined the boycott. If he married into a 'good Rajput family' he would certainly attend the wedding 'but not if you marry into that family', he said.[18]

Unaware of the behind-the-scenes machinations, Indira, Ayesha and her siblings plunged headlong into making preparations for the wedding. Thanks to Indira's foresight, most of Ayesha's wedding trousseau had been purchased in Europe before World War II broke out—sheets and towels from Florence and Czechoslovakia, shoes and matching bags at Ferragamo, nightgowns in *mousseline de soie* from Paris. A special shopping expedition was arranged to Calcutta to buy saris. Indira left her daughter alone to make her selection, only to be shocked on her return at the garish colours she had selected. Indira herself ended up choosing 200 saris in silk and chiffon, some embroidered with gold thread. Ayesha's presents included a black Bentley from the Nawab of Bhopal that Jai would later make her swap for a much older blue one, and a two-seater Packard from a Jaipur noble. Chimnabai gifted her a house in the Himalayan hill station of Mussoorie.

In Cooch Behar arrangements were being made to host the 200 or so wedding guests, each with their own entourage of servants. The numbers would have been larger had fewer trains been requisitioned for the war effort. Archways were erected under which the bridegroom would pass and bunting and lights were hung from houses and public buildings. Jai's retinue alone consisted of forty nobles from Jaipur. Each was supplied with a richly caparisoned elephant for the wedding procession.

Ayesha spent 8 May 1940, the day before the wedding, fasting, bathing in scented oils and having her skin rubbed with turmeric paste. She then performed the traditional pujas required of a bride. Nerves took over and, instead of sleeping, she spent much of the night talking to her sisters. In the morning she heard the firing of a nineteen-gun salute to announce Jai's arrival. 'Only then did I believe with total conviction that after all the years of waiting I would actually marry my beloved.'[19]

Unlike her mother's Brahmo Samaj wedding, Ayesha's was replete with ritual and symbolism. Her forehead was smeared with sandalwood paste to indicate the virtuous life she was expected to lead as a wife. After Jai's arrival, the customary presents from the groom to the bride were brought in a ceremonial procession to the palace and laid out in the durbar hall. They included traditional jewellery, a dozen sets of women's clothes and auspicious food items. Symbols of good fortune, auguring longevity for her husband, her children and herself, such as a conch shell bound in silver and a silver mirror, were wrapped in a banana leaf and carried by Ayesha to a shrine where she offered up prayers to Ganesha.

Jai's appearance at the ceremony was heralded by the booming of cannons and the music of marching bands. Ayesha was carried into the main courtyard of the palace in a silver palanquin and was given away by Bhaiya. After the religious rites, Ayesha and Jai went upstairs where their families were waiting for them. After touching their feet, they were offered a traditional thali to share. Ayesha offered Jai the first mouthful of rice and he reciprocated. It was then that the champagne came out. In the end the only Rajput ruler to boycott the wedding was the Maharaja of Dungarpur. Udaipur's maharana, the senior-most Rajput, did not attend because he was too frail to travel, but he sent two representatives—a gesture which amounted to a formal seal of approval to the marriage. One factor that brought Udaipur to the table was Jai's promise that if Ayesha had a son, he would never succeed to the Jaipur throne. Cooch Behar's British Resident defied the Viceroy's orders and was present at the ceremony.

The celebrations in Cooch Behar went on for a week, but the newly-weds left after two days for their honeymoon in Ootacamund, or Ooty. The journey to the hill station gave Ayesha her first taste of purdah. Her railway coach was surrounded by canvas screens and the car waiting for them at Calcutta had curtains separating the driver from the passenger seats. At Woodlands all the male servants were sent away, even those she had known most of her life. Indrajit, who was accompanying her, kept asking if she was going to live like this for the rest of her life. In the end Ayesha could not hold back the tears.

Things were more relaxed in Ooty, where the couple enjoyed rounds of tennis, horse riding, picnics and dinner parties. Ayesha, however, was forbidden from attending formal receptions at Government House. 'Although I wasn't exactly in purdah, still, on occasions where there might be older and more orthodox princes among the guests, Jai didn't want to put me in the embarrassing position of being the only Maharani to show her face in public,' Ayesha would later write. 'He told me that this would also be true in Jaipur in the beginning because I hadn't yet met the people.' To put his new wife's mind at ease, Jai told her there was no question of her remaining in purdah for her entire life. 'Let's wait for a year or so. When people gradually get used to the idea, you can drop purdah altogether.'[20]

Jai left Ayesha in Ooty to go to Bangalore to play polo and to be with Jo and their children, Joey and Pat. After a few days he wrote to say he was missing her and that she should join him. When she arrived in Bangalore, she went straight to their apartments, too fearful to meet Jo again, this time not as a friend but as Jai's third wife. After half an hour, Ayesha's ADC returned to say that Jo had invited her for tea. The meeting was a tense one that the two women tried to cover up with small talk. Only after Jai returned from his polo match did the mood relax somewhat. That night Jai, Ayesha, Jo and Bhaiya dined together.

Ayesha maintains that even if Jo resented her presence, she never showed it and always treated her with kindness. Jo's sons insist that everyone got on well. 'In those days, lots of people had two wives,' Joey would later recount. 'We were all treated the same. We never felt "this is my mother, and this is not my mother". Our father got on well with all of them.' The children distinguished one mother from another by saying big mama, middle mama and little mama. 'I can't remember any of the parents giving us a long lecture about a new mother coming to the house,' continues Joey, speaking of Ayesha's arrival. 'In our family, if your father and mother did something, it was all right. It was something that was built into our culture.'[21] To this day many people in Jaipur remember Jo as being lively and mischievous, a person with a good sense of humour. Some insist that she was far more beautiful than Ayesha.

Quentin Crewe writes that in the early years of Ayesha and Jai's marriage, Jo was seen as spoilt and an intriguer. Now in her mid-twenties, she had little to look forward to apart from the pleasure she got from her sons. Whenever she was in the City Palace there was no question of anything other than living in purdah. Within that world she did exercise a degree of power, being in charge of the zenana deorhi and holding the keys to Jai's private treasure vaults at Moti Doongri, a small family fort on the outskirts of the city. But the moments of freedom she enjoyed in England would not return. She never went back to Jodhpur after her marriage—offended by the palace's refusal to give her a gun salute equal to that of her aunt, First Her Highness. The constant problem of not knowing who to believe in Jaipur makes it difficult to draw conclusions about Jo or for that matter anyone else in the extended family. 'One cannot be sure that those who speak ill of her do not do so out of some obscure loyalty to Jodhpur, or because she may have reprimanded them—and these things are long remembered,' warns Crewe.[22] Although Jo continued to write regularly to Virginia, she never saw her again. As a token of their friendship, she sent Virginia a bronze cast of her slender arm. 'And I did keep it with me. In over fifty years, I've never forgotten Jo,' Virginia later said.[23]

* * *

Ayesha's arrival in Jaipur as the maharaja's new wife began with a seemingly endless round of ceremonies and receptions, with her being driven to the locations each time with curtains drawn to maintain purdah. At the Rambagh Palace, she was given a suite adjoining Jai's. Recently redecorated by a London firm, it had high ceilings and an airy bedroom painted pink, with pale voile curtains, pastel divans and chaises longues, as well as an oval bathroom with the bath set in an alcove. There was a large sitting room filled with objets d'art from the Jaipur collection and a panelled study. She had access to a marble veranda overlooking the Mughal garden–style central courtyard of the palace with its watercourses and gushing fountains. Today guests wishing to stay in the Maharani Suite can expect to pay over £5,000 a night.

A few weeks after her arrival on a day deemed auspicious by pandits, Ayesha was driven to the City Palace accompanied by Jai's personal bodyguards and then carried in a palanquin to the zenana deorhi for a special women's durbar. The women of the zenana and the wives of Jaipur's nobility filed past her, lifting up her veil to see her face for the first time and commenting on such things as the fairness of her skin and the size of her nose. She was allocated her own apartment, which was decorated in blues and greens and had a small square courtyard and a private durbar hall. Stays at the zenana quarters were for ceremonial occasions and lasted up to a fortnight. Ceremonies were meticulously performed and all formalities were observed. At the durbars her behaviour was watched by the family and their retainers and the ladies of the nobility. There was no room for anything to go wrong.[24]

After being a self-confessed tomboy in a large and carefree family, Ayesha found her introduction to palace life with its arcane traditions and rules of purdah frightening and oppressively formal. Normal conversation was impossible. She pleaded with those women in the zenana who spoke English to talk freely to her, to argue with her, to call her Ayesha in private. They ignored her requests.[25] Overly protective, Jai forbade her to learn Hindi on the grounds that if she started speaking to one group of women rather than another in the zenana 'rumour or intrigues would start'.[26] There were many in the court who had opposed her marriage to Jai and who might create rifts between her supporters or friction between her and Jo. There was even the threat of physical violence from those who considered her too privileged and pampered and too close to Jai.

Ayesha's first years of married life were spent in a state of apprehension. 'I couldn't have managed it all if Jai hadn't been there to encourage me, make fun of my doubts, laugh off my mistakes.'[27] Her flippancy hid a deeper, more fundamental shift in her personality and outlook on life. When her brother Indrajit visited her at Rambagh, he was shocked to see the change in her. 'The formality and grandeur must have had an effect on me ... He was stunned by the transformation and exclaimed, with characteristic brotherly directness, "Who the hell do you think you are? Queen Mary?"'[28]

Aware of the strain that purdah was having on his wife, Jai made sure that they socialized as much as possible with his teammates and their wives after polo matches. But such breaks were short-lived. Writing to her in December 1941, he conceded: 'It must be pretty awful for you at home shut up and surrounded by evil thoughts all the time. Please darling, go [to Calcutta] and enjoy yourself and remember that I just live for you and you alone.' Then, almost as if correcting himself, he warned her to be circumspect and not go alone to official parties at the viceroy's residence or Government House, 'but you can go to both places with Ma [Indira] to private parties. Don't go to any ruling Prince's house. Anyhow use your discretion and don't let Ma mislead you!'[29]

Jai's letter reveals at best a double standard. There is no evidence that his philandering paused for more than a few months after their marriage. Margaret Kumari, who comes from the thikana of Barwara and whose father, Man Singh or 'Rabbit', was Jai's best friend, remembers as a young girl in the 1940s hiding behind the hedge next to the polo ground with her brother and watching Jai pursuing a Parsi woman. 'He was so close to my father. Anything wrong he did [with his girlfriends] and he would come to our home—on the quiet.'[30]

* * *

The outbreak of World War II in September 1939 would eventually see thousands of Indians fighting alongside Allied forces in numerous theatres in Europe, the Middle East and North Africa. Jai was determined to be among them—but he would have to wait. In late 1940, he was sent to Risalpur on the North-West Frontier with the 13th Lancers. Ayesha was allowed to accompany him. She described living in a small bungalow in the cantonment, running the house herself while pandering to her husband's needs, as blissful. 'I got no special privileges or deference, I was just a captain's wife.'[31] Ayesha used her secretarial skills to type Jai's confidential correspondence and managed to do some sightseeing, visiting the Khyber Pass, Attock Fort and Peshawar. But when Jai and his regiment were sent to Bannu on the Afghan border, she had to return to Jaipur. Writing to his friend the Raja of Barwara from Bannu, Jai described it as 'damn good fun'. 'We were in the thick of trouble and I had a chance of opening fire with MC and shot some of those fucking tribesmen and wild M ... [illegible]! We lived in tents and were sniped at most nights.'[32]

Jai's dream was to join the Life Guards, the senior regiment of the British Army and part of the Household Cavalry. After pestering the Viceroy with requests, he was finally granted an emergency commission as a lieutenant in the Household Cavalry Overseas Composite Battalion in April 1941, the first Indian to be so honoured. There was opposition to him being sent on active service from almost all quarters, except for his wife. The Rajput Sabha pleaded with him to reconsider his commission—insisting that if he did go, he should be alongside Jaipur troops to boost their morale. On 9 May 1941, almost a year to the day since marrying Ayesha, he set sail from Bombay for the Middle East.

His hopes of seeing active service were dashed when he missed his rendezvous with his regiment and was instead attached to the Royal Scots Greys. He was then appointed a liaison officer with the Indian State Forces and given the rank of major general. A further setback came when he was pronounced unfit for service. His string of polo and flying accidents had left their mark and four months later he was back in India. Though his service was limited, Jai was to receive the highest praise after the war from Sir Arthur Lothian, Resident of the Rajputana states, who wrote: 'War is no longer picturesque or of limited danger. So, to elect of his own free choice, as His Highness did, to go to the front as an active officer of the Household Cavalry, displayed a sense of duty to King and Country well worthy of his famous ancestors.'[33]

When Jai returned to Jaipur, domestic politics took centre stage. Jaipur's diwan, Gyan Nath, who had been appointed in 1939, had the full support of the British for his hard-line stand on the pro-Congress Praja Mandal. Nath had a knack for rubbing Jai up the wrong way, at one point reporting to his British masters that the maharaja was meeting some of his 'unbudgeted expenses' from Jaipur's general revenues.[34] According to Robert Stern, the British finally accepted that forcing 'an obnoxious diwan on the shrewd and headstrong Maharaja of a state whose defects included the durbar's well-earned reputation for intrigue was to invite administrative chaos'.[35] Gyan Nath was permitted to resign in 1942, but to the consternation of the Rajputana Agency, Jaipur's obstinate ruler picked as his replacement Sir Mirza Ismail. Widely seen as progressive, Sir Mirza had just completed his term with Maharaja Krishnaraja Wodyar of Mysore. Early on in his administration he wrote to the Residency requesting that the maharaja and his family be referred to as 'royal', earning a sharp rebuke for his impertinence. Only the king-emperor and his family could be referred to as royal. Sir Mirza was a 'dictator of the "national socialist" variety' and the sooner he was dismissed the better.[36]

As far as Jai was concerned, Sir Mirza was a competent administrator and he was more than happy to let him get on with his work. The diwan set about cleaning up the overcrowded and dirty walled city. Encroachments on public roads were cleared and many buildings got their first coat of paint in more than a quarter of a century. Although he was a Muslim he even succeeded in removing Hindu temples from the middle of streets without the opposition of Brahmin priests. Writing in *Vogue* after a visit to Jaipur, Cecil Beaton called him 'the arch enemy of corrugated iron sheets, brass bands (Indian) and of almost everything that is crude and vulgar ... Already the metamorphoses he has achieved in a short time are incredible, but his plans are as countless as his inspirations.'[37] Jai enthusiastically embraced Sir Mirza's enthusiasm for modernizing his city and flew around in his Gypsy Moth to get ideas for new developments outside the city walls—until one day the propeller fell off.

Among the reforms initiated by Jai and supported by his prime minister were the Village Panchayat Act that gave administrative functions to local bodies, thus ensuring the protection of farmers and the poor; as well as the Municipality Act that guaranteed that half the seats in the Jaipur Municipal Board would be filled by election. At the urging of Sir Mirza, Jai ordered the establishment of a Legislative Council with an elected majority and a Representative Assembly to provide a platform for rural representatives. The former replaced the council of ministers established by Ram Singh in 1860, whose powers largely rested with thakurs selected and appointed by the maharaja. Together the new bodies were among the first moves towards democratic government in any princely state. Jai also took care to cultivate Marwari magnates to set up industries. Although many of India's leading business families such as the Birlas, Goenkas, Piramals and Poddars had their ancestral homes in the Shekhawati region, there had been almost no investment in the state. The *New York Times* correspondent Herbert L. Matthews described Jaipur as an example of what could be achieved under the right leadership. 'Here it is a case of a young Maharaja choosing an efficient Premier, turning the government over to him and enjoying himself.' Matthews noted that Sir Mirza was one of those rare Indians who wanted the British to stay and 'collaborate on an equal footing of equality in the future process of freeing the country'.[38] In 1946, at a time when anti-British feeling in India was at its height, the Viceroy, Lord Wavell, was greeted by cheering crowds and showered with flowers while driving through the walled city. The Viceroy's warm reception prompted expressions of outrage from the Indian National Congress. Sir Mirza also had to weather criticism from the Hindu Mahasabha, which objected to a Muslim holding such a high office in a predominantly Hindu state and lobbied unsuccessfully to eject him. One of his final achievements was to establish the University of Rajasthan in Jaipur in 1946.

For his part, Sir Mirza considered Jai 'an enlightened ruler, who true to his promise, gave me his full support', as well as 'a leader who would not allow intrigue of any kind to raise its ugly head'.[39] Addressing a joint session of the Representative Assembly and Legislative Council on 17 September 1945, he praised Jai for his courage in taking 'so great a step forward in a State where representative institutions have been non-existent for all practical purposes'. While stopping short of full democracy, it represented 'a bold advance on the road which leads to the goal of popular government'.[40]

Such enthusiasm was not shared by the British. Despite his warm reception in Jaipur, Lord Wavell wrote to King George VI complaining that while Jai had 'great personal charm' and was an 'attractive character', he took very little interest in the affairs of the state. 'The only subjects on which he asked my support during my visit were to obtain vacancies for his sons at Eton and to retain on the Reserve the commission in the Life Guards, which he was given during the war.' As for Sir Mirza, he was considered 'untrustworthy'. The Viceroy's only positive words were reserved for Ayesha, whom he described as 'pretty, attractive and sophisticated'.[41] The Rajputana Agency was also scathing in its assessment of Jai. He was 'selfish and lazy ... and not interested in the administration of his state'. His primary objective was to be away from Jaipur 'as much as possible' and 'leave everything to Mirza'.[42] Stern dismisses such criticism as being based on the 'contemptuous and uncritical' acceptance of Jai's reputation as a playboy prince.[43] Crewe takes a more sanguine view: 'It was always Jai's misfortune that, because of his great capacity for enjoyment and because he was always smiling, people were inclined to think that he was not a serious person.'[44]

While Jai was undertaking the serious business of transforming himself from an autocratic ruler into a semi-constitutional head of state, Ayesha was taking advantage of the war to create a new space for herself. She started attending Red Cross work and fundraising parties at the Ladies' Club where she met a range of women she had not encountered before, such as teachers, doctors and wives of government officials whose company was more stimulating than that of the purdah-ridden palace ladies. Together with Jo, she persuaded some of the zenana women to start knitting socks and sweaters for the Jaipur State Forces in the Middle East. Raffles, tournaments and collections were organized. A silver trinket fund raised contributions for the war effort.

Ayesha also used her husband's prolonged absences to take control of the management of the Rambagh household, with its 400 servants responsible for everything from keeping Jai's fleet of cars running to organizing hunting trips. There was a military secretary to oversee arrangements for entertaining guests and another to ensure the building was kept in perfect condition. Although Jai prided himself in running Rambagh along military lines, Ayesha found evidence of extravagance, wastage and petty corruption wherever she looked. The palace storerooms were 'like some fantastic parody of Fortnum and Mason's', overstocked with everything from Egyptian cigarettes to liqueurs, lipsticks, toffees and preserves ordered 'not just by the crate but by the dozens of crates'. Storeroom staff proffered the excuse that the quantities were needed so nothing ran out—an explanation Ayesha wasn't buying. 'There wasn't the least attempt to keep track of who helped himself to what. The palace had been supplying all the staff, the guests, the ADCs and their families, and anyone else who happened to want something.' Specially imported Evian water was being given to the governess's dogs, two pounds of cream went into one dish of creme brûlée on the pretence that 'for the Maharaja no amount of cream was too much'.[45] Within a year, Ayesha had managed to halve expenses at Rambagh, in the process establishing for herself a reputation for ruthless efficiency.

Despite Jai's hopes that his wife's more liberated outlook might lead to a relaxation of purdah, centuries of tradition were not about to be erased overnight. Frustrated by the resistance of Jaipur's nobility to change, Ayesha decided to open a girls' school primarily for the daughters of the noble families and the higher echelons of society. It was their women who were the most cloistered, spending their lives going from one zenana to another. Reasoned Ayesha: 'If they came to my school, I thought, in ten years' time we might see a break-through.'[46] Once a few nobles enrolled their daughters and saw that their education was a success, others would follow.

The Maharani Gayatri Devi (MGD) School opened on 4 July 1943, amid the chanting of Sanskrit shlokas invoking the blessings of Lord Ganesha and Goddess Saraswati. It had just twenty-four pupils and was housed in Madho Vilas, once a garden retreat of the Jaipur maharajas outside the walled city. Its first principal was an imposing Scotswoman, Lillian Donnithorne Lutter, who began her teaching career in Maymyo in Burma and later moved to Moulmein, where she became commissioner of the Girl Guides. In 1942, she had led a group of eighty children through the jungles of Burma and into India to flee the Japanese advance. Her contribution to women's education earned her both a CBE and a Padma Shri. The school's initial curriculum included English literature, Hindi, maths, geography and Indian and world history. There was also a strong emphasis on sports such as tennis and swimming.

Today MGD School covers twenty-four acres on Sawai Man Singh Road. It enrols 3,000 students, all of them girls, neatly attired in maroon pleated skirts with buttoned down straps, blue blouses, white socks, black buckled shoes and maroon ribbons. Students from grade one to twelve have access to gyms, a swimming pool, tennis courts and basketball courts. The school's motto, 'Our utmost for the highest', is carved into the plinth of a marble statue of Ayesha in front of the school. 'There are old ladies in Jaipur today who say that Ayesha was their liberator, that she opened up for them a world they might otherwise have never seen. While some were grateful, others were horrified.'[47] The school would remain her enduring passion and in her later years she could be found sitting on the steps reading Dickens to the students or taking them for spins in her chauffeur-driven car.

Ayesha's more ebullient mood, brought about by her increasing engagement in Jaipur society, was checked by a series of family tragedies. First Her Highness, Marudhar Kanwar, died on Christmas Day in 1944 from a liver ailment brought on by heavy drinking. Jai was away at the time and Bubbles, then thirteen, had to light his mother's funeral pyre. 'My heart went out to him in his shock and sadness, and I promised myself that whatever might happen in the future I would always look after him,'[48] wrote Ayesha. A few months later Jai's mother died. Jai had been much closer to her than to his father and would write her touching letters requesting his favourite achar and puri every time he visited. Then it was Ayesha's turn to experience tragedy in her own family when her sister Ila, aged thirty, died of ptomaine poisoning, leaving behind three children.

* * *

The end of the war in September 1945 brought a brief period of much-needed repose before the urgent issue of India's likely independence and the role of the princely states began to occupy the minds of political leaders in London and New Delhi. The princes were derided for having an average of 'eleven titles, 5.8 wives, 12.6 children, 9.2 elephants, 2.8 private railway cars, 3.4 Rolls-Royces and 22.9 tigers killed', but the reality was that no solution to the future political evolution of India would work without their participation.[49] When Queen Victoria was proclaimed the Empress of India in 1877, the princes acknowledged her rule and declared their unflinching loyalty. By and large they were happy with the status quo. The British did little to rein in their extravagant lifestyles or peculiar fetishes. Only the most debauched or corrupt feared dismissal. The rest were left to maintain their feudal traditions. In 1921, King George V reaffirmed as 'inviolate and inviolable' Lord Canning's 1862 pledge that the integrity of the states should be preserved by perpetuating the rule of the princes whose power to adopt heirs should be recognized.[50]

In the same year, the Chamber of Princes was inaugurated by the Duke of Connaught. From its very beginning the Chamber was belittled as being a collection of squabbling autocrats more concerned about hierarchy than actual change. Attempts by the Congress to politicize the populations of the princely states also met with little success. Meeting in Delhi in 1929, the forty Indian rulers making up the Chamber unanimously declared their loyalty to the Crown and distanced themselves from calls for independence. Although Jaipur was one of the Chamber's founding members and Jai attended its meetings when not abroad, he did so only reluctantly. Peter Muir, the New Delhi newscaster for the CBS, whose emotionally charged broadcasts were fed into the American mainland networks, remembers Jai and Bhaiya in early 1942 as being 'very young, very Oxford, and very much in khaki'. They took the Chamber's proceedings lightly, 'emitting almost audible sighs of relief when the opportunity came for them to slip out for a drink'.[51]

In theory the princely states were independent of British India but in reality they had conceded their paramountcy to the Crown by surrendering their right to declare war or conduct their own foreign policy. They were also beholden to it in many other ways. Whether it was the schooling of their children, their travel abroad or their choice of marriage partners, the Crown had the final say.

In 1946, the British government assured the princes that when they yielded control of India, paramountcy would not automatically be transferred to the new Indian union. Each state would be free to negotiate its terms. They could accede either to India or to Pakistan or remain independent. This was bitterly opposed by the Congress on the grounds that the states were not truly independent and when paramountcy lapsed it should automatically transfer to the new government of independent India. Sir Conrad Corfield, who headed the Government of India's political department, vetoed that possibility with the inclusion of a clause in the India Independence Bill that would see paramountcy lapse when India became independent, creating an autonomous body of 562 states, home to more than 90 million people out of a population of about 340 million. When Louis Mountbatten became viceroy in 1946, he consulted not with Corfield but with his constitutional adviser, Vappala Pangunni Menon, who argued that the princely states should sign treaties of accession to the new government. Responsibility for foreign affairs, defence and communications would be transferred to the Indian state in return for assurances that their domestic autonomy would be scrupulously respected.

In May 1947, Jai left India for his annual summer sojourn in England despite an urgent plea from his brother-in-law Yadhavendra Singh, the Maharaja of Panna, to remain in order to maintain 'cohesion and unity in Rajputana and the neighbouring region'. The situation was nearing its climax and the states might be faced with a formula not to their liking, he warned Jai. 'You are in that enviable position to give an inspiring lead in regenerating that constructive spirit of mutual understanding and cohesion which would bring about the desired solidarity of Rajputana and its neighbours.'[52] Jai ignored his entreaties.

By the time Jai returned in July, a states department under Menon and Sardar Vallabhbhai Patel, the home minister, had been set up to conduct negotiations with the princes, who by now were hopelessly split between those willing to join a Constituent Assembly and those wanting independence. Patel had long been an outspoken critic of the princely states, once describing them as 'disorderly and pitiable', with 'no limits to their slavery'.[53] In a speech on 5 July launching the states department, he appealed to the 'proud heritage' India's princes shared with its people and warned that 'the alternative to co-operation in the general interest is anarchy and chaos which will overwhelm great and small in a common ruin'.[54] Destined to be remembered as a 'Hindu Cromwell courteously decapitating hundreds of little King Charleses',[55] Patel would be the key figure in pulling the majority into line by working closely with Mountbatten. Corfield, however, urged the princes to maintain their solidarity in order to give them a stronger negotiating position after Independence. Mountbatten responded by sidelining Corfield and conducting negotiations with the princes himself. Without the Viceroy's knowledge but with the permission of the Attlee government, Corfield ordered the destruction of more than four tonnes of secret files, spelling out some of the more salacious depravities of the princes. His rationale for this bonfire of vices was that the files could have been used to blackmail the princes if they found their way into the hands of the administrations of independent India and Pakistan. No longer able to guarantee their future, Corfield was determined to protect, at least, their past.

On 25 July 1947, only twenty days before India and Pakistan were to become independent nations, Mountbatten called a special meeting of the Chamber of Princes after promising Patel he would deliver 'a full basket of accessions'.[56] It would be the last time 'the world's most exclusive fraternity' would be assembled together. Reminding the princes that he too was a blue-blooded royal, Mountbatten then set about trying to woo each of the individual princes to sign the Act of Accession. Repeating Menon's offer, he begged them to 'look forward ten years and consider what the situation in India and the world would be then and have the foresight to act accordingly'. If they signed the Act of Accession, Patel and the Congress would allow them to continue to receive from his cousin the king those honours and titles they so cherished. Do not 'turn your backs on the India emerging on the 15th of August', he urged them.[57]

While states such as Bhopal, Hyderabad and Travancore were mulling the idea of rejecting Mountbatten's offer and declaring their independence, Jaipur, Bikaner, Patiala and Gwalior began filling Mountbatten's 'basket'. The most dramatic scene occurred when the Maharaja of Jodhpur, piqued at being bullied into signing away his sovereignty, pulled out a pistol concealed behind the nib of a very large fountain pen. With a theatrical flourish he pointed it at

Menon and screamed he would 'shoot him down like a dog if he betrayed the starving people of Jodhpur'.[58] He later gifted the gun to Mountbatten. Of all the rulers of the major states, Jai was perhaps the most pro-British. He had a special rapport with Mountbatten, whom he had known since the 1930s, and was the only Indian ruler who called Mountbatten by his pet name 'Dickie'. They had a common love of polo and were both proud soldiers. Mountbatten would later tell Larry Collins and Dominique Lapierre that Jai and Ayesha 'were under no illusion whatsoever that this [princely India] could continue'.[59]

On 12 August 1947, Jai signed the Instrument of Accession handing the Dominion of India control of his state's external affairs, defence and communications. Simultaneously, he signed a Standstill Agreement to set out matters of common concern to the Dominion of India and Jaipur, such as communications and customs.

The partition of India on 15 August was accompanied by unbelievable communal bloodshed. Jaipur had begun accommodating refugees from Sindh, Punjab and frontier districts from early 1946, with the total number eventually reaching 40,000 two years later. Sawai Jai Singh's vision for Jaipur as a 'universal city with multiple communities coexisting peacefully' had not always been followed to the letter, but compared with many other northern Indian cities, communal violence was rare.[60] Anxious to prevent post-Partition violence spreading to Jaipur, Jai toured the city every night accompanied by a Muslim colonel from one of his regiments. Despite efforts by the Pakistani army to persuade Muslims from military families in Jaipur to move to Pakistan, few if any did.

* * *

Four months after Independence, Jai celebrated his silver jubilee as the Maharaja of Jaipur. He was weighed in silver which was then distributed among the poor. The culmination of the festivities was a huge durbar attended by Lord and Lady Mountbatten. Jai was invested as a Grand Commander of the Star of India. In return for the honour, he presented Mountbatten a jade-handled dagger set with rubies and emeralds that had been captured by his ancestor Man Singh I from an Afghan warrior.

Once his jubilee celebrations were over, Jai, Jo and Ayesha began preparing for Mickey's marriage to the Maharajkumar of Baria. She was Jai's oldest child, his only daughter, and the first Jaipur princess to be married in more than a century. The wedding was a grand affair, still remembered as one of the last and most opulent displays of princely pageantry in India. With the Jaipur royals related to most of the large Rajput families, and through Ayesha to the family of Cooch Behar, the number of relatives invited ran into the hundreds. Each family had its own car and ADC and each guest was given a two-inch-thick instruction book detailing all the ceremonies, entertainments and receptions. 'The tables glowed with the bright gleam of gold and silver thalis, bowls and goblets. Throughout the meal, as thalis were filled and refilled, the palace musicians played.'[61] For the first time in years the City Palace was filled with people. The poor were fed and prisoners were released. Henri-Cartier Bresson captured the wedding in photographs and on film. The *Guinness Book of Records* declared it the most expensive ever staged.

In 1950, Jai took Ayesha to England for her first visit since 1938. They bought a house near East Grinstead called Saint Hill and a 400-acre farm to go with it. Ayesha maintained that the farm was purchased to ensure their children who were attending school in England had supplies of butter and milk, both of which were rationed. The uncertain political situation in India and the desire to have a bolt-hole in England must have also weighed heavily on their minds. Their fears were about to be realized.

Almost as soon as the Indian tricolour was raised, Menon and Patel started to renege on their earlier promises. Interference in the internal affairs of princely states became the norm and border states were taken over on the pretext of ensuring India's security. Junagadh was blockaded because its nawab wanted to be a part of Pakistan and Hyderabad was invaded when it refused to accede. The pressure on the princely states to merge into the Indian Dominion intensified. Many were so small they had no practical purpose in remaining autonomous. Jaipur was one of eighteen states considered to be viable and therefore left alone, based on assurances by Nehru and Patel. In January 1948, Jai and several other princes met with Mountbatten and were given undertakings by Menon that the principle of merger would not apply to viable states.

Jaipur's hopes of maintaining its autonomy were undermined when on 25 March 1948 nine smaller states headed by Kota agreed to merge with the Dominion. A month later Udaipur, one of the so-called viable states, joined Kota as did several other states to the north and west of Jaipur. 'Were there no men of cool common sense, who considered the main duty of state leadership to be the preservation of the states entrusted to their care?' Jai wrote in a private note. These rulers, who 'had seen themselves as suns round which the whole of Hindustan revolved' were nothing but 'weak characters', he despaired.[62]

Using a mix of diplomatic skills and subterfuge, Patel and Menon now began to woo Jaipur, Jodhpur, Jaisalmer and Bikaner to merge with the new state of Rajasthan. Patel tapped the rulers' phones and enlisted the help of their ministers to play them off against one another. Unity never being a strong point of the princely states, Jodhpur was the first to break ranks, soon followed by Jaipur, with Jai accepting the inevitable conclusion that its days as an independent entity were numbered. At a time when 'all the forces in the country are moving towards democratic ideals', he wrote to his son Bubbles, 'the sacrifice which seems so great today may prove in the end to be no sacrifice at all'.[63]

Discussions between Jai and representatives of the Indian government continued throughout November 1948 until they were interrupted by Jai's involvement in yet another plane crash. A couple of American pilots had wanted to demonstrate a new twin-engine plane that could land and take off using only one of its motors. Instead of watching from the ground, Jai insisted on flying with them. The demonstration ended with the aircraft plummeting to the ground a short distance from Jaipur airport. When Ayesha reached the site of the accident she found Jai lying unconscious, his head resting in the lap of a villager and blood trickling from the corner of his mouth. Fortunately, his injuries were not life-threatening.

Menon arrived in Jaipur on 11 January 1949, proposing a deal that would see Jaipur integrated into the new union of Greater Rajasthan with Jai as the hereditary governor or rajpramukh. Three days later, Patel announced that the last four states had agreed in principle on integration. More negotiations followed and more concessions were withdrawn. Instead of the office of rajpramukh being held in perpetuity by the ruling family to whom it had been given, it was now only to be held for life. Nor would Jai be the commander-in-chief of the provincial forces.

On 29 March 1949, Patel boarded a plane at Palam airport in Delhi together with the Maharaja of Jodhpur to attend ceremonies marking the formal inauguration of Jai as the rajpramukh of the union of Greater Rajasthan. When it was approximately sixty kilometres from Jaipur one of the plane's engines failed, forcing the pilot to make an emergency landing on a riverbed. There were no injuries and taking out a seat from the plane Patel sat and waited while the other passengers went to look for help. At one point the party attempted to secure a horse and cart to take them to Jaipur, but according to a report on the incident in the *Times of India*, 'the pony proved stubborn'. They eventually made it to Jaipur at 11 p.m. in an All India Radio equipment van that happened to be passing by.[64]

The transition from princely state to administrative unit was accompanied by the usual pomp and splendour of the Jaipur court. Aside from the rulers of the various princely states that were now to be a part of Rajasthan, the ceremony was attended by about a thousand nobles and civil servants. On either side of the carpeted passage that led to the dais where Jai and Patel sat, members of Jai's private bodyguards stood with drawn swords. Halfway through his inaugural address, Patel congratulated Jai for his elevation from being 'the first servant of Jaipur' to becoming 'the first servant of Rajasthan'.[65] Not everyone was in such a celebratory mood. Embittered by the proceedings and the failure of Patel to remain in Jaipur to attend the opening of the new state legislature, Sadul Singh, the Maharaja of Bikaner, retorted bluntly: 'Ties of blood extending over the last five centuries have been severed by a stroke.'[66] By November 1949, only six out of more than 550 states that had acceded to India remained as separate political entities within their old boundaries.

For Jai, the cost of the merger was considerable. He was forced to give up cash, property and goods worth an estimated ten million pounds in return for a privy purse worth about twenty thousand pounds. The Government of India acquired Jaipur's railway infrastructure including rolling stock for a pittance. All official buildings were handed over as well as many historical monuments such as

115

Amber Fort and Jai Singh's observatories in Jaipur and Delhi. He also had to give up his army which was merged with the Indian armed forces. Jai's obligations included looking after the several hundred women still living in the zenana, a similar number of servants and at least half a dozen temples and their staff. He also set up a trust to establish a museum at the City Palace to preserve the family's collections of carpets, paintings, arms and other historically important items.

* * *

In the early sixteenth century the Hindu saint Krishnadas Payahari gifted Queen Bala Bai, wife of Prithviraj Singh I, the ruler of Amber, an image of Narasimha in the form of a holy ammonite. According to legend, the saint predicted that as long as the idol remained in the Narasimha temple, Prithviraj and his descendants would hold on to their kingdom. If it left the shrine the kingdom would be lost. Just before Jai signed the documents of merger, the idol was stolen and with it went centuries of princely heritage.[67]

6

'A COMBINATION OF SITA, LAKSHMI
AND THE RANI OF JHANSI'

Jaipur as a state had ceased to exist and Jai had relinquished his powers as maharaja in favour of the largely ceremonial office of rajpramukh. Gone were 'the good old days', as Ayesha called them. Jai's duties now included presiding over the state legislative assembly sessions, swearing-in of ministers and resolving political deadlocks. Mundane matters took up an inordinate amount of time. In August 1949, for example, the Nawab of Tonk wrote to him about the difficulties he was having with the zenana ladies of the late ruler. 'One begum in particular ... is living in a manner not becoming to a member of a ruling family,' he complained.[1]

As far as the people of Jaipur were concerned, Jai was still their ruler. Shouts of 'Maharaja Man Singhji ki jai' greeted him as he drove through the capital on his thirty-seventh birthday in August 1949. Reflecting on the celebrations that included a vast party in the garden of the City Palace, he wrote: 'It was just as happy and gay as the ones I had as Ruler of Jaipur and the display of love, loyalty and devotion shown by all the people greatly touched my heart.'[2] Such adulation did not go down well with Congress leaders who continuously found themselves outshone by the maharaja. But his position of rajpramukh also worked to their advantage by preventing him from becoming actively involved in politics. In India's first elections held in 1952, the Maharaja of Jodhpur won a convincing victory standing as an independent, but he died in an air crash just two days before the results were announced. There is little doubt Jai would have performed just as well had he contested an election.

117

After a difficult pregnancy, Ayesha gave birth to a son in October 1949. In keeping with an astrologer's advice that their son's name should start with 'J', they named him Jagat. Traditional gun salutes were fired, an official holiday was proclaimed in Jaipur city and ministers and nobles came to the Rambagh Palace to congratulate the couple. The servant who announced the birth to his father was rewarded with a car; the woman who told his grandmother Indira was given a pair of diamond and ruby earrings.[3] The joy of motherhood, however, was tempered by the tragic death soon after of Ayesha's brother Indrajit, who succumbed to horrific burns when the house in Darjeeling he was staying in caught fire.

Indrajit's death barely rates two paragraphs in Ayesha's memoir and the background to the tragedy is left out completely. Like his father, uncles and brothers, Indrajit was an alcoholic. A couple of years before his death, he met Billie Evelyn Bridges, a Texan woman doing social work in India. The two fell in love and she succeeded in curbing his drinking temporarily. According to Billie, they were married in a Hindu ceremony, but Indira, who objected to the liaison, pulled strings with officials she knew and had her expelled from India. Indrajit immediately went back to drinking. When Indira begged her to return, Billie demanded that their marriage be officially recognized.[4] In June 1949, Indrajit checked himself into a clinic for alcoholics in Bihar and promptly tried to run away with his doctor's wife. While at the clinic, his servants were forbidden from giving him alcohol. Desperate for a drink, he knocked out his driver, got into his car and drove eight hours to Darjeeling. Later that night, a cigarette he was smoking in bed set fire to the blankets. His servants did not go to his rescue when they heard him shouting because he could be violent when drunk.[5] Billie turned up in Cooch Behar the day after his death but was refused entry into the palace. 'She put up a holler, claiming she was the widow and entitled to her rights as such, but she got no farther than the doorstep. The family didn't need her anymore,'[6] Arthur Watson wrote in the *Daily News*.

Indrajit's elder brother, Bhaiya, also had a weakness for foreign women and alcohol but managed to keep the latter in check for most of his life. His adjustment to the new India, however, was much more difficult than Jai's. 'Bhaiya was a remnant of another age, brought up to be modern in some ways and unable to be free of the past in others; it left him stranded between two worlds,' writes the historian Lucy Moore.[7] In 1947, he flew to Los Angeles to meet his old friends Tony Martin and Richard Benjamin. Martin, one of America's most popular actors and singers in the 1930s and 1940s, had served in Assam during the war as a technical sergeant in the Air Transport Command. He also joined the Entertainment Production Unit performing for troops stationed in bases around the region. Bhaiya had handed over Cooch Behar's airstrip to American aircrews flying 'The Hump'—the dangerous route from north-east India to Kunming in southern China to supply Chinese troops fighting the Japanese. 'We want to repay him as best we can for the favours he did us during the war,' Benjamin told the *Los Angeles Times*.[8] The official purpose of Bhaiya's visit was to buy farm machinery for his state, but the real reason was to conduct a 'scientific expedition to the stars of Hollywood'. Martin and Benjamin were there to take care of the 'vacation' angle.

The idea for the 'expedition' had been hatched a few months earlier at the 300 Club in Calcutta. The club was founded in 1947 by Boris Lissanevitch, a Russian former ballet dancer who had escaped the Bolshevik revolution in 1917, seeking asylum in Paris before eventually settling in Calcutta. The 300 Club was housed in a building known as Phillip's Folly, whose former owner was an Armenian eccentric who had a steam car shaped like a gigantic swan that hissed steam from its nostrils, honked, shook and laid eggs of pure gold every time it stopped. Aside from Bhaiya and Prithi Singh, who was the Maharaja of Baria and a star polo player, regulars at Lissanevitch's club included Jai and Ayesha, the Aga Khan, the rulers of Kapurthala, Burdwan and Baroda as well as wealthy businessmen such as J.C. Mahindra.[9]

Lissanevitch, an exiled Nepali general, Mahabir Rana, and Maharaja Prithi Singh accompanied Bhaiya on his 'expedition'. No report was ever prepared on 'agricultural machinery' for Cooch Behar, but so much money was spent on flowers for female friends, drinks and parties that their funds were quickly exhausted. 'Nobody in America ever had heard of Cooch Behar. But the starlets vied for dates with the Maharajah. Martin made the spiel and introduced them to his highness,' the gossip columnist Leonard Lyons reported.[10]

The image of the handsome, sporty and flirtatious Bhaiya contrasted sharply with his demeanour when in Cooch Behar. 'The

Cooch Behar that I knew in Calcutta was an entirely different man from Cooch Behar the Maharaja in his own state. The moment he entered his land Bhaiya became a serious, respected administrator,' Lissanevitch would later recall, without elaborating on what, if anything, he had done for his state.[11] The contrast had a lot to do with Bhaiya's domineering mother. H.J. Todd, the British Resident for eastern India, described him as 'shy and tongue tied'. 'The reason of course is obvious,' Todd wrote. 'I was horrified to hear Indira say that when the Maharaja next went on tour in the villages she proposed to accompany him and teach him to take the centre stage. I suggested the Maharaja would do better if his mother was not always in the offing.' When Todd asked Indira why at the age of thirty her son was still unmarried, she explained that he wanted to choose his own wife. 'She must be a real stunner—or if he could not find such a girl, [one] with a very large dowry.'[12]

Indira's frustration with her son's attitude to women was matched only by her despair at his approach to ruling. 'Take my poor Bhaiya's case,' she wrote to Jai in 1951. 'He will be thirty-six this December and no wisdom, it breaks one's heart to see such deterioration. These two years of sitting idle since the merger [of Cooch Behar with India] have done their damage ... I could not be more disheartened and without hope.'[13] On another occasion she snapped at his refusal to eat prasad at a formal dinner. Indira's grandson Habi Deb Burman of Tripura would later recall her saying that if he did not follow state custom and tradition he should abdicate and relinquish his title and privileges. 'Bhaiya left the table quietly but Granny [Indira] continued relating [to the guests] how her son was weak—mixed with whores and jockeys and never with foreign women of his own status like Doris Duke and Barbara Hutton who admired him.'[14]

Indira's primary object of derision was Nancy Valentine, the daughter of a New York commercial artist and a small-time actor who had appeared alongside Elizabeth Taylor in the movie *Father of the Bride*. She also was reputed to be the best rumba dancer at New York's Mocambo nightclub. Gossip columnists called her Howard Hughes' 'favourite dancing partner'. While on his 'scientific expedition', Bhaiya, who was known in cafe society as 'Coochie Boy', had been introduced to her by Martin and he immediately fell in love with her blonde charms. He was in his thirties and she was nineteen. But Nancy had other plans and in August 1948 married Omar Dejany, the UN representative of King Abdullah of Transjordan. The marriage collapsed within months of the pair cutting the wedding cake. Shortly afterwards, Nancy travelled to England and then stayed with Jai and Ayesha in Jaipur. By early 1950, reports of her engagement 'to a well-known Indian playboy' had begun to circulate. After meeting Jai for tea, the society writer Earl Wilson asked him about Bhaiya's imminent marriage to Nancy. Denying the rumour, Jai told him: 'We're expected to marry within our own family.'[15]

Nancy travelled to Cooch Behar in July 1950 and the pair took their vows at a simple ceremony officiated by a Hindu priest, the bride wearing slacks instead of a sari. The couple went to America in September, but to the frustration of Hollywood watchers they refused to confirm that they had tied the knot. Instead, Valentine announced plans for a formal wedding the following year and said that she had started 'instruction in the Hindu faith'. In October 1951, she was spotted in New York sporting an eternity wedding ring that sparkled with rubies, sapphires and diamonds. 'We'll go through another ceremony,' she told Earl Wilson, who interviewed her at the Hotel Elysee, where she introduced herself to callers as the Maharani of Cooch Behar. 'I'll probably wind up wearing Levi's. I wore slacks the other time.' She said the wedding ceremony was going to be kept simple 'so as not to excite any Communists'. Asked whether she was worried about Bhaiya taking other wives, she answered: 'I don't think the Hindus do that so much anymore. But, oh gosh—an uncle of [Bhaiya's] had thirty-five wives or was it 135?'[16]

Despite numerous assurances from Nancy, the second wedding never happened. Her application to the Indian government to recognize the marriage and accept her status as the Maharani of Cooch Behar was dismissed. Nancy's mother, who described Bhaiya as 'about the most wonderful man I've ever met', refused to blame her de facto son-in-law for aborting the plan. 'I figure she's leaving because she doesn't want the Indian Government to spit in her eye.'[17] Before departing from India, Nancy told the press she was returning to America because her mother was ill. The real reason was Indira's jealousy. She was vehemently opposed to the relationship, once telling a friend of Nancy's that if they married, Bhaiya would lose his title and she would never be a maharani. Nancy would later tell the United Press that an American girl couldn't expect to find a more devoted husband than an Indian prince. 'They're fabulous, they know how to make a girl feel like she's the tastiest creampuff in the bakery. I only wish the one I got could still be mine ... With the Maharaja it was *Some Enchanted Evening* every day in the week.'[18]

By 1953, Bhaiya had given up on Nancy and was rumoured to be courting the singer Alicia Cortelli. Then on 16 July 1953, newspapers in England reported that his midnight-blue Bentley had collided with a truck near Baldock in Hertfordshire. Bhaiya suffered a broken collarbone and five broken ribs and was rushed to hospital in a serious condition. His passenger, who had concussion and leg injuries, was named as 'Miss Martin' of London. Her real name was Valerie Mewes. She was a twenty-one-year-old model and had changed her name to Vicki Martin at the suggestion of Stephen Ward. Vicki and Ward had met a couple of years earlier in the doorway of a shop in Oxford Street, where they had taken shelter in a rainstorm. Ward was a London osteopath whose clients included the billionaires William Averell Harriman and Nubar Gulbenkian, as well as Elizabeth Taylor, Douglas Fairbanks and a clutch of Indian princes including Sayajirao of Baroda, Jai and Bhaiya. Vicki was a homeless waif who had escaped from a broken home in Staines, Middlesex. For a few brief years she would become the love of Bhaiya's life, while Ward would become the scapegoat in the Profumo affair. John Profumo, secretary of state for war in the Macmillan government, used Ward's flat to have sex with the call girl Christine Keeler. Ward had also introduced Christine to the dashing Soviet diplomat Yevgeny Ivanov. When Profumo lied to the House of Commons about his love life, the resulting scandal threatened to bring down the government. But it was Ward who stood in the dock at the Old Bailey—a scapegoat for the establishment. He later committed suicide.

When Vicki met Ward, she was sharing a room with Ruth Ellis, who would later achieve notoriety by becoming the last woman to be hanged in England for the murder of her lover. Both were working at the Court Club in Mayfair, a fashionable venue that doubled as a brothel and was owned by the infamous crook and vice king Morris Conley. Ward was captivated by Vicki. He described her as having the 'most exquisite smile you have ever seen ... spontaneous, uninhibited and genuine'.[19] He took her to his flat, dressed her in some clothes that his ex-wife Patricia had left behind and promised to introduce her to people who could help her become a model.[20] Vicki stayed in Ward's flat for nearly a year. As well as convincing her to change her name to the catchier Vicki Martin, he coached her on how to iron out the harshest parts of her cockney accent and gave her tips on walking like a model. It worked. As Ward's friend the petty criminal Bobby McKew would later say, 'She had the look that launched a thousand lusts.'[21]

Her introduction to Mayfair society was at the opening night of the Fine Arts Club on Charles Street run by Ward's friend Siegi Sessler. After Ward helped her land a role in the film *It Started in Paradise*, she began receiving invitations to high-society dinners and parties. Her suitors were many, as Noel Whitcomb, a gossip columnist with the *Daily Mirror* wrote: 'There was always a regiment of rich men, showmen, playboys and peers, queuing up to take Vicki to luncheon or dinner.'[22]

Bhaiya, who was in London setting up a travel agency to lure millionaires to Cooch Behar for £1,000-a-head tiger shoots and trying to promote professional boxing in India, was one of those attending the opening of the Fine Arts Club. He was captivated by Martin the moment he set eyes on her. She was immediately attracted to him. The following evening, Bhaiya, Vicki and Ward dined together at Les Ambassadeurs, or Les A as the club was known by the international smart set. To demonstrate his affection for Vicki, Bhaiya went to the Dorchester Hotel, bought the entire contents of its flower shop and sent them to her at Ward's flat.[23] Within a month, she had moved into her own flat in Upper Berkeley Street, paid for by Bhaiya. To please him, the natural blonde dyed her hair black and the pair were frequently spotted at the Milroy, London's most fashionable nightclub, where regulars included Noel Coward, Vivien Leigh and Princess Margaret.

After the car crash at Hertfordshire, Bhaiya and Vicki recuperated in adjacent wards. Her room was crammed with so many flowers sent by him that the press could hardly squeeze in. 'I am so very fond of him as I feel he is of me but there is little hope of our romance coming to anything,' she told one reporter while showing off a gold Cartier tiger brooch—a gift from Bhaiya. 'You see it is the Tigre's mother who is putting her foot down,' she explained, referring to Indira.[24] Tigre was Bhaiya's nickname, while he called her *méchante*, French for a naughty girl. Despite her denials, newspaper headlines were soon declaring 'London Model to Wed Prince' and 'Vicki's Romance with the Maharaja'. Marrying Vicki, however, would go against the wishes not only of his mother but of his entire family. He also feared it might mean an end to his privy purse. When Bhaiya told her she would have to live with him in India, Vicki consulted Ward, who said that a headstrong, capricious and fun-loving woman like her would soon tire of the strictures of palace life and miss the freedom she enjoyed in London. He also pointed out that Bhaiya had grown used to his ostentatious lifestyle and that if he had to give it up, he would blame it on her.[25]

When Bhaiya came out of convalescence, Vicki confessed she could not marry him. He responded that if they could be married without him losing his privileges he would do so. The couple spent the next several months together, driving to Newmarket for the thoroughbred sales, attending polo matches at Windsor or flying to Paris for horse races at Longchamps. He then commissioned Vasco Lazzolo to paint her portrait. She never made her last sitting. At 3.30 a.m. on 9 January 1955, the car she was travelling in collided with another just outside Maidenhead. Vicki died from massive injuries on her way to hospital.

Bhaiya heard the news when the plane he was taking from Calcutta to Jaipur stopped in Delhi for refuelling. When waiting reporters told him of Vicki's death he collapsed in tears and whispered, 'Vicki ... Mechante ... my naughty little girl.'[26] Too distraught to attend the funeral himself, he asked Jai to go on his behalf. Jai arrived at the public funeral at Golders Green Crematorium, carrying a giant wreath of flowers tied together with a large red ribbon on which were printed the words 'Goodbye to Mechante. My love always, Tigre.' According to the *Daily Mail*, those attending were mostly 'Mayfair sprinkled with mink and titles'.[27] In the afternoon the ashes of Valerie Mewes were buried at the family grave at Englefield Green in a much more low-key affair. Among the small number of mourners was Stephen Ward.

* * *

Jai returned to India from the funeral with a brother-in-law to console and an increasingly hostile government to confront. In September 1953, Jawaharlal Nehru had written to the princes making blunt observations regarding the 'anachronisms' of the privy purses and the lifetime appointments of the rajpramukhs. 'How long can we justify to our people the payment of large sums of money from the public funds to the Princes, many of whom discharge no functions at all,' he wrote in a letter to Jai.[28] In his polite but firm rejoinder, Jai pointed out that both rights had been inscribed in the Indian Constitution. It should never be altered merely to consolidate the position of the party in power 'or to suit its administrative convenience'.[29] Nehru responded by suggesting that 15 per cent of the privy purses would go into a National Plan Loan to be used for development activities. Jai countered with the fact that no other grouping, including zamindars and business magnates, were being asked to make a similar contribution to public funds. The exchange of letters continued into 1955 with Jai eventually cautioning Home Minister Govind Ballabh Pant against any hasty action that might damage India's international reputation.

While the Congress equivocated over the privy purses, the concept of holding the office of rajpramukh for life was looking increasingly anachronistic. Governors and the President could only hold their offices for a period of five years. In October 1956, Jai received three letters, one from President Rajendra Prasad, one from Nehru and one from Pant. They carried the same message. From 31 October, Jai would no longer be rajpramukh. He was deeply hurt by the news. He had been neither consulted nor warned about the change. Writing to Nehru he said it was 'most distressing that in spite of sincere co-operation and unflinching loyalty on my part throughout the last seven years, my official connections with the administration should cease so abruptly'.[30] Jai was now without a job or an official role. As Crewe writes: 'The British Government, with little justice, had so often accused him of doing too little for his people; the Indian Government, in the name of justice for all, made it impossible for him to do anything.'[31]

Jai's initial response to his sudden demotion was to plunge back into polo, assembling a team for a series of international matches in England. After the war he had bought Kings Beeches, a mansion set on forty-five acres of landscaped gardens with large stables in Sunningdale so he could be near the Smith's Lawn polo ground at Windsor. It was also close to Ascot.

Another outcome of his loss of office was his decision to turn the Rambagh Palace into a hotel. The first time Ayesha heard of the plan was an off-the-cuff remark made at a lunch party in early 1956 hosted by the Oberois, who went on to become among India's leading hoteliers. When she and Bubbles confronted Jai, he gave one of those smiles that Ayesha knew so well, indicating that the story was true. Times had changed and it was no longer possible to keep the Rambagh the way it was, he explained. The family would instead live in the Rajmahal, the former British Residency. 'I was wretched, and so was Jo Didi when she heard the news. We had both come to Rambagh as brides. For nearly half my life—longer for Jo Didi—Rambagh had been the centre of my activities and of my allegiance. It was my home. We both pleaded with Jai to change his mind, but he remained determined.'[32] In the end Jo never left Rambagh. On 30 April 1958, she died aged just forty-two of complications brought on by a gall bladder disease. In her loneliness she had increasingly taken refuge in alcohol. She had refused to see a doctor and despite the seriousness of her condition, her ladies-in-waiting complied with her wishes rather than taking their own initiative. Jai and Ayesha had left Jaipur the day before. Eight-year-old Jagat, who remained behind, kept asking for a doctor, but no one took any notice of his demands. His parents were about to board a plane to London when the news of Jo's death reached them. They drove back to Jaipur for the funeral and the traditional mourning period. It was the last time the family stayed at the Rambagh Palace.

The leasing of the Rambagh Palace would have long-lasting consequences. So too would the gifting of the Jai Mahal Palace to Jagat on 5 May 1956. More than sixty years later, various branches of the family would still be squabbling in court over their shares in both properties.

* * *

While Jai did not inherit his adoptive father's religious devotion, he took his ritual duties seriously. The maharaja of a Hindu state was traditionally seen as the defender of the faith and would lead the people for any religious ceremony or festival. Pamela Mountbatten recalls attending Jai's week-long silver jubilee celebrations in 1947 at the City Palace. The festivities began with a grand parade for the festival of Dussehra. Pamela watched as men in turbans and courtly dress carried huge brass horns and trumpets and magnificently caparisoned elephants sauntered through the palace courtyard. She was shocked to see Jai sacrifice a goat and then dip his fingers into little bowls filled with its blood that he flicked at a long line of decorated horses, oxen and elephants. Inside the palace Jai sat on a huge silver throne as a procession of nobles paid homage, 'kept cool as they waited by the ministrations of servants with huge plumed fans'.[33]

The ritual slaughter of goats would also take place at the temple to Shila Devi at the entrance to the Amber Fort. Whenever Jai left the state for any length of time, the first thing he did on returning was offer prayers at the temple. The other important shrine for Jaipur's rulers was the Govind Devji temple within the City Palace precincts. The temple houses a statue of Krishna that was originally brought from Vrindavan and installed there by Jai Singh in 1735. A third significant temple was the Jamma Mataji temple approximately twenty-five kilometres from Jaipur city. When travelling Jai always carried with him an image of the goddess Durga to which he prayed daily. Flowers were placed in front of the image before any polo match.

Although Ayesha's Brahmo Samaj upbringing gave her a more secular outlook, there are numerous references in her memoir to observing Hindu rituals. At her mother's insistence, she performed the Shiv puja to obtain a good husband. She also made offerings to Ganesha before her wedding. Jai and Ayesha became followers of a Hindu sanyasin named Shraddha Mata. A Sanskrit scholar from

Varanasi, Shraddha Mata was rumoured to have had an affair with Nehru and by some accounts gave birth to his son in 1949 in a convent in Bangalore. In 1953, Jai 'gifted' her Hathroi Fort, built to protect Jaipur against invaders but now surrounded by back-packer hostels. According to Khushwant Singh, who met Shraddha Mata there, the fort was infested with 'flying foxes, rock pigeons and sand lizards'. She told Singh she first met Nehru in the early 1950s. They established an instant rapport 'which seemed to indi-cate we had known each other in our previous lives'. She claimed to have had an affair with the prime minister but could not marry him because he was a Brahmin and she was a Kshatriya.[34] In 1952, she travelled to Europe, America and East Africa, giving discourses on the Gita, which attracted large crowds. On her return, she con-verted Hathroi Fort into the headquarters of her Mahashakti Peeth. When not in Jaipur she lived at Nigambodh Ghat, Delhi's main cremation ground, in a tent erected among burning corpses. Her followers believed she was a reincarnation of Kali.

* * *

In January 1957, Jai wrote to Jawaharlal Nehru to ask for his guid-ance about standing for Parliament. The letter must have come as a surprise to the prime minister, who wasn't sure if Jai was consider-ing joining the Congress, which would be of great benefit to the party, or running as an independent. Nehru's response implied that Jai was in fact considering standing as an independent, something which would have had negative consequences. Dissuaded by the brush-off from Nehru, Jai formulated a plan to put Ayesha up as a Congress candidate. Instead of approaching his wife directly he instructed Rajasthan's Chief Minister Mohanlal Sukhadia to broach the idea with her. Jai's ancestors had always forged alliances with whoever occupied the throne in the imperial capital whether it was the Mughals or the British. By going directly to Nehru he was merely following Jaipur state tradition, believing that a political alliance would protect him and his family.

Since the early 1950s, Ayesha had been taking on more public duties. She was president of the Badminton Association of India and vice president of the Tennis Association of India. In addition to the

MGD School, she now added a second institution to her portfolio—
a school for teaching women refugees from Pakistan embroidery
and sewing. She also followed her Baroda grandmother's lead and
became involved in the All India Women's Conference, India's largest women's organization, which agitated for rights to education,
owning property, remarriage and divorce.

Her motives for enhancing her public profile were varied. Her
love of sport was clearly one, as was her involvement in education.
But even at this early stage, there were hints of her political ambi-
tions. Unlike Jai, she never disguised her contempt for the Congress
party and the blatant corruption that had been allowed to fester
under its rule. She was genuinely aghast at the decay and rampant
development that was scarring Jaipur's old city and the state government's refusal to do anything about it. In her frustration, she
wrote to Nehru, who supported her cause.

That Jai failed to recognize his wife's political leanings is extraordinary. It was no wonder that when Sukhadia asked her if she would
consider standing for Parliament as a Congress candidate, she
answered that doing so would be dishonest as she did not approve
of its policies or record in government.[35] Explaining her decision to
Jai, she said that with Gandhi at the helm it had been a great party.
'Having won power, however, it was attracting people who were
more concerned with a lucrative career than with achieving good
for India.' At a time when the Congress was urging people to tighten
their belts, 'party members seemed to regard themselves as a privileged class and were becoming more and more affluent every day'.
She had been personally affronted by Nehru's bald justification for
abolishing the post of rajpramukh on the grounds that 'the Constitution cannot be petrified'. 'I began, then, to question the integrity
of a government that could go back, so casually, on an agreement
enshrined in the Constitution. Certainly, if it was necessary for the
good of the country, changes should be made, but surely not without consulting all the parties involved.'[36] The priority should be to
form a strong opposition that would keep the Congress accountable.
For her to join the party would be tantamount to propping up a
corrupt and ineffective administration.

Though she declined the offer to be a Congress candidate, Ayesha
now began to think about politics in a new way. Both her Baroda

grandparents had been actively involved in civil society. Cooch Behar had always been one of India's most progressive states and Indira's role as regent and her fierce independence were also inspirations. In 1959, Chakravarty Rajagopalachari, Mountbatten's successor as Governor General, formed the Swatantra Party. He had broken away from the Congress over Nehru's utopian socialism and his attempt to impose collective ownership of land. Rajaji, as he was known, stood for freeing India from the grip of a socialist interventionist government and believed that the future prosperity of India lay in private ownership of property and economic freedom. 'At last someone was speaking up against excessive state control and the disastrous results of the Congress Party's economic policies and asking for a practical approach that wasn't shackled to visionary dogma,' Ayesha noted.[37] 'She felt she must do something to serve the people in their plight,' her friend Sher Ali Khan said after she wrote to him asking his advice. 'I supported her desire in this noble cause.' However, he warned her that knowing politics was different from practising it. 'The rules were different. The techniques were different. Sometimes they played football with the rules of polo, in which there was no off-side.'[38] Taking Sher Ali's advice and believing that Swatantra would be a sensible, non-extremist opposition to the Congress, she decided to join the party. 'I had great respect for Pandit Nehru but didn't like his policy of nationalising everything. Free India, swatantra Bharat, swatantra janata was what I believed in,' she later explained.[39] Firstly, though, she had to ask Jai's permission. His response was immediate, telling her she was the obvious choice.

The official announcement that Ayesha had joined the Swatantra Party had to be delayed because of the impending visit by Queen Elizabeth and the Duke of Edinburgh to India in February 1961. The royal tour, which included a stop in Jaipur, was putting the government on edge. India was an independent nation and the last thing it wanted was a former maharaja entertaining an English monarch and her husband in a way that harked back to the colonial era. Nehru interpreted the wording of an invitation to a reception in honour of the British royal couple as an invitation to a princely durbar, which Jai vehemently denied. Nehru also demanded to know why guests had been asked to come in full dress and wearing their turbans. Jai replied that that was the traditional costume in Jaipur. Nobles always attended any ceremonial occasion dressed in their achkans and turbans and carrying swords.

Elizabeth and Philip's stay in Jaipur stole the limelight from the other stops on their tour. The *Tatler*'s correspondent described the sight of the queen riding an elephant into the Pink City as 'unforgettable'. 'The Queen looked as happy as if she were leading in a Derby winner. The elephant, his face a mass of bright tracery, with bracelets of brass tinkling on his feet, was Moghul splendour as only India can do it. This ancient pageantry has in no way suffered from the country's socialist philosophy. The Indians prize and cherish it as the English do.'[40] A photo of the queen waving to the crowd from her elephant with Jai sitting next to her made the front page of the *Illustrated London News*, which noted that 700 noblemen were present at the durbar 'attired in the court dress of the time of Sawai Jai Singh, the eighteenth-century ancestor of the present Maharaja'.[41] The home affairs ministry in Delhi was fuming.

Not all the publicity was positive. When an official photograph showing a nine-foot, eight-inch tiger shot by Prince Philip was released by Buckingham Palace, an Indian government spokesperson branded it 'astonishing'. 'After the fuss in England we are most surprised that the Queen has allowed publication of this picture because it seems to sum up the reaction of certain sections of British opinion,' the spokesperson told the *Daily Herald*.[42] The photo showed a beaming Prince Philip standing near the tiger's head. Beside him was ten-year-old Jagat while Jai and Ayesha were on either side of the queen. Two hundred beaters had lured the tiger to a position where the prince was able to mow it down from the top of a twenty-five-foot-high hunting platform. One newspaper derided it as the most choreographed shoot ever staged. A second tiger was shot by the duke's treasurer, Rear Admiral Christopher Douglas Bonham-Carter, though it was rumoured that the animal was actually shot by the queen. The photo opportunity was followed by a champagne lunch in the jungle. In a front-page commentary, the *Mirror* blasted the hunt, saying it was high time 'that those who advise the Royal Family on these matters should take some heed of public opinion. The Royal Family do not seem to have caught up with the modern enlightened view on the killing of animals for pleasure.'[43]

Many of those attending the durbar saw the pomp and pageantry as demonstrable proof that the aristocracy was still strongly attached to its traditional ways and might even presage a resurgence of the royal families. Congress politicians were only too aware of how the aristocratic front led by the Maharaja of Jodhpur in the 1952 general elections had threatened their dominance in the state. With Ayesha's entry into politics, there were doubts that the Congress in Rajasthan could withstand another assault. 'The feudal snowball threatens to be turning into an avalanche,' said one politician after the maharani's decision was announced.[44] At a national level, Congress members of Parliament began discussing a ban on princely participation in politics. Rajaji hoped that the House of Jaipur's association with Swatantra would win over other ruling families and their followers. But there was plenty going against Ayesha. She was an outsider, which lessened her appeal among other Rajasthani nobles or princes who might have been tempted to also join the party. Nor could she speak Hindi or any of the local dialects that she would need to use on the hustings. Rajasthan's Congress chief minister declared in the state assembly that royals who went into politics should immediately lose their privy purses.

Ayesha's initial intention was to help the party by canvassing for candidates and raising funds, rather than openly campaigning, let alone standing as a candidate. She described her first public appearance as a party member—introducing Rajaji at a public meeting in Jaipur—as nerve-wracking. In the autumn of 1961 she was formally invited to stand for election the following year. She was also given responsibility for securing Rajasthan for Swatantra, which meant ensuring that four Lok Sabha seats and forty state assembly seats were won by the party. Jai toyed with the idea of standing himself but decided to stay out of the fray. Pat and Joey, however, stood alongside their stepmother. Pat ran for a Lok Sabha seat, while Joey campaigned for a seat in the state assembly. Only Bubbles, who had by this time joined the army, did not stand. No sooner had she thrown her hat into the ring than Rajaji was enthusiastically describing Ayesha as 'a combination of Sita, Lakshmi and the Rani of Jhansi'.[45]

For the foreign press, Ayesha's entry into politics spiced up what was an otherwise lacklustre campaign. Most of the coverage of royals in the fray did not go beyond clichéd depictions of their gilded but fading lifestyles. A Reuters dispatch described Ayesha's normal routine as consisting of riding, tennis, social engagements and entertaining house guests. A typical day usually ended with drinks at the Jaipur Club, while weekends were often taken up with watching her husband and his sons by his first two wives shoot tigers at Sawai Madhopur's royal hunting lodge. Summers were spent in Europe to escape the desert heat. 'Unlike most Hindu wives, she drinks, smokes, and likes to lounge in slacks and a blouse instead of the traditional chiffon sari.' As to her appeal as a candidate, 'once we could not even look at her; she lived like a fairy', a Jaipur camel driver was quoted as saying. 'Now she comes to our home and all she asks is our vote. It was the least we could do.'[46] *Time* magazine took the adulation a step higher: 'Not in the fourteen years of Indian independence has there appeared a candidate with her aura and appeal: she is rich, beautiful, intelligent, and a first-rate politician ... The Maharani represents the most striking example so far of the return of India's one-time ruling class to national politics.'[47] By allowing *Time* to follow her on the campaign trail Ayesha had temporarily set aside her disdain for the media. The move was as strategic as all her other public forays. She knew her entry into politics would resonate throughout the world. When it came to image-building, she was the gold standard among Indian royalty—a queen with a cause, ready to toss away the comforts of palace life for the heat and dust of electioneering.

Life on the hustings was far removed from her palace routine. Ayesha travelled from village to impoverished village in her 1948 Buick, switching to an open jeep where there were no proper roads. To begin with, Jai accompanied her to offer confidence and support, but for most of the campaign she was escorted only by her party workers. Her day began at six and ended at midnight. Villagers garlanded her with marigolds, smothered her with rose petals and pushed coconut sweetmeats into her mouth seven times in a traditional welcome. She performed pujas at local temples and took the blessings of priests. Priming her attack on the Congress, she likened the party's economic policy to 'growing a babul tree and expecting to get mangoes. They come to you when they need your vote; when they are returned to power, they become little monarchs who levy taxes on you as they please, make you quarrel with each other, and swell their bank accounts.'[48] She made a special pitch to village women, who listened to her segregated behind bamboo fences, calling them sisters and urging them to vote in favour of the Swatantra Party. 'Everywhere she went, thousands of voters turned out to see her. People would remain transfixed and continue to gaze in her direction even after her cavalcade had left,' the veteran journalist Sita Ram Jhalani, who covered the 1962 elections, remembers. After Ayesha's election rallies, party workers would throw into the crowds plastic badges with the Swatantra Party's symbol, the star, embossed on them. 'Old men and young boys would scramble to collect the badge. They would proudly wear it, calling it a gift from the Maharani.'[49]

On the final night of the election campaign, Jai addressed a huge gathering in a square outside the City Palace in support of his wife. 'The new government has taken my state from me, but for all I care they can take the shirt off my back as long as I can keep that bond of trust and affection. They accuse me of putting up my wife and two of my sons for election. They say that if I had a hundred and seventy-six sons [the number of electoral seats in the Rajasthan assembly] I would put them all up too. But they don't know, do they, that I have far more than only one hundred and seventy-six sons.'[50]

When the counting of votes was over, Ayesha had snatched the seat of Jaipur from the Congress candidate Sharda Devi in a landslide, piling up the biggest majority in India's history and earning a spot in the *Guinness Book of Records*. All ten of her opponents were forced to forfeit their deposits. Both Pat, contesting the Lok Sabha seat of Dausa, and Joey, who ran for the state assembly seat of Malpura, also had comfortable wins. As the large and noisy victory parade filed past the City Palace, Jai stood on top of one of the gateways throwing gold and silver coins to the crowd as he did when he was ruler.

On 16 April 1962, the Maharani of Jaipur took the oath of allegiance in the Lok Sabha, her pearls and perfume contrasting sharply with the homespun khadi of many of the chamber's 456 elected members. Also taking his oath in the Lok Sabha was Pat. After being nominated for a seat in the Rajya Sabha, Jai was also now a parliamentarian. Bubbles, who was an adjutant in the President's

Bodyguard in Delhi, was the fourth family member attending the occasion. The election had established the Swatantra Party as the largest opposition group in Parliament. A backbencher, Ayesha nevertheless was outspoken, criticizing the Congress government on new taxes that had increased the price of basic commodities and were hurting lower- and middle-income earners.

Despite openly backing his wife's landslide victory, there is evidence that Jai was lukewarm about her political career. His outward support concealed an inherent conservativism. As was the case with his attitude to purdah, Jai encouraged his wife to rock the boat—but as gently as possible. This time, Ayesha was having none of that. 'Her entry in politics ... changed their daily routine and style of living,' wrote her long-time confidant Sher Ali Khan. '[Jai] did not like it. He wanted to get away from it all but could not express it in so many words for fear of hurting her.'[51]

* * *

To rub salt into Nehru's wounds over the drubbing the Congress had suffered at the hands of the royals, the House of Jaipur was once again about to grab the limelight. Shortly before the inauguration of the new Lok Sabha, Jackie Kennedy and her sister Lee Radziwill arrived in India. As with the Queen a year earlier, Jai had extended a personal invitation to Jackie to visit Jaipur. And as before, the government was adamant that the Jaipur stopover should not overshadow the official part of her tour. Nehru was particularly sensitive to any breaches of protocol. According to the US ambassador to India, John Kenneth Galbraith, the prime minister had fallen 'deeply in love' with the First Lady ever since dining with her at the White House a couple of months earlier. Galbraith informed President Kennedy of the Indian government's protocol concerns, only to be told that Kennedy never interfered in his wife's private arrangements. The Indian government did not help matters by trying to micromanage every aspect of the tour. Their concerns included fears that she might be photographed in front of the Sun Temple's highly erotic sculptures during her visit to Konark. Galbraith suggested to Jackie that the temple visit be left out of the formal programme in favour of an 'unheralded and suitably discreet visit' later.[52] He despaired at the media's obsession with the First Lady's wardrobe, lamenting that the 'radioactive pink suit' she wore on her arrival grabbed the headlines and the lavender dress she sported while visiting a Banaras silk factory 'could be picked up at any range up to five miles'.[53]

The ambassador was also tasked with keeping the Indian government happy by limiting Jackie's exposure to princely India. This was impossible in Udaipur, where a boat trip on Lake Pichola to visit the Lake Palace provided the perfect photo opportunities. In Jaipur, Jai arranged for elephants bedecked in velvet and silver to take Jackie and Lee up to Amber Fort. Also on the programme were cocktail parties, polo and the City Palace visit. '[Jai] is suspected by the Indian government of wanting to make political capital of the visit. The Indian government has been determined to thwart this effort. I have been in the middle and most unpleasantly so,' Galbraith recorded in his journal. In particular, the government feared that a visit to the City Palace 'would provide an occasion for a triumphal tour through the city' and enable Jai to present himself as still being the ruler of Jaipur.[54]

After taking in the magnificence of Amber, Jackie and Lee, with Galbraith in tow, went to the polo ground to watch a demonstration match. That evening Jai and his teammates threw a party for the Americans at which Ayesha started teaching the First Lady how to dance the twist. In contrast to her obvious boredom in Udaipur where all she could think of asking her hosts was 'What is your annual rainfall?' Jackie was in her element in Jaipur. 'The conversation was on horses, mutual friends, social events, and polo,' Galbraith wrote, adding, 'I did have a long talk with the Maharani. She is in favour of free enterprise and also more and better government services; for protection of all existing feudal privileges but also more democracy. She is vivacious and extremely good looking, and I detect a certain determination to inform herself.'[55] Around midnight the group drove to the City Palace, where they spent several moonlit hours exploring the courtyards, durbar halls and gardens with their illuminated fountains. Even the apprehensive Galbraith admitted: 'It was all most romantic, and it was plain Mrs Kennedy enjoyed it immensely.'[56] The lateness of the hour and the private nature of the tour was a face-saving relief for the Indian government.

In October 1962, Jai and Ayesha took up Jackie's invitation to visit her and her husband at the White House. The visit coincided with the Cuban missile crisis, forcing Kennedy to cancel a dance in their honour. Instead they held a dinner for them attended by Lee Radziwill, several diplomats and journalists. Kennedy greeted Ayesha with a broad smile and the words, 'Ah, I hear you are the Barry Goldwater of India,' a reference to the maverick Republican and Kennedy's main challenger.[57] Their daughter, Caroline Kennedy, was so overawed by Jaipur's First Lady that she told her mother 'she's more beautiful than you'.[58] As the royals departed for New York, they were given the news that India and China were at war.

On 20 October 1962, the People's Liberation Army launched a full-scale invasion of India's north-eastern borderlands and Ladakh, catching poorly equipped Indian troops by surprise. Some of the fighting took place just a couple of hundred kilometres from Cooch Behar. The war sparked a furious debate in Parliament. Ayesha took the first opportunity she could to attack the government's conceal-ment of repeated incursions into India by China over the past several years and Nehru's use of the Defence of India Act to silence opposi-tion to government policies. Nehru responded by ridiculing the opposition, prompting Ayesha to blurt out: 'If you had known any-thing about anything, we wouldn't be in this mess today.' When Nehru pretended to ignore her remark, she repeated it in 'more parliamentary language'. This time the prime minister responded: 'I will not bandy words with a lady,' to which the opposition mem-bers called out, 'Chivalry,' in mocking tones.[59] Jai was much softer in his approach in his Rajya Sabha speech, emphasizing the need for compromise and accommodation, urging better relations with Pakistan and calling on India to form an alliance with the United States and Great Britain.

On the day of her outburst, Khushwant Singh recalls seeing Ayesha at a private party at the home of the Swatantra Party's leader in the Lok Sabha, Minoo Masani, where the peace activist Jayaprakash Narayan was the chief guest. Narayan was giving a briefing on the progress of negotiations with Naga tribals wanting to secede from India. Ayesha turned up late, her entry heralded by a 'whiff of expensive French perfume'. She was wearing a turquoise blue chif-fon sari with sliver sequins that sparkled 'like stars on a moonless night'. As Khushwant Singh would later write: 'She looked around her with large almond eyes. Everyone stood up. As Hilaire Belloc once described someone, "her face was like the king's command when all the swords are drawn".'[60] After asking everyone to sit, Ayesha sank down on the carpet, took out a mauve-coloured cigarette from a gold case and started smoking, prompting Narayan to remark in Hindi: '*Dekho zamana kaise badal gaya hai*—see how times have changed—a maharani sits at the feet of a commoner.' She then addressed the meeting in English, apologizing that her Hindustani was not good because her mother tongue was Bengali and she was married to a Rajput. As she was speaking, the man sitting next to Khushwant Singh leaned over and said: 'Her Bengali and Rajasthani are worse than her Hindustani. She can only speak English and French.'[61] Later that day, Jai and Ayesha were spotted at a cocktail dance at the Gymkhana Club, where they drank French champagne. Jai did not sign the drinks bill. 'It was the gift of erstwhile subjects and admirers,' Singh wryly noted.[62]

A fierce critic of Ayesha's political style was the journalist L.M. Eshwar, who described the Rajasthan chapter of the Swatantra Party as the 'Quinquennial Party of the Glamour Queen'. 'Once in five years during voting season, it is here, there and everywhere. Afterwards it is not seen or heard anywhere for another five years.'[63] Eshwar, who doesn't hide his anti-monarchical views in his 1968 book, *Sunset and Dawn: The Story of Rajasthan*, claims there were bitter divisions within Swatantra between the 'Maharani's group' and those opposed to Ayesha's high-handedness in running the affairs of the party and insistence on nominating her candidates for assembly and Lok Sabha elections. Local party workers complained to the party's national leadership about her autocratic style but got nowhere, so entrenched was her position. Thanks to her, claims Eshwar, there was no opposition worth the name in Rajasthan.[64]

While such criticism might be expected from a leftist, there were also rumblings of discontent from within Swatantra. Masani took a dim view of Ayesha's commitment to politics despite her popularity among voters. 'He was constantly fed up with her,' says his son, Zareer Masani. 'When she was needed for electioneering she was holidaying in England or the South of France.' Nor was she a conventional politician. 'She didn't pay much attention to Parliament.

My father used to contrast her unfavourably with the Maharani of Gwalior [Vijayaraje Scindia], who was much more engaged. The Maharani of Jaipur was primarily a socialite, whereas the Maharani of Gwalior was primarily a politician.'[65]

Despite her differences with Nehru, Ayesha, along with the majority of Indians, mourned his death in 1964. At a Swatantra meeting she told the party members that she felt his loss deeply. 'He had given up an easy life to work for the independence of his country. While there were those who disagreed with some of his policies, no one could argue with the fact that he loved India and India loved him.'[66] Nehru's replacement was Lal Bahadur Shastri. Shortly after taking office, he offered Jai an ambassadorship, probably in the hope that Ayesha would follow him and thereby leave politics. Of the three countries he could choose from, Jai opted for Spain. A shared love of polo was one obvious reason.

His decision to take up the post also reflected Jai's disillusionment with local politics. In October 1965, he addressed a meeting of the Rajput Sabha of which he was president, attacking them for their weakness, their lack of 'trustworthy loyalty' and their 'mental, spiritual and political bankruptcy'. Justifying his decision to go to Spain he said: 'I am convinced that I can serve our country better in other ways than by remaining and vegetating in the senseless and useless morass of petty local politics of Rajasthan.'[67]

Rajaji was against Jai accepting the ambassadorship as it implied loyalty to a government his party opposed. There was also opposition from other princes, who believed Jai should stay and help them fight for the retention of their privy purses. Believing that her activities in the opposition might make it more difficult for Jai in his posting, Ayesha sought a meeting with Shastri to ask his advice and to air her concerns. As she left the meeting Shastri asked her, 'Must you really be in the Opposition?' Ayesha responded by saying, 'Surely, in a democracy there must be some form of opposition?' To this Shastri said, 'Don't you think I have enough opposition already?'[68]

Shastri's tenure was brief. He died in January 1966 in Tashkent while attending peace talks with the Pakistani president, Ayub Khan, soon after Jai took up his post. His replacement was Nehru's daughter, Indira Gandhi, who had turned down the prime ministership after her father's death. In the 1967 elections, Ayesha stood for the Lok Sabha seat of Jaipur and the state assembly seat of Malpura, which Joey had contested and won five years earlier. When Indira Gandhi arrived in Jaipur to deliver an address to her supporters, she took a swipe at Swatantra followers who were staging a noisy protest outside. 'Those who raise slogans now were shouting for the perpetuation of the British rule. They did nothing in the fight for our independence, and what have they done in all the years since? They must learn that they can't rewrite history.'[69] Although Ayesha won her Lok Sabha seat comfortably, she lost Malpura to Damodar Lal Vyas by 10,000 votes, even though her opponent was too ill to do any campaigning. It was a drubbing she conveniently leaves out of her memoir. 'By 1967, the voters formed an impression that erstwhile rulers were a misfit in politics,' Vyas's son reflected later. 'Despite the fact that SMS [Jai] had told her that my father was a strong contender, Gayatri Devi decided to contest the election.'[70]

The worse-than-expected performance of Swatantra left the state assembly result on a knife-edge. Although the Congress had the largest number of seats, a united opposition was in a position to form the government. But their chance to prove their majority on the floor of the assembly was delayed by the governor of Rajasthan, who was a Congress appointee, so that the party could bribe opposition members to switch sides.[71] Ayesha responded by corralling opposition MPs in the City Palace and then taking them to Kanota Fort about eighteen kilometres from Jaipur. One of those holed up at Kanota later told the press they had been threatened with 'dire consequences' by one of Jai's employees if they dared to support the Congress.[72] The governor then imposed anti-riot regulations that banned gatherings of more than five people in the area where the governor and ministers lived. The following day he asked the Congress leader to form the next government. Ayesha and other opposition politicians decided to defy the ban and march to the governor's house to ask him to reverse the decision. A large crowd that had already gathered to protest against what they saw as a denial of democracy joined the march. When they reached the area where the ban was in force, police opened fire with tear gas and beat them back with lathi charges. All opposition leaders except for Ayesha were arrested and a curfew was imposed on the entire city.

Jai, who had flown back from Spain, accompanied his wife to New Delhi to plead their case before the President and the home minister. This was somewhat unorthodox as Jai's diplomatic role precluded any involvement in politics and thus provided further proof, as far as his critics were concerned, that he did not take his ambassadorial duties seriously. The pair received assurances that opposition members would have a chance to prove their majority when the assembly met. The curfew was also lifted. But when people began returning to the streets, police who had been brought in from neighbouring states opened fire, claiming they had not been informed that restrictions on assembly had been lifted. Nine people were killed and forty-nine wounded. A senior Rajasthan government official accused Jai of misusing his rank as an honorary lieutenant, dressing in uniform and trying to quell the mob only to inflame the situation.[73]

As Ayesha and her supporters gathered to consider their next move, the Government of India in Delhi imposed President's Rule in Rajasthan. Efforts to hold together the opposition continued with desperate Swatantra Party members reduced to entertaining the demands of a communist MP for a berth in any future ministry in return for his support. Rumours started circulating that Ayesha was coveting the position of chief minister. Her main rival was Dungarpur's Maharaja Lakshman Singh. A Mewari Rajput, Lakshman Singh was implacably opposed to the Jaipurs because of their past alliance with the Mughals. With the opposition growing increasingly divided, the Congress leader Sukhadia was able to cajole enough defectors to give him a comfortable majority.[74]

Having railed against the darker side of politics, Ayesha was now seeing it first-hand. 'Nepotism and corruption have reached the limit ... and the victims as always are the innocent poor. And this from a party that claims to be Socialist,' Ayesha wrote in her diary in early January 1967. Raw and unabashed, the entry reflects both her anger and her convictions much more honestly than her memoir's sanitized tone. 'Proud good people sacrificed for the greed and lust of a few. Justice does not exist. Truth is a thing to laugh at. Honesty is a fool. But hunger and want are real. If I ever give up politics, it will be because it hurts too much to see all this. I could easily lose myself in the pleasures of travel and international society and bury my head like an ostrich and not look at what is happening, but I love too much and too deeply. I love these people. I love those children. I want a bright future for them. They are India.'[75]

* * *

On top of Ayesha's increasing disillusionment with politics came another series of personal losses affecting those close to her. In 1966, Bhaiya's horse fell and rolled on him while he was playing polo in Jaipur. He had accepted a last-minute invitation to play but did not have his regular pony with him. His helmet came off and he suffered brain damage. He spent weeks in intensive care, but never fully recovered and would spend the rest of his life confined to a wheelchair. Since 1956, he had been married to Gina Egan, an English fashion model, who was fifteen years younger than him. According to Phillip Knightley's book on the Profumo affair, Gina was Vicki Martin's best friend and had worked with her at the Mayfair Club. She had played a beauty queen contestant in the 1951 British film *Lady Godiva Rides Again* in which Ruth Ellis also had a part. In her unpublished autobiography Gina makes no mention of Stephen Ward, a central figure in the Profumo affair, and claims she never met Vicki Martin. Bhaiya used the same techniques to woo Gina as he did with Vicki, sending her flowers, not by the bouquet but by the shopful. He would study her work schedule and plan romantic getaways in her breaks to places like Paris, where they always stayed in the Hotel Lotti and would have drinks in a small bar at the back of the Ritz.

Bhaiya was so terrified of his mother's reaction he kept the marriage a secret for three years. Jai and Ayesha were the first to be told. Both had met Gina before (Jai had even flirted with her), but the news that she was now the Maharani of Cooch Behar came as a shock. 'They were not pleased. As it was a fait accompli, they agreed to make the best of a bad job—a fact that did nothing for my self-esteem and an unfortunate foundation for my future relationship with my internationally known sister-in-law,' Gina wrote.[76] Ayesha omits Gina's name in *A Princess Remembers*, referring to her merely as her brother's 'English wife'. Jai, however, was more understanding and unsuccessfully tried to convince the Indian authorities to recognize her as the maharani.

The most hostile response came from Indira. When she heard that her son was seeing Gina, she kept feigning various illnesses and made him come to Rome or wherever she happened to be to look after her—a now familiar ruse. Her reaction to their marriage was to demand an immediate annulment. Rather than backing down as he had done with Nancy Valentine twenty years earlier, Bhaiya stood his ground, telling his mother there would be no divorce. A few weeks later, on 6 August 1959, news of their marriage was splashed on the front page of the *Daily Express*. The revelation came as such a shock to Indira that she fell ill in Bombay. 'She had hoped her son would marry someone of suitable rank, although how she could have cherished that illusion is a mystery, because for years he has dated show biz chicks and other Occidental glamour girls with no titles in their backgrounds,' surmised the American gossip columnist Don Dedera.[77]

Bhaiya's relationship with his mother was never the same again and when Gina came to live in Cooch Behar, Indira moved out permanently. He also saw less and less of Jai and Ayesha. When Sher Ali Khan visited Bhaiya in hospital after the fall, Bhaiya told his old friend he was bitter about the attitude of his family towards Gina. He also complained about Ayesha, who had made it clear that Gina and he were 'not welcome' any longer.[78] 'Bhaiya was a real gentleman,' wrote Khan. 'He defended the actions of marrying the person that he did, stubbornly. He got upset when his wife was slighted in any way.' He was also a sensitive man who 'never hurt anybody but got hurt himself many times, even that was kept hidden within himself and [he] tried to drown his hurt with drink'. Asked why he had not married a woman from a princely family, Bhaiya told Khan: 'Much safer to be chummy with the kind I cannot marry.'[79] As for Indira, she couldn't bear the fact that Gina was now in control of looking after her son.

After her falling-out with Bhaiya, Indira spent much of her time in Calcutta, where she became close friends with Anne Wright, whose husband, Bob, was working for a British managing agency and then went on to become the manager of the Tollygunge Club. Anne had first gone to Cooch Behar as a young bride in the 1950s, and at the age of ninety can vividly recall landing on the state's grass airstrip in the dilapidated DC3 being operated by Jamair. On arrival, guests of the royal family would be met by elephants that would transport them and their luggage to the palace. 'As time went on Ma [Indira] couldn't bear to be alone, so she would come over to us and ask if she could take our Tibetan spaniel Kulu to stay with her at night. So, every evening she would send her car to pick him up and take him to her house in Ballygunge. Kulu was her night watch dog.' Indira was someone to be reckoned with, adds Anne. 'She would take her cook, who was the ex-ballboy, to Paris and go to these Michelin star restaurants and demand that the chef teach him. They wouldn't do it for anyone else, but they did it for her.'[80]

In the final years of her life, Indira moved to a large art deco flat in Bombay. She was wheelchair-bound, suffering from gout and cardiac asthma. 'I felt that she knew she didn't have much time left,' says Zafar Hai, Khusro Jung's nephew, who was a frequent visitor to her flat just off Carmichael Road in a complex known as Kamal Mahal owned by the Baroda royal family. 'She was coming to terms with certain things, and once asked me about religion and what books to read. She was interested in Islam. She was really searching for something.'[81]

Concerned about her mother's worsening health, Ayesha flew from Madrid to India on 6 September 1968. Ma was being cared for in Bombay by her youngest daughter, Menaka. Ayesha was to fly there on 11 September, but electoral work in Jaipur delayed her departure by one day. Early on the morning of 12 September, Menaka rang to tell her that their mother's condition had suddenly worsened. Just before Ayesha was about to leave for the airport, the phone rang again with the news that Indira had died. Jai joined her in Bombay for the funeral before returning to Spain. 'That was the worst part. Both of us, as well as the visitors, I'm sure, could so easily imagine the room with Ma in it, the centre of an endless stream of guests, filling the place with her easy warmth and fun. Even when she was ill, her involvement with life had been so intense it was impossible to grasp the fact that she was dead.'[82] In her memoir, Ayesha expresses pride in the fact that her mother had lived life to the fullest without being in her husband's protective shadow.[83] When it came to how she would deal with her own ultimate widowhood, she closely followed her mother's example. Unfortunately, she also mimicked her attitude to the upbringing of her only son.

Just as the distance between Indira and Bhaiya would ultimately lead to tragedy, Ayesha's hands-off approach to Jagat would come at a huge personal cost.

* * *

A few weeks after Indira's death, Ayesha joined Jai in Spain. She admitted to feeling 'uneasy' about being unable to spend more time in Madrid because of her electoral duties. Her uneasiness would not have been helped by Jai's letters, laced with references to his care-free lifestyle. When not attending receptions at General Franco's fairy-tale castle at La Granja, he had plenty of time left over for polo, partying and partridge shoots. One hunting expedition with the Marquess of Blandford and the Greek shipping tycoon Stavros Niarchos netted 2,272 birds. Jai was so well known for his reckless disregard for road rules that when the Spanish police pulled his Mercedes over for speeding, they saluted and laughed.

As part of his less-than-onerous diplomatic duties, Jai opened a Hispano-Indian Chamber of Commerce and introduced the Spanish people to the artistry of Zubin Mehta and Ravi Shankar. He was not an active ambassador and was rarely to be found in his office, taking every opportunity he could to be in England. The couple brought with them servants from Jaipur who would touch their foreheads to the ground when they went to receive them at Madrid airport. 'They were generally very feudal in their behaviour to embassy staff,' recalls an Indian diplomat. 'A young Indian Foreign Service officer invited to a grand dinner they gave was asked to usher in the guests. But when the dining room doors were opened he was told he could not sit at a table and would have to eat in the corridor outside. He stomped off, outraged, saying he was not their ADC or servant.'[84]

For Ayesha, southern Spain's arid mountains topped with castles and crenellated walls were reminiscent of Rajasthan. In the southern resort town of Marbella, the smell of jasmine made her homesick for Jaipur, while the gypsy music of Granada reminded her of Indian folk tunes. She also welcomed the break from some of the unwelcome aspects of life in India. 'For once I was relieved to be out of India, not only because I was away from continual reminders of Ma [Indira] but also because further defections in our legislatures had increased my disillusionment with politics and I badly needed a change of atmosphere,' she wrote. 'Besides all this, I had begun to realize that my extensive engagement in politics had led me to neglect Jai and Jagat. I was now resolved to give them all my attention.'[85]

* * *

The setbacks suffered by the Congress party in the 1967 election led to a renewed attack on the rights of the princes. In his 1956 book, *The Story of the Integration of the Indian States*, V.P. Menon justified the privy purses by arguing that the Indian state had to give something in return for the princes unconditionally giving up their kingdoms. 'It could not be "heads I win, tails you lose".'[86] After cataloguing the assets surrendered by the rulers—everything from railway networks to fleets of cars, from public buildings to horse stables—he concluded: 'If these are weighed against the total amount of the privy purse, the latter would seem insignificant.'[87]

In the decade since Menon wrote those words, attitudes had changed. The princes were increasingly seen as being incompatible with the egalitarian social order India aspired to. Moreover, they were proving to be highly popular among the electorate. They had wiped out the Congress in Orissa and the party feared it might lose its majorities in Madhya Pradesh and Rajasthan to candidates from royal families. In this atmosphere, privy purses were the low-hanging fruit. More than 240 princes were receiving payments ranging in value from the £20,000 a year that the Maharaja of Mysore enjoyed to about £40 for the talukdar of Katodia. Even these lesser amounts were considerable when the average annual per capita income in India in the 1960s didn't rise much above 200 rupees. Jai's assets were reported to include twenty forts, more than 80,000 acres of farming land and a garage that housed two Cadillacs, three Bentleys, six Buicks, three Rolls-Royces, one Ford, one Pontiac as well as a selection of Studebakers, Packards, Chevrolets, a command car and eight jeeps. Why would anyone with such wealth need public funding to subsidize their lifestyles, his detractors asked.

The first meeting of the Congress Working Committee after the 1967 election agreed on a broad policy resolution, later known as the ten-point programme, which called for an abolition of princely privileges. A month later this was amended by the All India Congress Committee to specially include the elimination of privy purses. Indira Gandhi's legal basis to do so was questionable. They were part of the Instruments of Accession signed after Independence by the ruling princes. Whether the Constitution of 1950 changed the relevant provisions in the Instruments of Accession was up to the Supreme Court of India to decide. The response of the princes was to assemble a national organization known as the Rulers of Indian States in Concord for India. Despite the grand-sounding title, the princes once again failed to put up a united front, with the concord split between hardliners who thought they had nothing to gain by agreeing with the government's terms and moderates seeking a negotiated compromise.

The reigniting of the privy purse issue was one factor that prompted Jai's resignation from his post as ambassador to Spain. Now that the rights and privileges of the princes were coming under increasing attack, he felt the need to spend more time in India. Jai sided with the moderates in the concord and used his personal connection with Mountbatten to put international pressure on the Indian government not to renege on its undertakings regarding the privy purses. Never one to miss an opportunity to strut his connections, Mountbatten wrote to Indira Gandhi and Indian government officials questioning the legality of the move. Jai's communications with the former viceroy were sent via the British High Commission's diplomatic bag because the Indian postal service was considered unreliable and letters could easily be intercepted. Joey, who was attending the concord when Jai was abroad, also used the bag to communicate with Mountbatten until high commission staff put a stop to the practice. They feared that if the government discovered that diplomatic channels were being used for non-official correspondence it would be seen as 'interference in India's internal affairs'.[88]

The concord appointed three moderators to represent them in negotiations with the government—the Maharajas of Dhrangadhra and Baroda and the Begum of Bhopal. For the wealthier and more business-savvy princes the cash component of the privy purses did not matter much at all. Nor for that matter did it count for more than a drop in the bucket of India's budget—some 0.2 per cent by most estimates. Because the original agreement laid down that the privy purses be reduced with each new succession to the title, the list of beneficiaries had been almost halved to 283 and the amount paid out was a third of the original figure. Some of the other entitlements the government wanted to abolish, such as the right to fly flags from their cars and houses and to hunt animals on their private reserves, seemed trivial. However, when put together they amounted to an assault on their pride and tradition. Responding to a letter from Indira Gandhi asking the princes to 'assist the government in doing away with certain institutions', Bhagwant Singh, the Maharana of Udaipur, wrote:

> I need not tell you that the institution of 'maharana' has a history of fourteen centuries behind it. A history which is universally admitted as glorious and unsullied ... I am merely its trustee and servant—for such time as it pleases God. Please consider, please reflect for a moment, whether it would be worthwhile for me to live, whether I would deserve to live, whether those who value history and traditions would own me as an Indian, if I were to acquiesce in the degradation of this institution. It is not my private possession. It belongs to the people. If the traditions created by the people of Mewar, or of any other place, are not preserved, what will there be left to inspire the nation and invigorate our self-reliance, self-respect and integrity? ... Hardships are to be endured, but not dishonour.[89]

Jai's return to India prompted speculation that he was about to plunge into politics, take the leadership of the Swatantra Party and seek the overthrow of the Congress government in Rajasthan in retaliation for what he believed was its illegal usurpation of power in the state. The speculation followed the publication of an article in the January 1969 edition of the Bombay journal *Current*. According to Ayesha, however, her husband never harboured any desire for a political career. Quite the contrary. He was so disillusioned with India that he was toying with the idea of turning everything over to his sons and retiring to England.

For now, Jai's intention was to remain in India and stave off the anticipated attack on princely privileges. His lobbying efforts, however, were interrupted by the death of Bhaiya. His health had been steadily deteriorating since his fall, exacerbated by heavy drinking.

Ayesha had planned to meet him in Calcutta, but she too was in hospital for an operation. On 11 April 1970, she received a phone call from Woodlands saying that Bhaiya had suffered a heart attack and died. He was fifty-four. Despite their earlier closeness, Ayesha almost skirts over her brother's death in her memoir, only noting that he and his (unnamed) wife had no children. Since Bhaiya had no natural heir, it was decided that Indrajit's son, Viraj, would be appointed the next maharaja by the priest at the Cooch Behar palace. Jai had to lobby hard for the home minister in New Delhi to endorse the succession.

That Gina was never accepted as part of the extended family was just one factor behind Ayesha's apparent indifference about her latest loss. Brother and sister were at loggerheads over their mother's inheritance. Indira had never disclosed her will to her children and had refused Bhaiya's request for his share of the proceeds from her estate.[90] Most of her private correspondence was also destroyed by Ayesha, probably because it could have revealed embarrassing details about her mother's affairs, including possibly with Jai. An element of mother–daughter rivalry was also at play—with Indira being more liberated than her daughter. Indira had taken on the might of the Raj, which wanted to remove her as regent, and cared little about what the public and those in authority thought of her. Ayesha had taken on the Congress party—a much milder foe—and was more interested in protecting her persona as a politician and a faithful wife.

* * *

After Bhaiya's funeral, Jai left for England for his usual round of polo matches and parties. Ayesha did not accompany him immediately but joined him in time to celebrate her fifty-first birthday on 23 May 1970. The mood was more sombre than usual. Five days earlier the government had introduced a bill to abolish the privy purses. At the same time, she was becoming increasingly concerned about Jai's health. Two days after complaining of feeling tired at a cocktail party, he fell off his horse while umpiring a polo game at Windsor. Still, he insisted on attending a party at their home Kings Beeches, given every year after the Queen's Cup. The Queen,

Prince Philip and Lord Mountbatten were there. Jai spent much of the evening talking with Dickie about how to thwart the Indian government's plans to abolish the princely order.

On 24 June, Jai decided to play a polo match at Cirencester. Heavy drizzle kept Ayesha and Bubbles in their car while Jai took to the field. Suddenly they saw him lying on the ground. He had fallen from his horse. As the players dismounted and stood around him, Ayesha ran over. 'I remember noticing in some part of my mind that someone had kicked his helmet out of the way and this, irrationally, angered me very much.' Jai was lifted into an ambulance but was pronounced dead on arrival by a doctor at Cirencester Hospital. 'I pleaded with him to do something, but he merely shook his head.'[91] Before leaving India on this final journey, Jai had told his friend Yashwant Rao Pawar that he had no intention of cutting down on his polo. 'Knowing as you do what the game means to me in every sense of the word, I ask you: what more can I now ask for or expect of life? Therefore, my last wish is that my end should come on the polo field, in the midst of a chukka, with my friends around me, my pony under me, my polo stick in my hands and my boots on.'[92] Jai had got his wish.

That night his body was taken to Kings Beeches and placed in a sandalwood coffin and on the following day it was flown to Jaipur. Only when Ayesha reached home did she realize that her husband was gone forever. The entire city plunged into mourning and thousands filed past his body as it lay in state at the Chandra Mahal, opposite the Govind Devji temple. His sons, Bubbles, Joey, Pat and Jagat, kept vigil throughout the night. The funeral procession started at nine o'clock the next morning. Wrapped in a red shawl and wearing a scarlet turban, his body was lifted on to a gun-carriage. The five-kilometre-long procession was led by a mahout on an elephant carrying the Mah-e-Muratib, the ceremonial rod that had been given by the Mughals to the rulers of Amber as a token of special distinction and honour. It was followed by more mahouts on elephants who threw coins into the crowd. Overhead, a plane of the Jaipur Flying Club showered mourners with rose petals. Men carrying lighted torches and a military escort of 600 officers and soldiers accompanied Jai's body as the carriage made its way through the rain-soaked streets of the old city. A dozen former rulers and the chief minister of Rajasthan together with his two predecessors and senior cabinet members joined the procession. At the rear walked Jai's favourite polo horse, Zorawar, carrying his cap and fifteen of his medals. A crowd of more than half a million people lined the route to the cremation grounds at Gaitore, many of them having come from remote villages the previous night. When the procession reached Gaitore, Jai's body was placed on a funeral pyre. The last rites were performed and Bubbles, the heir apparent, lit a pyre of sandalwood, tulsi and peepal twigs as chants of 'Maharaj ki Jai' and 'Maharaj Amar Rahe' rang out and a nineteen-gun salute fired from Nahargarh Fort, high above the cremation ground, echoed around the hills.

From her room in the City Palace Ayesha could hear the sound of the guns. 'I could hear, too, the sound of the wailing ... Grief seized me almost like a physical spasm.'[93]

* * *

In 1938, an unnamed British official reached for a leather-bound copy of Shakespeare's *Hamlet*, before speculating in a confidential cable to his superiors in London whether Jai would be a bulwark for his state or proceed down 'the primrose path'—in other words a path marked by lassitude, sensual pleasure and ultimately self-destruction.[94] At the time, the British were at the peak of their frustration with Jaipur's maharaja. His repeated absences and his reluctance to take a hands-on approach to the administration of his state would lead them to conclude that he was 'an absentee ruler by inclination'.[95] Jai surrendered to temptation's lure, playing Prince Charming and plunging into endless rounds of polo. Courting Ayesha while pursuing his very public affair with Virginia Cherrill left little time for his other wives. Lonely and with no real role to play in Jai's life, both would succumb to alcoholism before they reached their mid-forties. Rather than confront the regressive social norms of Rajput society, Jai preferred to escape to Europe to seek the solace of its privileged aristocracy.

To his credit Jai was also willing to stand up to his British over-lords, as evidenced by his appointment of Sir Mirza Ismail as prime minister in 1942. He enthusiastically and emphatically embraced

Ismail's ideas for modernizing the state, progressing towards a model of popular representation and reaching out to the Congress. His protection of his Muslim subjects after Partition revealed remarkable compassion and bravery, and had earlier injuries not disqualified him from service during World War II, he would have almost certainly pursued a successful career in the army. When in 1949 Jai inspired his eldest son, Bubbles, to join the military by writing a letter that stressed the importance of making sacrifices for one's country, he also revealed his awareness that change was inevitable and that democracy should be welcomed. If India's princes thought they could continue to live as they did fifty years ago, they would be 'asking for trouble and be wiped off the map', he wrote. Sacrificing the independence of Jaipur may prove to be 'no sacrifice at all' if it meant greater democracy.[96]

But aside from his brief tenure as rajpramukh and a not particularly memorable stint as India's ambassador to Spain, Jai's record as a public figure was unremarkable. His distaste for politics and the manner in which the socialist Nehru government treated the princes were obstacles, but they were not insurmountable. The outpouring of grief at his funeral still leads some to believe that had he not died prematurely and entered politics, he would have reached even greater heights than Ayesha. That seems highly unlikely. The steady erosion of princely power had worn him down. And, as revealed in a letter written by Louis Mountbatten to Ayesha two days after her husband's death, there were other things on his mind—and they had little to do with representative democracy. The government's attempt to abolish the privy purses, he had told his old polo-playing buddy at their last meeting, was an 'unacceptable insult' for former rulers like him. Should it happen he would never want to live in such 'humiliating circumstances' in India again.[97]

Top: Gayatri Devi and Sawai Man Singh ll of Jaipur, known to their friends as Ayesha and Jai, shortly after their wedding. She was his third wife.

Bottom: Man Singh II and his Queen Gayatri Devi.

Top: Maharani Gayatri Devi on her wedding day with Sawai Man Singh II Bahadur, May 1940.

Bottom: Gayatri Devi, described in *Vogue* as one of the most beautiful women in the world, at the Rambagh Palace.

Top: Portrait of Maharani Indira Devi of Cooch Behar (Gayatri Devi's mother) by Philip de Laszlo, c. 1928. 'There is a delicate, studied, almost insolent self-assurance about her pose.'

Bottom: Gayatri Devi and Man Singh ll with Queen Elizabeth and Prince Philip in Jaipur, 1961. The nine-foot, eight-inch tiger was shot by Prince Philip. This photo op was followed by a champagne lunch in the jungle.

Top: US First Lady Jackie Kennedy with Gayatri Devi and Man Singh ll at a polo exhibition match in Jaipur, 1962. Man Singh ll would die on the polo field in 1970, aged fifty-seven.

Bottom: Jagat, the only child of Gayatri Devi and Man Singh ll: the playboy prince, whose circle of friends included Imran Khan and Mick Jagger, would die of alcoholism at forty-seven.

Top: Gayatri Devi campaigning as a Swatantra Party candidate during the Lok Sabha elections in 1962. She won with what was then the biggest margin in India's history.

Bottom: Gayatri Devi and her stepson Bhawani Singh (Bubbles) in 1998. Though the two had become estranged over inheritance disputes, they reconciled in her later years.

Top: Jaipur's last maharaja, Bhawani Singh, (front) with (left to right) Jagat's children, Devraj and Lalitya; his wife, Padmini Devi; Jagat's ex-wife, Priyanandana; and his only child, Diya Kumari, in 2006. Bhawani Singh won the Maha Vir Chakra for his gallantry during the war with Pakistan in 1971.

Bottom: A view of the Maharani Gayatri Devi Girls' High School, Jaipur.

Top: Maharani Gayatri Devi at the Polo Ground, during the Maharaj Prithi Singh Foundation Polo Cup in Jaipur.

Bottom: Diya Kumari and her mother, Padmini, during Holi celebrations at the City Palace, 2018. Padmini proved to be a formidable fighter for her family's interests.

Padmanabh Singh during his eighteenth birthday celebrations in 2016 when he became 'titular maharaja' of Jaipur, succeeding his grandfather Bhawani Singh.

7

'NO TIME TO PLUCK AN EYEBROW'

Indira Gandhi never passed up an opportunity to express her visceral contempt for India's princes. It was something she inherited from her father, who loathed the 'gilded and empty-headed maharajas and nawabs who strut about the Indian scene and make a nuisance of themselves'.[1] Of all those she despised, she held the Rajmata of Jaipur in most contempt. As Khushwant Singh so eloquently observed: 'Indira could not stomach a woman more good-looking than herself and insulted her in Parliament, calling her a bitch and a glass doll. Ayesha Devi brought the worst out in Indira Gandhi: her petty, vindictive side.'[2] Ayesha's entry into politics on the ticket of the vehemently anti-Congress Swatantra Party and her election victory margin that far eclipsed her father's only deepened Indira Gandhi's animosity. 'Go ask the Maharajas how many wells they dug for the people in their States when they ruled them, how many roads they constructed, what they did to fight the slavery of the British,' she told a rally in Jaipur in 1967. 'If you look at the account of their achievements before Independence, it is a big zero there.'[3]

In September 1970, Indira Gandhi put an amendment to the Constitution before Parliament to rescind the privy purses. The Lok Sabha passed the amendment 339 votes to 154, but the bill was defeated in the Rajya Sabha by one vote. A few days later, she sought a Presidential proclamation based on a clause contained in the original accession provisions that gave the President the right to derecognize a prince who misbehaved or committed a serious crime. On 6 September, a compliant President V.V. Giri wrote to each of the princes, derecognizing them on the basis of this clause, thereby stripping them of their allowances, their privileges and also their titles. Bubbles was in London when Giri sent the letter. Barely eight weeks had passed since he had received a copy of India's official gazette confirming him as the new Maharaja of Jaipur. Now he was officially the last maharaja, as were the maharajas of all the princely states. While he was awaiting the arrival of the letter informing him he had been derecognized, a journalist from the *Observer* asked what that would mean in practical terms. Bubbles declined to answer, but Ayesha's then twenty-year-old son Jagat, who was present for the interview, was quick to spot the implications as he saw them: 'It means we can't race around Jaipur the wrong way in one-way streets. Now we can be taken to court for traffic offences. We couldn't before—that was one of our privileges.'[4]

Back in India, far more serious concerns weighed on the minds of the princes than 100 rupees traffic fines. Arguing that the proclamation derecognizing them with the stroke of a pen violated the Constitution and was a breach of their fundamental rights, the concord of princes filed an appeal in the Supreme Court. In a shock decision, the court pronounced in their favour on the grounds that the government had no right to flout the mandates of the Constitution. 'If it is held that it can, then our hitherto held assumption, that in this country we are ruled by laws and not by men and women, must be given up as erroneous,' Justice K.S. Hegde remarked.[5] The ruling followed the overturning by the Supreme Court of the government's bank nationalization legislation, another popular leftist measure Indira Gandhi was trying to push through Parliament. On 27 December, at the urging of advisers that she needed popular endorsement of her policies, she announced that elections would be held one year early, in February 1971.

By now Ayesha was considering retiring from politics and public life altogether. As the *Times of India* noted, she was 'no longer the political figure she once was'.[6] She had not only lost her assembly seat in the 1967 election, she had also failed to secure Pat's seat of Dausa in a by-election in the following year. At the last civic poll in Jaipur, Swatantra had retained just two of the forty-three seats.

She was also still adjusting to life without Jai. A few months after his death, she called on an old friend, the poet and art collector Momin Latif. 'She said, "I have absolutely no money. So I better make some money ... I've got these hundreds of saris, could you kindly help me sell them."' Latif was bemused by the request. 'She was a multi, multi-millionaire, but she thought she was penniless. She was the princess of Cooch Behar for god's sake, she wasn't some kind of maid who suddenly came into money.'[7] While Jai was alive, he had looked after all aspects of her finances, met the running costs of their various properties and paid the staff. Financially she was well off. Before his death, Jai had set up trust funds in the UK, the US and the Bahamas. He also had undisclosed investments in the Rothschild Trust, the global wealth management vehicle of several Indian princely families. The couple were close friends of the trust's chairman, the English billionaire Sir Evelyn Rothschild. Had Jai left a will, things would have been more transparent, but that was not the Jaipur way, says Latif. 'Everything was fixed. He was the king of Jaipur, why should he leave a will? In his lifetime he had given everything he had to give to his children. Everything was in proportion.'[8] Now that she no longer had Jai to fall back on, Ayesha asked her stepson, Pat, to look after her financial affairs.

Slimly built and self-effacing, Pat inherited little of his father's sporting prowess or love of partying, leaving it to his elder brother, Joey, to carry on that tradition. Instead he preferred to position himself as the Jaipur family's wealth manager, controlling his stepmother's financial affairs, his half-brother Jagat's assets, and becoming the director of several family companies. A dressed-down royal seen mostly in a short-sleeved shirt (his friends speak of a limited wardrobe), he lives in a modest flat not far from the Rambagh Palace. In person, he is very much an Anglophile, a legacy of his schooling at Harrow and his frequent visits to Britain. When he speaks it is in measured tones, a habit born from the fact that much of his dealings with the family have been embroiled in years of litigation. Considering him the only member of the family who seemed to grasp the complexities of the financial morass Ayesha had inherited, she decided to put her trust in him. It was a decision that would have long-running consequences.

As she grappled with the aftermath of her husband's death, other tragedies followed in quick succession. Jai's daughter Mickey died though she was still in her early forties. Her grand wedding had resulted in an unhappy marriage and she drank heavily. Jai's brother Bahadur Singh passed away shortly afterwards.

At the urging of the grandmother of the Maharaja of Jodhpur and the Rajmata of Bikaner, Ayesha stood for Parliament once again. This time she threw open the gates of the hitherto forbidden City Palace to the general public, where she would sit like a commoner and hold talks with visiting constituents. On the hustings, she warned voters against the 'deceptive slogans of Socialism' being peddled by the Congress party. Twenty-three years of Congress rule had only made the rich richer and the poor poorer, she insisted.

Although she won her seat of Jaipur by a comfortable margin of 50,000 votes, Swatantra lost three-quarters of its thirty-four seats. Indira Gandhi was returned with a landslide, giving her a two-thirds majority in Parliament. The Swatantra Party's main ally, the Jana Sangh, blamed the opposition's association with politicians such as Ayesha and the issue of the privy purses for the humiliating losses.

Her initial reluctance to stand for election was reflected in her rather lacklustre performance in Parliament during her third term. Her interventions in the Lok Sabha were largely confined to the question of the privy purses and the government's apathy at not doing more to promote India as a tourist destination. 'We should give an opportunity to the ladies of the oldest profession in the world' to sing and dance for tourists, she recommended, arguing it would also help in their rehabilitation.[9] Not willing to be upstaged, Indira Gandhi attacked a speech by Ayesha defending the rights of the princes, saying: 'It is easier to shed tears than privy purses. These vestiges of feudalism cannot last long.'[10]

With Indira Gandhi now commanding the lair, any chance the princes had of retaining their privileges had all but vanished. As Ann Morrow writes: 'They were as vulnerable as the deer they had tied up between two lighted posts to be pounced on by a tiger at vicere-gal shoots.'[11] Using her electoral mandate Gandhi pushed through Parliament the Twenty-Fourth and Twenty-Fifth Amendments, giving the government the power to alter the Constitution without the necessity of judicial review. In August, she introduced the Twenty-Sixth Amendment which now contained the clause that 'all rights, liabilities and obligations in respect to the privy purse are extinguished'. 'We may be depriving the princes of luxury,' she told the Lok Sabha, 'but we are giving them the opportunity to be men.'[12] During an emotional parliamentary debate, Fateh Singh, the

Maharaja of Baroda, pleaded: 'Twenty-two years ago we were referred to as co-architects of independence. Today we are branded as an anachronism and even reactionaries obstructing the path towards an egalitarian society.'[13] His words were to no avail. The amendment received the assent of the President on 28 December 1971. India's centuries-old princely order was no more—the death knell sounding ironically on land that Madho Singh II had ceded to the British in exchange for some villages in the Punjab and was now the core of Lutyens' Delhi. When Ayesha went to renew her passport shortly afterwards, she was described in it as Gayatri Devi of Jaipur (MP) and her husband was listed as the 'Late Sawai Man Singhji of Jaipur'. When she protested that at the time Jai had died he was still maharaja, the passport was amended.

As she slowly came to terms with the loss of her husband, Ayesha re-engaged with her public work. Following a split in Swatantra and the death of Rajaji, the party's leader and founder, she now sat as an independent in Parliament. She moved into Moti Doongri, a small ancestral fort on the outskirts of Jaipur that from a distance resembled a Scottish castle save for the protruding white spire of a Hindu temple. The fort had been gifted to her by Jai. The construction of Lily Pool, the house in the grounds of the Rambagh Palace that Jai had commissioned just before his death, was not yet complete.

Though Bubbles was now the maharaja, his military duties kept him away from Jaipur and its palace politics. Unlike his half-brothers Pat and Joey, who had both been sent by their father to Calcutta to work in the private sector, Bubbles had upheld the Rajput martial tradition. In early January 1949, Jai wrote a letter to his eldest son in which he agonized about whether Jaipur should give up its status as a separate entity and join Rajasthan. 'I personally feel that every sacrifice is worth making if you can serve your country better and for a greater cause,' Jai wrote.[14] According to Bubbles's biographer Sajjan Singh Rathore, the letter had a profound effect. On his return from Harrow he told his father he had decided to join the army and 'get a taste of life without the comforts royals were used to'.[15] In 1952, after passing his entrance exam, he joined the 3 Cavalry regiment as a second lieutenant. Army service complemented his passion for polo. He took the Indian team to its World Cup win in 1957 and went on to become the president of the

Rajasthan Polo Club. From 1955 until 1963, he served with the President's Bodyguard. After being posted as an adjutant at the Indian Military Academy in Dehradun, he joined 10 Para (Special Forces) as second-in-command, where he carried out high-altitude parachute jumping in Ladakh without the help of oxygen. In 1968, he became the unit's commanding officer.

The closing months of 1971 saw an escalation of tensions between East and West Pakistan. Bubbles helped train soldiers of the Mukti Bahini resistance movement in East Pakistan before it was brutally crushed by the Pakistani army. When East Pakistan proclaimed independence and renamed itself Bangladesh, it was immediately supported by Indira Gandhi and the Indian Parliament. In December 1971, India declared war against Pakistan and officially recognized Bangladesh as an independent state. It was their third war in less than a quarter of a century. As a lieutenant colonel leading the 10 Para unit, also known as the Desert Scorpions, Bubbles executed one of the most daring operations of the war, infiltrating his battalion eighty kilometres inside enemy territory to attack the headquarters of the Pakistan Rangers at Chachro as well as nearby positions at Virawah and Mehendale. In his memoir of the war, the then deputy secretary (home), Ganesh Narayan Vyas, describes how Bubbles strategized to launch an attack on the enemy in the middle of the night. During one raid, he ordered the removal of silencers from their Jonga jeeps and had them driven in a line with their headlights on. The roaring of the engines and the sight of the headlights on the meandering roads made the enemy think that a large tank-led force was heading towards them. 'This scared the enemy forces and they had to retreat, running away from the battle.'[16]

For his bravery, Bubbles was awarded the Maha Vir Chakra, India's second highest military honour. At the time there were rumours that the prime minister had tried to block the awarding of the medal because of her animosity towards the Jaipur family, but reneged under pressure from the chief of army staff, Sam Manekshaw. The story has never been proven. Those familiar with the Pink City's endless intrigues dismiss it as just another rumour.

* * *

In *A Princess Remembers* Ayesha provides few details of her first few years without Jai. The sudden interest in the lives of India's potentates in the lead-up to the abolition of the privy purses had largely died down, but when royalty made the news, the papers milked the stories for all they could. On 26 October 1974, Ayesha and her friends, Viscountess Harriet de Rosière and her husband Paul, spent the evening dining at the Waldorf-Astoria Hotel and dancing at the El Morocco, a nightclub famous for its zebra tiles and swanky guest lists just off Second Avenue in Manhattan. It was 2 a.m. when they left the club and were being driven to Sutton Place, where Harriet and Paul were staying. When Paul got out of the car, a man armed with a revolver demanded that he get back inside. He then forced the chauffeur at gunpoint to drive to York Avenue and 72nd Street, where he made Ayesha and Harriet hand over their jewellery. 'I couldn't believe it at first. It seemed like a bad joke. But I really did not think that I was in danger. It was all over quickly,' Ayesha said later.[17] The gunman grabbed whatever jewellery the women were wearing, including Ayesha's pearl necklace, before escaping in a yellow car. Police later put the value of the jewellery stolen at $50,000. They believed the robber and his accomplice had been staking out the club and followed the group when they left. Brushing off the incident she told *People* magazine: 'Where else could I have had such a fantastic experience for the cost of just a pearl necklace?'[18] A few months later *Time* magazine carried an article insinuating that the Maharani of Baroda and her sons had accumulated more than $300 million abroad and were busy teaching 'the natives how to play marbles with emeralds the size of tiger's eyes' while drinking 'Dom Perignon from Waterford crystal mugs'. The stories might have passed unnoticed had they not been seized on by Ayesha's political enemies.[19]

On the morning of 11 February 1975, as she sat down to breakfast after yoga, Ayesha's maid announced that some visitors had arrived. The visitors turned out to be officials from the tax department who had come to search her premises at Moti Doongri. Simultaneous raids were being conducted at the Rajmahal and Jai Mahal palaces, the Rambagh Palace Hotel, the City Palace and Museum, Pat's and Joey's private homes in Jaipur and Ayesha's official residence in New Delhi. Raids were also carried out in

Gwalior at properties belonging to Rajmata Vijayaraje Scindia who, like Ayesha, was an opposition MP. Ayesha asked if she could phone her lawyer and accountant, but the request was denied. She was told she could not leave the premises.

After a day's searching, all the investigators could find that was remotely implicating was correspondence relating to a fundraising cricket match. Every bottle of perfume, powder box and lipstick was examined in minute detail, as was her collection of saris. Eventually a woman rummaging through Ayesha's belongings found £19 in English currency and an assortment of foreign coins. On the second day their luck changed. An official who had been hacking through a stone floor made an astonishing discovery. Hidden in an underground storeroom were hundreds of kilos of gold. The hoard included 50,000 gold mohars, gold bars and biscuits, studded and unstudded gold ornaments as well as a solid gold parrot weighing 183 grams, decorated with flat diamonds set in enamel work. Gold was also found at the Rambagh Palace Hotel and Jai Mahal Palace as well as Jaigarh Fort, where a locked storeroom revealed a small quantity of silver, jade and coral articles and almost 3,000 weapons consisting mainly of old firearms. When the weight of the various seizures of gold was added, the total came to 868 kilos, worth an estimated tens of millions of pounds. Searchers also discovered 1,728 silver coins weighing nineteen kilos.[20] A safe concealed behind a false bookcase in Moti Doongri contained heirlooms Jai had intended for Bubbles to inherit, comprising mostly emeralds, the largest of which weighed an incredible 523 carats. The items included two pen-shaped engraved emerald beads weighing 732 carats, gold ornaments encrusted with diamonds, rubies and pearls and over a dozen other items classified as dynastic heirlooms that were later valued at four million pounds. Valuables and other assets worth another five milllion pounds were seized from other properties. Investigators also found a chequebook of an American bank and evidence of a Swiss bank account in Ayesha's name. It was later claimed that 75 per cent of the Jaipur family's movable assets had not been declared to wealth tax and estate duty authorities.[21]

The excitement of officials at the discovery of the gold hoard quickly gave way to disappointment when they realized that it corresponded almost exactly to what Jai had declared as the contents of his private treasury at the time of the merger of the states to form Rajasthan, less what had been sold legally on the open market in the mid-1950s. In April 1949, the state's ministry had drawn up an approved list of private properties of Jaipur's maharaja. The gold reserves included in the list were denoted as ancestral properties which meant they would become part of a trust for the ruler's family and successors.[22] Since the gold had been declared at the time of the merger and every piece was recorded in the documents of the covenant signed between Jai and the Government of India in 1949, the only illegality that may have been committed was that wealth tax had not been paid. It was not Ayesha who was responsible for that but Bubbles as the head of the family. After the searches, Bubbles issued a statement saying he was ignorant of the treasure at Moti Doongri because he had spent most of his time on army postings.

Jai's gold and jewellery had originally been kept at Nahargarh Fort but was moved to Jaigarh in 1942. Shortly afterwards, a seal at one of the storerooms was discovered to have been broken and ransacked. The guards belonging to the Mina tribe, who had traditionally guarded the fort, were dismissed and replaced by Rajputs. 'The army marched into Jaigarh Fort with their drums beating and gave them half an hour to move out. They knew if they remained there they would be slaughtered,' says Pat.[23] Jai decided to move his personal treasure to the kapadwara in the City Palace, a large windowless building located behind what is now the posh Baradari restaurant. Approximately half the gold was then packed in regular suitcases and sent to Bombay by train (the porters complained about the weight, Pat recalls), where it was sold. The proceeds, approximately a million pounds, were used to buy shares. Because the roof of the kapadwara was in poor condition the remainder of the gold and other items were moved to Moti Doongri. Every time Jai left Jaipur, Jo moved into the fort to deter thieves.

Ayesha's political opponents pounced on the tax raids for maximum political mileage. The communist MP Bhupesh Gupta told the Rajya Sabha that Ayesha had hurled abuse at officials when they demanded entry into her home. 'The most courteous language she used for them was "bastard".' Gupta demanded that she be locked up in Tihar Jail and that the Ministry of Broadcasting make a film of the seizures so it could be shown around the country. He also called for the toshakhanas, or treasuries, of all the royal families to be sealed before their contents were removed and hidden. 'Shrimati Gayatri Devi seems to be a very interesting person,' he charged. 'She is all gold and diamond! The moment you touch Gayatri Devi, gold comes out and she delivers gold! The moment you touch Gayatri Devi, you get diamond!' Calling it disgraceful that she had a seat in Parliament, Gupta accused her of 'heading a gang of cheats and swindlers of the national exchequer, who are cheating the Government and who are cheating the public in this manner'. Midway through his impassioned speech Gupta thundered: 'Jaipur Maharani goes to America more frequently than I go to Karol Bagh!'[24]

* * *

At three in the afternoon of 12 June 1975, the ticker machines at Indira Gandhi's office on Safdarjung Road in New Delhi went into overdrive. Press agencies were sending out news flashes that the Allahabad High Court had ruled that the prime minister was guilty of electoral malpractice in the 1971 election campaign. Her election as MP for Rae Bareli had been invalidated and she was debarred from holding elective office for six years. Since the election, there had been increasing disillusionment with her rule. The monsoon had failed for the third year in a row, there were food shortages and the price of basic commodities had skyrocketed. In 1974, the trade union leader George Fernandes had crippled the country by declaring a railway strike. Indira Gandhi appealed against the high court ruling, but all she was granted was the right to remain in office without a parliamentary vote.

For Indira Gandhi the stakes could not have been higher. She had worked too hard to get to this point. She had too much to lose. On the night of 25 June, without consulting her cabinet and with the acquiescence of a compliant President, she declared a state of Emergency. Power was cut to newspaper offices and censorship was imposed. Opposition leaders were arrested by the dozens in pre-dawn raids. The following morning, she delivered a broadcast to the nation on All India Radio. After assuring people there was 'nothing to panic about', she said there had been a 'deep and widespread' conspiracy brewing ever since she had begun to introduce reforms 'of benefit to the common man and woman of India'. The Emergency, she insisted, was necessary to restore stability, peace and order and to safeguard democracy and national unity. Her broadcast ended with an assurance that internal conditions were expected to improve quickly and the Emergency would be dispensed with 'as soon as possible'.[25]

Ayesha, who was fifty-six, was undergoing medical treatment in Bombay when the Emergency was declared, thus escaping the initial wave of arrests. At the end of July, she travelled to the Indian capital to attend Parliament, only to find that the opposition benches were practically empty. When she reached her New Delhi home on the night of 30 July, the police came to arrest her under the Conservation of Foreign Exchange and Prevention of Smuggling Activities (COFEPOSA) Act—the evidence against her being the loose change in pound notes and various coins found at Moti Doongri. The proclamation of the state of Emergency had strengthened the government's powers so that suspects could be detained indefinitely. Bubbles, who had been staying with Ayesha in her Delhi residence, was arrested at the same time. Both were taken to Tihar Jail. It would later emerge that the decision to arrest Ayesha and Bubbles was made on 24 July. The Intelligence Bureau believed they were in Patna and were preparing to flee to Nepal, but this information was not passed on to the home ministry and the first attempt to detain them was made in Jaipur. The Shah Commission, set up by the Indian government in 1977 to investigate excesses during the Emergency, would remark that 'a striking feature concerning these arrests seems to be the urgency with which the whole matter was processed in the course of one day—i.e. 24th July 1975 itself.'[26] What transpired on that day to make their arrest so urgent was never explained.

Bubbles was allocated a cell with washing facilities. Ayesha was placed in a smelly room with a single tap but no running water, normally used by visiting doctors. She had expected the jail to be clean 'like an army barrack'. Instead the conditions were appalling. Outside her cell was a putrid open drain that prisoners defecated in. 'There were no fans and mosquitoes seemed to devour us.'[27] The room was

163

already occupied by Srilata Swaminathan, a Communist Party activist who campaigned for the rights of Dalits and Adivasis. She had earned Indira Gandhi's ire by organizing labourers working on the sumptuous farmhouses on the outskirts of Delhi belonging to the capital's elite, including Indira's son Rajiv, to demand higher wages. There was only one bed in the room. Swaminathan gave it to Ayesha, while she slept on a durrie on the floor. After a few days, Srilata was moved to another cell and Ayesha had the room to herself. Thanks to her status she was given privileges including a daily newspaper—heavily censored—and a cup of tea in the morning. She was also allowed to walk in the prison grounds in the evening with Bubbles. A fellow prisoner, Laila Begum, cleaned her cell and Laila's two sons brought her roses. 'It was like a fish market with petty thieves and prostitutes screaming at each other,' she recalled.[28] Heavily pregnant women were sent to hospital at the last moment. A baby had been born in the jail's lavatory while another was delivered as the woman was being rushed to the hospital in a taxi. There were lunatics too. One woman was always stark naked and covered in flies. Another talked to herself all day long and threw bricks at everyone. 'One brick missed my head and another, my leg,' Ayesha later said.[29]

On the same day as Ayesha was arrested, Louis Mountbatten wrote to Britain's deputy high commissioner in India, Oliver Forster, expressing concern about rumours that Ayesha was about to be detained. The letter, dated 30 July, ended with a 'PS' confirming the news that she had been 'flung into jail'. Mountbatten said he would raise the matter with the Queen over lunch that day, though he admitted that any action 'from this end ... would probably be counter-productive'. The PS ends by asking Forster if he could 'get a message of affection to her'.[30] A week later Mountbatten's private secretary wrote to the British high commissioner, Sir Michael Walker, on the subject of Ayesha's imprisonment. Mountbatten intended to write to Indira Gandhi on the grounds that he had been friends with the Jaipur family 'for so very long and asking whether she would consider granting bail in this case, particularly as the Raj Mata is not in jail for "political offences"'.[31]

Mountbatten then made contact with Pat and Joey as well as with Jagat who was living in London. Jagat, who had been told not to return to India in case he was arrested, advised Mountbatten that any intervention would anger Indira Gandhi and she might react by taking away his mother's hard-won privileges.[32] Jagat's view was shared by officials at the British High Commission in Delhi, who were clearly less than enthusiastic about Mountbatten firing off loose cannons just a few years after his fumbled attempt to intervene in the case of the privy purses. 'I think he will only collect a rebuff, though he probably will not do any harm,' Forster wrote to his superiors in London. 'It is difficult to judge since I'm sure the Lady's harassment of the Raj Mata is in the nature of personal vendetta; pressure from Lord Mountbatten may simply strengthen the Lady's determination to keep the Raj Mata locked up.'[33]

From England Jagat sent his mother embroidery material, books and the latest issues of *Vogue* and *Tatler*. On his twice-weekly visits Joey brought her food, fresh laundry and updates on efforts to free her and Bubbles. He also smuggled in a transistor radio for her to listen to uncensored news from the BBC. Ayesha asked for friends to send textbooks and slates so she could teach the children in jail, and she got them a cricket set and a football. She set up a badminton court and played with the younger women, who were mostly prostitutes or pickpockets. Though she sometimes received food from outside, she normally ate the same vegetables and lentils served out of buckets as other prisoners. 'The *sabji* didn't have any *aloo* and the *daal* didn't have any *daal*. It was all water,' recalls Virendra Kapoor of the *Financial Express*, one of the many journalists incarcerated in Tihar.[34] Although Ayesha bonded well with her cellmates, she remained a princess. 'She was superior to all that she surveyed,' a jail official later recalled. 'She was nice, but always aloof. She maintained her distance from the other women who were in awe of her. She treated them as her subjects. She smiled at them, sometimes spoke to them but never mixed with them.'[35]

After about a month, the prison authorities told Ayesha that another political dowager maharani, Vijayaraje Scindia, the Rajmata of Gwalior, was being transferred to Tihar. The central government had complained to the authorities in Gwalior that the rajmata was 'living in great pomp with an entourage' and considered Tihar to be a more appropriate punishment.[36] When they told Ayesha she would have to share her room with Vijayaraje, she protested. An extra bed would leave no room to stand. Moreover, she needed somewhere to do her yoga and stayed up late at night, reading and listening to music.[37] Persuaded, the prison superintendent arranged for another cell to be made ready. In the meantime, Vijayaraje slept on Ayesha's veranda. Because they were still MPs, the rajmatas continued receiving parliamentary papers that brought stories of more politicians being jailed. From newly arrived political prisoners they learned how Indira Gandhi and her son Sanjay were perpetuating the Emergency. 'Both of us at times feared that we would be poisoned to death and when we told the jail superintendent about it, he rubbished it.'[38]

For all her stoicism and bravado, Ayesha missed her regal comforts. Stories about her requests for pink toilet paper are probably apocryphal, but there was no question of doing without her colognes and favourite outfits. Virendra Kapoor remembers how during the times assigned by the authorities for prisoners to meet visitors, Ayesha 'would come wearing her chiffon sari, the fragrance of her perfume wafting through the air. She would also wear jewellery during the meeting sessions. While [Rajmata Vijayaraje Scindia] had moved on to cotton saris, she stuck to her classic ones.'[39] He recalls Vijayaraje as being less traumatized by her experience than Ayesha. 'There was a glow on her face. The Rajmata of Jaipur on the other hand looked haggard and shell-shocked.'[40]

In August 1975, Ayesha and Bubbles wrote to the finance ministry appealing for their release on health grounds. They also stated in their representations that they had never indulged in any antinational or smuggling activities. Ayesha pointed out that whatever foreign exchange she was receiving through trusts abroad was fully taxed by the Indian government and was declared in tax returns. The letter was passed on to Indira Gandhi with a note from the minister of revenue and expenditure, Pranab Mukherjee, recommending their release, but the prime minister rejected the recommendation. Meanwhile in England, Mountbatten ignored Jagat's advice and kept pressuring the British royal family to write directly to the Indian prime minister demanding Ayesha's release. Mountbatten's intervention was treated coolly by the British High Commission, which viewed her detention as an internal matter that would best be dealt with quietly. 'We believe that an informal initiative by a member of the Royal Family would be unlikely to do any good to the Rajmata. It would probably equally do her no harm, but it might irritate Mrs Gandhi,' a confidential cable suggested. The cable noted that she had declined the privilege of having food sent in on the grounds that the prison food was 'quite adequate'.[41] A couple of months later, Walker raised the subject of VIP detainees with the Indian high commissioner to Britain and a cousin of Indira Gandhi's, B.K. Nehru, who admitted he was concerned about the poor treatment that Ayesha was receiving and promised to personally look into it. When Walker told him he understood she was being 'held in reasonably good conditions', B.K. Nehru responded, 'I am glad to hear it. I hope we still know how to treat our prisoners in a civilised manner.'[42]

On 1 November 1975, Bubbles was unexpectedly released on parole. The following month, Joey urged Ayesha to write to Indira again. She had lost ten kilos and her blood pressure was very low. For someone whose visceral hatred of the Congress and all it stood for had guided much of her public life, her letter had a distinctly grovelling tone. 'As the International Women's Year is coming to an end, may I take this opportunity to assure you, Madam, of my support to you in person and your programme in the interest and betterment of our country'. She also stated she had decided to give up politics and promised to 'not take any further interest in politics as the Swatantra Party has already [become] defunct and I have decided not to join any political party. In view of what I have stated above, as well as my deteriorating health, in spite of the medical facilities allowed and provided to me, may I request you for gracious considerations that I may be released. If there are any conditions which you want to impose, I will try to abide by.'[43]

On Christmas Eve 1975, Ayesha sat alone in her cell listening to Cole Porter on a cassette recorder, eating Beluga caviar and a Fortnum and Mason Christmas cake sent to her by friends. A year earlier she had been in Calcutta, rushing from polo matches to hairdressers, from cocktail parties to Christmas dinners. Now she had sewer rats for company. A few days later she was admitted to the Govind Ballabh Pant Hospital, where doctors discovered she had gallstones. She refused to have an operation while still a prisoner. On 9 January 1976, Joey told her he hoped she would be released from jail because of her illness, but one more hurdle remained.

Shortly after their arrest, Ayesha's and Bubbles's lawyers had filed a writ petition challenging her detention before the Delhi High Court. Now the government was demanding that petition be withdrawn. She complied.

The order for her release was signed on 11 January 1976. Her sister Menaka and Joey picked her up from hospital and took her to Tihar to collect her belongings. After saying farewell to her fellow prisoners, including the Rajmata of Gwalior, the superintendent and prison guards, she returned to her home on Aurangzeb Road in Lutyens' Delhi. From there she drove to Jaipur, where 600 people were waiting to welcome her back at Lily Pool despite decrees banning public gatherings. An operation on her gall bladder in Bombay was followed by a lengthy recuperation in Bangalore.

Although Bubbles and Ayesha were no longer in jail, the authorities were still determined to pin whatever they could on them. One of Jaipur's most enduring legends concerns a massive treasure buried under Jaigarh Fort. Located 120 metres above Amber Fort, Jaigarh is named after Jai Singh, who renovated the fort in 1726. Beneath one of three large tanks in the fort's courtyard, where tourists dress up in traditional Rajasthani clothes and take endless selfies, is rumoured to be hidden gold and jewellery looted from Kandahar by Man Singh I, who led the Mughals in an attack on the city in 1600. While marching back to Delhi he is said to have diverted thousands of loot-laden camels to Amber and buried the treasure in Jaigarh as the fort was being built. Once in a lifetime when he was deemed to be of a suitable age, Jaipur's ruler would be blindfolded and taken through a maze of passages. Only the fort's traditional custodians, the Mina tribals, who were described in some press reports as being armed with 'cutlasses, muskets and bows and arrows', knew the treasure's location.[44] When the ruler reached the storeroom accompanied by a Mina chieftain and a member of the Barwara thikana, the blindfold would be removed and he would find himself in an Aladdin's-cave-like enclosure surrounded by gold coins and ingots, boxes of precious stones, silver goblets, bejewelled swords and other valuables. He was allowed to select one item only before being blindfolded again and let out of the fort. Jai's predecessor Madho Singh chose a bird of solid gold 'studded with rubies of extraordinary fire, so heavy that a woman could scarcely lift it'.[45] Jai kept it on his mantelpiece.

Other versions of the legend distinctly lack the *Arabian Nights* touch. One account has the Maharana of Udaipur sending an emissary to Amber offering to disclose the treasure's location in exchange for a cut of the contents. Most historians believe that the bulk of the loot was used to fund the building of Jaipur by Jai Singh in the 1720s and subsequently by Ram Singh and Madho Singh for welfare projects. Another story has Jai Singh ordering a man named Himmat Singh to make multiple fake maps showing different locations for the hoard and concocting a story that the treasure had been put back and added to. 'If you were a ruler, you needed credibility,' says Pat, recounting the story. 'One copy of these plans, which were essentially a confidence trick, found itself in the hands of the income tax department. They were all hot and bothered. The department thought if they can find this treasure it will solve all of India's economic problems.'[46]

Armed with what later turned out to be a fake parchment map given to them by a man purporting to be a descendant of a Mina tribal chieftain, the tax department called in the army engineers from Jodhpur and half a dozen other agencies, including the Geophysical Research Institute of Hyderabad, to search for the treasure. The state-of-the-art seismic equipment being used was so sensitive it picked up an earthquake in Russia thousands of kilometres away. 'At the bottom of one tank they found nine huge holes the size of this room where the treasure obviously could have been buried,' recalls Pat, who was present during the hunt, armed with his own metal detector. An 1878 Act provided that any wealth found below twenty feet would be shared by the government and the owners of the land, in this case the Jaipur family. Says Pat: 'There was access to these chambers from the side of the fort. Architects and engineers all said these chambers contributed nothing to the water tank, so they were obviously a depository for something.'[47] On 15 June 1976, the *Times of India* reported that the map showed the location of treasure worth over 100 million pounds, including jewellery valued at thirty to forty million. The newspaper quoted Pranab Mukherjee as saying the map had been examined by experts at the National Archives and appeared genuine. The key to the vaults was supposedly lying on a stone slab six metres below the ground and from this slab ran a ten-metre-long tunnel to the vaults themselves.[48] As the hunt dragged on, speculation as to the value of the hidden hoard shot up to 160 million pounds or enough to finance India's fifth five-year plan. 'It was the Emergency and Indira Gandhi was being told that any day this treasure will be found, but after six months they realized there was nothing,' says Pat contemptuously. 'Nobody was willing to bell the cat by telling Indira [Gandhi] that no treasure had been found. So in the end they packed their bags and left quietly in the middle of the night.'[49] All that was found were a few old coins and some heavy guns.

The Jaigarh treasure story refuses to die. Still doing the rounds of Internet chat rooms (usually in the same thread as narratives that Lal Bahadur Shastri was poisoned) is the rumour that Sanjay Gandhi ordered a seven-day curfew in the city of Amber, with police being given shoot-at-sight orders. While the curfew was in place, sixty truckloads of gold, silver and jewellery were dug out and transported to Delhi. The loot was transferred to two Boeing 747s and flown out of India, presumably to be deposited in an extremely large Swiss bank vault. No proof of such an operation has ever come to light. Then there is the curse of Jaigarh Fort. Ayesha was one of those convinced that every member of the party that raided Jaigarh met with a tragedy in their family because they had defiled a sacred place. 'They destroyed quite a lot of the beautiful fort. I think I am right in saying that everybody had a tragedy in their families,' she told the *Indian Express*.[50] Based on such logic, Sanjay's death in a plane crash in 1980 was also the result of the curse he incurred when ordering the looting of the fort's treasure.

* * *

In 1977, Indira Gandhi called a snap election, believing she would get a landslide majority for her party. In what remains the biggest political miscalculation in modern India's history, the opposite happened. She and Sanjay both lost their seats as a vengeful electorate delivered its verdict on the Emergency. The news reached Ayesha while she was throwing a party for English polo players at Lily Pool, prompting much popping of champagne corks. She had decided not to contest the election as the Swatantra Party was no longer a political force. Instead she campaigned for opposition parties in the state assembly elections. By now she was thoroughly disillusioned with politics. 'Politicians dirty the chairs they sit on, just like flies!' she told the historian and hotelier Aman Nath.[51] The Congress was defeated and Bhairon Singh Shekhawat, a Jana Sangh leader, was appointed chief minister of Rajasthan. Ayesha was made the chairperson of the Rajasthan Tourism Development Corporation.

Shortly after the 1977 election, the Morarji Desai government set up the Shah Commission. The commission found that under guidelines issued by the finance ministry, the COFEPOSA Act was intended for dealing with cases of 'smugglers, foreign exchange racketeers or such foreign exchange violations as were having a nexus with smuggling'. It was not intended for dealing with minor infractions under the Foreign Exchange (Regulation) Act. In the case of Ayesha and Bubbles, the commission found that there was 'no nexus whatsoever either with smuggling or with foreign exchange racketeering'. Their detention was 'in utter disregard of the policies and guidelines which had been laid down by the Finance Ministry'.[52] The commission also found that Finance Minister Pranab Mukherjee had committed acts of forgery and destroyed evidence by tampering with a note sent to Indira Gandhi recommending their release. Neither Mukherjee nor Gandhi ever testified before the commission. Their prosecution for refusing to testify was thrown out by the Delhi High Court in December 1979. Mukherjee went on to become the President of India in 2012.

Despite being vindicated by the Shah Commission, Ayesha nonchalantly insisted: 'I would never hold grudges. Besides, I would have been most insulted if she hadn't thought me important enough to put in jail.'[53] When Sanjay died, Ayesha phoned Indira Gandhi to express her condolences, but the former prime minister refused to take her call. Later she would insist there was nothing personal behind Gandhi's decision to put her in Tihar Jail. 'Whoever made that suggestion is a fool. Why should there be anything personal? We hardly knew each other, there could be nothing personal. She was very polite when we met,' she told Shekhar Gupta, the editor of the *Indian Express*, in 2006. 'I never regretted being in politics, I never regretted being in the Swatantra Party, I never regretted being a chela of Rajaji's. He believed that India should be really free.'[54]

* * *

Ayesha's other reason for staying out of politics was to spend time with Jagat, whom she hadn't seen for two and a half years. An only child, he had had a cloistered upbringing. The age difference between him and his half-brothers prevented the development of close familial bonds. In 1957, when he was seven years old, he was ceremonially adopted by Jai's elder brother, Bahadur Singh, who had two wives but was childless. The adoption meant that Jagat would become the Raja of Isarda on his uncle's death. 'I realize this is not an ordinary thing, even in my country, but after all, it was all in the family,' Ayesha said at the time. 'I was able to reassure Jagat that Mummy and Daddy had no thought whatever of giving him away, that his uncle, who had no boys of his own, wanted to give him a big present, when he was grown up, and that was all.'[55]

Jagat was twenty-one and living in London when his father died. He had been educated at Mayo College, followed by Ludgrove prep school in Berkshire, the alma mater of Princes William and Harry. Like the sons of many Indian royals he then followed a well-beaten path by attending Harrow. 'He was incredibly popular,' remembers Richard Goodhew, a school friend. 'He played squash with both hands, which made us all laugh, and was an excellent shot.'[56] After leaving school he lived at the Cheyne Walk home of James and Nuala Allason. James Allason had developed a close friendship with Jai, whom he met while serving at the armed forces' General Headquarters in Delhi during World War II. As well as polo, the two men shared a love of hunting. 'In the morning we would drive for tiger mounted on elephants, after lunch shoot crocodile from electric canoes, and in the evening hyena-bashing, where you ride after the animal with a polo ball fixed on the end of a polo stick and play polo shots at it. It was a mistake to fall off.'[57] James Allason is today best remembered as John Profumo's private secretary.

Jagat became closely acquainted with the Allasons' eldest son, Julian, a professional photographer, partygoer and later a travel writer for the *Financial Times*. '[Jagat] was an instant social success. He was immensely good looking, tall and slim with a huge amount of hair. He went out wearing his kaftan—and ladies just fell for him,' says Julian's brother, Rupert, who later became a Tory MP and spy writer under the pseudonym Nigel West. 'Photography was his way of knocking off seriously beautiful women—he'd stand there with a camera saying, "Stand over there ... can you take off a few more clothes please."[58] Jagat was especially known for his practical jokes. Friends staying in his Knightsbridge flat looking for towels in the bathroom cupboard were likely to find a tiger's head staring at them instead.

One of those enamoured with Jagat was Rajyashree Kumari, the daughter of Maharaja Karni Singh and Maharani Sushila Kumari of Bikaner. In the memoir *Palace of Clouds*, she recounts meeting Jagat in London, where she was studying. 'Like many other girls, I had a huge teenage crush on Jagat Bapji,' she writes. One evening her parents invited him to join them and their daughter for dinner at Gaylord, a popular Indian restaurant on Mortimer Street. He arrived in a silver sports coupe and offered to take her, but her parents disapproved and she had to follow in a taxi. 'As I recall there was no exciting conversation, my parents asked him about his life at college and what plans he had for the future and we ended up chatting about our respective dogs; he had a small whippet called Bugs.'[59] Over time, Rajyashree's parents warmed to Jagat, seeing him as a suitable Rajput boy for their daughter to marry. Despite Jagat showing no inclination to want to settle down, emissaries were entrusted to begin negotiations and horoscopes were compared, only for the court pandits to declare that there was no compatibility between the pair. They also predicted he would have a short life.[60]

Jagat's circle of acquaintances in London included Mick Jagger, Imran Khan and Mark Shand, all of whom visited him in Jaipur, where he would spend the north Indian winters. Shand, the brother of Camilla Parker Bowles, was seventeen on his first trip to India in 1968 when he met Ayesha and Jagat in Jaipur. He later described Jagat as 'the dazzling prince with flowing locks and flashing eyes, attired in jewels and jeans, turban and T-shirt'.[61] Recalls Belinda Wright, now executive director of the Wildlife Protection Society of India: 'He would never carry any money. If he arrived by taxi at a friend's house they would have to pay the fare ... He was the most infuriating human being on this planet and also the most lovable. And of all the friends I've lost, in many ways he is the one that I and his other friends talk about the most. He had this incredibly odd charisma.'[62] Others were less generous in their opinion of Jagat. 'I don't know why people kept defending an irresponsible man with rather juvenile behaviour,' says Aman Nath. 'He had that standoffishness which came from a spoiled kid's arrogance.'[63]

Though stripped of their titles and perks, India's royalty still lived the high life, mixing not only with global celebrities but also with their own kind, a postcolonial cocktail set that came together at the Ascot races and the casinos of Monte Carlo. In 1966, Jagat's father rented their Kings Beeches estate to Thailand's king and queen. A decade and a half earlier, Princess Vibhavadi Rangsit, who was the queen's lady-in-waiting, and her husband, Prince Piyarangsit Rangsit, had met Ayesha's mother, Indira, in Switzerland. She was visiting her son Indrajit, who was being treated for his drinking problem at the Beersham clinic. Indira invited them back to Calcutta to stay at Woodlands. The prince and princess had sent their daughter Priyanandana to Malvern Girls College in Worcestershire. Priya, as she was known to her friends, then enrolled to study Sanskrit at London University's prestigious School of Oriental and African Studies (SOAS). While she was studying in London, her mother appointed General Sir Rodney and Lady Moore as her guardians. Sir Rodney had been the commander-in-chief of British forces in Malaya and was the ADC to the queen. Priya remembers him as being an old-fashioned gentleman, dressing in black tie even when they were dining alone at their house in Ascot. In 1971, her mother introduced Priya to Ayesha. Priya wanted to take a year off from SOAS to go to Jaipur, employ a private tutor and continue her Sanskrit studies. She stayed with Ayesha at the Rajmahal Palace until the start of the rajmata's annual summer sojourn in England and then boarded with a Rajput army family.

Meeting Priya for the first time at her ancestral home on the upmarket Wireless Road in Bangkok, tastefully decorated with centuries-old Thai and Cambodian art, I am struck by the candour with which she talks about Jagat, her dark eyes sparkling as she relates episodes in their unconventional courtship. There is an understated elegance about her that must have appealed to Jagat, who was used to seeing the same quality in his mother. Priya's diminutive frame hides a steely resolve that would come to the fore much later when the royal fairy tale would start to fall apart.

'I was invited to a party at Moti Doongri where Gayatri Devi had moved,' Priya reminisces. 'I was so excited to go there and everybody kept saying Jagat lives here when he comes to Jaipur. I was pretty impressed. I fell in love with the place before the man!'[64] The two first met the following year when Jagat accompanied his mother on a visit to Bangkok at the invitation of the Indian ambassador. After returning to England to continue her studies at SOAS, Priya rang him from the Moores' house in Ascot. Jagat, who was staying close by at Kings Beeches 'came over like a shot'. 'Well, we clicked from there and much to my parents' horror I moved into Kings Beeches and then he moved in with me at my London flat.' Ayesha initially didn't say anything about their relationship, but Sir Rodney was less than enthusiastic. Jagat was working as a photographer at the time as well as advising the auction house Sotheby's on Indian arms and armaments, a subject that fascinated him. 'The only person he was afraid of was his father. The only person who could influence him was his father,' says Priya. 'Had his father not died he would have gone on to university, but his mother couldn't make him. He was spoilt. His mother couldn't make him do anything.'[65]

Jagat's uncle Bhaiya had had a similar upbringing, losing his father at an even younger age and then putting up with a mother who mostly neglected him except when it came to passing judgement on his choice of girlfriends. As an only child Jagat was more spoilt, with his mother turning a blind eye to what would soon become a serious drinking problem. His formative years were largely the responsibility of his schoolmasters or family friends, who indulged him on account of his royal roots.

In 1978, after a five-year courtship, Priya and Jagat decided to marry. Jagat didn't want a big Indian wedding, but his mother insisted that if Priya was to be accepted in Jaipur some formal ceremony was necessary. They settled on a tikka or engagement ceremony at the City Palace. Accompanied by his male friends, Priya's father asked for Jagat's hand by offering special gifts to Jagat's eldest half-brother, Bubbles, and other relatives.[66] Neither Priya nor her father wanted a big Thai wedding either. A year earlier, in February 1977, Vibhavadi was travelling in southern Thailand, representing the king on a morale-boosting mission visiting troops and villagers when her helicopter was diverted to pick up two wounded border patrol policemen who had been ambushed by communist insurgents. When the helicopter was coming in to land, the insurgents opened fire, wounding Vibhavadi, who died before the pilot could reach the nearest hospital in Surat Thani. In deference to her late mother, Priya and Jagat were married in a low-key civil ceremony at the Chelsea Town Hall on 10 May 1978. It was followed by a grand reception graced by Queen Elizabeth, Prince Philip, Princess Alexandra and Lord Mountbatten as well as royalty from India and Thailand. 'I think he felt he needed to marry someone who understood something of the royal way of life,' said Jagat's friend Princess Purna of Morvi, the wife of the Guinness heir Garech Browne.[67]

Back in Jaipur, the newly-weds moved to Moti Doongri, where their first child, a baby girl they named Lalitya, was born on 3 February 1979, followed by a son, Devraj, two years later. For Ayesha, Jagat's marriage altered a tenuous mother–son bond. After Jai's death, she had always insisted her son accompany her on her travels. 'He became her "walker",' says Anne Wright. 'She had to take a companion. Ayesha would control Jagat. If you come with me to so and so, you will get so and so. She controlled him. But she lost that control when he got married.'[68] The consequences were not all negative. With marriage also came responsibility, something that his mother welcomed. She also got on well with her new daughter-in-law, with whom she shared a love of horses. Priya recalls a trip they took together to the Pushkar Fair, where she bought a stallion named Tara. '[Ayesha] said: "You're a Rani of Jaipur, you can't ride here!" I paid no attention and I galloped the horse around the fair and I bought him myself.'[69]

* * *

The expectations of widowhood did not sit well with Ayesha. Her mother had shunned all conventions when Jit died, rejecting any notion of living the austere life of a widow, such as renouncing worldly pleasures, giving away her chiffon saris and not wearing jewellery. There was no question Ayesha would follow any other course. Although she was the rajmata, there was no let-up in her travels, her obsession with horses or her entertaining. In 1979, she told the American journalist Jane Leveret that the end of princely India had been a liberating experience. 'I did in fact gain my own independence. Before I had had a very high position as Maharani with restrictions. It was like I was a queen, I couldn't wander around on my own, everything was rather official. Now one is free to do as one likes,'[70] she said, omitting to mention that she had a dozen staff at her beck and call to make that freedom possible.

The writer Ann Morrow describes going to a party at Lily Pool in the mid-1980s, where the guests hovered in an air of anticipation, unable to concentrate on their conversations as they awaited Ayesha's fashionably late arrival. 'Suddenly the low buzz of conversation stops, and all eyes turn as the hostess flutters into the room.' She wears a blue-green chiffon sari. Her only jewellery is two large diamond rings. 'She is svelte, exotic and compelling, and there is a moment of absolute silence.'[71] As the silence dissolves and the atmosphere zings, 'she flits round, chats about "the ball in New Orleans," her fillies "at the stud farm" in America and the Arc de Triomphe, wafting about in a flirty conspiracy of fun'. At the end of the night she farewells her guests with kisses and promises to 'see you in Washington'. Suddenly she vanishes. 'In the morning she is leaving for Paris to mesmerise the French.'[72]

Lily Pool is featured in the *World of Interiors* and *Inside Outside*. Ayesha doesn't mind 'that swallows dirty my lampshades and chipmunks [squirrels] nibble the fringes of my curtains'.[73] She brings glamour to Jaipur. She revives the city's famous blue pottery and attends board meetings of the MGD School. Outwardly at least, an atmosphere of convivial familial solidarity wafts through the bougainvillea and past the peacocks that amble about in the garden. Mickey's daughter, Bambi, is minister for tourism in Gujarat and has a son studying hospitality in Switzerland. Bubbles has a beautiful daughter named Diya. Joey is married to Rani Vidya Devi, the daughter of Raj Kumar Rajendra Singh of Jubbal, and they have a son named Ajai. Pat and his wife, Devika, also have a son, Vijit. Ayesha spends her summers in England watching the polo at Smith's Lawn and Cowdray Park. She makes sure she returns in time for her pink-themed party on the roof of Lily Pool that coincides with the full moon festival of Sharad Purnima. 'We are the real India. The people trusted us for so long,' she assures Morrow, who laps up her statement uncritically, mesmerized by the perfumed, perfectly formed princess in front of her.[74]

The closed world of celebrity and constant adoration skews Ayesha's view of herself—something that comes out starkly in her memoir. 'When the flag goes up at Lily Pool people know I am at home,' she writes, as if the whole of Jaipur was waiting and watching for her return from another season of polo and parties in Europe.[75] When it came to image-making, no Indian royals came close to her. She was India's most photographed princess and one of the world's iconic beauties—yet she pretended to be oblivious about her reputation and indifferent about her looks. Asked once by a women's magazine to reveal her beauty secrets, she retorted: 'Tell them I drink a bottle of whiskey a day, and I dye my hair black with boot polish.'[76]

Another writer who called on Ayesha around the same time as Morrow was the *Washington Post*'s Elisabeth Bumiller. When she arrived at Lily Pool, she found Ayesha wearing 'an un-regal outfit' consisting of dark brown slacks and a plaid cotton shirt. 'I was always a tomboy,' she tells Bumiller in a throaty English accent that sounds like 'an Indian Tallulah Bankhead'. 'If I got up in the morning, it was "rush, rush, I've got to go riding". There was no time to look in the mirror and pluck an eyebrow.'[77] Bumiller starts the conversation by asking Ayesha about the two schools she runs in Jaipur, her rug business, the stud farm as well as her charity work. Ayesha tells the *Post*'s reporter that she has recently returned from a round of parties in New York celebrating the Costumes of Royal India Exhibition at the Met. Nearly half of the exhibits on show have come from the family's private collection. She then starts to pine for the not-so-distant past, when twenty or thirty guests would come to stay at Rambagh, beginning their days breakfasting on the marble verandas and ending them on the dance floor. Guests did whatever they liked. She continues:

> Some went riding, some went for an early morning shoot, some might get up late. After breakfast, I had a bath, changed, then went to my office. After a siesta there would be an afternoon polo match, followed by tennis on the lawns. And after that a lot of people would go play squash—really athletic, we used to be, come to think of it. Then there'd be time to change again for the evening. We'd have drinks, and dinner different places—sometimes in the summer it was on the lawn, and now and then we'd go up to Moti Doongri, that little fort in front there. It was a nice

life. Nothing can possibly be as good. After all, I've lost everybody I've loved, and everybody who made my life a happy life.[78]

And what about her attitude towards tourists paying $250 a night to stay in her old bedroom in the Rambagh, asks Bumiller. 'One's feelings change. You can't be static in your mind.'[79]

8

THE MAHARANI'S MERCENARIES

Behind the facade of Rambagh Palace balls, of garden parties with visiting celebrities at Lily Pool and the feigned acceptance of the inevitability of royalty in retreat, not all was right in the House of Jaipur. The warm bond between Ayesha and Bubbles had gone. 'You never meet them at each other's homes in Jaipur, though each is always curious to know if you have seen the other,' noted Anne Morrow.[1] While attending a high-society Jaipur wedding, Elisabeth Bumiller found out why. 'Among the topics at the wedding was a bitter lawsuit over an estimated $400 million estate that is splitting the family, pitting the widowed queen mother against her stepson, the current maharaja'[2]

At the heart of the quarrel was whether Jai's estate belonged to the whole family or to Bubbles alone. Family custom and the principle of primogeniture dictated that as the eldest son he should be the sole inheritor, insisted Bubbles. But under the Hindu Undivided Family (HUF) Act, all of Jai's offspring had the right to an equal share of his fortune. 'It's only he who is creating this problem,' Ayesha told Bumiller, referring to Bubbles. Admitting that the situation was 'sad', her stepson countered: 'It's not like I have everything and the rest of them are out on the street.' Nor did he think the family quarrel was historically cataclysmic. 'This is very much part of the old tradition. The family fights used to be much worse than they are today.' At this point Bubbles's wife, Padmini Devi, who had been listening to the conversation, interrupted: 'The estate doesn't belong to anybody else. It's very simple. Let the court decide.'[3]

Most veteran Jaipur watchers trace the evolution from royal love-in to litigation to Jai's death. '[Ayesha] had such charm for the boys: Joey, Pat and Bubbles. They all loved her. Then Jagat was there. It was a very close family,' says Anne Wright. 'When Jai was alive he completely controlled her and them, so everybody got on. The moment he died, the whole thing splintered.'[4]

While the Jai factor played a role, it does not account for why it took almost a decade and a half for the tension to boil over. Media reports at the time pointed to the deterioration in relations between Ayesha and Padmini as being the root cause of the conflict. The classic mother-in-law versus daughter-in-law 'saas–bahu' skirmishing that had been simmering for years suddenly took on palatial proportions. Like Donegild in Chaucer's *The Man of Law's Tale*, Ayesha was being blamed for wanting to split up her stepson's marriage, something that seemed incongruous given that she was responsible for them tying the knot in the first place. What she hadn't anticipated was Jai's premature death that would turn the tables on who was the House of Jaipur's leading lady.

Bubbles was thirty-four when he finally married Padmini on 10 March 1966. A close relative of the family remembers Jai's frustration at his eldest son's inability to settle down. 'He'd been through so many women he wanted to marry, he didn't want to marry. [Man Singh] and Gayatri Devi would not have objected if he had chosen some girl who was socially acceptable.' Potential partners for Bubbles included Harshad Kumari, the daughter of the Jam Saheb of Jamnagar, Digvijaysingh Ranjitsinghji Jadeja, and Usha Devi of Gwalior, the daughter of Maharaja Jivajirao Scindia. But according to a member of a Maratha princely family who watched the drama being played out, Ayesha objected to a union with either state for fear of being overshadowed. 'If there was going to be any competition, she wanted to have the upper hand.'[5]

Padmini's father, Maharaja Rajendra Prakash, was the ruler of the small Himalayan kingdom of Sirmaur, not the kind of state that normally supplied marriage partners for Jaipur royals. What clinched the union was his close friendship with Bhaiya. It probably helped, also, that Padmini was an exquisite beauty, described by one admirer as 'straight out of a fine Pahari miniature painting'. 'I don't know how much thought [Bubbles] gave to this. But he must have, otherwise he wouldn't have married [Padmini],' the close relative says.[6]

Initially, Padmini and Ayesha bonded well. 'She took her to London and got her educated in etiquette and so on. Because she was from Sirmaur, a very small state, she didn't have that finesse. She didn't have a chance to mingle,' says the relative. 'Padmini's social graces were not as good as Jaipur's.' Following the marriage, relations between the two women soured. 'Somewhere, something went wrong. Maybe they were both vying for Bubbles's attention.'[7] From Ayesha's perspective, says Aman Nath, it came down to the fact that '[Ayesha] hated the idea that Padmini could do anything better than her'.[8] With Jai's death, she was now the dowager, and Padmini, from a tiny Himalayan state most people had never heard of, was the maharani. Playing second fiddle was not in Ayesha's nature. Nor, as it turned out, was it in Padmini's. Moreover, unlike Ayesha, Padmini had an impeccable Rajput pedigree. 'Ayesha, who had hobnobbed in politics with Rajmata Gwalior, quite fancied that title which sounded closer to the Queen Mother tradition of England than a cloistered dowager in the zenana,' explains Nath, who recalls Bubbles once exclaiming: 'She is no Rajmata, certainly not the mother of the ruler!'[9]

The closest Padmini has come to revealing the tensions between the two came much later. In March 2009, she appeared on *The First Ladies*, an NDTV chat show where the designer duo Abu Jani and Sandeep Khosla tickled the egos of celebrity wives with mostly innocent questions about their tastes in decor and what their husbands liked to eat for dinner. When Khosla dared to point out to Padmini that she was the 'least-known queen of Jaipur' and asked: 'Is it intentional?', his clearly indignant interviewee responded: 'Least-known queen means what? As in my mother-in-law?' She regained her poise after Khosla corrected himself by saying Padmini was in fact the queen and Ayesha was the rajmata. Padmini then politely explained that she had been taught from the time she was a child that the first seat was always 'given to the elders'.[10]

After being married to Bubbles for just a few years, Padmini began to spend more time in New Delhi, prompting speculation that the couple were separating. But in 1983, she returned to Jaipur, bringing with her two of her most trusted advisers from Sirmaur, Amarendra Jit Singh Paul and Prabhu Jyoti Singh Paul. For all her lack of Westernized sophistication, Padmini would turn out to be a woman of steely determination, relentless in fighting for the rights of her husband, her daughter and her grandchildren. And once she was back in Jaipur, she took the reins firmly in her own hands. 'It was as if she wanted the world to know that she too came from a martial family,' says Aman Nath.[11]

Padmini's first priority was to overhaul the management of the City Palace. 'She told Bubbles: "You've messed it up. Now I want my people, not your people, to run it,"' recalls the Jaipur correspondent of the *Times of India*, Prakash Bhandari. 'For the locals, the so-called faithfuls, it was a palace rebellion.'[12] The Paul brothers quickly made themselves at home, even setting up a mini gurdwara in one of the palace's vacant offices. All financial and legal affairs came under their supervision. One person who watched their take-over described them as 'the Maharani's mercenaries. She had to assert herself and they were her means to do it.'[13]

Now that Ayesha and Padmini were living just a few kilometres apart, strains reappeared. Matters came to a head in late August 1985 when Bubbles gave his wife a general power of attorney with regard to all properties and then left on an overseas trip. 'Since relations between the Rajmata and Padmini Devi were far from cordial, Bhawani Singh's actions aroused Gayatri Devi's ire,' wrote Inder Sawhney in the *Illustrated Weekly of India*, adding that Ayesha felt that the Paul brothers would now start exerting too much influence over palace affairs.[14]

Others put the ruckus down to Bubbles and Padmini beginning to look to the future. They had a daughter, Diya, but no son, raising the possibility of the estate going to Diya and her future husband—a man who might have no connection to Jaipur. Now that princely titles had been abolished, they were faced with the reality that there would never be another formally recognized Maharaja of Jaipur or even a suitable head of the Rajawat clan. Although Indian law allowed a daughter to inherit an estate, this was anathema to people who still lived by the traditions of a royal court. Bubbles had also recently suffered a heart attack. This had changed his entire perception of life, he later told Ritu Sarin of the news weekly *Sunday*. 'I suddenly realized I had to safeguard the legal rights of my wife and daughter.'[15]

What had been a largely private tussle now went public. Granting Padmini power of attorney 'infuriated the other Jaipurs, who say Bubbles has been regally henpecked by his greedy wife', wrote

Bumiller. Padmini dismissed the charge as 'mischievous gossip'.[16] Regardless of who had henpecked whom, Ayesha and Jagat published a notice in local newspapers stating that any transactions conducted by the Paul brothers regarding palace properties would not be valid and they would not be held responsible in any manner. Two months later, on 31 October 1985, Padmini wrote to the administrator of the Jaipur Municipal Corporation complaining that bogus pattas, or deeds, were being issued by 'unauthorised persons' for land owned by her husband—an underhand swipe at the rest of the family.

These opening salvos were like poorly aimed muzzle loaders firing grapeshot compared with the heat-seeking missile that was about to be aimed at the House of Jaipur's gilded interiors. In April 1986, Jagat filed a suit in the Delhi High Court demanding that all property left by his father in the possession of Bubbles and Padmini be divided equally in accordance with the provisions of the HUF Act and that a receiver be appointed to prevent his family's heritage from being frittered away. Pat and Joey then walked into the Rajmahal Palace and handed Bubbles a copy of Jagat's petition. 'Articles of immense value are being removed from the strong rooms,' it read. The maharaja had mismanaged and misused the properties and, as a result, 'huge financial liabilities have accrued'. The demands of the Income Tax and Wealth Tax Departments over the properties had piled up over the years to the tune of tens of millions of rupees. The astronomical wealth left to him by his father was being squandered. Worse still, it was alleged Padmini's family 'was assisting the Maharaja in siphoning off the wealth abroad'.[17] The other party in the suit was Ayesha. All property left by Jai, the plaintiffs insisted, should be divided equally among his three sons and widow on the basis of the Hindu Succession Act. The law of primogeniture, under which Bubbles was claiming to be the sole beneficiary of the estate, was an 'obsolete concept and redundant'.[18]

The estate's value was pure conjecture as no valuation had been done, but it included the jewels in the House of Jaipur's crown. Accompanying Jagat's petition was a 526-page list of movable and immovable properties under dispute, ranging from the Rambagh and Jai Mahal palaces to a jade backscratcher. It included the Moti Doongri Fort, several bungalows in Jaipur, as well as hundreds of acres of agricultural land, a hunting lodge and bungalows in Sawai Madhopur and Jaipur House in Mount Abu. The ten items for which exemption was sought under the Wealth Tax Act included a pair of emerald drops weighing 75 carats, two carved emerald beads weighing 732 carats, two pieces of gold and enamel pendants studded with eighteen pieces of emeralds, sixteen flat diamonds and what were described as 'some very cheap pearls and rubies (gross weight 82.200 gm)'. Other objects for which exemption was claimed under the Estate Duty Act included more than 175 daggers, walking sticks, mirrors and pendants. Altogether 11,365 pieces of jewellery, antiques, paintings, furniture and other household items were listed in the annexure.[19]

Aside from undisclosed funds lying in various tax havens, the most valuable part of Jai's estate was the 1,120 acres of land in Jaipur that the authorities alleged was owned by Bubbles, most of which was locked in land ceiling disputes with the state government. Bubbles had initially claimed all the property as owned by the HUF with himself as the karta, or head of the family, in order to get around the Urban Land (Ceiling and Regulation) Act that barred holding more than 1,500 square metres (0.37 acres) by an individual. When Jagat filed his writ petition, Bubbles was forced to write to the urban land ceiling authorities claiming that all the lands were owned by him personally and not by the HUF. He said that the amount of land owned by him was much less than listed by the Revenue Department. The authorities responded by asking the former maharaja why he was claiming a change of ownership ten years after filing the initial tax returns. They also demanded to know whether there had been any concealment or misinformation about ownership in the past.

Lawyers for Bubbles countered by arguing that Jai was the 'owner and had full and absolute right over the private properties' as provided under the covenants he signed at the time of the accession of Jaipur state on 2 June 1949. Since Bubbles was recognized as his father's successor by the President of India on 7 July 1970, only he had the right to dispose of these properties. Moreover, there was no HUF, nor could there ever be because Jagat and Joey belonged to different families, having been given away by adoption to other royal houses 'as per the law, practice and customs prevalent in the

Jaipur Royal Family'.[20] Jagat had no locus standi to move the court because he was adopted by the thakur of Isarda in 1957. Joey, who was given away to the thakur of Jhalai in 1937, was also disqualified for the same reason. To compensate them for their ineligibility to succeed to the throne on the basis of primogeniture, Joey's and Pat's sons had been granted jagirs and other movable and immovable properties by their father. Bubbles's lawyers also objected to the filing of the suit in Delhi since none of the disputed property was in the Indian capital.[21]

The argument over whether Jagat and Joey had been legally adopted (by the thakurs of Isarda and Jhalai respectively) would become particularly complex with both parties going to extraordinary lengths to prove their respective cases. Lawyers for Bubbles combed through the court records and found reference to a suit Jagat had filed in the district court in Jaipur against one 'Sambharmal Lohia' for a property in the Isarda thikana. In the suit, Jagat allegedly described himself as the son of Bahadur Singh. Included as evidence were pages from Ayesha's memoir where she describes giving Jagat for adoption, as well as an article from the London paper *Tanfield's Daily* reporting the event. Photographs of the adoption ceremony showing Jagat as a rather sad-looking eight-year-old and Jai laughing and joking with his elder brother, Bahadur, were also presented, together with records of Jagat's landholding in Isarda that show him as Bahadur's son.[22] Jagat's lawyers argued that although adoption was a Jaipur tradition, it had no legal basis. Jai had always treated Jagat as his son, and after Jai's death, Bubbles treated him as his brother. Evidence presented to support their contention included an invitation from Bubbles to Jagat's tikka ceremony in January 1978, which refers to him as his brother. Any claim to the contrary, Jagat's lawyers argued, was a 'figment of imagination'.[23]

Bubbles responded to Jagat's case by launching a counterclaim to annex the properties and possessions belonging to his half-brothers and stepmother. 'When the team came from Delhi to seal my strongrooms, I told them to simultaneously seal the properties of my brothers. After all, where has their furniture come from? It has come from the City Palace, not from their own earnings!' he told *Sunday* magazine.[24]

As the war of words escalated, the attacks became more personal. 'There is no point in behaving like a gentleman with them,' Bubbles told the press, referring to his half-brothers. 'All of us had the same opportunities, background and education. But what can I do if they have not been able to achieve anything?' Breaking another taboo, he questioned his widowed stepmother's moral standing. 'One would have expected that with her background and experience, she [Ayesha] would behave in a more dignified manner. What she does privately is her prerogative. If she is running a stud farm with an army major, it is her affair. But she knows what my father wanted. Now the courts have to decide the outcome. The only hope is that the end of the tunnel will be bright for all of us.'[25]

Not content to leave things there, Bubbles took on the family over the running of the Rambagh Palace. Back in 1972, he had signed a twenty-year agreement with the Taj Group to manage the forty-seven-acre property. In return, the family would receive 3 per cent of the gross operating profit and between 7 and 10 per cent of the return from room occupancy. According to his advisers, the Rambagh earned a profit of only £8,000 in 1985–86 out of which Bubbles, who owned 6,260 shares out of the total equity of 33,260 shares, received a pittance. One of the culprits, he alleged, was Ayesha, who was not paying rent for Lily Pool, which was located in Rambagh's grounds. This, Bubbles told *Sunday* magazine, was 'an oppressive activity by itself'. He also accused the other family members of 'utilising company funds and property for purposes of financing themselves, including litigation transfer, journey fare and stay in India and abroad'.[26]

On 5 September 1986, the Delhi High Court responded to Jagat's suit by ordering a commissioner to inspect and seal the contents of eighteen storerooms housing everything from shamianas to priceless Mughal era carpets and a centuries-old elephant carriage. Lawyers for Bubbles disputed the order, claiming that the contents of the storerooms had been bequeathed by Jai to his successor as maharaja and his immediate family and did not form part of the HUF. The court-appointed commissioner, R.S. Chhabra, undertook three inspections between early September and late October 1986. His reports swing between the factual and the surreal as he pursues what is often a wild goose chase through the City Palace,

Moti Doongri and other disputed properties. Seals affixed with paper on locks at the City Palace Museum were deemed unsuitable because they could be torn 'by the monkeys present in the area', he noted.[27] Was a banquet hall actually a living room, a storeroom or part of the museum? Was a room exempt because it was Diya's bedroom regardless of what priceless treasures were in it?

One store consisted of seven rooms and contained so many tents, durries, howdahs, hookahs, mirrors and other items that he was told it would take five museum staff and half a dozen labourers at least a month to prepare a proper inventory. Another store contained nothing but varieties of saddlery, walking sticks, spears, guards' uniforms, pickle jars and chandeliers. The carpet storeroom contained more than 150 valuable carpets preserved in neem leaves. In Moti Doongri, one room was so infested with bats that Chhabra ordered the lighting of a fire to smoke them out, though this proved unsuccessful. In the 'library-cum-study', a false floor-to-ceiling bookshelf concealed the entrance to a strongroom. Though it had been raided in 1975 by income tax officials, its existence was denied by Jagat's lawyer. Chhabra's inspection of Moti Doongri was interrupted when Amarendra Jit Singh Paul, who was acting as the legal representative for Bubbles, ran inside alleging that a pack of dogs had been let loose on him. He also claimed someone had threatened to shoot him and that he had a tape-recording to prove it (the dogs were found to be tied up and the recording was never produced). At Lily Pool, purdah was used as an excuse to prevent Paul entering rooms where 'ladies were residing'. The building's basement contained nothing but crates of empty soft drink bottles and a basket of onions—all of which was duly recorded in Chhabra's report. After three such visits he asked to step down as commissioner on health grounds.[28]

As the dispute over Jai's estate began to inch its way through the courts, another fracture in what was once a close-knit family exploded. On the evening of Saturday, 19 July 1986, a brawl erupted between two groups of employees at the City Palace. The Hindi-language newspaper *Rashtradoot* reported that the clash began when employees loyal to Ayesha, Jagat, Pat and Joey began to attack those working for Padmini and Bubbles. According to a statement given at Manak Chowk police station by Amarendra Jit Singh Paul, who was Padmini's principal private secretary, the trouble began when he went to lock the residence of Colonel Virendra Singh, the administrator of the Museum Trust. Paul claimed that one of Virendra Singh's employees threatened to kill him and another hit him on the head with a sharp object.[29] An affidavit filed by Kesri Singh, the museum's assistant security officer, blamed a group of 'hooligans' led by Paul for starting the fight. Kesri Singh alleged that the attackers, who were armed with weapons, ransacked his house and threw his belongings outside. He suffered cuts to his hands in the incident. Four others were hospitalized. 'They have ousted our men from the place and threatened us for [sic] finishing our lives,' he declared in his statement.[30] Twelve days later, a confidential note to Joey penned by Virendra Singh alleged that on 30 July Paul and two other museum employees barricaded themselves in the kapad-wara for four and a half hours. Paul was later seen driving out of the City Palace in a jeep at high speed. Jagat would later claim in court that articles 'the value of which cannot be calculated in terms of money' had been stolen.[31]

Tensions surrounding the City Palace Museum had been simmering for months, allegedly exacerbated by the actions of the Paul brothers, who had sacked many of the staff in their overhaul of the City Palace. Jai had set up the Sawai Man Singh II Museum Trust in April 1959 with a view to preserving for posterity valuable items of jewellery, paintings, manuscripts, armoury and other treasures. Its 10,000 or so objects included a pair of life-size parrots carved out of a single emerald with rubies the size of marbles as eyes. Among the trust's best-known objects are the two gigantic silver pitchers, weighing 350 kilos each, that Madho Singh used for transporting Ganges water when he sailed to England in 1902.

Jai was the trust's chairman until his death in 1970. When Bubbles succeeded him to the post it was already a troubled institution. In January 1969, workers at the City Palace had discovered that a storeroom containing rare paintings had been broken into. Thieves had gained entry into the Surat Khana by cutting the bars of a ventilator. Altogether 1,830 paintings were taken. Several months later police searching the home of the museum's director, Sangram Singh, found around 2,000 paintings of which thirteen were identified as those stolen from the museum's collection. A court subsequently found that Sangram Singh had paid three men to carry out the theft, including a petty criminal named Ayodhya Singh, who smuggled out a valuable collection of early-eighteenth-century Gita Govinda paintings by concealing them under his dhoti. Most of the stolen paintings were never recovered and were probably sold to foreign collectors and museums. Others were put in a trunk and buried in the desert near the town of Jhunjhunu. In 1973, Sangram Singh was sentenced to five years' imprisonment, though some of the charges against him were set aside.[32] It was an ignominious end to a stellar career. Sangram Singh had been one of the leading experts on Rajasthani painting, discovering the distinct styles of various thikanas and helping to teach scholars in the field such as Stuart Cary Welch, Mark Zebrowski and Terence McInerney.

After Jai's death the Museum Trust's board included Ayesha, Bubbles, R.P. Agarwal, a former director of the Archaeological Survey of India, and the Maharaja of Kota, Brijraj Singh. In February 1986, Ayesha issued a public notice on behalf of herself and four of the museum's seven trustees to prevent the sale of Atish Market, which occupied a prime location in the heart of the walled city, fearing that the property would be misappropriated. The Paul brothers had instigated the sale as part of their restructuring of the palace's finances. The notice warned all concerned that none of the properties, movable or immovable, could be 'transferred, assigned, alienated, disposed of or parted with', except by a unanimous resolution of the board.[33]

Privately, Bubbles was furious. He had transferred a large part of his own property to the trust by a settlement deed in 1972. As well as Atish Market, the trust now controlled much of the City Palace, the Town Hall, the guards' enclosure and Jaleb Chowk. But his right to do what he wanted with his properties was now under threat. It was time to take revenge. On 17 November 1986, he sacked Ayesha from the board and replaced her with Padmini. Agarwal was ousted at the same time. Ayesha challenged her stepson's authority to sack her in a suit seeking a permanent injunction and declaration in the Jaipur district court.

Out but not down, Ayesha followed up by filing a case in the Supreme Court on 20 April 1988 challenging the participation of certain 'illegally' appointed trustees in the functioning of the trust and the 'unauthorised' removal of certain members of the board of trustees. 'The whole act reeks of mala fides and appears to be the work of a warped mind whose sole intent and purpose seems to be to bring down the high ideals of the great and honourable family of Jaipur,' the petition stated. It asked for the court's intervention to replace Bubbles with a person who was knowledgeable and of high character and dignity as the trust's chairman 'so that the properties of the Trust are not frittered away to the detriment of the interests of the State and the country which, when it loses these fabulous works of importance and pricelessness, would not find them elsewhere'.[34]

Things deteriorated further when musclemen from both sides of the divided family fought pitched battles in Sawai Madhopur and Ramgarh to occupy buildings. More than a dozen people were injured in the melees. 'It is very unfortunate and we would not like to wash our dirty linen in public,' Pat told *India Today* when asked about the incidents.[35] Amarendra Jit Singh Paul, meanwhile, used the power of attorney granted him by Bubbles to file a case against Ayesha for misappropriating 500,000 rupees from the Sawai Jai Singh Benevolent Trust. Paul alleged that she had taken a loan from the bank for herself by mortgaging the fixed deposits of the trust. On 15 September 1988, she applied for anticipatory bail believing she would be arrested.

The increasingly bitter court and street brawls, not to mention the public mudslinging, seemed out of character with the widely shared view, current even today, that Bubbles was a non-vindictive, kind-hearted gentleman. It also went against the Rajput ethos, something he himself highlighted in an interview with the *Ottawa Citizen* in 1988. 'We are Rajputs, we have always taken care of our people. That's our history, we don't forget that. We still take care of our old pensioners, we can't forsake them.' As for close associates of the family, many were appalled and saddened at the turn of events, torn as they were between their loyalties. 'They have embarked on the path of self-destruction. At the end of it there will be no winners.'[36]

* * *

On an early November afternoon in 1989, a motorcade suddenly descended on the small village of Jatwara about thirty kilometres east of Jaipur. A plump figure in a bright turquoise T-shirt alighted from an Ambassador car decorated with the saffron, white and green colours of the Congress party. Local volunteers had put up bunting and flags, giving the otherwise dour-looking village a festive air. The party's symbol, the hand, was everywhere. The Congress candidate cut 'an incongruous figure', wrote the *Times* of London correspondent Christopher Thomas, who had accompanied the motorcade. Sweating gently, the candidate blinked through tinted glasses at the swirling dust kicked up by the adoring crowds. 'Everybody wanted to drape garlands around his neck, and orange marigolds were soon stacked up to his nose. He looked decidedly uneasy.'[37]

In May 1988, Bubbles stunned Rajput society by announcing that he was joining Congress, now headed by Rajiv Gandhi. 'I offered my services for the party and he welcomed it,' he told *India Today* after meeting Rajiv in New Delhi. His intention, he added, was 'to do something creative'.[38] The flirtation with politics had begun several years earlier. On 31 October 1984, he had gone to the capital to meet Indira Gandhi to discuss the modalities of joining her party. But the meeting was cancelled because she had an interview scheduled with Peter Ustinov and his film crew that morning. After Indira's assassination at the hands of her Sikh bodyguards on that very morning in 1984, Bubbles put his political plans on hold because the situation was too fluid. In November 1986, he was back in the fray, seeking endorsement for his decision at a meeting of forty-two former jagirdars of Jaipur state and ten members of the Mina community. Having served the country as a soldier, it was fitting he should enter active politics, those present agreed. One of his first priorities was to tour drought-affected areas of the state.

Not everyone accepted his motives. 'He is entering politics to save his disputed fortunes with Congress patronage,' thundered Janata MLA Manak Chand Surana. Bubbles rejected the charge: 'The family disputes have been going on for years. If I were looking for patronage, I would have got into politics much earlier.'[39] More cynical observers saw it as another case of Jaipur rulers always securing their interests by being on the right side of the Delhi durbar. 'First there were the Mughals, then the British and now the

Congress (I).'[40] Others thought it suicidal. Why would Bubbles join a party that had jailed him and his stepmother during the Emergency? Many voters had not yet forgiven the Congress for incarcerating their rajmata and their maharaja. Former palace employees speaking on condition of anonymity insist it was Padmini who pushed her reluctant husband down the path of politics on her return from New Delhi, believing it would be in the family's interests.

After filing his nomination papers, Bubbles went to his stepmother's house to take her blessings rather than support. 'Her effect as far as political mileage goes has worn off now,' he told *Sunday* magazine. 'The people are considerably upset that she has taken sides in a family quarrel. She, being the Rajmata, should have stayed neutral.' Padmini concurred, saying, 'What good has she ever done for the people? Even today Jaipur lacks basic amenities, a sorry state for the first planned city in the country to be in.'[41] Speculation that Ayesha would take her feuds and legal disputes with her stepson to the electoral battleground by contesting on behalf of the opposition proved unfounded. Instead, she threw her support behind the BJP's Girdhari Lal Bhargava. On 1 November 1989, she inaugurated the BJP's state election office in Jaipur, saying that Bhargava was 'with the people' and that a non-Congress government was the only way to establish a just and true democracy.[42] 'He has no touch with the people,' Bhargava said of Bubbles. 'Even if he was successful he couldn't serve the people of Jaipur city who would never be able to see him.'[43] Bubbles responded by saying it would have been much more dignified if Ayesha had gone elsewhere to campaign.

Despite the curious crowds turning up at villages such as Jatwara and at various locations in Jaipur city to hear him speak, 'Durbar Saheb', as Bubbles was respectfully called by many Jaipur citizens, turned out to be a poor orator, his audiences listening in reverential silence rather than enthusiastic rapture. Most came to catch a glimpse of their mythical maharaja rather than to hear what promises he was making. Padmini supported her husband, telling the faithful that 'our *izzat* [honour] is now in your hands and it is your duty now to ensure that the Durbar Saheb is not disgraced before the eyes of the world'. Nothing would drive a wedge between them and the people of Jaipur, she said. 'The doors of the palace will always be open to you,' she assured the crowds.[44] The appeals and pledges were to no avail. Bhargava would defeat Bubbles by nearly 100,000 votes—a crushing result for both the maharaja and the Congress. The party lost every seat it contested in Rajasthan.

The political humiliation of Bubbles was a moment of sweet revenge for Ayesha. When two years earlier he had publicly accused her of behaving in a less-than-dignified manner by 'running a stud farm with an army major', he had crossed a red line. Of all the taboos in Jaipur, the greatest is to publicly besmirch the character of Gayatri Devi, who is still considered the real Queen of Jaipur, almost saintly in stature, more than a decade after her death. In off-the-record interviews, a different picture emerges. It is not unusual to hear her described as being petulant and arrogant and even acting like a bully at times. Her distrust of the prying media was legendary. One journalist who tried to approach her for an interview likened her rejection to being 'whacked with a yak's tail'.[45]

As for her personal life after Jai's death, the details remain hidden behind a veil of discretion. As a woman who retained her beauty and regal aura well into her old age she had many admirers. Bubbles had once hero-worshipped his stepmother, keeping a photograph of her propped up on the dashboard of his car. But she was also an intensely private person. Unlike her philandering husband, 'Gayatri Devi didn't have muddy affairs,' says author and curator, Kishore Singh. 'She always behaved with a sense of dignity, grace and poise.'[46]

* * *

Kuldeep Singh Garcha, or Colonel Garcha to his friends, is passionate about polo. Barrel-chested and boisterous, with a neatly brushed white beard, the former commandant of 61 Cavalry speaks with ebullient self-confidence about his career, his love of polo and the charity that he runs for underprivileged children. At his house near Jaipur's Army Cantonment, every room, wall, cabinet and table is crammed with memorabilia. Photographs, trophies, plaques and certificates jostle for space, perfectly curated with matching frames like regimental rows of soldiers lined up with well-drilled military precision. At seventy-five, he still plays regularly, though he no longer enjoys the handicap of five he had when he captained the

Indian polo team. Prince Charles, with whom he played in the Blues and Royals, features in many of the photos, as do other polo-playing potentates and global celebrities, including Sylvester Stallone. He coached the *Rambo* star for a brief period until his Hollywood producers pronounced the sport too dangerous.

Garcha was the anonymous army major targeted in the now infamous swipe of disapproval from Bubbles when he accused his stepmother of behaving in an undignified manner. To some the swipe still sounds like the angry words of an admirer who has been usurped by another. Garcha insists Ayesha and he were merely close friends, brought together by their mutual love of polo. In 1979, he helped her set up and run the Gee Stud Farm in the grounds of the Rambagh Palace, using stables that Bhaiya had built. Garcha was the managing director of the company with 50 per cent ownership. 'I used to meet her at the stables every day. She used to come and see every horse, every day, feed them grass and sit there with a cup of tea. Then her car would come and she would go for a round of the town. Go and see the statue of late His Highness [Jai]. Every day she would drive around it. Then maybe go to Gem Palace [Jaipur's premier jeweller] and have a cup of coffee there.' Even after Jai's death Ayesha never missed a chance to watch a game in India or abroad. 'Her enthusiasm for watching polo was such that she would become quite annoyed if people came and started talking to her while watching a match,' says Garcha, who credits himself with reviving the sport's former glory days by getting corporates to sponsor tournaments and a crop of new players to take up the game.[47]

It's easy to understand why the two got along. Aside from their shared love of horses and polo, Garcha has no time for niceties, frequently asking me to turn off my recorder before launching into a potentially defamatory story about people in Ayesha's inner circle, knowing full well that he too has been the subject of much innuendo. 'She was not diplomatic at all. I used to tell her: "You're so upfront. People know where you're coming from." She called a spade a spade. She would avoid fools. It's like, if I don't like you why would I want to hang out with you, rather than keep talking. She was true royalty in that sense.' Without naming names, he recounts an incident where a chief minister of Rajasthan came to her seeking a favour. Her response, given in front of her staff, was: 'I'm not going to help you. You are a thief.'

Like her other admirers, Garcha has his pet stories about her kindness and generosity. In 1995, a rare silk Persian carpet was stolen from Lily Pool. Two years later police apprehended a member of her staff after he tried to sell the carpet to a curio dealer in Jaipur. 'She was in England. So, she called her secretary and told him: "Please go and get him out of jail." When she came back I asked her, "Why did you do that?" She said: "His grandfather worked for me, his father worked for me. So, he's stolen something, whatever, that's okay."' The staff member was allowed to resume work at Lily Pool.

She was meticulous when it came to entertaining, checking the seating, the table layouts, the food to be served. Garcha recalls one dinner party where a thakur had been invited. She was busy preparing things herself and asked him to help. He told her he couldn't because he was a guest. 'She called her servants to pack up his things and tell him to leave and he had to go.'[48]

* * *

If there was one topic that Ayesha would never talk about, not even to a close confidant such as Garcha, it was the turmoil in her son's life. In January 1985, Priya applied for a divorce that was granted by the Supreme Court of Thailand nearly six years later on 24 December 1990. 'My husband had a drinking problem. My mother-in-law Gayatri Devi was a solace, but she used to be abroad most of the time. Jagat's philandering ways distanced us,' Priya told the *Bangkok Post* in 2015.[49] Ayesha saw it differently, telling Dharmendar Kanwar, her biographer, that her son's alcoholism, and later death, was the result of the divorce and Priya's refusal to allow their children to see him. 'Unfortunately, he had a lot of unhappiness after his marriage broke up,' she told Kanwar. 'He was not allowed to see or communicate with his children who were the most important part of his life and he missed them terribly. The pain of not being able to meet them is what led to his deterioration. He took to drinking to offset his unhappiness and in the end this caused his liver problem and eventually his death.'[50] When the comments were published in Kanwar's authorized biography of Ayesha, Priya threatened to take Kanwar to court.[51] 'It was totally untrue,' says Priya. 'Jagat started drinking at school, long before he met me. In fact, it was his drinking problem that was one of the reasons for the marriage to break down. Even though I knew and everyone warned me at the time of marriage that he drank, I thought that I could change him. I hoped that he would become more responsible after getting married and having a family, but of course that didn't happen.'[52]

Close friends of Jagat also support Priya's claims that his problems with alcohol started well before their break-up. 'He was an alcoholic, not an aggressive alcoholic but I imagine it would have been quite difficult to be married to him,' says Nick Spencer, who first met Jagat in Bangkok in the 1980s. 'He used to hide his vodka in Coca-Cola bottles that he would have at breakfast. He tried to dry out but clearly it was a genetic thing.' Long periods when he would rarely see his parents added up to a difficult childhood. 'Jagat was rather abandoned in Jaipur while his father, when he was still alive, and his mother were jetting around the world. I think he regretted [that] and held it against his mother—a charming woman but quite a selfish woman ... who was never far from a mirror.' Ayesha had a commanding personality but lacked maternal instincts. The bonds between them were strong, but it was a 'love–hate relationship', Spencer says. Jagat was drawn to Spencer and his Thai wife, Kai, because they had two children similar in age to Lalitya and Devraj, and he would often stay with them in Bangkok. 'When he broke up with Priya he missed his children. Clearly, he loved a family life. He wasn't a playboy in that sense.'[53]

Spencer took Jagat trekking in Nepal where, despite the effect that alcohol was having on his health, they climbed to an altitude of 18,000 feet. In Chitwan National Park they rode on elephant back while stunning rhinos with tranquillizers so they could be moved to another park. 'He was a very good shot even when he had the shakes and he was pretty ropey that morning. [But] his shooting was impeccable,' Spencer recalls. In Nepal, Jagat was treated like a Rajput prince at the highest echelons of society. At a dinner in his honour 'he pitched up two hours late totally unconscious of the fact that people were waiting just for him. He wasn't in any way arrogant or princely or anything like that. But he was hopeless at punctuality.' At the time Jagat was living in Moti Doongri with a pet sheep named Mutton and an Irish wolfhound called Genji. 'We'd retire at around 10 p.m. to the Rambagh bar which was Jagat's nursery originally. So he started off on the right track.'[54]

Stripped of close parental ties and nearly twenty years younger than his next older half-brother, Pat, Jagat developed a familial relationship with Maharaja Gaj Singh of Jodhpur, 'Bapji', becoming a frequent visitor at Jodhpur's Umaid Bhavan Palace and socializing with him whenever the pair were in London. 'Cousins and brothers and sisters, all of that didn't exist there [in Jaipur]. From the Indian side, I became his closest friend,' Gaj Singh explains. 'He was good looking, quite athletic, a good sportsman, and women took him too seriously.' Like others, Jodhpur's maharaja recalls a charismatic young prince who shouldered his responsibilities lightly. 'Once I happened to be on the same flight from Delhi. This flight used to stop in Jaipur first. Suddenly he said: "I'll come on with you." I said "Okay." Those days they didn't have headcounts; otherwise someone would have told him to get out. That evening I got a call from a rather stern Rajmata of Jaipur who asked: "Is Jagat with you? Well, he's supposed to be here. I have a houseful of guests for his birthday."'[55]

Being the child of such celebrity parents 'was an unfortunate combination', says Gaj Singh. He was only twenty when his father died, and the onus for guiding his development fell squarely on his mother's shoulders. 'Ayesha didn't know how to cope with him. It wasn't healthy,' says Belinda Wright, Anne Wright's daughter. 'She wanted him to be something else. But he was difficult and he didn't like being controlled.' The domineering side of her character didn't help. 'Jagat hardly had any privacy in his life. Ayesha always knew what girlfriends he had, what time he got home, how much he had to drink. That made him even more rebellious.'[56] The charge that Ayesha neglected her son is borne out by a female member of an Indian royal family he pursued relentlessly after divorcing Priya. 'She [Ayesha] was too busy being the glamour girl of the world. It was: "Good morning darling, good night darling" and nothing in between.'[57]

After his separation, Jagat divided his time between Jaipur and London. 'He didn't show any great unhappiness,' Princess Purna of Morvi told the *Daily Mail* in February 1997. 'But it was as if he was saying: "I love drinking and partying and I'll do it often."'[58] He also found refuge in the companionship of women. 'He wasn't really into sex. He was into falling in love. He liked the process of falling in love and he loved to pine,' says Wright.[59]

There was no shortage of women in Jagat's life. Nor was there a shortage of broken hearts. Nick Spencer recalls him turning up one day with the British actor Jenny Seagrove, who was starring in the television series *A Woman of Substance*, where she played the young Emma Hart. 'Jagat's reason for bringing her around was that she was a heroine of my then teenage daughter, Sam.'[60] Other girlfriends included *Train to Pakistan* director Pamela Rooks and Sarah Dyer, the granddaughter of General Reginald Dyer, who was infamous for ordering the 1919 Amritsar Jallianwala Bagh massacre. 'Sarah was divorced, pretty and fun, quite well off and frightfully happy to have a drunken prince around and more than happy to pay his taxi bills,' remembers Wright.[61] Another of his girlfriends was the London socialite Zenia Singh, who recalled his endearing, though at times peculiar, zest for life. When Holi was being celebrated he would divide the household between guests and servants. 'But, whereas everyone else used washable paint, he used carpet dye which was impossible to remove.'[62]

In late January 1997, Jagat boarded a flight from London for New Delhi, taking his seat in the first-class cabin at the front of the plane while his two servants sat at the back in economy. Maharaja Gaj Singh alludes to some kind of altercation with an air hostess. 'He had long hair and a leather jacket, and I think he was carrying a penknife or something. Anyway, the pilot threw him off.' Not knowing what had happened, the servants flew on to Delhi, while Jagat went back to his flat at Cadogan Square. According to Kishan Sen, the family's cook, Jagat then went to a pub on Kings Road, started drinking heavily, got into a fight with some locals and staggered back home. When the police found him next morning he was unconscious.[63] 'He had a medical record, but no one knew it, so when they took him to hospital they did the normal [treatment] which wasn't the right one and he went into a coma,' says Gaj Singh.[64] Hearing he was in hospital, Priya and her children offered to fly to London, but Ayesha said there was no need. The last time they had spoken to him was a couple of months earlier in December 1996 to plan a long-overdue reunion. It never happened. After two strokes and a brain haemorrhage, Jagat died on 5 February. He was forty-seven. 'I shall never forget seeing him lying on his bed in the hospital, not breathing and I knew Jagat was no more,' Ayesha would later tell Kanwar. 'I cannot describe the pain of that moment and every now and then it comes back, and I blame myself and I wonder about life and death.'[65]

As well as his mother and half-brothers, mourners at Jagat's funeral included Mark Shand, Mick Jagger, James Allason and other friends and admirers. Shand was so close to the family that he had named his daughter after Ayesha. Huddled in a group at the funeral were several of Jagat's female acquaintances who were 'all crying, all behaving like widows'.[66] On 8 February, a specially chartered plane flew his body to Jaipur, where it was taken to Lily Pool and kept overnight for mourners to pay their respects. By now Priya, Devraj and Lalitya had arrived from Bangkok. 'She [Rajmata] told me: "I want to sit with Jagat for a while, please leave me alone,"' recalls Ayesha's private secretary, Ayub Khan. 'I had never seen her crying. But that time she was crying.'[67]

The following day the body was transported to the royal crema-tion ground at Gaitore. Sixteen-year-old Devraj lit the funeral pyre. Lalitya and Priya returned to Bangkok, but Devraj remained for the twelve-day mourning period. At the end, Bubbles performed the pagri dastur, the ceremony recognizing Devraj as Jagat's heir. Shamianas were set up on the lawn in front of Lily Pool, and in the presence of his uncle Pat and his cousin Vijit, Devraj received nazars from the Jaipur nobility. Vijit, accompanied by Bubbles, then took Jagat's ashes to Haridwar to be immersed in the Ganges. 'I'm not supposed to do so as ruler. My logic: I'm going as a brother,' Bubbles later explained.[68]

*　*　*

If there was one positive outcome to the piteous end of a tragic life, it was the first sign of a rapprochement between Bubbles, his step-mother and her grandchildren since the start of their court battle over Jai's will. Bubbles had just completed a three-year posting as India's high commissioner to Brunei. As he later confided to a friend, he was happiest when abroad and far removed from what he called 'clandestine court politics'.[69] The oil-rich sultanate was also a place where Indian royalty was taken seriously. Now that he was back in Jaipur it was time to mend fences and bring Ayesha and her grandchildren closer together. Devraj and Lalitya began spending their school holidays with her in Jaipur and summers at her London flat.

Overshadowing the reconciliation was the question of Jagat's inheritance. Since he had died intestate, Devraj, Lalitya and Ayesha jointly petitioned the Jaipur district court in 1998 claiming to be his three legal heirs. Jagat's three half-brothers, Pat, Joey and Bubbles, gave no-objection certificates. Pat had been managing Ayesha's financial affairs and Jagat's assets and was the director of most of the family companies. He was also in possession of a power of attorney given to him by Jagat. A few weeks after Jagat's death, he asked Priya to sign papers disclaiming her rights to her ex-husband's estate. 'I willingly did so,' she said. 'I gave up my own legal rights, but I did not give up the rights of my children.'[70]

Now childless—as well as widowed—Ayesha redoubled her social work. She raised funds for women's education and oversaw the activities of the Sawai Man Singh Benevolent Trust, set up to help the poor and needy of the erstwhile Jaipur state. In addition to MGD School there were two new schools to look after, the Maharaja Sawai Man Singh Vidyalaya and the Lalitya Bal Niketan, named after her granddaughter and located in a village outside Jaipur. The village was chosen because her driver came from there. Khushwant Singh remembers Ayesha inviting him to address MGD students on Parents' Day.

> I told the students, 'Don't let your fathers choose your professions, choose what you like the best; don't let your mothers choose your wives or husbands, choose your own. If it does not work out, get a divorce and try again. Learn to make your own mistakes. Don't waste your time on prayer; it's a lot of mumbo-jumbo. Instead, read, work, have a good time.' And so on. Needless to say, it went down very well with the boys and girls. Parents were appalled and protested to Gayatri Devi. She was amused.[71]

Ayesha also had more time to visit Cooch Behar where the people still regarded her as amader rajkumari, our princess.[72] But the visits brought her little joy. Her birthplace was now a shadow of its former glory. Because Bhaiya and Gina were childless, they had adopted Bhaiya's nephew Virajendra, who became maharaja in 1970. It was a poor choice. Viraj died in 1992, also without an heir, upholding the family tradition of drinking himself to death but not before he had squandered whatever was left of his uncle's wealth. After almost six centuries of often enlightened rule, Cooch Behar, eastern India's most glamorous dynasty, was extinct. Stripped of its treasures by looters and debt collectors, Ayesha handed over the palace in which she and her siblings had grown up to the West Bengal government. Today the few heirlooms that have been recovered form a rather forlorn museum.

Perhaps fearful that a similar fate might await some of her own treasures, Ayesha donated a large collection of her jewellery to the British Museum in the mid-1990s on the condition that the provenance not be revealed until 2029. Palace insiders talk of a large suitcase containing necklaces, earrings, bracelets, pendants and other pieces, many of them set by Cartier, being sent to London. Today's much stricter regime of museums being required to give the provenance of art objects would have made the donation much harder. In 2019, a cabinet containing necklaces, brooches, earrings and a ring, all set with emeralds, together with other Cartier pieces donated by Ayesha was quietly unveiled in the British Museum. Their provenance is not listed.

9

A WEDDING, A WILL AND AN ADOPTION

As the volume of plaints, depositions and declarations relating to Jai's estate continued to climb, another dynastic drama was unfolding in the House of Jaipur—this time a very public spectacle that pitted entrenched medievalism against modernity, custom against reform and community against individual choice. The very future of the thousand-year-old Kachchwaha ruling family was at stake— or so it seemed.

In 1984, Bubbles asked his friend Budh Singh Rajawat to help him run the City Palace. Rajawat was a sarpanch from a village near Sawai Madhopur and for the next five years he worked in the palace mainly as the household controller and then alongside Bubbles during his 1989 election campaign. In return for his help, Bubbles gave his twenty-three-year-old son, Narendra Singh Rajawat, a job in the accounts section of the Sawai Man Singh II Museum Trust. Narendra's office was next to the maharaja's and the two talked frequently over cups of coffee. The urbane and softly spoken young man whose life was about to become inextricably entangled with the Jaipur royal family says he was welcomed with open arms by Bubbles. 'If anyone came to his office to meet him he would bring that guest to my office. It's not that he would press the bell, he would bring them to meet me without any ceremony.'[1]

Princess Diya Kumari was a precocious eighteen-year-old when she too walked into Narendra's office unannounced. 'It was certainly not love at first sight or anything like that in our case. I don't believe in love at first sight,' Diya would later explain. But she admitted taking an instant liking to him. 'What appealed to me about Narendra was his simplicity and sincerity. He came across as being very considerate and caring—qualities that you rarely find in Indian men.'[2] Their courtship was low-key. It had to be. Diya's parents were expecting her to marry a blue-blooded royal, preferably from one of the higher pedigree Rajput princely states. She was their only child and potentially the heiress to a vast fortune. Newspapers estimated the estate's value at several hundred million pounds, an amount plucked from thin air, an unlikely tenfold increase from the figure being quoted just a decade earlier, but one guaranteed to capture the public's imagination. Loyal staffers turned a blind eye to surreptitious meetings at friends' houses. Innocent shopping trips provided precious moments of privacy. 'Up to this time it was just a very nice, strong friendship. It was only when I accompanied my parents on a trip abroad, when I missed him unbearably, that I realized things went deeper than a mere friendship. I wanted him to be with me always. That was when I realized how serious my feelings for him were.'[3]

When Diya told her mother about Narendra, she was so upset that her daughter was going against family tradition that she kept the news from her husband. Guilt-ridden, Diya felt that as an only child she was letting her parents down. 'When you are faced with a situation like this, the turmoil, the struggle just gets too much at times. Your heart and your instincts are totally obtuse to what your brain says.'[4] The pair stopped seeing each other for several months, hoping that 'things may fizzle out'. They didn't. In February 1994, almost taking a leaf out of Indira of Baroda's courtship with Jitendra of Cooch Behar, the couple eloped, marrying in an Arya Samaj ceremony in New Delhi and getting the marriage registered in a court. 'We had a commitment towards each other and both of us felt it was time we honoured it.'[5]

It would be another two years before Diya mustered the courage to tell her parents about their marriage, the delay in part because Bubbles had suffered a stroke while he was India's high commissioner to Brunei. It also meant two years of torture of being married yet not being able to live with Narendra. 'We wanted to live together but what could we do? I could not ditch my parents just when they needed me the most—at a time when my father was recovering. Besides, the doctor had advised us not to upset dad.'[6] Finally, in January 1997, she told her parents she was married, fully prepared to leave the family home if they rejected her new status. 'They were more hurt than furious,' but in the end accepted the situation.[7] Others recall a more dramatic scenario with Bubbles threatening violence. 'Padmini had to smuggle Narendra out of the palace,' says Jaipur hotelier Durga Singh Mandawa. 'Finally, they accepted the situation because Diya was their only daughter.'[8]

By now the romance was Jaipur's worst-kept secret. When Narendra crashed his motorcycle en route to his village home, the local police found letters from Diya and her picture in his wallet. Assuming he was a relative, they rang up the City Palace at Jaipur informing them of the 'royal' accident. 'Money, contacts, familial regard for royals helped put the lid on that scandal,' the journalist Sunil Mehra wrote at the time.[9] Realizing privacy was no longer an option, plans were made for a re-enactment of the marriage as public acknowledgement of their already legalized status. On 25 July 1997, the palace announced that the couple were going to be married on 5 August, the Hindu festival of Teej, which celebrates the celestial union of the gods Shiva and Parvati.

No one, it seemed, had anticipated the reaction. The protocol surrounding the private lives of Jaipur's royal family evaporated as quickly as water on hot bitumen after a monsoon shower. Press reports described Narendra as the museum's cashier or as Diya's ex-driver and labelled his father as a palace guard. To hide his 'commoner roots' it was rumoured that Bubbles had given Narendra vast sums of money to build himself a grand residence. Gossip swirled that Ayesha, Pat and Joey were pressuring Bubbles to adopt a male nephew to prevent Diya and Narendra's child from inheriting the vast legacy. 'For the Jaipurs, no one was good enough for Diya. Not the local chieftains' boys, not the bright beautiful men she was allowed to see but not come out of her fish-bowl to meet and be with,' a palace insider told Mehra.[10] The gloves were off and suddenly everyone wanted to have their say. 'They're livid. All that lolly and a nobody from nowhere walks off with the dame AND the drachmas.'[11]

Two days before the wedding, a 500-strong crowd gathered outside the City Palace, burning effigies of Bubbles. Most were members of the Rajput Sabha. Set up by Jai in 1939, it was tasked with maintaining the centuries-old traditions of the Rajputs, as well as looking after the welfare and uplift of the community. Clashes over land, family feuds and marital disputes occupied much of the time of its elected officials. Its largely rural base translated into a highly conservative stand on religious and social issues. When seventeen-year-old Roop Kanwar died on her husband's funeral pyre at Deorala in 1987, the sabha appropriated her sati as a 'glorious saga' in Rajput history. The organization's president, Narendra Singh Rajawat (no relation to Diya's husband), described widow self-immolation as a 'supernatural force which comes out of dedication, devotion and attachment in absolute terms. It is not like nirvana but close to it.'[12] Shortly after Roop Kanwar's death, Rajawat formed the Sati Dharma Raksha Samiti (Committee for the Defence of Sati), which was forced to change its name to the Dharma Raksha Samiti (Committee for the Defence of Religion) after a Rajasthan High Court ruling. For his outspokenness, Rajawat was one of sixteen people charged with glorifying sati, though he, together with the surviving co-accused, was acquitted more than a decade later.

The day after the wedding date's announcement, Rajawat met with Bubbles at his office at the City Palace. As the maharaja and senior-most member of the community, Bubbles was the permanent president of the sabha. Brushing hierarchy aside, Rajawat demanded that the marriage ceremony be called off. Diya and her husband belonged to the same gotra, or clan, and therefore shared the same bloodline. In Rajput tradition that made them the equivalent of brother and sister. When Bubbles pointed out that the 1955 Hindu Marriage Act permitted intra-clan marriage and that Rajputs were Hindus first and foremost, Rajawat retorted: 'Legal laws are not primary. Social laws are. We Rajputs take pride in preserving our culture, our social norms.'[13]

Rajawat had known about Diya's plans to marry Narendra before she had told her parents. When she had broached the subject with him he had assured her he would 'handle the rest of the Rajput community', provided Bubbles agreed to the marriage. Now those assurances had been thrown out of the window, Diya would later assert.[14] What started out as a matter of ethics quickly got highly personal. Bubbles claimed 'misguided' Rajputs were trying to extract mileage out of the wedding for their petty gains. 'Rajawat should pay attention to Rajput poverty, lack of education, instead of railing like an obscurantist if he's a community leader,' he added.[15] A phone call between Rajawat and Padmini only escalated the row. The sabha chief told her 'to become Muslim if she wanted to conduct this marriage'. Padmini's riposte was 'not to meddle in what was a purely personal affair'.[16]

Diya's parents stood their ground and the kanyadaan ceremony to solemnize the wedding went ahead, not in Jaipur as originally planned but in the New Delhi neighbourhood of Jor Bagh. By Indian standards it was a low-key affair with only about 200 guests. Among those attending were the Maharajas of Kota, Kapurthala, Kishangarh and Jodhpur as well as thikana families of the erstwhile Jaipur state such as Sewar, Samode, Bissau and Barwara. The BJP MP Jaswant Singh and the former ruler of Jammu and Kashmir, Karan Singh, were also on the guest list. 'They [the Rajput Sabha] couldn't do much. All our relatives, all our Maharajas attended the wedding in Delhi,' says Narendra. 'Legally we were in the right.'[17] His parents did not make it to the ceremony after being blocked from going to the capital by Rajput Sabha supporters.

Undeterred by its failure to stop the kanyadaan ceremony or prevent senior members of the community from attending, the sabha continued its offensive. A day after the ceremony, Rajawat told a rally outside the City Palace that 'performing a socially unacceptable marriage is setting an offensive precedent'. Bubbles and all those maharajas who defied the sabha's edict should be excommunicated. 'As head of the Rajput clan how can they set an unheard-of precedent? We'll oust him from the community and related organizations, even anoint a new King.'[18] Bubbles blamed the ongoing agitation on the sabha's chairman, Devi Singh Mandawa. 'This is politically motivated. Mandawa, who's leading the agitation, was once in my mother's Swatantra Party, he is now with the BJP. He had a factory he's sold. Now he has nothing to do. Hence this.'[19] To head off further agitations, Bubbles dissolved the sabha's executive committee and appointed his own. When Rajawat refused to hand over the keys of the sabha's premises, Bubbles's ad hoc committee took out a case against him.

According to Diya, threats against her and Narendra continued for months. 'We have been receiving all sorts of threats from people we know and those we don't. In fact, we had started receiving threats immediately after the wedding date was formally announced in Jaipur—mainly from this Narendra Singh Rajawat, ironically, my husband's namesake, and his henchmen—telling us that we will be harmed, that they will send suicide squads. They have threatened to kidnap my husband and me and to not let us enter Jaipur.' Rajawat, she said, had even warned her that he would blacken their faces if Bubbles did not step down. 'In this day and age such talk is shocking. I mean, is my marriage the prime issue facing the community today?' The couple were allegedly even warned to remain celibate and not have children. 'I do believe traditions must be followed and kept alive. But traditions cannot rule your life. They change with times. Having more than one wife was a Rajput tradition, but can anyone do it today? I honestly never imagined that they'd make such an issue of it all.'[20]

At the age of eighty, Narendra Singh Rajawat is no longer the firebrand leader he once was. He speaks with difficulty and relies on his daughter, Chhavi, to help him express himself. Chhavi has also broken with tradition, becoming India's first female sarpanch and the first with an MBA, something that her parents are rightly proud of. 'Changes that once took fifty years now take place in one,' her father says of the transformation of Rajput society. Two decades on from Diya and Narendra's marriage, he remains steadfast in his opposition to the union. 'Action had to be taken. If he was a commoner no one would have cared but marrying within the same gotra was wrong.' He does concede, however, that people with a vested interest took advantage of the controversy for their own ends and condemns the threats made against the couple. 'They didn't want it to settle down quietly,' he insists.[21]

* * *

By solemnizing their wedding, Diya and Narendra could at last live as husband and wife in the City Palace. Diya made one of her priorities transforming her family home into a world-class museum. 'There is so much restoration work to be done. I would like to put new works on display. And yet I am not being allowed to. Obstacles are being placed at every step.'[22] Those obstacles related to various court cases that by now had been running for more than a decade

and showed no sign of ending soon. One casualty of the legal wran-
gling over Jai's inheritance was the Rajasthan High Court order to
seal the Kapadwara. For more than forty years, some of the most
valuable artworks, manuscripts, jewellery and armoury accumu-
lated over the centuries by Jaipur's rulers have been off limits to
the public, historians and the family, and are likely to remain so
indefinitely. The treasures include the first Persian translation of
the *Mahabharata*, known as the *Razmnama* or the *Book of War*.
Commissioned by the Mughal Emperor Akbar for his personal
library, it comprises eighteen richly illustrated volumes and the
translation of tens of thousands of Sanskrit verses. Sixteen of the
greatest artists of the time are believed to have worked on the
illustrations.[23] The *Razmnama* was purchased from the Mughal
court by Sawai Madho Singh I in 1753 and last put on display during the Jaipur Exhibition of 1883. Other valuable items under lock
and key and in an uncertain state of preservation include a Persian
translation of the *Ramayana*, thousands of valuable miniature paintings as well as court records.

Other movable parts of Jai's estate had also fared badly. In
January 1993, R.S. Chhabra, joint registrar of the Delhi High Court,
was ordered to inspect the seals he had put on six strongrooms and
seventeen godowns back in 1986. Chhabra found that several of the
seals had been tampered with. A wall of the Kapadwara appeared to
have been knocked down and restored. In several cases keys to the
storerooms and godowns could not be located. A year later,
B.J. Divan, who had been appointed the receiver and administrator
of Jai's estate, carried out his own inspection of the strongrooms
and godowns and verified most of Chhabra's findings. Amarendra
Jit Singh Paul, representing Bubbles, dismissed Divan's report as
'partisan' and 'biased' and called for him to be replaced. Denying
the administrator's findings, he blamed 'red-faced and black-faced
monkeys' that infested parts of the City Palace for removing wiring
and tampering with locks. He also rejected the charge that entry had
been gained into the Kapadwara, where the most valuable items
were stored as its walls were nine feet thick and therefore impossible to tamper with.[24]

In October 1993, Divan undertook an inspection of the carpet
store inside the Mubarak Mahal Chowk of the City Palace. After

gaining entry into the store he found the carpets in a 'pitiful condition, under layers of dust', making them extremely difficult to examine. They included large pieces woven in the Mughal karkhanas of Lahore and Agra, as well as some that were exclusive to the court of Amber. The City Palace collection, he wrote in his report, was considered 'the most important and comprehensive in the world'. However, when he compared the carpets in the inventory against those in the store he found that forty-six of the 189 listed had disappeared. Most of those missing were made in Lahore and Herat in the seventeenth century and were of a size and quality 'not to be found anywhere in the world and are priceless'.[25] Of the remaining pieces many were infested with moths despite the use of neem leaves to keep insects away. At a further inspection of a storeroom in the Rajmahal Palace, by now used by Bubbles as his residence, he found that all of the seventy-two shikar trophies listed on the inventory had disappeared. Divan also raised concerns that the 11,653 paintings listed in Schedule II of Jai's estate were suffering the same fate as the carpets, having been stored without airing or cleaning for more than eight years. The jewellery in the strongrooms had not been inventorized despite all the pieces being antique and 'part of our national and cultural heritage'.[26] Based on Divan's reports, Jagat's lawyers declared that there was 'a strong apprehension that all the valuable articles lying in the strong rooms and the godowns, the value of which in today's date will run into several crores of rupees, have been removed'.[27]

In January 1994, Divan carried out more inspections including at a property known as Aramgah on the road from Jaipur to Ramgarh. Aramgah had been built by one of Jaipur's former rulers as a rest house for guests making their way to the Ramgarh forest for hunting. At its entrance was a signboard that read 'Guest House Prencess [sic] Diya Rersorts [sic] Private Ltd.' When he inspected the rooms, he found them stripped bare of all furniture and fittings. Dust and bird droppings covered the floors and all the doors and windows had been removed. In the open ground behind the main buildings were more than 130 neem trees, their branches and leaves chopped off. The caretaker told him that the leaves and branches had been sold and the money had been deposited with Bubbles's office in the City Palace. On checking the palace's books, no record of any company running the resort could be found. The whole operation, Divan wrote in his report, was 'a sham, bogus and invalid'. In a separate report filed with the Delhi High Court, Divan accused Bubbles in connivance with Paul of receiving income from properties in Mount Abu, Sawai Madhopur and Jaipur city instead of depositing that money with the high court in accordance with its order of April 1986.[28]

Narendra had wanted to concentrate on his construction business rather than involve himself in family matters, but he soon found himself under pressure to overhaul the management of the City Palace. 'You've married our only child,' his in-laws told him. 'People who work for us are taking us for granted, we have so many battles.' When Diya also insisted on lending a hand, he had no choice but to comply. 'In those days things were not very good at the palace because people were not handling the affairs properly. Being a commerce graduate I started helping them. Firstly I reorganized the whole museum which was running at a loss, then we started a lot of new businesses.'[29] On 3 January 2000, a durbar was recreated at the City Palace to celebrate the 1,000th anniversary of the Kachchwaha clan. Looking fresh after getting its first new coat of paint in almost forty years, the City Palace was lit up for the occasion. Bubbles sat in the courtyard holding his faux durbar as shehnai players greeted gawking tourists who were showered with flower petals.

Diya's marriage, her parents' initial opposition and the Rajput Sabha's agitation once again turned attention to the perennial problem of what to do about an heir to the dynasty. Tradition, or what was left of it, would have normally seen Bubbles adopting a nephew. With Jagat's death, that left Pat's son, Vijit, who was working at the Rambagh Palace, or Joey's son, Ajay.[30] But with the family bitterly divided by numerous legal battles and Bubbles clinging to the principle of primogeniture to keep the spoils of Jai's estate within his line, these options were ruled out. Then on 12 July 1998, Diya gave birth to a baby boy named Padmanabh. 'You have to meet my grandchild,' an ebullient Bubbles told Anne Wright shortly after the birth. 'He produced this little baby and said: "This is the future Maharaja, I don't care what people say or do, but this is the future Maharaja."' Wright later recalled.[31]

* * *

On 22 November 2002, for only the second time in more than eighty years, Sanskrit shlokas and hymns rang out from the durbar hall of the City Palace as temple pandits and the head priest of the Jaipur royal family performed the hour-long adoption ceremony for the next head of the Kachchwaha dynasty. As Narendra placed his young son in his father-in-law's lap, an eighteen-gun salute announced to the outside world that Jaipur had a new crown prince. A display of fireworks lit the night sky. At the age of just four years and four months Maharajkumar Padmanabh Singh may not have had much inkling of what was happening around him. Tradition dictated that he remain with his biological parents until the end of the ceremony, but every time he made eye contact with his grandmother Padmini Devi he ran over to her and had to be restrained.[32]

Bubbles was quick to defend the break with tradition: 'After much thought and deliberation, I have decided to adopt my grandson,' he declared. 'I do not have a son, and the dynasty needs a male heir to inherit the family's assets.'[33] The galaxy of erstwhile Rajasthani princes and dignitaries attending the adoption ceremony included the former ruler of Mewar Arvind Singh, which observers saw as a sign that the centuries-old animosity between the Sisodias and Kachchwahas was finally consigned to the dustbin of history. Among the many congratulatory messages was one from Prince Charles, Padmanabh's godfather.

Notable in her absence was Ayesha, a sign that the same royal observers took as proof that the relations between Bubbles and his stepmother were still icy. Prior to the ceremony, Ayesha had sent a letter to Bubbles in which she urged him not to go through with the adoption. 'Dear Bubbles, I have given much thought to the ceremony of adoption,' she wrote. 'I would like to remind you that in your position you have an obligation to live up to and with the traditions and customs of the House of Jaipur. I want you and your family to seriously reconsider your plans.'[34] Ayesha's excuse for not attending the ceremony was that she was in Cooch Behar.

The adoption had also irked the Rajput Sabha, with Narendra Singh Rajawat declaring that adopting a daughter's son was against traditions. 'Because it was a first and concerned such a prestigious family it caused considerable disquiet,' says Durga Singh Mandawa. 'The Rajput social order from eternity has always been that a nephew or a first cousin was adopted, as in the case of Isarda.'[35] Diya defended the adoption, telling journalists that it was a moment of pride for her. 'My husband and I are proud to be honoured by His Highness's grace,' she told the media, brushing aside the Rajput Sabha's allegations that the adoption was 'unconstitutional'. 'Daughters are as much a part of the parents as the sons. By adopting his daughter's son, the Maharaja has taken a progressive decision which has opened avenues for our community's women,' she said.[36] Padmini also responded to the criticism, saying: 'We cannot be expected to adopt the son of someone who has filed a case against us.'[37] Among the wider Rajput community, there was relief that the Kachchwaha line would continue. 'There was heartfelt happiness instead of opposition,' Durga Singh Mandawa insists. 'At least we had a person instead of law suits and court cases.'[38]

It was a view not shared by Padmanabh's grand-uncles, Pat and Joey, who issued a high court writ alleging that Bubbles had broken an ancient Rajput tradition by failing to name an heir from the male line of the family. Padmanabh's father, Narendra Singh, admitted the feud was damaging the family. 'There is no reason for this fight, and no reason for the constant accusations. The Maharaja has chosen his successor and that should really be the end of the matter, but some people will not let it go. It could have terrible consequences.'[39]

A decade and a half on, the adoption still raises eyebrows. 'Bhawani Singh was able to break a rule because his daughter had broken another,' says a long-time observer of Jaipur affairs, referring to the adoption and Diya's marriage. 'To put it another way: a double fault gets you back in court.'[40] Others, however, point to Padmanabh's qualities even at an early age. 'Even as a three-year-old, Pacho could sit for two or three hours at a time observing all the ceremonies happening around him,' says family friend Shivina Kumari, referring to Padmanabh by his nickname. 'His grandparents passed on all these traditions from hundreds of years ago.'[41] Diya said she had no qualms about the adoption. 'I didn't have a brother and all social responsibility needs a Maharaja. So the next best heir was Padmanabh. But there is no special treatment for him. He's just like our other two children, but only being made responsible so as to take care of things later.'[42]

* * *

Padmanabh's adoption as the heir apparent signalled yet another seismic shift in intra-family relations. In April 2002, Priya and her children made their first visit to Jaipur since Jagat's death. This time Bubbles opened up the doors of the City Palace to them and insisted they stay as his guests. Foes had become friends even though the original legal wrangles over Jai's estate were still progressing languidly through India's labyrinthine legal system. Fault lines had been redrawn. Although Devraj and Lalitya were close to their grandmother Ayesha, Priya was not on speaking terms with her. The bonds between Ayesha and Pat, meanwhile, appeared to be getting stronger, with the ageing rajmata increasingly relying on him to manage her legal and financial affairs.

Priya used her visit to ask Pat about the status of the succession certificate. At the time of Jagat's death in 1997, his children were too young to take over his estate. Despite Pat's and Joey's declarations back in early 1998 that they had no objection to succession certificates being issued in favour of Ayesha and her grandchildren, there had been no progress in the matter and the Thai family's patience was running out. When Priya and Devraj met Pat, he explained that the formalities had been held up because of a claim on Jagat's estate 'by a family member who was not a legal heir'.[43] Priya and her children were also growing suspicious about Jagat's shares in the company that controlled the Jai Mahal Palace Hotel. Concerned about the delays in the case caused by the absence of original documentation, Devraj and Lalitya wrote to Pat on 24 April 2003, asking for clarification. Pat's response, dated 6 May, expressed surprise at the letter's innuendos and legalese and declared it was 'high time' they perceived matters 'in the right perspective'. He denied that he had looked after all of their father's affairs, saying that Jagat was 'capable and confident' of managing things for himself, and that Priya's decision to hire lawyers had unnecessarily exacerbated tensions. As for the share certificates pertaining to the Jai Mahal Palace Hotel, Pat admitted they might have been misplaced. In the meantime, he would continue to conduct matters pertaining to the estate on behalf of Ayesha.[44]

The roots of the House of Jaipur's latest spat began in 1956, when Jai gifted his youngest son the Jai Mahal Palace. Built in 1745, it was known as Natani ka Bagh after its owner, Hargovind Natani, the commander-in-chief of Maharaja Ishwari Singh's army. From 1874, it was the home of the British resident surgeon, Thomas H. Hendley. When he moved out, it became the residence of three successive prime ministers of Jaipur, the last being Sir Mirza Ismail. In 1954, it was renamed Jai Mahal and run, rather unsuccessfully, as a hotel by the proprietors of Gem Palace. In May 1981, Pat and Jagat set up Jai Mahal Palace Hotel Pvt. Ltd with the two of them as the directors. The eighteen-acre property, boasting one of India's best-preserved Mughal gardens, was handed over to the Taj Group in 1984 on a seventy-five-year lease. The Taj invested heavily in the property, adding a couple of wings built in faux-Rajasthani palace style. The old floors were ripped out of the original structure and replaced with white marble. It wasn't the cash cow with cachet that the Rambagh was, but it ranked in the top ten of Jaipur's hotels. It was also the most valuable asset in Jagat's estate.

While Jagat was alive he owned 5,050 shares or 99 per cent of Jai Mahal Palace Hotel Pvt. Ltd against 50 shares or less than 1 per cent held by Pat and his son, Vijit. When Priya conducted a search of the Registrar of Companies she found Jagat's shareholding had been diluted to 7 per cent and that Pat and his son now owned 93 per cent of the company. Jagat's shares in the Rambagh Palace Hotel had also been reduced from 27 per cent to about 4 per cent. Devraj called his grandmother to protest. He claims she was unaware of the situation. 'She told me my uncle would explain, but he never did.'[45]

The dilution of shares, Priya alleged, started as early as 2001. She also charged Pat with using his full control over the company to get interest-free loans worth tens of millions of rupees from the Taj group for the company.[46] When Devraj wrote to his grandmother in August 2005 informing her of the dilution of the shares, she told him not to involve her in the matter and 'go directly to Pat'.[47]

On 30 March 2006, Devraj and Lalitya fired the first shot in what would be a bitter and drawn-out legal fight by filing a petition with the Company Law Board (CLB). In the petition they charged Pat and Vijit with committing 'illegal and fraudulent acts' in Jai Mahal Palace Hotel Pvt. Ltd and Rambagh Palace Pvt. Ltd. As their father's legal heirs, they demanded management rights and their share of the company's profits. They also alleged that Pat and Vijit had illegally delayed the transfer of shares to them on 'false pretexts' and misled them 'with oblique motives'.[48] By filing the petition with the CLB they hoped the matter would be expedited more quickly than in India's notoriously slow civil courts. They were wrong.

Pat and Vijit's response was swift. On 27 April, their lawyer U.K. Choudhary spelled out the reasons why the CLB should dismiss the petition. Prominent among them was the allegation that since Devraj and Lalitya were not Indian citizens they had no legal entitlement to Jagat's estate or his shares. After presenting his arguments to the judge and the opposing legal team, Choudhary dropped a bombshell. Scanning the courtroom, he picked up a typewritten note from Jagat to Ayesha on the Rambagh letterhead. Dated 23 June 1996 and only two paragraphs long, it began with the words 'My dear Mummy'. The letter, which had allegedly lain forgotten among Jagat's papers at Lily Pool for nearly a decade, cut his own children out of his will and bequeathed everything to his mother:

> As you are aware, I have not been keeping too well. I telephoned Devraj and Lalitya but as usual they refused to speak to me. I am very disturbed by the children's attitude, no doubt influenced by their mother. I know that Priya will grab my property through the children.
>
> Therefore, on my demise, I hereby disinherit my children Devraj and Lalitya from getting/claiming any part of my estate. I hereby bequeath all my movable and immovable properties and assets to you solely.[49]

The signatures of the two witnesses were illegible and unattested. Developments now moved quickly. Three days later Ayesha's lawyers filed an application at the district court in Jaipur for a succession certificate in respect of her late son's entire estate. She followed up with an application for transmitting all the shares owned by Jagat in Jai Mahal Hotels Pvt. Ltd and Rambagh Palace Hotels Pvt. Ltd into her name. Priya's initial response was that the will was a forgery. 'Jagat left many signed blank letterheads with Pat at the Rajmahal office for convenience since he liked to live in England.'[50]

The appearance of the will signalled yet another fracture in the House of Jaipur. The day before Choudhary's surprise tabling of Jagat's statement, Ayesha had filed a court statement admitting the right of Devraj and Lalitya to inherit their father's estates in equal shares along with her. Now she was depriving them of what they believed was their share of their father's estate—effectively disinheriting her grandchildren from her own bloodline. The two questions uppermost in the minds of Jaipur's Rajput elite now were: did she do it because she detested Priya, or was she being manipulated by others? Her vacillation also suggested a deeper antipathy towards her grandchildren that was a by-product of her own estrangement from Priya. Alleged Dalip Malhotra, Devraj and Lalitya's advocate: 'It's clear to the grandchildren that Gayatri Devi's decisions are being influenced by those surrounding her and [she is] signing papers without understanding the implications. How can anyone go against their own blood?'[51]

10

'A BROTH SPICIER THAN A THAI CURRY'

Jaipur royal tradition dictated that displeasure was normally conveyed indirectly—politely declining an invitation to another family member's function or issuing a bland public notice in a newspaper. 'Whatever tension there was, it was all under the rug,' Dharmendar Kanwar, Ayesha's biographer, de facto spokesperson and close friend, commented. 'It was not something that outsiders would know about.'[1] Central to the maintenance of this decorum was Ayesha's indomitable sense of entitlement and her cast-iron doctrine of never commenting on family conflicts, especially to pesky reporters. Now her ability to control the narrative was eroding rapidly. The restraint that had kept slander from triumphing over the facade of dignity was about to be abandoned.

In late July 2006, Priya, Devraj and Lalitya returned to Jaipur, once again staying at the City Palace as guests of Bubbles and Padmini. The discovery of the alleged will and Ayesha's move to disinherit her grandchildren was the last straw for the Thai side of the family. On 28 July, a media release arrived at the Jaipur Press Club, an ugly run-down concrete edifice where hardened hacks wash down greasy masala omelettes with double pegs of Teacher's Scotch. A media conference was to be held at Lily Pool the following day fronted by Princess Priyanandana Rangsit and her children, Devraj and Lalitya. It was Priya's first visit to Jaipur with her children since 2002. Devraj was now twenty-five and working on one of the Thai king's rural development projects. Lalitya was twenty-seven. She had a master's in archaeology from Cambridge University and worked as a heritage conservationist in Thailand.

Their Thai heritage coupled with the fact that neither of them had spent much time in India had endowed Devraj and Lalitya with a degree of reticence that was about to be tested by the rapacious Indian media. In photographs scattered around Lily Pool, their father, Jagat, reminded me of a young, long-haired Freddie Mercury when the fashion of the day was tight flared jeans and body-hugging shirts. Devraj had inherited his father's looks but his manners and dress were distinctly restrained. He had only a halting command of Hindi and his Thai humbleness was out of step with the brashness associated with much of the younger generation of Indian royalty. Lalitya carried her mother's allure as well as her sense of dignity and restraint, assets that were to be put to good use in the coming weeks and months as what the press was terming the 'battle royale' moved out of the courts and into the public arena.

Prior to their arrival, Priya had hired the PR firm Perfect Relations to drum up coverage. There was no need. Jaipur's royals always made good copy and very little had been heard from the Thai side of the family. No one wanted to miss an opportunity to get their version of what was fast becoming the most sensational story to engulf the family since the jailing of Ayesha and Bubbles more than two decades earlier.

Delivered on Lily Pool's sparkling green lawns, the message from Jagat's ex-wife was blunt: wicked uncles were cheating her children of their inheritance. Allegations of a forged will and murky share dealings were laid out for all to see. An estate worth hundreds of millions of pounds was being pillaged illegally. Never had anyone in the family fronted a full-blown press conference. Never had such serious allegations been made outside of a courtroom. What was just another story of a litigious royal family bickering over the spoils of their princely past suddenly became, as one journalist put it, a 'broth spicier than a Thai curry'.[2] The gloves were off and in the next few months reports of schisms and palace intrigues, coercion, alcoholism and a messy divorce exploded into public view. 'A frontier had been crossed,' conceded Kanwar.[3]

Priya told the assembled media that the 'forged will' came to light only after she demanded certain rights for her children. Ayesha, she claimed, had been coerced by Pat and Joey. 'The Rajmata has been manipulated, she is not infirm, but she is dependent, and easily influenced. When she is alone, she is one person, when she is with Patbapji and Joeybapji, she becomes another,'

Priya alleged. 'I don't know what's in her mind … If she thinks this is my way of trying to grab Jagat's property, she should think again. My children are not minors, what comes to them is theirs. To cut them off like this is heartless.'[4]

Priya cast herself as acting with no ulterior motive other than to seek justice for her family. Referring to Ayesha's move to disinherit Devraj and Lalitya, she said: 'Perhaps Rajmata does not like me. But the children should not be made to suffer.'[5] Since Jagat's death, she alleged, his half-brothers had attempted 'to replace him in Rajmata's affections at the same time as taking the rightful inheritance from his heirs. I am here to seek justice in India for Jagat's and my children. As a mother I feel that it's my duty to try to claim my children's patrimony and legal rights for them as I am sure their father would have wished.'[6] Speaking on behalf of his family, Devraj asked: 'How this will suddenly appeared nine years after my father died is perplexing. I had performed my father's last rites in Jaipur in 1998. As tradition goes, the former ruler, Brig. Bhawani Singh handed over my father's sword to me, making me the legal successor.'[7] So intense was the barrage of questioning by journalists, Priya and her children had to seek refuge on the first floor of Lily Pool. 'It rather got out of hand and we had to run upstairs to hide from the hordes of press,' Priya recalls.[8]

Now that the press conference was over, it was time to go public on their fence-mending with Bubbles and Padmini. 'Filing the suit against the "durbar" [Bubbles] was a mistake … that led to differences within the family with no one getting benefit,' Devraj told the *Times of India* the following day. Added Priya: 'While the two [uncles] have caused enough damage, Bhawani has shown his regal character by being supportive of us. He has extended all support, as we are new to this country and not familiar with the legal system.'[9]

Pat waited until Priya and her children had left Jaipur before commenting on the sudden appearance of the will and the accusations levelled against him regarding his shares in the Jai Mahal Palace. Contrary to Priya's insistence that she knew nothing about the alleged will until Choudhary produced it in the CLB, he claimed his stepmother had informed her grandchildren about its contents just after its discovery. According to Pat, Ayesha asked Priya and her children to find a mutually beneficial solution. 'But they weren't interested in discussing it. If they had, it wouldn't have become a legal issue.' Added Pat: 'The matter can be resolved. The lady is 87, there is no dearth of wealth.'[10] Addressing the question of the changes in shareholdings, Pat claimed he had a right to dilute Jagat's stake in Jai Mahal Hotels Pvt. Ltd in order to borrow from lending institutions to expand the company's activities. The money, however, was not borrowed, because the project it was meant for had fallen through.[11] In later court proceedings Pat's lawyers would also argue that Jagat had only attended twelve of the sixty-two board meetings held since the Taj takeover, 'establishing his non-interest in operation/management of the company'.[12]

Anjali Puri, who was reporting for *Outlook* magazine at the time, says the Thai side of the family was the clear winner in the public relations war. 'Priya and the kids came across better because they seemed less decadent and more normal than the palace-wallahs. She was bitter and angry and had a slightly cutting manner and imperious, entitled air about her, but she didn't speak in riddles and didn't come across as steeped in palace intrigue. And the kids were likeable.'[13]

Hoping to dilute some of the sympathy the Jaipur elite was feeling for Priya's family, Pat agreed to be interviewed by Puri at his Rambagh office. Midway through the meeting, he produced a yellowing fax message allegedly written by Priya to Ayesha in December 1996. The message warned the rajmata against 'scheming again and planning to come to Bangkok after the New Year to surprise us and the children'. Wrote Priya: 'Let me tell you that your plan won't work. How many times do I have to tell you that if you want to see the children, the only way to do so is with my consent and good will. Do you think that sneaking in on the children will do that? There WILL be trouble for sure and it would forever ruin any chances you may have of a reconciliation. You will be even sadder and more bitter than before.' The alleged fax ends with Priya speculating that Ayesha had been manipulated by 'troublemakers who want to harm me and don't care a bit about the children or even your feelings. Please reconsider.'[14]

On 2 August, Pat issued a statement denouncing Priya and her children's 'mala fide intentions to grab property and defame the Rajmata' and accused Bubbles of 'provoking' them.[15] Jagat had been disturbed by the behaviour of the children, who had even refused to accept gifts from him, Pat's statement continued. '[He] made repeated efforts to meet his children, but his divorced wife always prevented it and this pain was the reason for his untimely death'.[16] Priya responded with a statement asserting that Jagat had died because he was an alcoholic and accused her ex-brother-in-law of 'lying through his teeth'.[17] She also denied Pat's claim that she was trying to acquire Jagat's assets through her children, saying that when they separated they signed an agreement not to make any demand on each other's properties.[18] Her relationship with Ayesha had become strained only after she filed a case against Pat.[19]

Padmini also weighed into the controversy over the will, telling Puri: '[Pat] did it to us, now he's doing it to these kids.' The claim that Jagat had disinherited his children because of his estrangement from them was unbelievable, she added. 'The Rajmata personally told my husband and myself that Jagat had started keeping in touch with the children before his death ... Maybe she is financially under the control of Maharaj Prithviraj Singh and has to keep him satisfied more so than her own grandchildren.'[20] In an interview with the *International Herald Tribune*, Padmini expressed her dismay at the lurid details of the family saga being aired so publicly in the press. 'We have a moral obligation not to go into these gory details in public. We belong to good families, and we owe it to ourselves to behave with restraint,' she continued. 'This has not been dignified.'[21]

On 5 August 2006, Ayesha finally broke her silence, telling the *Indian Express* from her London residence: 'My son made a will, and I will stand by it.'[22] The statement prompted Devraj and Lalitya to write to their grandmother. In the letter they urged her not to let her differences with their mother colour her love for them. 'Perhaps our parents didn't get along well. You didn't like our mother because she is strong-minded, but why do we have to take the blame?' they wrote. 'All this makes our father seem so unjust and cruel. You say he was a kind and sensitive person, so how could he be heartless enough to disinherit his children without taking you into his confidence? He knew our mother will not ask for anything. We were teenagers at that time and we can't believe that he hated us as you claim, rather we know that he loved us as we thought you do,' their letter proclaimed.[23]

Despite the pleas of her grandchildren, Ayesha instructed her lawyers to apply to the district court in Jaipur asking to consolidate the 1998 case for the issue of a succession certificate and the dispute over Jagat's will. Lawyers for Devraj and Lalitya responded by arguing against the consolidation of the cases on the grounds that the proceedings were distinct and independent.[24] 'This was a sad time for me as our grandmother misunderstood us, and for the first time since our father passed away, Lalitya and I did not get to go and stay with her at Lily Pool,' says Devraj, reflecting on the strained relationship with his grandmother. 'During those two years when I was in Jaipur, it was Uncle Bubbles who gave my mother and me huge apartments in the Chandra Mahal at the City Palace. He was kind and the most caring of us among all of our uncles.'[25]

* * *

In the breezy bar of the Jaipur Polo Club, where polished silver trophies and framed black-and-white photographs speak of past glory and less litigious days, speculation about the alleged motives of the competing parties dominated discussions. Why would Jagat disinherit his children if he was about to start seeing them again? Why was the will written on the Rambagh Palace letterhead, given that he had never stayed there? Was the letter disinheriting his children ever sent? If it had been sent, it would have been read by Ayesha back in 1996, so why had she forgotten about the contents? Why were the signatures of the witnesses not verified? Was Jagat even sure that his mother would outlive him? Both she and Jagat were known to go on vacation leaving signed blank papers with trusted aides. Could one of these have been used to forge the will?

Ayesha's apparent determination to validate Jagat's will also prompted speculation about the extent to which she was controlling the court proceedings herself or being directed by others. Friends concede she had little knowledge about legal issues. She was now eighty-eight years old. After suffering a broken hip in a fall, she needed a wheelchair to get around. Given her advanced age and the fact that she spent several months abroad each year, was she even aware of the implications of the legal actions taken in her name?

Laying claim to Jagat's estate also seemed gratuitous, given that Ayesha had considerable assets of her own. Although Lily Pool was one of the dozens of properties whose ownership was under dispute (the management of the Rambagh Palace claimed she was a tenant who hadn't paid her rent rather than an owner) she had a spacious apartment in London's Knightsbridge, the Moti Doongri fort, share portfolios and access to the proceeds of various trusts. The only major asset of Jai's she no longer owned was Kings Beeches in Britain, which was sold in the early 1970s. After briefly being occupied by peace campaigners during the Gulf War, the property had burned down. The vacant land was bought by a Saudi sheikh.[26]

Dharmendar Kanwar tried to hose down such speculation by putting the best spin possible on the rajmata's relationship with the rest of the family. 'She loved them and always tried to keep the family together, notwithstanding the legal battles.'[27] Ayesha had been particularly close to Pat's wife, Devika Devi of Tripura, who was the daughter of her elder sister, Ila. She maintained contact with her even though she was estranged from her husband and lived in Delhi. Joey's wife, Vidya Devi, had been entrusted with the administration and management of MGD School and the Sawai Man Singh School. 'Whenever there was a function, both came together and relations seemed cordial,' said a teacher.[28]

Others, however, linked the legal disputes to the sudden rise in real estate prices. 'The family has been at each other's throats for donkey's years,' an unnamed relative was quoted as saying at the time. 'But in the last eighteen months, property prices in India, and particularly in Jaipur, have gone through the roof. Much more is at stake now.'[29] According to one estimate more than forty property disputes between various members of the Jaipur royal family were being contested in local courts.

In September 2008, Bubbles had sent Devraj an urgent letter saying that his grandmother was gravely ill and they should come to Jaipur as soon as possible. When Devraj and Lalitya arrived at Lily Pool they learned that Ayesha had been bedridden for weeks. 'She was indeed happy to see us, and promptly ordered supper. She barely ate but came down to the dining room in her wheelchair, it was nothing short of a miracle and the staff could hardly believe it as she had not been out from her room for over a week,' Devraj recalls.[30]

The grandchildren's visit to Jaipur marked the beginning of their reconciliation with their grandmother, with Bubbles playing a key role. 'Our grandmother urged us to go and visit Uncle Bubbles often, so going to the City Palace to have lunch with him at the Baradari Café was also our regular routine during those days,' says Devraj. 'She wanted us to be close to his care and protection.'[31] For the first time in years, Ayesha started visiting the City Palace, spending time with Bubbles and Padmini as well as their daughter, Diya, and her husband, Narendra. 'The old misunderstanding between us and our grandmother melted away, and Lalitya and I gradually tried to explain to her what had happened with regard to our late father's estate.'[32]

In November 2008, Devraj and Lalitya were summoned to Lily Pool. Barely a year and a half had passed since Ayesha had disinherited them. Only eight months previously they had accused their grandmother of acting with 'mala fide and oblique' motives to delay the issuing of a succession certificate and deny them their legal right to inherit their father's estate.[33] Now, in the presence of their lawyers, the three of them signed a settlement dividing Jagat's estate evenly among themselves. Ayesha pledged not to make any claim on Jagat's disputed will and to ask the courts to dispose of any matters arising out of any previous disputes. The meeting ended with the rajmata handing over Jagat's turban and sword to Devraj, symbolically making him his father's heir. Three months later the Jaipur district court ordered the issuing of a succession certificate on the basis of the settlement.

* * *

On a sunny Sunday afternoon in early February 2009, a 1937 blue-and-white Bentley with the numberplate 'Rajasthan 4' stood parked alongside a 1923 Austin Chummy, a 1947 Sunbeam Talbot convertible and a scrum of Rolls-Royces, Chevrolets, Cadillacs, E-Type Jaguars and other luxury makes on the lawns of the Jai Mahal Palace Hotel. Aside from the Jaipur polo season, the other fixture on the city's social calendar that Ayesha never missed was the Vintage and Classic Car Rally. The Bentley with its crystal rooster mascot designed by Lalique and silver polished door handles was a pre-wedding gift to her from Jai. Her favourite car, a white 1968 280S Mercedes Saloon that Jai had imported from

Spain using his diplomatic privileges, was also there, as was her 1956 Jaguar XK. Both cars normally sit in a garage behind Gem Palace on MI Road and are now owned by Sudhir Kasliwal, scion of the iconic 150-year-old jewellery store. An eighth-generation jeweller, Kasliwal is also the rally's organizer and vice president of the Rajputana Sports Car Club.

With a clientele ranging from curious Japanese tourists to Arab sheikhs, Gem Palace is arguably Jaipur's best-known non-royal landmark. Surrounded by photographs of regular clients, including Bill and Chelsea Clinton, the Mountbattens, Mick Jagger, Pierce Brosnan, Giorgio Armani, Lady Diana, Prince Andrew and numerous other greater and lesser royals, faded film stars and up-and-coming celebrities, Kasliwal reminisces about the many afternoons Ayesha used to spend in his showroom sipping coffee and talking about jewellery and cars. When he told her about the forthcoming car rally she accepted his invitation without hesitation. 'In my heart I thought, how can she come? She can barely walk. But she did. She came for both days.' Instead of being driven around the grounds of Jai Mahal, she made Sudhir push her wheelchair so she could personally inspect all the cars, including her own. 'That's the kind of spirit she had, even at her age and her condition.'[34]

As the sapping desert heat started to descend on Jaipur with its flame-thrower intensity, Ayesha began making plans for her annual pilgrimage to England. But before leaving there was some important business to attend to. On 27 April 2009, she wrote to the board of directors of the Jai Mahal Hotels Pvt. Ltd advising them that she had executed a deed transferring her entire shareholding in the company to her grandchildren. Whether Jagat's will was authentic or not no longer mattered. Its provisions were now effectively null and void.

Two weeks later, on the morning of 10 May 2009, Ayesha asked Bubbles to come to Lily Pool. Her personal secretary, Ayub Khan, remembers them spending half an hour together in her study with the door closed. He was then told to come in. As Khan sat at Ayesha's desk, they dictated her final will, which he typed out on the Lily Pool letterhead. Sipping tea on the lawn in front of Lily Pool, where he still works, Khan remembers the moment clearly. 'Gayatri Devi made her signature on the will, Bhawani Singh and I signed the document as witnesses,' he tells me. Titled 'My Last

Wish', it read: 'Life is uncertain so I wish to make provisions for my properties to avoid any disputes in the family. While revoking all previous Wills or codicils, now I declare that on my death all my properties, jewellery, cash including control of schools shall go to Devraj & Lalitya absolutely forever as per my this last wish. I am sure that H.H. Maharaja Bhawani Singh, Maharaj Prithvi Singh and Maharaj Jai Singh will give full support to my grandchildren by honouring my above wishes in all respect.'[35] 'She was perfectly in her senses,' says Khan, referring to the rajmata's mental condition. Nor was there any coercion involved. 'You can give her suggestions, but she was such a strong-willed lady that you cannot influence or guide her or dictate [to] her.'[36] The contents of the will were a game changer, but so too was the fact that Ayesha had asked Bubbles to help her draft it. Decades of acrimony had been set aside. Stepmother and stepson were now reconciled.

That evening Ayesha flew to New Delhi before boarding a flight for London. Prior to leaving she told Joey she believed the trip might be her last and she wanted to see her friends one more time.[37] Her doctors had warned her against going to England, which had been something of an annual pilgrimage, interrupted only during World War II and the years immediately afterwards. On her previous trips she had been accompanied by her maid or other staff. This time, she travelled alone.

Once again, her indefatigable energy saw her entertaining friends at her Cadogan Square flat, attending parties and watching polo at Cowdray Park and Windsor. In June, she co-hosted with Sir Evelyn de Rothschild and Sarah, Duchess of York, a fundraising event in London for Mark Shand's Elephant Family charity. The event, organized by the Indian philanthropists Priya and Cyrus Vandrevala, was to raise funds to buy land to protect endangered Asian elephant habitats. Shand and Rothschild were among her closest friends in London. It would be her final social engagement.

In early July, Ayesha complained of gastric trouble and was admitted to King Edward VII's Hospital in London. One of those who made regular visits as she lay in the intensive care unit was her old friend and confidant Momin Latif. Stoking the marble fireplace in his haveli overlooking the Qutb Minar to soften Delhi's winter chill and insisting on adding more whisky to my morning tea, Latif described her pitiful state. 'She was lying there. I felt so sorry for her twisted up in a corner. I asked: "How do you feel?" She said: "I'd love a whisky and I'd love a cigarette." I ran out to Marylebone Road and I got her twelve of those little bottles and I said to her: "I'm going to hide these under your pillow." She had one sip and one puff and ... in walks this dreadful English nurse. She yelled: "Who has been smoking in here!" I said: "I have and Her Highness has."' Latif gently suggested to the nurse that the rajmata be allowed the occasional indulgences. 'She's dying. There's no reprieve. It's a death sentence, so be kind, be human.'[38]

On 17 July, after fifteen days in intensive care during which time she ate no solid food, Ayesha was flown to Jaipur in an air ambulance accompanied by Pat. 'I called her from Thailand when she was in London. I could easily make out from her voice that she was unwell and was desperate to come back to Jaipur,' says Devraj. 'She said, "I am bored of the hospital and just want to go back to Jaipur. I want to see you there."'[39] Devraj and Lalitya flew from Bangkok to Jaipur, but when they saw her at the Santokba Durlabhji Memorial Hospital, she could hardly utter a word. Doctors in Jaipur detected obstructions in her intestines and cleared them with a stent, but she remained in intensive care for twelve days. By now the Indian media was reporting daily on her condition. A steady procession of well-wishers called on her, but many of the staff who had worked for her and Jai over the decades were prevented from saying their good-byes.[40] On Tuesday, 28 July, S.C. Kalla, the doctor in charge, told reporters she had requested to be allowed to go home as her condition had improved, but later in the evening she complained of breathlessness. 'She was having breathing problems since Tuesday night. Around 10 this morning, we put her on a ventilator. But, her condition deteriorated later in the day after a blood clot blocked the vessels in her lungs.'[41]

The third wife of Sawai Man Singh II and India's most recognizable royal died at around 4 p.m. on Wednesday, 29 July 2009 in the presence of her grandchildren and stepsons. She was ninety. The same apartment in the zenana deorhi of the City Palace that had been arranged for her when she arrived as Jai's wife almost seventy years earlier became her final resting place. Her dying wishes had included having a pedicure and listening to her favourite Frank

Sinatra songs. 'Bhawani ensured all the respect was given to her and he personally monitored all the arrangements,' Ayesha's close friend Tripti Pandey recalls.[42]

The following day thousands of mourners lined the route from the City Palace through Tripolia Bazaar, Badi Chaupar, Hawa Mahal Bazar and Chandi ki Taksal in the walled city, many climbing on to shop terraces to get a better view. As the two elephants leading the procession emerged from City Palace, followed by a column of royal guards on foot, a brass band and members of 61 Cavalry on horses, the city's busy markets came to a standstill. Traders emerged from their shops and threw rose petals at the decorated military truck on which the rajmata's body had been laid. The silence of the crowd was broken only by occasional shouts of 'Maharani ki Jai' as the procession made its way to the cremation ground at Maharaniyon ki Chhatri on Amber Road. To the sound of priests chanting Vedic hymns, Bubbles lit the funeral pyre. Police and army squads presented salutes and reversed their arms as a mark of respect. Those present included government ministers and dozens of titular rulers of the erstwhile princely states. Thousands more people waited outside as a forty-gun salute sounded. Two days later, Devraj immersed his grandmother's ashes in the Ganges at Haridwar. Across on the other side of India, the communist government of West Bengal declared a public holiday as a mark of respect.

Newspapers in India and around the world mourned the passing of the 'Desert Queen'. An obituary in the *New York Times* described her as 'one of the last remaining symbols of India's feudal past'. Her life had been one 'of novelistic dimensions, part E.M. Forster, part Jackie Collins'.[43] The *Times* of London labelled her a woman who 'had it all: Swiss education, schooling in England, hunting, riding, European summers, social seasons in Paris, a palace with 500 staff— and beauty'.[44] 'She was a princess, and a princess who could make Jackie Kennedy appear almost a frump,' declared *The Economist*.[45]

In one of her last interviews before her death, Ayesha declared she had 'no regrets'. 'I'm not a nostalgic person. I live in the present. I just try to do what I can, when I see unhappiness around me. Why grumble about things that don't go your way. Make the most of life. Don't make me sound arrogant or extraordinary.'[46]

* * *

After speaking to dozens of friends, family members and employees, after numerous rereadings of *A Princess Remembers* and a forensic perusal of her public statements, I still feel conflicted about the late rajmata. There was much about her memoir that I found disturbing, in particular her almost indifferent attitude to the many tragedies that beset her life—aside, of course, from the deaths of Jai, Jagat and her mother, Indira. It is as if she shed her physical purdah but was incapable of removing her emotional one, denying the reader any sense of real intimacy. The daughter of Indira Devi, the most liberated Indian princess of the twentieth century, never once questions her husband's orders or her role as his third wife. Nor does she take issue with his philandering. That the memoir was ghost-written by Santha Rama Rau clearly had a sanitizing effect, as did her need for privacy. 'The more you kept your distance the more she respected you,' says Timmie Kumar, executive director of the Clarks Amer Hotel in Jaipur, before adding: 'Jaipur without Gayatri Devi is not really Jaipur. She loved this city ... She had grace, dignity, intellect, and a wonderful sense of humour.'[47]

Such opinions are commonplace among those to whom she extended her regal hand of friendship. Prem 'Gudu' Patnaik, a Delhi-based industrialist and brother of Odisha chief minister Naveen Patnaik, takes a more nuanced view, remembering her as being 'prone to pettiness' and at times 'quite impervious'. She was also used to getting her own way, he adds, from masterminding the marriage of Bubbles and Padmini to demanding that guests attending her fancy dress parties got changed if she did not approve of their costumes. But, like others, he lauds her style and panache. 'Jai was zero. She brought the glamour and the class.'[48]

Historian, architectural restorer and hotelier Aman Nath, who collaborated with Ayesha on a number of projects, describes her as a 'conqueress' with several well-aimed weapons at her disposal. 'She wore her beauty like an ancestral brooch, a physical chip on her bony shoulder. Most often, this first layer was enough for instant victory: at Cooch Behar, Calcutta, London, wherever she went, victory was close at hand. Her stature as Jaipur Maharani number three only added a new halo to her angelic beauty. The other Maharanis just ceased to exist.' Born a princess and well trained in etiquette, her second sword of conquest was her informed conversations carried out with a range of affectations. 'She knew what and how to say it and usually bullied her opinions on others. Her Hindi was spoken only in masculine gender, much as the British memsahibs did, and her French was used not so much to communicate but for social intimidation.' Her other weapon was 'snubbery for snobbery. She could ignore people into oblivion.' Adds Nath: 'Anachronistic as it may sound, Ayesha was the most stubborn chameleon of our times, as endearing as she was annoying, a grand royal who could be commoner than most commoners. I don't think she forgave anyone easily, but when it was prudent she preferred to be conveniently forgetful. Her life had taught her that. This was to remain her strength in the changing times she straddled like a female colossus. In her estimation *she* was Jaipur—and indeed there was that international moment when she was. Then time passed her by.'[49]

To me Ayesha remains an enigma—and I have no doubt that she liked to project herself that way. She could be arrogant and opinionated but detested such traits in other people. Entitled and self-absorbed, she nevertheless worked for the betterment of women and the rights of her constituents. 'There was intense resentment against Ayesha when she came to Jaipur. She was not royal enough or, as they defined it, she was too modern,' says Kishore Singh. 'Her entry into politics added to her confidence and stature among the people, but her acceptance across the Rajput community was a long time coming. Ladies would emulate her style, but constantly diss her for how she did her hair, for the fact she smoked and wore slacks.'[50]

To her credit she could sometimes be generous to a fault. In 1965, Amancio D'Silva, a Goanese guitar player who cut his teeth in Bombay playing at Parsi weddings and local clubs with Nellie and her Swing Band, arrived in Jaipur with his Irish-born wife, Joyce. When Ayesha saw him performing at the Rambagh Palace Hotel (his signature style combined jazz guitar with ragas) she made him her 'court musician'. While travelling to the United States, she bought D'Silva his first Western-made instrument, a Gibson guitar. Shortly after their son, Stephano, was born, he was diagnosed with a rare blood condition and was constantly in and out of hospital. Ayesha suggested that the family seek treatment in England and paid for

Stephano's medical expenses as well as the move. His father's career blossomed and Stephano himself went on to become an accomplished musician.[51]

Ayesha's memoir, in which she comes across as unblemished as her studio-portrait complexion, masks other contradictions. Her decade-long stint in politics and her incarceration in Tihar Jail are convincing portrayals of self-sacrifice in the name of civic duty whereas her motives were much more complex and not always for the benefit of the Swatantra Party. She claimed to believe in democracy while defending feudal privileges, seemingly oblivious of their incompatibility. Both she and Jai were obsessed with cultivating their rich and aristocratic friends in the West. How much more could they have done individually and collectively had they spent more time in Jaipur? In assessing the rajmata's legacy I am drawn back to a remark she made to Ann Morrow in the mid-1980s when, after a particularly lavish party, she told the writer: 'We are the real India.'[52] Her comment reflects what the journalist Madhu Trehan once described as Ayesha's 'often alarming naivete as well as blind loyalty to her class and kind. She seems completely ignorant, one suspects deliberately so, of the economic connection of her position.'[53]

The atmosphere of sycophancy that pervaded the Jaipur durbar was hardly conducive to self-reflection and there is little evidence that Jai was any less ignorant of the realities that underpinned their privileged existence. Their formative years came at a time when feudalism was well entrenched. 'Before Independence, the princely states of Rajasthan like Jaipur and Udaipur were essentially "of the Rajputs, by the Rajputs, for the Rajputs",' says the historian Akshay Chavan. 'Other communities had very few rights or privileges.'[54] In Ayesha's case, there was little incentive to change her attitudes or her lifestyle following Jai's death or after the abolition of the privy purses. The people still trusted her, she told Morrow—letting slip another revealing comment that underlined her limited capacity for contemplating a time when the lifestyles of Indian royals would be replicated only in museums.

11

'A TYPICAL PALACE INTRIGUE'

Ayesha's last journey from the City Palace to the ghats of Haridwar briefly quelled a combustible combination of litigation and personal animosity that had come to define internecine relations in the House of Jaipur. But even before her ashes had floated a few kilometres down the Ganges on their way to the river's confluence with the sea in the Bay of Bengal, the acrimony resurfaced. Each death in the family had created a new skirmish. Jai had died intestate, precipitating a legal dispute over whether Bubbles would be heir to his fortune or whether it should be divided equally among his offspring. Jagat had also died intestate, or so it seemed until a will surfaced a decade later that disinherited his children, who claimed it was a forgery. Now Ayesha had died leaving a will whose contents were known only to the two men who had witnessed it—Bubbles and her private secretary, Ayub Khan. The twelve-day period of mourning, when a dead person's family was expected to respectfully offer prayers for the departed, for themselves and for their household, counted for nothing. Battle lines were being redrawn. Motives were being questioned. Loyalties cast aside.

In his study of Jaipur state, Robert Stern noted how the negative aspects of the Rajput ethos came to the fore as rival power centres scrambled to fill the vacuum caused by the collapsing Mughal empire:

> Wherever it was possible and in every possible combination and permutation, Rajput clansmen and non-clansmen, princes and princes, princes and barons, barons and barons did violence to one another and on behalf of one another. They seized one another's

lands and defended them, laid waste to another's estates and died protecting them, honoured and defamed one another, rescued and betrayed one another and in glorious battle met and mangled one another. They fought over land and honour because they were warriors.[1]

Three centuries later, the spoils had changed, no blood was being spilled and the arena of conflict had shifted to the law courts, but the same Byzantine tropes of usurpation, betrayal and dishonour remained. Now with Ayesha's death, all sides were honing their tactics for the next assault.

A week after lighting his grandmother's funeral pyre, Devraj broke his silence, telling the *Times of India* that he would remain in Jaipur until all the formalities relating to her death had been completed. 'I have been overwhelmed by the support that I received from the nobles and distant relations of the family in these sad and testing hours. I have no idea whether Rajmata Gayatri Devi has left a will and who is the executor. We shall cross the bridge when it comes, and we are not giving any thought on it.'[2] Devraj's statement was his attempt to deflect attention from the unseemly behaviour of individuals closely connected to his grandmother. Some reports claimed that the looting of Lily Pool started the moment Ayesha's air ambulance landed in Jaipur on 17 July and that its rooms, except the one where Devraj was staying, had been sealed. Other reports spoke of her prized polo ponies being sold at auction and of valuables being spirited away. On 4 August, a wall suddenly appeared, blocking access to Lily Pool's swimming pool. Devraj refused to comment on the construction, but a palace source told the *Economic Times* it was erected mainly to stop occupants of Lily Pool's servants' quarters going to the Rambagh Palace.[3] Around the same time, locks were placed on the gate leading from Lily Pool to Rambagh. Some saw it as a land grab by parties connected with the hotel operators. Complicating matters was an ongoing legal dispute with the JDA, which had acquired part of the land adjacent to Lily Pool in 1993. The case was before the Delhi High Court but had barely progressed for more than a decade.

On Sunday, 9 August, the twelfth and final day of mourning, family members and invited guests observed the rang ka dastur in the courtyard of the City Palace. Nobles and well-wishers filed into the palace, with men and women taking up separate places to watch the ceremonies. Three pandits performed the final rituals before replacing Bubbles's white turban with a saffron one reserved for the maharaja. Devraj, Diya's husband, Narendra, and Pat's son, Vijit, then replaced their turbans with yellow headgear to mark the official end to the mourning period.

Kept away from the ceremonies and forced to wait in the sodden monsoon heat outside the City Palace were dozens of increasingly impatient journalists. Rumours that Ayesha's will would be read out on the final day of mourning had been sweeping Jaipur since her cremation. Estimates of the value of Ayesha's estate ranged from From almost ninety million pounds to 180 million pounds, with the value of her jewellery adding another thirty million pounds to the potential jackpot. But as darkness descended on the walled city, it became increasingly unlikely that an announcement would be made. 'Twelfth-day ceremonies are meant to overcome sad days of demise,' Lokendra Singh Kalvi, a thakur who had attended the rang ka dastur, said angrily as he left the palace, brushing aside the sweaty scrum of waiting reporters. 'It's [the] media that coined the will matter.'[4] Ayesha's lawyer G.K. Garg hosed down conjecture about the value of her estate, pointing out that only those properties handed over to her through gift deeds by Jai could be considered as her private property and could be named in her will. Much of that property had already been disposed of during her lifetime. 'She has gifted much of the land of the Moti Doongri hillocks to a trust, while the Lily Pool is apparently a part of Rambagh given to her on a ninety-nine-year lease,' Garg explained.[5]

On 20 August, Devraj and Lalitya faced the media at Lily Pool. This time it was Lalitya's turn to read out a brief statement. 'In order to put an end to all speculations we would like to announce that our grandmother Rajmata Gayatri Deviji left behind her last "Will" in favour of us, giving us all her properties and rights. We are also the only natural legal heirs entitled to succeed to her estate ... and the same is in the knowledge of all family members. We sincerely hope to receive full support of all family members—Brig Bhawani Singh, Prithviraj and Jai Singh.'[6] She concluded by saying: 'We have been told by our family elders to speak this much only.'[7]

Once again, what appeared to be a cut-and-dried case contained the seeds of its self-destruction. Although the will was clear about

Devraj and Lalitya being the sole inheritors of their grandmother's estate, it lacked any detail as to what that estate comprised. When asked how the grandchildren would know what they had inherited, Devraj and Lalitya's lawyer D.K. Malhotra explained that a list of the moveable and immovable properties ought to be provided by Pat, who had had the power of attorney for both Ayesha and Jagat when they were alive. The brothers had 'been successful in their mischief when the Rajmata was not well', Malhotra added. 'Her step-son Bhawani Singh was not well. The children were kept away in Thailand. They [Pat and Joey] have enjoyed others' inheritance.' The onus was on Pat to provide an account of Ayesha's properties and papers. 'We will take action if he does not. It is an offence under Indian law punishable by ten years in jail,' Malhotra warned.[8] Commenting on the appearance of the will, Pat refuted the claim that 'all family members' had knowledge of it, saying that the first he knew about its contents was when he saw a news report on television. 'If the will is in their favour it's good. They are her grandchildren and she [Rajmata] had every right to decide in their favour,' he told *Daily News & Analysis*.[9]

Despite Pat's conciliatory tone, Devraj accused his uncle of actively working against him. 'I think he would rather I was not here. There is a lot for him to gain if I am not around,' he told Andrew Buncombe of the *Independent*. His uncle had not expected that Ayesha would pass her estate on to her grandchildren. 'There was a time when there was a rift between ourselves and her. Everyone was surprised by her last move, not just the uncles,' Devraj said. 'The end of an era for our family was with the death of my grandfather in 1970 and since then, for each branch of the family, the survival instinct has been to get as many resources as possible. That leads to collective downfall.' To underline how far the family had fallen, Devraj took Buncombe to a garage at the front of Lily Pool. Protected by canvas covers were his grandmother's baby-blue Bentley, believed to have been built in the 1920s, and her 1949 Jaguar sports car. Shrugging his shoulders he said to Buncombe, 'My uncle has the keys to these.'[10]

Taking the keys of the rajmata's vintage cars was just the first volley in what was about to become a no-holds-barred brawl for dozens of ancestral properties, company shares, family trusts and even the garbage left behind in Ayesha's London flat. Court summons would be ripped up as soon as they were served, allegations of judges being bribed were traded like volleys on Rambagh's tennis courts and grievances were hung out to dry like soiled dupattas for the media and their scandal-hungry consumers to ogle at.

On 15 February 2010, Pat's legal team served a notice on Devraj and Lalitya to vacate Lily Pool, their grandmother's home for the last three decades of her life. Pat claimed he was in possession of a deed signed in 1977 between Ayesha and the Rambagh Hotel Pvt. Ltd according to which she agreed to pay 3,000 rupees per month as rent for five years and was to vacate the property after the deed lapsed. Her grandchildren had until 15 May 2010 to pack up and leave, failing which legal action would follow and they would be held liable to pay 50,000 rupees per month as rent. Devraj and Lalitya responded by rubbishing the rent deed's legal standing. They warned Pat that any action he took against them on the basis of his notice 'will solely be on your risk and consequences'.[11]

In April 2010, Ayesha's apartment at Cadogan Square in London was listed on the property market. It was prime London real estate, a stone's throw from Harrods and a favourite hangout for despots like Muammar Gaddafi and the billionaire Indian fugitive Lalit Modi. The Rothschild Trust put the flat on the market for an asking price of £2.1 million, somewhat below the average of £3.7 million for property in the area. Once sold, Bubbles, Pat and Joey were entitled to 25 per cent each, with Jagat's children splitting the 25 per cent that would have gone to him had he still been alive. Wanting to see the flat one more time, Priya and Devraj flew to London only to find it empty. 'I went into her bedroom and I could smell her lingering perfume there. Everything had been packed up very hurriedly and sent into storage,' says Priya. When they were finally able to sort through her belongings in 2017, they found that six of the twenty-one containers contained rubbish—even avocado seeds had been wrapped carefully in tissue paper.[12] Many of Ayesha's most precious belongings had allegedly gone missing but her full-length portrait by the Italian painter Pietro Annigoni was still there.

* * *

Until the mid-1990s the main protagonists in the litigation wars had been the heads of the three branches of the Jaipur family: Bubbles, Pat and Jagat. But with the death of Jagat and Ayesha, the declining health of Bubbles and the appearance of new wills and succession certificates, the zones of combat had been redrawn. Devraj and his sister were now fighting Pat on several fronts, the main one being the ownership of shares in the Jai Mahal and Rambagh properties which was before the CLB. Now a new flank was about to open and a new litigant or 'bounty hunter', as one royal spectator put it, was entering the fray.

Urvashi Devi was the sixty-year-old daughter of Bubbles's sister, Prem Kumari, or Mickey. It was her mother's wedding to Maharaja Jaideep Singh, the ruler of the former princely state of Devgadh-Baria in eastern Gujarat, that had earned a *Guinness Book of Records* mention for its extravagance. Known in the family as 'Princess Bambi', Urvashi was a Congress party politician who had served as tourism and environment minister in the Gujarat government. She was also an animal lover. To mark the twenty-fifth anniversary of her father's death, she organized a dog show, presenting her prized miniature schnauzers and Caucasian sheepdogs. Recently she had given sanctuary to 197 abandoned donkeys in a reserve adjacent to her palace, where they were regally fed on a diet of chana churi, wheat flakes and green and dry fodder twice a day. She was with Pat when Ayesha was hospitalized in London. The rajmata, she said, had been her inspiration for joining politics.

On 1 May 2010, Urvashi joined Pat in filing a petition before the sessions court at Jaipur, disputing Ayesha's will and claiming a share in Jai's properties. In addition to what were now well-rehearsed arguments that Jagat had been adopted by the ruler of Isarda and that he had disinherited his children in 1996, they charged Devraj and Lalitya of taking advantage of their dying grandmother to force her to sign a document she did not understand. They told the court that the rajmata had been unable to talk or walk when she allegedly signed the will and that her estate could not have been bequeathed to her grandchildren because 'of the hostile relationships that they shared'. They also argued that the will should have been witnessed by Pat, who was her power of attorney, rather than Bubbles and Ayub Khan. 'In such a situation the aforesaid settlement is clearly proved to be manipulated, concocted and fabricated.'[13]

Devraj's response to the petition filed by the 'Urvashi Group', as it was known in court parlance, was to argue that his father, Jagat, had always remained a part of the HUF of Sawai Man Singh II and not of his elder brother, Bahadur, the thakur of Isarda. For Pat to claim otherwise, Devraj argued, was misleading the court. Countering the allegation that the rajmata was mentally unsound when she made her will, he presented evidence about a series of public functions she actively participated in between December 2008 and March 2009.[14]

The new legal case cast a pall over the first anniversary of Ayesha's death. Absent from the prayer meeting organized by her grandchildren were Pat and his son, Vijit. In London a special service marking the anniversary proceeded without rancour, with most participants unaware of the enmity clouding Ayesha's legacy back in Jaipur. The Gayatri Mantra was sung by an English soprano, while Joey, representing the Jaipur family, read verses from the *Bhagavad Gita*. Lord Patrick Beresford of the Guard's Polo Club, one of Ayesha's closest friends, recounted numerous anecdotes before taking a stab at Indira Gandhi for locking her up during the Emergency 'in a stinking hole with a drain running through her cell'. His choice of music for the occasion included 'The Flower Song' from *Carmen* by Bizet and the 'Waltz' and the 'Dance of the Swans' from Tchaikovsky's *Swan Lake*. Mark Shand delivered readings from the Corinthians, Chapter 13. The congregation then filed out of the church to the accompaniment of three of the rajmata's best-loved Frank Sinatra classics: 'Moon River', 'A Nightingale Sang in Berkeley Square' and 'My Way'. She had chosen the songs during her appearance on BBC Radio's *Desert Island Discs* programme in 1984.[15]

Once again, the solemnity of the anniversary quickly gave way to squalidness as litigation intensified and accusations flew. The succession certificate dividing Jagat's estate three ways issued by a lower court on 19 February 2009 was challenged by the Urvashi group on the ground that it ignored various property disputes pending before the high court. That tactic failed when a month later the Rajasthan High Court dismissed their challenge to strike down the succession certificate. Despite the high court's ruling, Devraj and Lalitya's position was still precarious. Having spent most of their lives in Thailand, they were considered outsiders in Jaipur. For the past two years, they had relied on Bubbles and his family to negotiate the jungle of lawsuits and palace intrigues. Now that support network was about to collapse.

In late March 2011, Bubbles was admitted to a hospital in Gurgaon, suffering from high blood pressure and a lung infection. Already frail after a heart attack and a series of strokes over the past several years, his condition steadily worsened. He died of multiple organ failure at around 1 a.m. on 17 April, aged seventy-nine.

The body of Jaipur's last maharaja was brought home in a motor-cade and was laid out in the courtyard of Chandra Mahal at the City Palace dressed in his military uniform. Less than two years after the death of his stepmother, a now familiar parade of nobility, celebrity and friends filed through Tripolia Gate to pay their respects. Once again, the normally hectic bazaars around the City Palace came to a halt as thousands of people watched the gun carriage with his body slowly wind its way through the walled city and then to Gaitore, the royal cremation ground. As an army bugler sounded the 'Last Post', twelve-year-old Padmanabh, wearing a white bandhgala and turban, lit his grandfather's funeral pyre. Watching the flames consume the body was a particularly poignant moment for Devraj and Lalitya. Bubbles had given them a refuge in Jaipur and supported their legal battles. Now they were on their own. 'I cried. I lost my durbar, my head, not just my uncle,' says Devraj.[16]

The funeral prompted an outpouring of reminiscences about a humble man who in the 1960s was instantly recognizable in the streets of New Delhi driving his white Ford Thunderbird convert-ible. 'Army was his life. He was in touch with his regiment after retirement,' said Colonel V.S. Chandraval, who served alongside Bubbles in 10 Para Brigade. 'He would shake hands with all the 300 soldiers.'[17] Kuldeep Singh Garcha, whom Bubbles had pilloried years before because of his close relationship with Ayesha, praised the man who had mentored him early in his polo career. 'As a human being, he never let the child in him die. He was very com-fortable with the aam aadmi [common man] ... He was one of the best human beings. It's an irreparable loss'.[18] Digvijay Singh, secre-tary of the Rajasthan Polo Club, described him as a 'godfather for polo across the globe. Such was his renown that everybody would ask about him at polo events ... He never used to isolate himself from the team. He would eat with them, play with them, and would even take them along on his social dos. Whatever exposure we have got today is totally because of him.'[19]

* * *

To many in Jaipur, the death of Ayesha and Bubbles signalled the end of an era. Bubbles was the last prince to be recognized as a maharaja before such titles were officially abolished. Ayesha was not the last of India's maharanis, but her life story had made her perhaps the most enduring symbol of princely India. But only the most nostalgic royals were prepared to accept what happened next.

On the twelfth day of mourning, royalty from all over Rajasthan, local and national politicians and the family's priests, closely followed by a press pack, descended on the City Palace for the raj tilak, or coronation ceremony, of the class eight Mayo College schoolboy, Padmanabh Singh. After the family's head priest marked his forehead with vermilion, the newly anointed maharaja, accompanied by two liveried attendants holding fly whisks and another carrying a decorated parasol to protect his head from the glaring sun, inspected a guard of honour. The flags of the Kachchwaha dynasty that had been at half-mast were hoisted again above the City Palace amid the sounding of drums. A customary visit to the zenana to seek the blessings of the ladies of the royal family was followed by prayers at the Govind Devji temple.

By law the title Padmanabh inherited meant nothing, its only value measured in the gravitas it generated among his peers and the tourist spending it might bring. He was the heir to a rich lived history, but as Kishore Singh noted at the time, India's princely line 'probably deserves the same endangered World Heritage status as an architectural site, or natural wonder'.[20] The new 'Maharaja's' unpretentiousness was highlighted. His tutor at Mayo described him as an ordinary boy who performed well in classes and at sport. 'Padmanabh Singh has no airs of being a royal,' Yash Saxena said. 'He is down to earth and has adapted very well. He mixes very well with all other students, and his classmates are very fond of him.'[21] In a 2018 interview Padmanabh credited Mayo for defining his character. 'It was a tough life with strict discipline and no luxuries. We had a dormitory of ten, with just one slow-moving fan in the room in peak summers. Then we used to have army camps in July at places full of mosquitoes, and I would spend my birthday there. I was a chubby little kid with my fancy shirts signed by Ronaldo. Nobody at the school has any privileges, the family backgrounds do not matter and then you get teased because you are so-and-so.'[22]

Others, however, criticized the first such ceremony in Jaipur in more than forty years as regressive and feudal. 'The incident was highly repulsive and deserved condemnation as all the privileges including the titles of the former rulers were done away with through a Constitutional amendment some four decades ago,' said R.K. Pant, former head of the history department in the University of Rajasthan. Joining the chorus was the historian and author Dr Ram Pandey, who called it 'a naked and vulgar dance of feudalism'.[23]

India's princes may have been consigned to the dustbin of history, but the clash of tradition and modernity had yet to run its course. In the late spring of 2013, another coronation sparked a further controversy. This time it was the turn of Diya and Narendra's nine-year-old son, Laksh Raj, to become the titular Maharaja of Sirmaur. Laksh Raj's ascent to Sirmaur's throne was courtesy of his maternal grandmother, Padmini Devi, the daughter of the last ruler of Sirmaur, Rajendra Prakash. On 13 April, Padmini held a small tikka ceremony at the City Palace, where her grandson's paternal gotra was changed from 'Manav' to 'Attri' of the Sirmaur dynasty. It was followed a month later by a formal coronation at Nahan, the capital of the former sub-Himalayan princely state.

Enter, once again, the murky world of adoption and succession— a Jaipur speciality made more complicated by multiple wives and no male heirs. Rajendra Prakash died in 1964 without a male successor despite having two wives, Durga Devi and Indira Devi, who was Padmini's mother. Durga Devi's daughter, Nalini, had one son, Udai Prakash, who claimed he had been adopted by Durga Devi in 1965 and was therefore the rightful heir to the late maharaja's properties. 'Hindu law and custom does not allow a daughter to declare a successor to her father once she is married into another family. She can do so in regard to her own property and family that is in Jaipur alone,' Udai Prakash told the *Pioneer* from his home at Sirmaur House in Dehradun on learning that a nine-year-old schoolboy was about to usurp him. 'Ever since her marriage into the Jaipur Royal Family, [Padmini] has neglected her part of the Nahan Palace and has brought it to a state of ruin. She has barely visited Nahan four or five times in the past four decades,' he alleged. Udai Prakash also claimed that during the past thirty years Padmini had jointly contested a number of property cases where she had admitted he was the late maharaja's adopted son and heir. 'She was with me against all adversaries and now those adversaries have gone over to her side and are supporting her in her bid to declare her grandson the crown prince of Nahan. She cannot legally adopt a second grandson as she has already adopted Padmanabh Singh, Laksh Raj's elder brother,' he said, adding that both the central ministries of law and home affairs had recognized him as Rajendra Prakash's successor.[24] What he neglected to mention was that two other relatives had also staked their claim to the late maharaja's property. Brushing aside the controversy, Padmini went ahead with the ceremony in Nahan, which was graced by the usual swathe of dignitaries and celebrities including, most newspapers noted, the Bollywood actress Dimple Kapadia.

Padmini's insistence on first Padmanabh's and then Laksh Raj's ascension to the 'thrones' of two erstwhile princely states reflects the steely resolve of the dowager rajmata. Her first priority has been protecting her family's interests, even if it has meant going to court to pursue her aims. Palace insiders speak of a woman who spends long hours playing cards and enjoys partying and dancing to Michael Jackson tunes until the early hours of the morning. At her surprise seventy-fifth birthday party in September 2018, guests wore masks of their favourite actors and actresses from the 1950s as she arrived. 'Hand-engraved perfume jars, cut-glass decanters, silver hand mirrors and delicate hand fans were subtly incorporated in the decor, and the royal crest was embroidered onto cushions and napery too. The evening was scented by oversized bouquets of tuberoses, which, as it turns out, are her favourite flower,' *Vogue* magazine reported.[25] Among the invitees were her best friends: Amitabh and Jaya Bachchan, the designer Farah Khan Ali, the actor and politician Beena Kak, the playback singer Kanika Kapoor as well as Jyotiraditya and Priyadarshini Scindia of the Gwalior royal family.

* * *

With both her sons now appending their royal titles on their school report cards, it was Diya's turn to step into the limelight. A decorative arts graduate, she turned her attention to the City Palace's museum and its galleries, sprucing up displays and refreshing its website. Education was another priority. In 2001, she had established the Palace School, whose curriculum was based on the Montessori system. Now she set her sights on starting another school on a thirteen-acre site near the airport, to be named after her father. When not attending fashion launches, giving away trophies at polo matches or flagging off vintage car rallies, she dedicated herself to her charities. At an event organized by the Eye Bank Society of Rajasthan, she announced she would be an eye donor. A few weeks later, flash bulbs popped as she graced a clinic to fit twenty-five amputees with the 'Jaipur Foot'. She was now the chairperson of the Rajasthan chapter of the business grouping ASSOCHAM. In New Delhi she organized an exhibition called Treasures of Rajasthan with Vivek Nair of the Leela Group of Hotels. Jaded Jaipurians smelled a political career was in the offing. They were right.

Diya's first experience of politics was as an eighteen-year-old campaigning for her father during the 1989 parliamentary elections when he lost to the BJP. She was a fast learner. 'The campaigning experience with my father would surely help me and I would take care of the mistakes that he unconsciously committed during the elections that led to his defeat. And his biggest mistake was contesting the elections on a Congress ticket,' she said in an interview in September 2013.[26]

A few days earlier, Diya had stood before a crowd of 200,000 people at Amrudo ka Bagh in Jaipur, sharing the stage with the chief minister of Gujarat, Narendra Modi, and Vasundhara Raje, the BJP's opposition leader in the Rajasthan legislative assembly. Wearing a sky blue and crimson sari she bowed gracefully before Modi as she was officially inducted into the party. Standing alongside her was another star Rajasthani Rajput recruit for the saffron cause, the 2004 Olympic silver medallist Rajyavardhan Singh Rathore. Modi was in a fighting mood and roused the crowd with a forty-five-minute-long speech in which he tore into the Congress-led UPA government for its 'rampant corruption and irresponsible governance'. A week later he would be chosen as the BJP's prime ministerial candidate in the 2014 Lok Sabha elections and would win his seat of Vadodara by more than half a million votes. Diya's entry into politics was fast-tracked by Vasundhara Raje, whose father had been the Maharaja of Gwalior. Raje's mother, Vijayaraje Scindia, had spent months in Tihar Jail with Ayesha during the Emergency. Now their descendants were standing shoulder to shoulder to contest the upcoming assembly elections—Diya from Sawai Madhopur and Vasundhara from Jhalrapatan. 'Vasundhara Raje has been a great inspiration for all the women in the state and for me in Rajasthan,' Diya explained shortly after her induction. Asked why she opted to join the BJP rather than the Congress, the forty-two-year-old said the Congress party had 'become synonymous with corruption and scams. It is not the party which Rajiv Gandhi led.'[27] Her main objective in entering politics was 'to serve the people ... I shall do whatever the party high command considers the best for me.'[28]

What Diya lacked in campaigning skills was more than made up by a political spin machine that sought to strike the perfect balance between her royal roots and her common touch. Childhood, the electorate was told, was spent in army cantonments where her father was posted, or in a 'simple flat in Delhi'. 'It was only in Jaipur during vacations that I experienced the palace life. I am just as much a commoner as anyone else.'[29] A besotted media, charmed by her film-star looks and sophisticated fashion sense, spent more time describing her diet than her policies. By night she would rest in the family's former hunting lodge, now a Taj-run five-star hotel, outside Ranthambore National Park, but by day she eschewed her packed lunches for desi khana washed down with sticky sweet chai. 'My meals take place in the villagers' homes. I don't even carry bottled water,' she told the *Telegraph* after lunching on bajre ki roti, sagora and lahsun ki chatni at the home of a poor Gujjar family.[30]

Diya's chief opponent in Sawai Madhopur was Kirori Lal Meena, a veteran politician who had fallen out with Vasundhara's cabinet during the last election over ticket distribution. His National People's Party, an alliance of tribal leaders, BJP rebels and Congress dissidents, was determined to fight elections in at least 150 out of the 200 seats up for grabs. Meena was widely described as a potential 'kingmaker' in the formation of the next government. Early on in the campaign, Diya's poll prospects were boosted when she received the backing of the Rajput Sabha. Nearly fifteen years after the organization had tried to excommunicate her for marrying within her gotra, she was being seen as a standard bearer for the state's Rajputs. 'The gotra issue was a dispute within the community. But when a person from our community was fielded from the seat, how could we vote for a person from another caste or religion? We held a meeting with the samaj leaders and decided to support her. The gotra row has taken a back seat,' Raghuveer Singh Rajawat, the district president of the All India Kshatriya Mahasabha, said.[31] Rajputs made up only 10 per cent or so of Sawai Madhopur's electorate, but their support would prove crucial. Diya won her seat by a narrow margin of 7,000 votes. State-wide, the BJP won in a landslide, picking up a staggering 162 seats. Vasundhara Raje was sworn in as chief minister.

* * *

The electoral contest was a welcome distraction from the court disputes that continued along their unpredictable course. If there is one certainty about the Indian legal system, it is that no judgement is necessarily final. Jai's death intestate had, like a butterfly's beating wings, triggered a storm that was refusing to abate. Since the first hearings over the division of Jai's estate began in 1986, tens of thousands of pages of court documents had been added to the files of half a dozen courts. Some of the lawyers who had first taken on the initial cases had retired, as had some of the judges who had heard their plaints. In the case of the litigants, three had died, new ones had been added and allegiances had taken complete U-turns. But that did not stop the wheels of justice, however bent or broken, from moving on.

On 23 September 2015, corks popped as bottles of Cristal Champagne were poured into fluted glasses at Priya's Bangkok residence. It was time to get out the caviar. The trigger for the celebration was the Supreme Court's ruling that Devraj and Lalitya were their grandmother's rightful heirs. Jagat's 1996 will in favour of his mother was 'beyond any dispute' and Ayesha's grandchildren derived rights in the royal estate from the succession documents validly executed by their grandmother. In a scathing judgement, Justices Anil R. Dave and Adarsh Kumar Goel ruled that the Urvashi group 'abused its position' to deprive the children of their rights.[32] Commenting on the ruling, Devraj said his uncles had committed a grave mistake believing that he and his sister were not Indians and therefore not entitled to inherit anything in India. 'Their vicious plan did not work,' he said. Without their uncles' knowledge, they had become Overseas Citizens of India, giving them the same rights as any citizen except for owning farmland and voting. 'It was our trump card.'[33]

Two years later another judgement further put to rest the questions over their grandmother's estate. On 10 December 2017, the Delhi High Court ruled in favour of Devraj and Lalitya, confirming that they were the legal heirs to her property irrespective of the contents of Jagat's will. All that was left now was for the National Company Law Tribunal (NCLT) to once again take up the matter of the dilution of Jagat's shares in the three properties managed by the Taj Group—the Rambagh Palace, the Jai Mahal and the Sawai Madhopur Lodge. In 2012, the Delhi High Court had ordered the rectification of shares in the royal family's firms in Devraj and Lalitya's favour. But the Urvashi group had appealed to the Supreme Court, which put the rectification on hold. If the NCLT decided in their favour, Devraj and Lalitya would secure ownership of Jai Mahal and get a greater share in the other properties.

Company insolvencies and fraudulent share transactions leave little room for poetic licence. But on 1 August 2018, when R. Varadharajan delivered the NCLT's final order on the Jai Mahal dispute, he couldn't resist making a metaphorical swipe at both parties for their conduct. The case before him was nothing other than: 'A typical palace intrigue, in this case involving the royal family of Jaipur being a vestige of the colonial era and a monarchial past of India ... which would have otherwise been resolved a century back.'[34] The rest of Varadharajan's eighty-one-page ruling pulled no punches in nailing the guilty party. By illegally allocating themselves thousands of shares, Pat, Vijit and his wife, Meenaxi, had ousted Devraj and Lalitya from Jai Mahal Hotel Pvt. Ltd, denying them a say in the affairs of the company. Pat had also illegally siphoned off approximately £1m in relation to properties situated at Sohna in

Haryana and at Mussoorie. Varadharajan ordered that the shareholding structure that existed immediately after the death of Jagat when Devraj and Lalitya had 99 per cent of the shares be restored.[35] The wheels of justice were finally starting to turn.

* * *

At sunrise on 24 August 2016, guests in their £600-a-night luxury suites at the Sujan Rajmahal Palace Hotel were rudely woken by the sound of bulldozers. Those nursing hangovers from too many pineapple and cardamom martinis and expecting a *Second Best Exotic Marigold Hotel* experience were instead treated to the spectacle of a stand-off between Diya Kumari and lathi-wielding policemen protecting hundreds of workers who were busy sealing the hotel's entrances, pulling down a heritage building on its grounds and evicting its occupants, all with the television cameras rolling.

Originally a pleasure pavilion for Maharaja Jai Singh II's favourite wife, the 250-year-old property had seen many changes. In 1821, it became the official home of the British Resident before reverting to the ownership of the royal family at the time of Independence. After a major renovation that gave the building its current art deco look, it replaced the Rambagh as Jai and Ayesha's private home. Following Jai's death, Ayesha moved into the Moti Doongri Fort and then to Lily Pool. The Rajmahal was occupied by Bubbles but fell into disrepair after he passed away and became the property of his adopted heir, Padmanabh. In 2014, it was taken over by the Sujan Group, who turned it into Jaipur's most 'crushingly cool' hotel experience, featuring fourteen suites and thirty-seven different patterns of wallpaper 'as bright and graphic as a beach towel', the work of designer Adil Ahmad. Bubbles's Ford Thunderbird convertible with the number plate JAIPUR 1 is permanently parked out front, ready to whisk guests on sightseeing tours. But on this particular day it was not going anywhere.

As the dust rose from an eighteenth-century pavilion that was being pulverized by jackhammers near the hotel's perimeter, Diya was joined by her mother, Padmini. Both were waving court orders in the face of the JDA boss, Shikhar Agarwal, who ordered a temporary halt to the demolitions but refused to reopen the gates. The night before, the JDA had posted notices on the gates to the palace announcing the 'anti-encroachment' drive. The JDA claimed it had a 1993 court order on the acquisition of 10 acres of land occupied by the Rajmahal. Diya insisted she had papers proving a court had stayed the land acquisition and threatened to sue the civic authority. Agarwal insisted the JDA was acting in accordance with the law. That may have been the case, but it didn't explain why it had waited twenty-six years to carry out the orders and why its actions were timed to coincide with Chief Minister Vasundhara Raje's departure from Jaipur to attend a literary festival in Bhutan. After all, just a few days before, Raje had dined with Diya and Padmini. 'If this could happen to a BJP MLA from a royal family, you can imagine what would be happening to the common man,' Diya thundered. Added her husband, Narendra: 'It was the worst humiliation the Jaipur royals could have been subjected to.'[36]

A week later, Padmini proved that even at the age of seventy-three she had plenty of fight left in her. In a statement published in local newspapers, the rajmata announced she would lead a march from Tripolia Gate to the Rajmahal to protest the JDA's action. What happened was not only an insult to her family but also to the people of Jaipur. Sealing the Rajmahal was 'immoral and repressive' and an affront to the patriotism of her late husband.[37] Given the blessings of local Rajput associations, the march attracted hundreds of people. When protesters reached the Rajmahal, the rally was addressed by Padmanabh, who said: 'We have faith in the chief minister ... judiciary and justice will prevail.'[38]

The stand-off was finally settled after intervention from the BJP president Amit Shah, who reportedly accused Vasundhara Raje of treating the royal family like a 'land mafia'. After vowing never to talk to the chief minister again, Padmini met Vasundhara Raje on 4 September. The same night the entrances to the palace were unlocked. Two days later, a local court ruled against the JDA, ordering a return to the status quo and directing the authority to rebuild the demolished structures at its own cost. Agarwal and JDA Secretary Pawan Arora were removed from their posts two months later. Following a complaint by the royal family, a magistrate issued bailable warrants against Agarwal, Arora and other top JDA officials for the 24 August demolition.[39]

Although the dust had settled on the Rajmahal episode, Raje went into the December 2018 state assembly elections on a weak wicket. Diya was denied a ticket in Sawai Madhopur, prompting speculation that relations between her and the Chief Minister had yet to heal.

For her part, Diya cited unspecified personal reasons for not contesting Sawai Madhopur. Those reasons probably included her impending separation from Narendra. The couple applied for divorce in December 2018 and the court granted it the following month, dispensing with the usual six-month cooling-off period. In their joint application, the couple said that they had been living separately for about one and a half years and now wanted to part ways with mutual consent. By fast-tracking their divorce, Diya was able to file her nomination papers for the seat of Rajsamund in the 2019 Lok Sabha election without the shadow of the separation darkening her campaign.

Once again, the personable and highly photogenic princess became a favourite subject for media covering the Rajasthan chapter of the election campaign. 'The forty-eight-year-old does not mind getting her chiffons dirty as she revels in the heat and dust of politics,' cooed Sonia Mishra of *The Week*.[40]

When the ballots were counted, she had won by a staggering 550,000 votes—the third highest margin in the state and the second highest for a woman candidate. The BJP rode a 'desert storm', virtually eliminating the Congress in Rajasthan. Had she contested the state assembly she would have been sitting on the opposition benches. Instead, she was the second member of her family after Ayesha to take a place in the Lok Sabha and one of the thirty-eight women BJP MPs elected in Narendra Modi's second term.

With Diya's electoral maelstrom presaging a long and illustrious political career, and with a series of major court decisions going in favour of Ayesha's grandchildren, 2019 was shaping up as a watershed year. But decades of discord had left scars that were too deep to heal overnight. Politics and power made for uneasy bedfellows and there was no such thing as closure in India's labyrinthine court system. The House of Jaipur was still a house divided.

EPILOGUE

If signatures could speak, Jai and Ayesha's guestbooks would tell a thousand stories. The first signatures, dated 22 January 1961 when the Jaipurs lived at Rajmahal Palace, are those of Queen Elizabeth and Prince Philip. A little over a year later, Jackie Kennedy and her sister Lee Radziwill memorialized their visit, as did Jackie's children, John and Caroline, in 1982. Ambassadors, high commissioners, counts and countesses mingled with poets, playwrights and painters. Mexico's Octavio Paz was followed by the Italian photographer Pietro Francesco Mele, best remembered for his work in Afghanistan and Tibet. 'Reggie', 'Baby', 'Boopy' and 'Bunny' had a 'wonderful stay' in 1964. After Ayesha moved to Lily Pool, one guest filled a whole page of the guestbook with a watercolour of bougainvillea climbing up its sun-soaked walls. For some the experience bordered on the profound: 'One need not die to go to Heaven, just come to Lily Pool. It's a sensation in itself seeing a beautiful horse from your window and to think you are sharing a roof with the most beautiful woman of the century. The warmth felt here is not entirely due to the sun,' 'Raj' wrote in November 1984.

Ayesha's study at Lily Pool appears untouched. Her vast desk is strewn with ashtrays and stationery, photographs of Jai, Jagat and her grandchildren, her favourite horses and cars and a white marble statue of Ganesha. On the walls are paintings of Jai as a champion polo player and of her cantering past a church in a picture-postcard English village. A silver-framed photograph showing Queen Elizabeth and Jai riding in a howdah through the streets of Jaipur vies for space on the crowded side tables with photos of assorted European royalty and heads of state as well as numerous polo trophies. The dining room is dominated by a crystal Lalique dining table that fits perfectly with Lily Pool's art deco chic. The walls are hung with more portraits of Ayesha, Indira and Jai. A corner cabinet is filled with rose quartz statues that once graced her suite at the Rambagh Palace. The lounge room is more relaxed and breezy. Birds fly in and out but there are no squirrels nibbling on the curtains.

* * *

In May 2019, I attended celebrations to mark the 100th anniversary of Ayesha's birth, curious to see how Jaipur's most famous royal was being remembered. Reminders of that dignity and grace were evident at an exhibition of photographs, 'A Journey to the Hearts of People', at Jaipur's Birla Auditorium, which chronicled her extraordinary life frame by frame. The commemorative programme began with her grandson, Devraj, speaking to the capacity crowd about her legacy, before introducing a phalanx of luminaries and erstwhile maharajas, each with their own stories of the rajmata's influence and contributions to society. The Bollywood actress Simi Grewal spoke of her idol, a woman so beautiful she grew up looking at her photograph every day. The interview she conducted with Ayesha on her celebrity talk show in 2002, probably her most revealing, was played in full. Then it was the turn of class eight students from Jayshree Periwal International School, who staged a musical titled *Safar*. In song, drama and dance they acted out her life from growing up in Cooch Behar to her marriage to Jai, her entry into politics to incarceration in Tihar and her love of polo. Later, on that sweltering evening, a colourfully caparisoned elephant greeted hundreds of guests arriving at the Jai Mahal Palace Hotel's gardens for a commemorative dinner. As models strode down a catwalk in a dazzling display of chiffon chic, a sound system thumped out Ayesha's favourite Sinatra and Cole Porter tunes at a volume so high conversation was almost impossible, before switching to an even louder compilation of the latest Bollywood hits.

Once again, the celebratory atmosphere was little more than a veneer. An opportunity to pay tribute to Ayesha's indisputable legacy regarding the empowerment of women in Rajasthan, her contributions in the areas of arts, culture and fashion and her stellar political career was not enough to bury differences and bring the extended family together. None of Ayesha's stepsons or their families attended the Birla Auditorium or the Jai Mahal functions. The only person with any connection to the current royal family who took up Devraj and Lalitya's invitation was Narendra Singh Rajawat, who had recently divorced Diya. The MGD School, perhaps the most enduring symbol of Ayesha's influence on Jaipur society, was not involved. Rani Vidya Devi, Joey's wife, is the president of the school's board and Urvashi Devi, who together with her nephew Pat is still embroiled in litigation with Ayesha's grandchildren, is an ex officio member.

At the City Palace, where she arrived in 1940 as Jai's third wife, her memory has been almost entirely erased—copies of her memoir, *A Princess Remembers*, in the museum's bookshops and a brief vignette in the daily sound and light show are among the only reminders of her more than six-decade-long association with the Jaipur royal family. None of this comes as a surprise to Kishore Singh. 'There's an almost total lack of affection and warmth between much of the family. They are only too happy to put each other down.'[1]

* * *

India's princes and princesses once prided themselves on their pedigree and sense of exclusivity. Today a new social order has arrived, based more on celebrity. In November 2019, one clever headline writer declared Padmanabh Singh Jaipur's newly crowned 'Heirbnb'[2] after he became the first Indian royal to rent out part of his palace on the accommodation-sharing web platform. The one-bedroom Gudliya Suite with its own private pool and butler was previously only available to royalty, heads of state and A-list celebrities. Now anyone with a spare $8,000 can book it online and sleep in the room Oprah Winfrey once occupied. The price includes free parking and unlimited Wi-Fi, though most guests will probably prefer to avail of the complimentary chauffeur-driven limousine pick-up at the airport. 'My own travels with Airbnb have made me feel very welcome in new cities and cultures, and I am happy that the experience of quintessential Indian hospitality will be shared with others,' Padmanabh said in a press release.[3] Until 1 January 2020, the proceeds from each booking went towards his mother's project, the Princess Diya Kumari Foundation, a non-profit dedicated to supporting disadvantaged women and girls in Rajasthan.

The royal family now employs a PR agency to ensure that any public appearances serve to enhance rather than detract from the aura they strive to maintain. Some among the Jaipur elite privately scoff at the idea of relying on a PR firm, pointing out that Ayesha and Jai achieved their cult status purely on the basis of their personas and their work. In 2013, Christopher Miller, who has held senior communications and government relations positions with the World Bank and the International Finance Corporation, was appointed as a special adviser to Diya Kumari on her socio-economic development projects and to the family on the management of the City Palace complex, Jaigarh Fort and its other commercial, philanthropic and heritage preservation initiatives—tasks requiring additional oversight now that Diya is a member of the Lok Sabha. He also acts as a mentor of sorts to Padmanabh, the millennial 'maharaja' on whose shoulders—and Instagram account—Jaipur's legacy now rests.

Corporatization has yet to erase all the vestiges of the old feudal order. After he was given the title of maharaja, Padmanabh used to ask people not to touch his feet as a mark of respect, until his grandmother Padmini Devi told him, 'If it allows people to connect with your grandfather, don't crush their dreams.'[4] When Diya launched her 2019 campaign for the Lok Sabha seat of Rajsamand, almost all the palace staff, from the guides who show tourists around to drivers and kitchen staff, were expected to pitch in. Ancient caste loyalties still play a role in local politics. Rajputs account for about 12 per cent of the state's population and wield influence in at least two dozen assembly seats. Perhaps the most prominent member of the community in politics was the BJP's Bhairon Singh Shekhawat, who won three terms as Rajasthan's chief minister and later became vice president of India. Rajput allegiance to the party started to break down under Diya's political mentor, Vasundhara Raje (who is not a Rajput). Diya's thumping victory in Rajsamand has reversed that trend, fuelling speculation that she might make a run for the chief ministership at some time in the future.

Nor has corporatization interfered with playing the religious card. In August 2019, when India's Supreme Court was determining whether a temple to the Hindu god Ram existed on land once occupied by the Babri mosque in the holy city of Ayodhya, the judges asked if there were any descendants of the Raghuvansha dynasty who might want to stake a claim to the site. The first person to respond was Diya, a vocal supporter of building a Ram mandir at Ayodhya. Taking to Twitter she said that her lineage was well 'documented' and that she had 'manuscripts to prove it'. 'My father was the 309th descendant of Lord Ram. We have documents that show that we descended from Kush, Lord Ram's son. We belong to the Kushwaha or the Kachchwaha clan.'[5] Diya was followed by half a dozen erstwhile Rajasthani royals also claiming to be Raghuvanshis. A champion of the saffron cause, she had made such a claim earlier too, but the timing of her decision to reassert it was significant. In October 2019, the Supreme Court ruled that Hindus should be allowed to build a Ram temple on the disputed site, in what was seen as a major victory for the BJP.

Padmanabh's presence at many of his mother's rallies was viewed as his political baptism. 'Politics is power,' he told the *Mumbai Mirror* in 2015, when he was still a student at Mayo College. 'My ancestors were rulers on the strength of their might and military power. But times have changed, and you can be in politics only if people elect you to be their representative.'[6] If politics proves too distasteful, others predict a bright future for him on the catwalk for Dolce & Gabbana and other fashion labels. 'He is so comfortable in his skin, so confident about his style and so good looking. No doubt, he is going to be the next big fashion icon globally,' says Bollywood photographer Tarun Khiwal.[7] 'Pacho' (the nickname was given to him by Padmini, whose favourite Spanish soap opera was called *Gata Pacho*) has made the covers of numerous glossy magazines including *GQ, Hello!, Elle* and *Grazia*.

On a sunny Jaipur winter afternoon, I find myself being escorted up a gently sloping passage entered through a door at the back of the Baradari restaurant in the City Palace. As I turn a corner I'm led through a room whose walls are painted with portraits of Radha and Krishna in amorous embrace. Lying on the floor are more than a hundred broken polo sticks. 'The best quality bamboo comes from Malaysia and it's getting increasingly expensive,' Padmanabh points out.[8] It is not uncommon to go through several sticks in a tournament. Those that can will be fixed. Polo is the young maharaja's primary passion. He began playing competitively in 2015 and a year later, aged just sixteen, was appointed as the brand ambassador of high-end polo equipment and clothing maker La Martina. More recently Cifonelli and Ralph Lauren have added him to their portfolios. He is a member of India's national polo team as well as Britain's elite Guards Polo Club and has competed with Princes William and Harry. When the season is in full swing he sometimes plays in Mumbai in the morning, Delhi in the afternoon, and in Jaipur the following morning, each stop requiring a stable of several horses—and a ready supply of polo sticks.[9]

Padmanabh is still in his jodhpurs and black India Polo Team sleeveless vest when his mother arrives wearing a striking pink silk sari in Sukh Niwas of Chandra Mahal, a vast drawing room brimming with solid silver objets d'art and Rajasthani miniatures. The wardrobe mismatch between mother and son is more than made up for by the chemistry between them. The young maharaja is clearly in awe of his mother's charity work and meteoric political rise, while she worries about the dangers that a sport like polo entails. '[The princes] do get the votes because of what their ancestors did for the people and for what they are doing in the present,' she explains in answer to a question about the relevance of royalty today, before listing initiatives in education, charity work, hospitality and the promotion of handicrafts. 'In Rajasthan, the people still look up to you and consider you as a figurehead. But India is changing and when I'm in Delhi or Mumbai I don't expect any of that.' As a pair of liveried servants brings a fresh pot of tea and home-made biscuits, I ask her how she feels about the many controversies she has weathered, including her same-gotra marriage and Padmanabh's adoption by his grandfather. 'Because I belong to this family, anything we do, even if we sneeze, a story is made about that,' she concedes. 'You have to take it in your stride and not let it affect you negatively.'[10]

Pressed on his future plans, Padmanabh's response makes it clear that his views on politics have mellowed in the last few years. 'The way I would like to participate in politics and the future of this country is by supporting [my mother] and through other non-political means.'[11] His disarming style and genuine modesty bode well for any career he intends to pursue now that he has a fine arts degree from a university in Rome as well as an aptitude for championship-level polo. But good manners and a calm exterior cannot hide the fact that he is the de facto head—at least as far as traditional ranking goes—of a larger family unit that remains deeply split.

Three generations of litigation are spread across three branches of his nearest kin and there is no guarantee that the next generation will not inherit the detritus. Legal cases launched in the mid-1980s still clog the courts. In a 2018 ruling by the Delhi High Court on whether the law of primogeniture should apply to Jai's estate, the list of petitioners and respondents was six pages long, made up of different combinations of current and deceased members of the family who have fought the case for over three decades. More than a dozen advocates were listed as appearing for various parties. After taking into account the evidence before it, the court threw out what it termed the 'anachronistic' principle of primogeniture and ruled that Jai's estate be dispersed among all the legal heirs on the basis of the HUF Act.[12]

* * *

Slander and gossip feed on this festering quagmire of claims and counterclaims, while the assets at stake—palaces, jewels, share portfolios, trusts and antiques—steadily increase in value. 'They get you nowhere,' says Maharaja Gaj Singh of Jodhpur, referring to the legal disputes that plague so many of India's princely families. 'It's better to give up something and get on with life because otherwise it's very draining emotionally as well as financially. Basically, you're losing time.'[13] Maharaja Gaj Singh says the best solution is mediation rather than confrontation. It has worked elsewhere. In 2013, the Baroda royal family finally reached a compromise that settled a two-decades-long dispute over the ownership of property and companies valued at around 200 million pounds. The dispute between Sangramsinh Gaekwad and his brother Ranjitsinh Gaekwad involved more than twenty members of their extended families and included such prized assets as the Laxmi Vilas Palace set on 600 acres in the middle of Baroda. 'A Bombay lawyer once said to me, "I can resolve any family issue when it's to do with Marwaris but with you lot it's very difficult,"' chuckles Gaj Singh. 'His explanation being that with a Marwari businessman the priorities are purely financial, whereas with us there's a lot of emotion, egos and prestige involved.'[14]

Asked whether she believed Jaipur could ever follow Baroda's lead, Diya Kumari limits herself to saying: 'Of course it is unfortunate that this has happened ... and I do hope that it gets sorted out, that we come to an understanding.' Her uncle Pat insists he has held out the olive branch to the other branches of the family regarding the dispute over Jai's estate and the Jai Mahal Hotel share transfer. On the former, he and his brother will settle provided they are safeguarded against all the tax liabilities relating to the estate. On the latter, he blames Devraj, Lalitya and their mother for their intransigent stand. 'They are not willing to compromise. I think their lawyers are very keen that the litigation should continue for the obvious reason that the lawyers stand to benefit most.'[15] Priya denies the charge, saying that Pat's proposed share transfer is unacceptable. 'Jai Mahal is full of debt. Rambagh is the cash cow. It's better to hang on to the 27 per cent Jagat had rather than end up with 100 per cent of debt-ridden Jai Mahal.'[16] As for the definitive 2018 Delhi High Court ruling on the HUF case, the Supreme Court, at the time of writing (March 2020), is considering an appeal launched by lawyers for Padmanabh, Diya and Padmini. Also heading for the Supreme Court is an appeal against a March 2020 National Company Law Appellate Tribunal that dismissed the NCLT's earlier ruling granting Devraj and Lalitya's ownership of the Jai Mahal Palace. The authenticity of Ayesha's will is also being challenged before the district judge in Jaipur.

And on and on it goes.

* * *

The Diggi Palace Hotel may not have the five-star rating of the Rambagh, Rajmahal or Jai Mahal hotels, but it can claim more visitors in any winter season than the other three combined. For the past twelve years, it has hosted the Jaipur Literature Festival, the annual free literary love-in that celebrates some of the best writing from India and the world in a Woodstock-like atmosphere. In recent years, the number of footfalls over the five-day festival has exceeded

300,000, so it's almost disconcerting to arrive at the hotel without seeing crowds surging from shamiana to shamiana. It's early September and peacocks outnumber paying guests.

Ram Pratap Singh, the scion of the Diggi royal family, is the archetypical Rajput—ramrod-straight posture, chiselled features, aquiline nose and piercing brown eyes. His ancestors were Khangarwat Rajputs who served with distinction in the Jaipur army during the eighteenth and nineteenth centuries. When Jaipur was established, the most important thikanas such as Diggi, Chomu, Kanota and Samode were given land grants outside the walled city, ostensibly to act as a first line of defence in case of an enemy attack. Today most of their palaces have been turned into heritage hotels.

Ram Pratap Singh traces the current disputes back to the time of the Mughals, who encouraged rulers to take multiple wives and concubines, complicating matters of succession and inheritance. Nor does he hide his bitterness over the way India's ruling families were treated after Independence when they found themselves in the crosshairs of Nehru's socialist experiment. 'Every revolution needs a bete noir. In India, the British were removed through a peaceful revolution, but after Independence they still needed someone to flay. So who do you beat up but the princes. Every law of the land was made to cut us down to size.' Before the privy purses were abolished, land reforms that put a ceiling on the amount of agricultural and urban holdings forced royal families to set up religious and family trusts to protect their feudal property. 'That set in place all the infighting. If you can't fight the state, then the best persons to fight are your brothers and sisters.'[17] As a seasoned Jaipur watcher, he views the ongoing schisms in the Jaipur family with a mixture of bemusement and dismay. 'When the monkeys fight, the dog takes the rotis,' he quips, reaching—like so many in this city—for old Rajput sayings that deliciously illustrate the contemporary state of affairs. 'The primary aim in these intra-family disputes is to create strife between everyone so that you are never free of your problems,' he adds. 'You have to rise above it. In the Jaipur family no one ever did.'[18]

Victimhood is an all too common trope in the palaces and havelis of Jaipur. Some like Ram Pratap Singh have moved on, becoming successful businesspeople or hoteliers. Others still pine for the good old days. Jaipur's royal family was not alone in weathering the transition from feudalism to imperialism and ultimately surrendering itself to democratic rule. Hundreds of other princely states shed their anachronisms and adjusted to India's new reality, not as museum pieces to be gawked at by tourists but as proud and self-confident ambassadors of their regal past.

* * *

Generational change is the greatest hope for the House of Jaipur. Princess Diya is making her mark with her charities and educational initiatives as well as in the political sphere, and Padmanabh looks set to follow his mother's example. Devraj and Lalitya have their Thai ancestry to draw on and are keen to preserve Isarda's heritage and honour their grandmother's legacy. Ayesha's aura has endured because she mostly remained aloof from the litigation that dragged down her stepsons and their families and continues to drain their energies and finances on largely avoidable litigation.

Nearly two centuries ago, James Tod observed the disdain of Rajputs for negotiation and their refusal to surrender. 'To sheath the sword' before 'a feud is balanced' would be an eternal blot on a family's reputation, 'hence feuds are entailed with the estates from generation to generation'.[19]

When it comes to settling family feuds, time has largely stood still in the House of Jaipur since those words were written. But in most other respects the world Tod wrote about has been transformed unrecognizably and so have the lives of India's princes. Power has passed from the palaces to the people, putting an end to centuries old privileges. Today there are no kingdoms at stake, no borders to protect. With the abolition of the princely states, the stupendous wealth that flowed from their revenues, enabling the royals to buy emeralds the size of hens' eggs or gift their girlfriends diamond tiaras, is gone. Hundreds of business tycoons in India far outshine the erstwhile princes in opulence and extravagance, notably on display at the lavish weddings they hold for their offspring.

The present generation of Jaipur royals, unlike the previous ones, no longer run off to the playgrounds of the West to escape their responsibilities at home. They have challenged the old traditions and social order to further the cause of women's rights, to promote education and other charitable pursuits. They have become mature, professional managers of their estates and assets, turning their gilded palaces into luxury hotels. Their magnificent forts now house exhibitions of art and sculpture, and the City Palace Museum, overhauled under their direction, has become one of the finest in India. In politics, at the polo ground and even on the fashion catwalk, the House of Jaipur has begun to map out a new set of traditions, deftly harnessing their royal aura as they reinvent their roles and their relevance in twenty-first-century democratic India.

NOTES

IOR: India Office Records, British Library
NA: National Archives, London
NAI: National Archives of India, New Delhi

INTRODUCTION

1. *Vogue*, 15 September 1965.
2. Rosita Forbes, *India of the Princes*, 141.
3. Following the abolition of princely titles in 1971, Padmanabh Singh is the titular Maharaja of Jaipur and derives no entitlements from the designation.
4. In August 2019, Diya Kumari tweeted: 'My family is the descendant of Lord Ram. My father was the 309th descendant of Lord Ram. We have documents that show that we descended from Kush, Lord Ram's son. We belong to the Kushwaha or the Kachchwaha clan.' *Outlook*, 15 August 2019.
5. Giles Tillotson, *Jaipur Nama: Tales from the Pink City*, 17.
6. Thomas Roe and John Fryer, *Travels in India in the Seventeenth Century*, 445.
7. James Tod, *Annals and Antiquities of Rajasthan*, vol. 1, 162.
8. Jason Freitag, *Serving Empire, Serving Nation: James Tod and the Rajputs of Rajasthan*, 38.

1. A BOY NAMED MORMUKUT

1. Ibid., 181.
2. John F. Richards, *The Mughal Empire*, part 1, vol. 5, 23.
3. Robert Stern, *The Cat and the Lion: Jaipur State in the British Raj*, 45.
4. James Tod, *Annals and Antiquities of Rajasthan*, vol. 1, 169.
5. Ibid., 90.
6. Rudyard Kipling, *From Sea to Sea: Letters of Travel*, 12.
7. Louis Rousselet, *India and Its Native Princes: Travels in Central India*, 229.
8. NAI, Foreign and Political Department Proceedings, January 1883, A-Political I, nos. 105–10.

9. Robert Stern, *The Cat and the Lion: Jaipur State in the British Raj*, 175.
10. Quentin Crewe, *The Last Maharaja: A Biography of Sawai Man Singh II*, 14.
11. Vibhuti Sachdev, 'Negotiating Modernity in the Princely State', *South Asian Studies*, 173.
12. 'Proud Descendant of Line of Kings', *The Times*, 22 June 1902.
13. 'Beautiful Indian City', *Aberdeen Press and Journal*, 9 July 1902.
14. John Bodley, *The Coronation of Edward VII*, 252.
15. *Boston Globe*, 17 August 1902.
16. Quentin Crew, *The Last Maharaja: A Biography of Sawai Man Singh II*, 8.
17. Robert Stern, *The Cat and the Lion: Jaipur State in the British Raj*, 225.
18. Quentin Crewe, *The Last Maharaja: A Biography of Sawai Man Singh II*, 9.
19. Ibid., 10.
20. NAI, Foreign and Political Department Proceedings, 1922, no. 605–P(S).
21. Nandakisora Parika, *Jaipur That Was: Royal Court and the Seraglio*, 78.
22. Quentin Crew, *The Last Maharaja: A Biography of Sawai Man Singh II*, 16.
23. NAI, Foreign and Political Department Proceedings, December 1921, Secret I, nos. 1–2.

2. 'THE LYING COURT'

1. Rudyard Kipling, *From Sea to Sea: Letters of Travel*, 20.
2. Anil Chandra Banerjee, *The Rajput States and the East India Company*, 159.
3. Robert Stern, *The Cat and the Lion: Jaipur State in the British Raj*, 239.
4. Ibid.
5. Aman Nath, *Jaipur: The Last Destination*, 121.
6. N.C. Pahariya, *Political, Socio-Economic and Cultural History of Rajasthan*, 295.
7. Iris Butler, *The Viceroy's Wife: Letters of Alice, Countess of Reading, From India, 1921–25*, 68.
8. Kesharlal Ajmeria Jain (ed.), 'Our Present Ruler', *The Jaipur Album*, 5.
9. Ibid., 7–8.
10. Quentin Crewe, *The Last Maharaja: A Biography of Sawai Man Singh II*, 10.
11. Gayatri Devi, *A Princess Remembers: The Memoirs of the Maharani of Jaipur*, 104.
12. Robert Stern, *The Cat and the Lion: Jaipur State in the British Raj*, 238–9.
13. James Tod, *Annals and Antiquities of Rajasthan*, vol. 1, 307.
14. Rajasthan History Congress Proceedings, December 2017.
15. Interview, Aman Nath, 16 March 2020.
16. Quentin Crewe, *The Last Maharaja: A Biography of Sawai Man Singh II*, 19–20.

17. Ibid., 22.
18. Ibid., 21–2.
19. Ibid., 22.
20. Aman Nath, *Jaipur: The Last Destination*, 117.
21. NAI, Foreign and Political Department Proceedings, May 1921, no. 605 (II)-P.
22. Quentin Crewe, *The Last Maharaja: A Biography of Sawai Man Singh II*, 49.
23. Ibid., 50.
24. Interview, Maharaja Gaj Singh of Jodhpur, 7 September 2019.
25. NAI, Foreign and Political Department Proceedings, 1928, no. 376–P(S).
26. James Tod, *Annals and Antiquities of Rajasthan*, vol. 2, 356–7.
27. Rosita Forbes, *India of the Princes*, 120.
28. Rudyard Kipling, *From Sea to Sea: Letters of Travel*, 11–2.
29. Ibid., 10.
30. Ibid., 12. Kipling was of course wrong in saying that Jai Singh had been buried. The cenotaph marked the place where he, like all Rajputs, had been cremated.
31. Edwin Arnold, *India Revisited*, 143.
32. Rosita Forbes, *India of the Princes*, 134–5.
33. Ibid., 132–3.
34. Manisha Choudhary, *Journal of History and Cultural Studies*, 16.
35. Ibid., 19–21.
36. Robert Stern, *The Cat and the Lion: Jaipur State in the British Raj*, 236.
37. Ibid., 229.
38. Quentin Crewe, *The Last Maharaja: A Biography of Sawai Man Singh II*, 52.
39. Ibid.
40. *The Pioneer*, 24 December 1870.
41. Nasrullah Khan, *The Ruling Chiefs of Western India*, 9.
42. James Johnston, *Abstract and Analysis of the Report of the Indian Education Commission*, 82–3.
43. Caroline Keen, *The Power Behind the Throne: Relations between the British and the Indian States, 1870–1909*, 108–9.
44. Quentin Crewe, *The Last Maharaja: A Biography of Sawai Man Singh II*, 56–7.
45. Ibid., 60.
46. Ibid.
47. Ibid., 69.
48. Ibid., 62.
49. Ibid., 70.
50. Robert Stern, *The Cat and the Lion: Jaipur State in the British Raj*, 234–5.

51. *The Times of India*, 19 March 1931.
52. Robert Stern, *The Cat and the Lion: Jaipur State in the British Raj*, 235.

3. WHITE SATIN PYJAMAS AND A TRIPLE ROW OF PEARLS

1. Evelyn Waugh, *A Little Learning: An Autobiography*, 212.
2. Daphne Fielding, *Mercury Presides*, 108.
3. Fatesinhrao Gaekwad, *Sayajirao of Baroda, The Prince and the Man*, 47.
4. Caroline Keen, *The Power Behind the Throne: Relations between the British and the Indian States, 1870–1909*, 227.
5. IOR, Curzon to Hamilton, 4 June 1902, Curzon Collection, MSS Eur, F111, vol. 161.
6. Lucy Moore, *Maharanis: The Lives and Times of Three Generations of Indian Princesses*, 79.
7. The palace and its contents elicited mixed reviews from the press with one reporter writing that the throne room reminded him of the garish lobby of a New York hotel. *The Evening Standard*, 31 December 1910.
8. Lucy Moore, *Maharanis: The Lives and Times of Three Generations of Indian Princesses*, 50.
9. *The Times of India*, 12 July 1911.
10. Gayatri Devi, *A Princess Remembers: The Memoirs of the Maharani of Jaipur*, 42.
11. Lucy Moore, *Maharanis: The Lives and Times of Three Generations of Indian Princesses*, 10.
12. 'Serious Secession', *Chicago Daily Tribune*, 4 May 1913.
13. Gayatri Devi, *A Princess Remembers: The Memoirs of the Maharani of Jaipur*, 24.
14. Ibid., 28.
15. Edith Tottenham, *Highnesses of Hindostan*, 138–9.
16. Lucy Moore, *Maharanis: The Lives and Times of Three Generations of Indian Princesses*, 156.
17. Sunity Devee, *The Autobiography of an Indian Princess*, 209.
18. James Jupp, *The Gaiety Stage Door: Thirty Years' Reminiscences of the Theatre*, 65.
19. Gayatri Devi, *A Princess Remembers: The Memoirs of the Maharani of Jaipur*, 43.
20. 'Life Size', *Lethbridge Herald*, 21 May 1932.
21. IOR, Cooch Behar: Succession 1922; Minority Administration, L/PS/11/222, P 4985/1922: 20 December 1922–3 January 1931.
22. Ibid.
23. *The Modern Review*, April 1926, 495–6.
24. Gayatri Devi, *A Princess Remembers: The Memoirs of the Maharani of Jaipur*, 52.

25. Ibid., 52.
26. Interview, Ali Khusru Jung, 28 January 2020.
27. Ahmed Lateef, *Hyderabad to Hollywood*, 20.
28. Interview, Indira Dhanrajgir, 12 September 2019.
29. Ahmed Lateef, *Hyderabad to Hollywood*, 20.
30. Interview, Prithviraj Singh, 4 September 2019.
31. Interview, anonymous.
32. Gayatri Devi, *A Princess Remembers: The Memoirs of the Maharani of Jaipur*, 86.
33. 'A King's Story', *Life Magazine*, 22 May 1950, 127.
34. 'More Women Join in Fox Hunting', *Springfield Leader and Press*, 23 November 1927.
35. *The Courier and Advertiser*, 14 January 1928.
36. 'A Yankee Abroad', *Arizona Daily Star*, 20 September 1928.
37. Lucy Moore, *Maharanis: The Lives and Times of Three Generations of Indian Princesses*, 188.
38. William Gerhardi, *Memoirs of a Polyglot*, 372.
39. Lionel Tennyson, *From Verse to Worse*, 211.
40. IOR, telegram from secretary of state to viceroy, 12 March 1929. Cooch Behar: Maharani of Cooch Behar; guardianship and schooling of the minor Maharaja of Cooch Behar L/PO/5/15, 6 January 1929–16 December 1930.
41. IOR, Cooch Behar: Succession 1922; minority administration L/PS/11/222, P 4985/1922, 20 December 1922–3 January 1931.
42. Lucy Moore, *Maharanis: The Lives and Times of Three Generations of Indian Princesses*, 182.
43. IOR, Cooch Behar: Succession 1922; minority administration L/PS/11/222, P 4985/1922, 20 December 1922–3 January 1931.
44. Ibid.
45. IOR, Cooch Behar: Regent and restrictions on her control over the family budget, R/1/1/1786, 1929.
46. NAI, Home Political, Proscribed Publication under Section 124 99-A, F-48–4, 1933.
47. Ibid.
48. IOR, Irwin 18/2/29, interview with Indira at Bikaner House Cooch Behar: Maharani of Cooch Behar: Guardianship and schooling of the minor Maharaja of Cooch Behar, L/PO/5/15, 6 January 1929–16, December 1930.
49. IOR, C.C. Watson record of interview with Maharani Regent and restrictions on her control over the family budget, 22 February 1929, R/1/1/1786, 1929.
50. IOR, Maharani of Cooch Behar: Financial arrangements by the state;

proposed curtailment of the allowances of the Cooch Behar family; tutor for Maharaja of Cooch Behar; powers of Maharani as Regent to be curtailed; unsatisfactory behaviour of the Maharani, L/PO/5/14 (I), 2 July 1928–25 February 1930.

51. *The Sunday Times*, 8 September 1929.

52. IOR, Cooch Behar: Maharani of Cooch Behar; guardianship and schooling of the minor Maharaja of Cooch Behar L/PO/5/15, 6 January 1929–16 December 1930.

53. Ibid.

54. Ibid. Telegram from viceroy, 20 March 1929.

55. Ibid. Letter by unknown author to the king's private secretary Lord Stamfordham, 20 March 1929.

56. Gayatri Devi, *A Princess Remembers: The Memoirs of the Maharani of Jaipur*, 87–8.

57. Ibid., 87.

58. 'Maharanee in Air Mishap', *Daily Mail*, 5 November 1929.

59. Quentin Crewe, *The Last Maharaja: A Biography of Sawai Man Singh II*, 100.

60. Ann Morrow, *Highness: The Maharajas of India*, 25.

61. Quentin Crewe, *The Last Maharaja: A Biography of Sawai Man Singh II*,

62. 'Derek Brown, 'The Common Woes of Bubbles and Wankie', *The Guardian*, 29 November 1992.

63. Giles Tillotson, *Jaipur Nama: Tales from the Pink City*, 221.

4. POLO AND PINK CHAMPAGNE

1. Gayatri Devi, *A Princess Remembers: The Memoirs of the Maharani of Jaipur*, 100.

2. Quentin Crewe, *The Last Maharaja: A Biography of Sawai Man Singh II*, 132.

3. Gayatri Devi, *A Princess Remembers: The Memoirs of the Maharani of Jaipur*, 101.

4. *Washington Post*, 22 April 1932.

5. 'Jaipur Ruler Weds Jodhpur Princess', *The Times of India*, 26 April 1932.

6. Quentin Crewe, *The Last Maharaja: A Biography of Sawai Man Singh II*, 93.

7. Gayatri Devi, *A Princess Remembers: The Memoirs of the Maharani of Jaipur*, 109.

8. Ibid., 102.

9. Quentin Crewe, *The Last Maharaja: A Biography of Sawai Man Singh II*, 133.

10. Gayatri Devi, *A Princess Remembers: The Memoirs of the Maharani of Jaipur* (1982), 94. The daydream is left out of the 1995 edition of Ayesha's memoir.

11. Gayatri Devi, *A Princess Remembers: The Memoirs of the Maharani of Jaipur*, 113.

12. Ibid.

13. Interview, Prithviraj Singh, 29 May 2019.

14. Gayatri Devi, *A Princess Remembers: The Memoirs of the Maharani of Jaipur*, 115.

15. Ibid., 120.

16. Ibid.

17. Ibid., 122.

18. Ibid., 143.

19. Ibid., 143–4.

20. Interview, Anne Wright, 29 August 2019.

21. Gayatri Devi, *A Princess Remembers: The Memoirs of the Maharani of Jaipur*, 144.

22. Miranda Seymour, *Chaplin's Girl: The Life and Loves of Virginia Cherrill*, 191.

23. Ursula d'Abo, *The Girl with the Widow's Peak: The Memoirs*, ebook.

24. Quentin Crewe, *The Last Maharaja: A Biography of Sawai Man Singh II*, 101.

25. Simon Fenwick, *Joan: The Remarkable Life of Joan Leigh Fermor*, 50. Pryce-Jones's hopes of marrying Joan were dashed by her father, who responded to his request in unambiguous terms: 'Having nothing, without prospects, without a home, you expect to marry my daughter, who has always had the best of everything.'

26. 'To Goings-On', *Bystander*, 27 February 1934.

27. Quentin Crewe, *The Last Maharaja: A Biography of Sawai Man Singh II*, 99.

28. Ibid.

29. Simon Fenwick, *Joan: The Remarkable Life of Joan Leigh Fermor*, 80.

30. *Western Daily Press and Bristol Mirror*, 20 May 1933.

31. 'Just Like a Prince out of "The Arabian Nights"', *San Francisco Examiner*, 27 August 1933.

32. *Tatler*, 19 June 1935.

33. *Bournemouth Weekly Post and Graphic*, 15 June 1935.

34. 'Great Films That Weren't Best', *Seattle Post Intelligencer*, 15 February 2010.

35. Miranda Seymour, *Chaplin's Girl: The Life and Loves of Virginia Cherrill*, 113.

36. Ibid., 123.

37. Ibid., 149.

38. Ibid., 169.

39. Ibid., 186.

40. Ibid., 192.

41. Ibid., 193.
42. Ibid.
43. Ibid., 194.
44. Ibid., 195.
45. Ibid., 199.
46. Ibid., 209.
47. Ibid., 208.
48. Ibid., 210.
49. Ibid., 212.
50. Ibid., 215.
51. *Liverpool Echo*, 13 April 1937.
52. Gayatri Devi, *A Princess Remembers: The Memoirs of the Maharani of Jaipur*, 127.
53. Elisabeth Bumiller, 'Family Feud in the House of Jaipur', *Washington Post*, 3 January 1987.
54. Miranda Seymour, *Chaplin's Girl: The Life and Loves of Virginia Cherrill*, 234.
55. Ibid., 237.
56. Ibid., 238.
57. Ibid., 239.
58. Ibid., 241.
59. Ibid., 242.
60. Quentin Crewe, *The Last Maharaja: A Biography of Sawai Man Singh II*, 113.
61. Ibid., 115.
62. Ibid., 116.
63. Barnett Rubin, *Feudal Revolt and State-Building: The 1938 Sikar Agitation in Jaipur*, 110.
64. 'Troops Rushed to Sikar from Jaipur', *The Times of India*, 26 April 1938.
65. 'Locked in a Tower to Make Sure He'll Wed a Princess', *San Francisco Examiner*, 24 July 1938.
66. 'Ultimatum to Mad Rajah', *Belfast Telegraph*, 20 July 1938.
67. Barnett Rubin, *Feudal Revolt and State-Building: The 1938 Sikar Agitation in Jaipur*, 63.
68. NAI, Foreign and Political Department Proceedings, 1938, no. 215–P(S).
69. Barnett Rubin, *Feudal Revolt and State-Building: The 1938 Sikar Agitation in Jaipur*, 54.
70. Ibid., 56.
71. *Hindustan Times*, 9 July 1938.
72. Barnett Rubin, *Feudal Revolt and State-Building: The 1938 Sikar Agitation in Jaipur*, 69.

73. Quentin Crewe, *The Last Maharaja: A Biography of Sawai Man Singh II*, 122.

74. Ibid., 123.

75. *Lincolnshire Echo*, 12 July 1938.

76. Barnett Rubin, *Feudal Revolt and State-Building: The 1938 Sikar Agitation in Jaipur*, 72.

77. Quentin Crewe, *The Last Maharaja: A Biography of Sawai Man Singh II*, 126.

78. Robert Stern, *The Cat and the Lion: Jaipur State in the British Raj*, 297.

79. Quentin Crewe, *The Last Maharaja: A Biography of Sawai Man Singh II*, 128.

5. 'WHO THE HELL DO YOU THINK YOU ARE? QUEEN MARY?'

1. Miranda Seymour, *Chaplin's Girl: The Life and Loves of Virginia Cherrill*, 247–8.

2. Ibid., 253.

3. Ibid.

4. Ibid., 257–8.

5. Gayatri Devi, *A Princess Remembers: The Memoirs of the Maharani of Jaipur*, 139–40.

6. Muhammad Sher Ali Khan, *The Elite Minority, The Princes of India*, 224.

7. Ibid., 217.

8. Ibid., 221.

9. Ibid., 228.

10. Ibid., 232.

11. Ibid.

12. Ibid., 212.

13. Ibid., 233.

14. NAI, Foreign and Political Department Proceedings, 1940, no. 21 (8)-P

15. Quentin Crewe, *The Last Maharaja: A Biography of Sawai Man Singh II*, 138.

16. NAI, Foreign and Political Department Proceedings, 1940, no. 26 (45)-P(S) and 11 (20)-P(S).

17. Quentin Crewe, *The Last Maharaja: A Biography of Sawai Man Singh II*, 140.

18. Ibid., 139.

19. Gayatri Devi, *A Princess Remembers: The Memoirs of the Maharani of Jaipur*, 148.

20. Ibid., 156.

21. Elisabeth Bumiller, 'Family Feud in the House of Jaipur', *Washington Post*, 3 January 1987.

22. Quentin Crewe, *The Last Maharaja: A Biography of Sawai Man Singh II*, 142.

23. Miranda Seymour, *Chaplin's Girl: The Life and Loves of Virginia Cherrill*, 248.

24. Gayatri Devi, *A Princess Remembers: The Memoirs of the Maharani of Jaipur*, 172.

25. Ibid., 179.

26. Ibid.

27. Ibid., 172.

28. Ibid., 181.

29. Quentin Crewe, *The Last Maharaja: A Biography of Sawai Man Singh II*, 143.

30. Interview, Margaret Kumari, 2 September 2019.

31. Gayatri Devi, *A Princess Remembers: The Memoirs of the Maharani of Jaipur*, 196.

32. Quentin Crewe, *The Last Maharaja: A Biography of Sawai Man Singh II*, 147.

33. Aman Nath, *Jaipur: The Last Destination*, 123.

34. NAI, Foreign and Political Department Proceedings, 1940, no. 3 (14)-P(S).

35. Robert Stern, *The Cat and the Lion: Jaipur State in the British Raj*, 305.

36. Ibid., 305–6.

37. Quentin Crewe, *The Last Maharaja: A Biography of Sawai Man Singh II*, 124.

38. Ibid., 157.

39. Mirza Ismail, *My Public Life: Recollections and Reflections*, 76.

40. R.P. Singh, and Kanwar Rajpal Singh, *Sawai Man Singh II of Jaipur: Life and Legend*, 100.

41. Quentin Crewe, *The Last Maharaja: A Biography of Sawai Man Singh II*, 167.

42. NAI, Foreign and Political Department Proceedings, 1942, no. 110–P(S).

43. Robert Stern, *The Cat and the Lion: Jaipur State in the British Raj*, 310.

44. Quentin Crewe, *The Last Maharaja: A Biography of Sawai Man Singh II*, 168.

45. Gayatri Devi, *A Princess Remembers: The Memoirs of the Maharani of Jaipur*, 206.

46. Ibid., 209.

47. Quentin Crewe, *The Last Maharaja: A Biography of Sawai Man Singh II*, 145.

48. Gayatri Devi, *A Princess Remembers: The Memoirs of the Maharani of Jaipur*, 216.

49. Larry Collins, and Dominique Lapierre, *Freedom at Midnight*, 131.
50. V.P. Menon, *The Story of the Integration of the Indian States*, 10.
51. Peter Muir, *This Is India*, 24.
52. Quentin Crewe, *The Last Maharaja: A Biography of Sawai Man Singh II*, 170.
53. Balraj Krishnan, *Sardar Vallabhbhai Patel: India's Iron Man*, 296.
54. Stanley Wolpert, *Shameful Flight: The Last Years of the British Empire in India*, 296.
55. 'Taming India's Princes', *The Scotsman*, 18 January 1949.
56. Ian Copland, 'The Princely States, the Muslim League, and the Partition of India in 1947', *The International History Review*, February 1991.
57. R.P. Singh and Kanwar Rajpal Singh, *Sawai Man Singh II of Jaipur: Life and Legend*, 109–10.
58. Alex von Tunzelmann, *Indian Summer: The Secret History of the End of an Empire*, 188.
59. Larry Collins and Dominique Lapierre, *Mountbatten and Independent India*, 14.
60. Catherine Asher, 'Jaipur: City of Tolerance and Progress', *Journal of South Asian Studies*, 2014. As Catherine Asher notes, despite Sawai Jai Singh's personal piety, he wanted to establish a city that would not give primacy to the followers of any particular faith, something that would not be possible if the city's many Hindu temples were visually dominant. The walled city's wide streets, suitable for processions by all communities, was part of this vision.
61. Gayatri Devi, *A Princess Remembers: The Memoirs of the Maharani of Jaipur*, 175.
62. Quentin Crew, *The Last Maharaja: A Biography of Sawai Man Singh II*, 178.
63. Ibid., 182.
64. 'Sadar Patel's Plane Landed in River Bed', *The Times of India*, 31 March 1949.
65. G.M. Nanundar (ed.), *Sadar Patel, In Tune with the Millions*, 69.
66. Ian Copland, *The Princes of India in the Endgame of Empire, 1917–1947*, 266.
67. Rima Hooja, 'The Garhs of Jaipur', https://www.indiaseminar.com/2014/660/660_rima_hooja.htm.

6. 'A COMBINATION OF SITA, LAKSHMI AND THE RANI OF JHANSI'

1. Quentin Crewe, *The Last Maharaja: A Biography of Sawai Man Singh II*, 187.
2. Ibid., 192.
3. Vicky Ward, 'Born to Fabulous Wealth, a Friend of Mick Jagger, the Playboy Prince who Died a Lonely Death from Drink', *Daily Mail*, 21 February 1997.

4. Arthur Watson, 'The Maharajah's Valentine', *Daily News*, 9 January 1952.

5. Lucy Moore, *Maharanis: The Lives and Times of Three Generations of Indian Princesses*, 247.

6. Arthur Watson, 'The Maharajah's Valentine', *Daily News*, 9 January 1952.

7. Lucy Moore, *Maharanis: The Lives and Times of Three Generations of Indian Princesses*, 247.

8. 'Maharaja Arrives Here to Buy US Machinery', *Los Angeles Times*, 4 September 1947.

9. Meena Vathyam, 'The Detours of Boris Lissanevitch: Shanghai, Shashlik and Tigers', academica.edu/38025433/The_Detours_of_Boris_ Shanghai_shashlik_and_tigers, n.p.

10. Leonard Lyons, 'The Lyons Den', *Salt Lake Tribune*, 8 December 1947.

11. Michel Peissel, *Tiger for Breakfast: The Story of Boris of Kathmandu*, 138.

12. IOR, Political Committee Memo, 9 May 1947, 13/1023.

13. Quentin Crewe, *The Last Maharaja: A Biography of Sawai Man Singh II*, 198–9.

14. Lucy Moore, *Maharanis: The Lives and Times of Three Generations of Indian Princesses*, 247.

15. Earl Wilson, 'The Maharaja', *San Francisco Examiner*, 12 May 1950.

16. Earl Wilson, 'Maharani From Smithtown Going to India to Join Mate', *San Francisco Examiner*, 31 October 1951.

17. Arthur Watson, 'The Maharajah's Valentine', *Daily News*, 6 January 1952.

18. 'Finds Indian Prince Makes Devoted Husband', *Daily News*, 12 December 1952.

19. Phillip Knightley and Caroline Kennedy, *An Affair of State: The Profumo Case and the Framing of Stephen Ward*, 38.

20. Ibid.

21. Douglas Thompson, *Stephen Ward: Scapegoat*, ebook.

22. Noel Whitcomb, 'The Vicki Martin I Knew', *Daily Mirror*, 10 January 1955.

23. Phillip Knightley and Caroline Kennedy, *An Affair of State: The Profumo Case and the Framing of Stephen Ward*, 40.

24. Douglas Thompson, *Stephen Ward: Scapegoat*, ebook.

25. Phillip Knightley and Caroline Kennedy, *An Affair of State: The Profumo Case and the Framing of Stephen Ward*, 40.

26. Noel Whitcomb, 'The Vicki Martin I Knew', *Daily Mirror*, 11 January 1955.

27. Noel Whitcomb, 'Good-bye to Vicki-From her Two Worlds', *Daily Mirror*, 15 January 1955.

28. *Selected Works of Jawaharlal Nehru*, Second Series, vol. 23, Jawaharlal Nehru Memorial Fund, New Delhi, 1998, 218.

29. Quentin Crewe, *The Last Maharaja: A Biography of Sawai Man Singh II*, 196.

30. Ibid., 201.

31. Ibid., 202.

32. Gayatri Devi, *A Princess Remembers: The Memoirs of the Maharani of Jaipur*, 265.

33. Pamela Mountbatten, *Daughter of Empire: Life as a Mountbatten*, 153.

34. Khushwant Singh, *Not a Nice Man to Know*, 120, 125.

35. Gayatri Devi, *A Princess Remembers: The Memoirs of the Maharani of Jaipur*, 258–9.

36. Ibid., 234.

37. Ibid., 273.

38. Muhammad Sher Ali Khan, *The Elite Minority, The Princes of India*, 208.

39. *The Indian Express*, 3 August 2009.

40. 'The Queen Sees the New India', *Tatler*, 8 February 1961.

41. *Illustrated London News*, 28 January 1961.

42. 'The Tiger That Started the Row', *Daily Herald*, 26 January 1961.

43. 'The Prince and the Tiger', *Daily Mirror*, 25 January 1961.

44. H.L. Erdman, *The Swatantra Party and Indian Conservatism*, 123.

45. 'Whistle-Stopping Maharani', *Time*, 10 November 1961.

46. 'Maharani Mixes Fun, Politics', *Chicago Daily Tribune*, 19 March 1962.

47. 'Whistle-Stopping Maharani', *Time*, 10 November 1961.

48. Ibid.

49. 'The Political Journey', *Daily News & Analysis*, 30 July 2009.

50. Gayatri Devi, *A Princess Remembers: The Memoirs of the Maharani of Jaipur*, 301.

51. Muhammad Sher Ali Khan, *The Elite Minority, The Princes of India*, 249.

52. Richard P.F. Holt (ed.), *The Selected Letters of John Kenneth Galbraith*, 198.

53. John Kenneth Galbraith, 'Plain Tales from the Embassy', *American Heritage*, vol. 20, no. 6, 1969.

54. Ibid.

55. Ibid.

56. Ibid.

57. Gayatri Devi, *A Princess Remembers: The Memoirs of the Maharani of Jaipur*, 314.

58. Lucy Moore, *Maharanis: The Lives and Times of Three Generations of Indian Princesses*, 265.

59. Gayatri Devi, *A Princess Remembers: The Memoirs of the Maharani of Jaipur*, 321.

60. Khushwant Singh, *Khushwant Singh's Book of Unforgettable Women*, 14.

61. Ibid.
62. Ibid., 15.
63. L.M. Eshwar, *Sunset and Dawn: The Story of Rajasthan*, 80.
64. Ibid., 80–1.
65. Interview, Zareer Masani, 16 January 2020.
66. Gayatri Devi, *A Princess Remembers: The Memoirs of the Maharani of Jaipur*, 324.
67. Quentin Crewe, *The Last Maharaja: A Biography of Sawai Man Singh II*, 218–20.
68. Gayatri Devi, *A Princess Remembers: The Memoirs of the Maharani of Jaipur*, 325.
69. Elisabeth Bumiller, 'Family Feud in the House of Jaipur', *Washington Post*, 2 January 1967.
70. 'The Political Journey', *Daily News & Analysis*, 30 July 2009.
71. L.M. Eshwar, *Sunset and Dawn: The Story of Rajasthan*, 71. Eshwar claims that Jai successfully pressured the Maharajkumar of Karauli to switch sides and join the Swatantra Party.
72. Ibid.
73. Ibid., 72.
74. Another sign that the House of Jaipur's allure was fading came in the 1968 by-elections for the state seats of Dausa and Chomu, both considered Swatantra strongholds. Ayesha nominated her stepson Pat to contest Dausa, but he was roundly defeated by Nawal Kishore Sharma, a Congress party worker running for his first election. Chomu also went to the Congress.
75. Dharmendar Kanwar, *Rajmata Gayatri Devi*, 107–8.
76. Gina Egan, unpublished manuscript, n.p.
77. 'Voice of Broadway', *Arizona Republic*, 3 September 1959.
78. Muhammad Sher Ali Khan, *The Elite Minority, The Princes of India*, 236.
79. Ibid.
80. Interview, Anne Wright, 29 August 2019.
81. Interview, Zafar Hai, 23 July 2015.
82. Gayatri Devi, *A Princess Remembers: The Memoirs of the Maharani of Jaipur*, 340.
83. Ibid., 57.
84. Interview, anonymous.
85. Gayatri Devi, *A Princess Remembers: The Memoirs of the Maharani of Jaipur*, 342.
86. V.P. Menon, *The Story of the Integration of the Indian States*, 477.
87. Ibid., 483.
88. NA (UK), India: Abolition of Privy Purses, New Delhi to Commonwealth Office, 14 August 1967, FCO 37/44, 1967.

89. D.R. Mankekar, *Mewar Saga: The Sisodias' Role in Indian History*, 179–80.
90. Gina Egan, unpublished manuscript, n.p.
91. Gayatri Devi, *A Princess Remembers: The Memoirs of the Maharani of Jaipur*, 349.
92. R.P. Singh and Kanwar Rajpal Singh, *Sawai Man Singh II of Jaipur: Life and Legend*, 171.
93. Gayatri Devi, *A Princess Remembers: The Memoirs of the Maharani of Jaipur*, 352.
94. Robert Stern, *The Cat and the Lion: Jaipur State in the British Raj*, 241.
95. Ibid., 240.
96. Sajjan Singh Rathore, *A Brave Son of Rajputana*, 83–4.
97. Quentin Crewe, *The Last Maharaja: A Biography of Sawai Man Singh II*, 232.

7. 'NO TIME TO PLUCK AN EYEBROW'

1. Jawaharlal Nehru, *Glimpses of World History*, 343.
2. Khushwant Singh, *Why I Supported the Emergency: Essays and Profiles*, 21.
3. Quentin Crewe, *The Last Maharaja: A Biography of Sawai Man Singh II*, 225.
4. 'The Last Prince', *The Observer*, 13 September 1970.
5. R.P. Singh and Kanwar Rajpal Singh, *Sawai Man Singh II of Jaipur: Life and Legend*, 180.
6. 'Keen Contest Likely in Jaipur', *The Times of India*, 11 February 1971.
7. Interview, Momin Latif, 19 January 2020.
8. Ibid.
9. 'Jumbos Will be Bought, Says Karan', *The Times of India*, 13 July 1971.
10. 'Productivity, More Jobs Linked: Karan', *The Times of India*, 3 April 1971.
11. Ann Morrow, *Highness: The Maharajas of India*, 236.
12. Gayatri Devi, *A Princess Remembers: The Memoirs of the Maharani of Jaipur*, 362.
13. D.R. Mankekar, *Accession to Extinction: The Story of Indian Princes*, 243.
14. Sajjan Singh Rathore, *A Brave Son of Rajputana*, 83.
15. 'Bubbles, The "King" who Tasted Life in the Trenches', *The Telegraph*, 23 January 2013.
16. 'Fearless and Fervent Armyman', *Daily News & Analysis*, 18 April 2011.
17. 'Holdup Man Gets $40,000 in Jewels', *The New York Times*, 27 October 1974.
18. Jim Shepherd, 'India's Modish Maharani Survives Even Armed Robbery in Style', *People*, 24 February 1975.

19. The *Time* story was cited by Congress member of the Rajya Sabha Kalyan Roy who erroneously linked it to Jaipur. See *Rajya Sabha Debates*, 25 February 1975, 35–6.

20. High Court of Delhi, *Col. Sawai Bhawani Singh & others* vs *Union of India & others*, 28 April 2010.

21. High Court, New Delhi, suit no. 870 of 1986, rejoinder affidavit, 14 January 1988.

22. 'Jaipur Gold Hoard', *The Times of India*, 18 March 1975.

23. Interview, Prithviraj Singh, 29 May 2019.

24. *Rajya Sabha Debates*, 6 May 1975, 233–4.

25. 'Speech and Proclamation', *The New York Times*, 27 June 1975.

26. Shah Commission of Inquiry Interim Report I, 11 March 1978, 81.

27. 'Rajmatas Narrate Tales of Political Vendetta', *The Times of India*, 15 November 1977.

28. Coomi Kapoor, *The Emergency: A Personal History*, ebook.

29. 'Rajmatas Narrate Tales of Political Vendetta', *The Times of India*, 15 November 1977.

30. NA (UK), Mountbatten to Oliver Foster, 30 July 1975, Political Situation in India, Confidential, FSE 1/2, Part G, 331–380, 1975.

31. Ibid., John Barrett to High Commissioner, 6 August 1975.

32. Ibid., Mountbatten to Forster, 5 September 1975.

33. Ibid., Forster to P.J.E. Male, 27 August 1975.

34. Coomi Kapoor, *The Emergency: A Personal History*, ebook.

35. Ananya Sengupta, 'Classic, Not Cotton, Saris in Tihar Jail', *The Telegraph*, 29 July 2009.

36. Ibid.

37. Although Ayesha records this in her memoir she would later deny it in an interview with Shekhar Gupta's *Walk the Talk* program on NDTV, saying not everything in the book was true. See *The Indian Express*, 3 August 2009 for a transcript of the interview.

38. 'Rajmata and the Dark Days of Emergency', *The Times of India*, 29 July 2009.

39. Ananya Sengupta, 'Classic, Not Cotton, Saris in Tihar Jail', *The Telegraph*, 29 July 2009.

40. Coomi Kapoor, *The Emergency: A Personal History*, ebook.

41. NA (UK), The Rajmata of Jaipur, Political Situation in India, Confidential, FSE 1/2, Part G, 331–380, 1975.

42. NA (UK), Political Situation in India, Michael Walker to FCO, 1 October 1975, FCO 37/1595, 1975.

43. Shah Commission of Inquiry Interim Report I, 11 March 1978, 81.

44. 'Indian Fort Reportedly Stuffed With Treasure', *Calgary Herald*, 29 September 1951.

45. John Lord, *The Maharajas*, 212.
46. Interview, Prithviraj Singh, 29 May 2019.
47. Ibid.
48. 'Hunt for Hidden Treasure in Jaipur On', *The Times of India*, 16 June 1976.
49. Interview, Prithviraj Singh, 29 May 2019.
50. 'I Don't Know Why They Go Back to Politics', *The Indian Express*, 3 August 2009.
51. Interview, Aman Nath, 28 August 2019.
52. Shah Commission of Inquiry Interim Report I, 11 March 1978, 82.
53. Ann Morrow, *Highness: The Maharajas of India*, 35.
54. 'I Don't Know Why They Go Back to Politics', *The Indian Express*, 3 August 2009.
55. Gayatri Devi, *A Princess Remembers: The Memoirs of the Maharani of Jaipur*, 246.
56. Vicky Ward, 'Born to Fabulous Wealth, a Friend of Mick Jagger, the Playboy Prince who Died a Lonely Death from Drink', *Daily Mail*, 21 February 1997.
57. 'Lt-Col James Allason', *The Independent*, 23 June 2011.
58. Vicky Ward, 'Born to Fabulous Wealth, a Friend of Mick Jagger, the Playboy Prince who Died a Lonely Death from Drink', *Daily Mail*, 21 February 1997.
59. Rajyashree Kumari Bikaner, *Palace of Clouds: A Memoir*, ebook.
60. Ibid.
61. 'Gayatri Devi', *The Independent*, 25 August 2009.
62. Interview, Belinda Wright, 29 August 2019.
63. Interview, Aman Nath, 20 March 2020.
64. Interview, M.R. Priyanandana Rangsit, 16 September 2019.
65. Ibid.
66. Ibid.
67. Vicky Ward, 'Born to Fabulous Wealth, a Friend of Mick Jagger, the Playboy Prince who Died a Lonely Death from Drink', *Daily Mail*, 21 February 1997.
68. Interview, Anne Wright, 29 August 2019.
69. Interview, M.R. Priyanandana Rangsit, 16 September 2019.
70. Jane Levert, 'Rajput Splendour Still Reigns in Rajasthan', *Hartford Courant*, 29 July 1979.
71. Ann Morrow, *Highness: The Maharajas of India*, 23.
72. Ibid., 36.
73. Gayatri Devi, *A Princess Remembers: The Memoirs of the Maharani of Jaipur*, 233.
74. Ann Morrow, *Highness: The Maharajas of India*, 36.

75. Gayatri Devi, *A Princess Remembers: The Memoirs of the Maharani of Jaipur*, 391.

76. Jessica Kerwin, 'Princess Grace', *W Magazine*, 1 December 2007.

77. Elisabeth Bumiller, 'Family Feud in the House of Jaipur', *Washington Post*, 3 January 1987.

78. Ibid.

79. Ibid.

8. THE MAHARANI'S MERCENARIES

1. Ann Morrow, *Highness: The Maharajas of India*, 35.

2. Elisabeth Bumiller, 'Family Feud in the House of Jaipur', *Washington Post*, 3 January 1987.

3. Ibid.

4. Interview, Anne Wright, 29 August 2019.

5. Interview, anonymous.

6. Interview, anonymous.

7. Interview, anonymous.

8. Interview, Aman Nath, 28 August 2019.

9. Ibid.

10. 'Padmini Devi: Living a Fairytale Life', *The First Ladies*, NDTV, 1 March 2009.

11. Interview, Aman Nath, 15 March 2020.

12. Interview, Prakash Bhandari, 7 September 2019.

13. Interview, anonymous.

14. Inder Sawhney, 'Family Feud', *The Illustrated Weekly of India*, March 1987.

15. Ritu Sarin, 'Royal Soap Opera', *Sunday*, 25 December 1986–1 January 1987.

16. Elisabeth Bumiller, 'Family Feud in the House of Jaipur', *Washington Post*, 3 January 1987.

17. Ritu Sarin, 'A Royal Soap Opera', *Sunday*, 25 December 1986–1 January 1987.

18. High Court of Delhi, *Maharaj Jagat Singh* vs *Lt. Col. Sawai Bhawani Singh & others*, suit no. 870/86, replication of the plaintiff on behalf to the written statement of defendant no. 1.

19. Ibid., index of schedule II of movable properties.

20. Ibid., replication of the plaintiff on behalf to the written statement of defendant no. 1.

21. Ibid., reply on behalf plaintiff no. 3 to the applications of plaintiffs nos. 1 & 2.

22. Ibid., list of documents attached to the affidavit of Smt. Urvashi Devi.

23. Ibid., replication of the plaintiff on behalf to the written statement of defendant no. 1.

24. Ritu Sarin, 'A Royal Soap Opera', *Sunday*, 25 December 1986–1 January 1987.

25. Ritu Sarin, 'A Royal Soap Opera', *Sunday*, 25 December 1986–1 January 1987.

26. Ibid.

27. High Court of Delhi, *Maharaj Jagat Singh* vs *Lt. Col. Sawai Bhawani Singh & others*, suit no. 870/86, report of the local commissioner, 8 September 1986.

28. Ibid.

29. Ibid. Statement by Amarendra Jit Singh Paul.

30. Ibid.

31. Ibid.

32. Rajasthan High Court, *Sangram Singh* vs *The State of Rajasthan*, 30 September 1977.

33. Pankaj Pachauri, 'Royal Battle Over Jaipur's Market', *The Times of India*, 22 February 1988.

34. Supreme Court of India, *Ramsharan Autyanuprasi* vs *Union of India & others*, 14 November 1988.

35. Pankaj Pachauri, 'Jaipur "Prince" Lt-Colonel Bhawani Singh Set to Join Congress (I)', *India Today*, 31 May 1988.

36. 'Ex-Maharaja Recollects Glory That was Jaipur's', *Ottawa Citizen*, 27 May 1988.

37. Christopher Thomas, 'T-Shirt Maharaja on Vote Chase', *The Times*, 31 October 1989.

38. Pankaj Pachauri, 'Jaipur "Prince" Lt-Colonel Bhawani Singh Set to Join Congress (I)', *India Today*, 31 May 1988.

39. Ibid.

40. Ibid.

41. 'Battle Royal', *Sunday*, 19–25 November 1989.

42. Reuters, 2 November 1989.

43. Reuters, 15 November 1989.

44. 'Battle Royal', *Sunday*, 19–25 November 1989.

45. John Fitzgerald, 'In Jaipur to Ogle the Ostentatious Palaces,' *The Globe and Mail*, 11 December 1996.

46. Interview, Kishore Singh, 17 January 2019.

47. Interview, Kuldeep Singh Garcha, 5 September 2019.

48. Ibid.

49. Jeerawat Na Thalang, 'Winning the Battle Royal', *Bangkok Post*, 18 October 2015.

50. Dharmendra Kanwar, *Rajmata Gayatri Devi*, 116.

51. *The Times of India*, 22 June 2004.
52. Interview, M.R. Priyanandana Rangsit, 26 February 2020.
53. Interview, Nick Spencer, 29 August 2019.
54. Ibid.
55. Interview, H.H. Maharaja Gaj Singh of Jodhpur, 7 September 2009.
56. Interview, Belinda Wright, 29 August 2019.
57. Interview, anonymous.
58. Vicky Ward, 'Born to Fabulous Wealth, a Friend of Mick Jagger, the Playboy Prince who Died a Lonely Death from Drink', *Daily Mail*, 21 February 1997.
59. Interview, Belinda Wright, 29 August 2019.
60. Interview, Nick Spencer, 30 August 2019.
61. Interview, Belinda Wright, 29 August 2019.
62. Vicky Ward, 'Born to Fabulous Wealth, a Friend of Mick Jagger, the Playboy Prince who Died a Lonely Death from Drink', *Daily Mail*, 21 February 1997.
63. Interview, Kishan Sen, 16 January 2019.
64. Interview, H.H. Maharaja Gaj Singh of Jodhpur, 7 September 2009.
65. Dharmender Kanwar, *Rajmata Gayatri Devi*, 116.
66. Interview, Belinda Wright, 29 August 2019.
67. Interview, Ayub Khan, 20 January 2020.
68. Sunil Mehra, 'Royal Knot', *Outlook*, 25 August 1997.
69. Interview, Aman Nath, 20 March 2020.
70. Jeerawat Na Thalang, 'Winning the Battle Royal', *Bangkok Post*, 18 October 2015.
71. Khushwant Singh, 'Beauty that Never Fades', *The Telegraph*, 8 August 2009.
72. Dharmendra Kanwar, *Rajmata Gayatri Devi*, 123.

9. A WEDDING, A WILL AND AN ADOPTION

1. Interview, Narendra Singh Rajawat.
2. 'A Royal Love Story', Rediff, https://m.rediff.com/style/nov/06diya.htm.
3. Ibid.
4. Ibid.
5. Ibid.
6. Ibid.
7. Ibid.
8. Interview, Durga Singh Mandawa, 31 August 2019.
9. Sunil Mehra, 'Royal Knot', *Outlook*, 25 August 1997.
10. Ibid.

11. Ibid.

12. *Trial by Fire: A Report on Roop Kanwar's Death*, Women and Media Committee, Bombay Union of Journalists, n.d., n.p.

13. Sunil Mehra, 'Royal Knot', *Outlook*, 25 August 1997.

14. 'A Royal Love Story,' Rediff, https://m.rediff.com/style/nov/06diya.htm.

15. Sunil Mehra, 'Royal Knot', *Outlook*, 25 August 1997.

16. Ibid.

17. Interview, Narendra Singh Rajawat, 28 May 2019.

18. Sunil Mehra, 'Royal Knot', *Outlook*, 25 August 1997.

19. Ibid.

20. 'A Royal Love Story', Rediff, https://m.rediff.com/style/nov/06diya.htm.

21. Interview, Narendra Singh Rajawat, 28 May 2019.

22. Rashme Seghal, 'Life is No Fairytale', *The Times of India*, 21 September 1997.

23. For a detailed description of the *Razmnama*, see Thomas H. Hendley, *Memorials of the Jeypore Exhibition, The Razm Namah or History of the War*, 1884.

24. High Court of Delhi, *Maharaj Jagat Singh* vs *Lt. Col. Sawai Bhawani Singh & others*, suit no. 870/86, report of the administrator-cum-receiver, B.J. Divan, 30 January 1994.

25. Ibid.

26. Ibid.

27. Ibid.

28. Ibid.

29. Interview, Narendra Singh Rajawat, 27 May 2019.

30. Pat said that Bubbles broached the subject with him only once. Interview, Prithviraj Singh, 29 May 2019.

31. Interview, Anne Wright, 29 August 2019.

32. Interview, Padmanabh Singh, 24 January 2020.

33. Rajeev Syal, 'Family Feud Erupts Over Heir to $1B Fortune', *National Post*, 30 December 2002.

34. Ibid.

35. Interview, Durga Singh Mandawa, 31 August 2019.

36. Siddharth Bose, 'Jaipur Royals Get a Crown Prince', *Hindustan Times*, 23 November 2002.

37. Rohit Parihar, 'Heir of Erstwhile Maharaja of Jaipur "Bubbles" Bhawani Singh Becomes a Contentious Issue', *India Today*, 9 December 2002.

38. Interview, Durga Singh Mandawa, 31 August 2019.

39. Rajeev Syal, 'Family Feud Erupts Over Heir to $1B Fortune', *National Post*, 30 December 2002.

40. Interview, anonymous.
41. Interview, Shivina Kumari, 30 January 2019.
42. 'Spreading the Royal Light', *Hindustan Times*, 6 May 2008.
43. High Court of Delhi, *Raj Kumar Devraj* vs *Jai Mahal Hotels Pvt. Ltd*, Co App 25 2011, pleading, 6 May 2003.
44. Letter from Prithviraj Singh to Tep Rangsit [Devraj Singh], 6 May 2003,
45. Anjali Puri, 'Jaipur's Siamese Twinge', *Outlook*, 14 August 2006.
46. Ibid.
47. Facsimile dated 14 August 2005, from Tep Rangsit [Devraj Singh] to the Rajmata of Jaipur.
48. High Court of Delhi, *Raj Kumar Devraj* vs *Jai Mahal Hotels Pvt. Ltd*, Co App 25 2011, reply on behalf of newly added respondent, being respondent no. 5 Urvashi Devi.
49. Ibid.
50. Interview, M.R. Priyanandana Rangsit, 16 September 2019.
51. Dean Nelson, 'Indian Royals Fight for Empire of the Hotels', *The Sunday Times*, 6 August 2006.

10. 'A BROTH SPICIER THAN A THAI CURRY'

1. Amelia Gentleman, 'India's Faded Royals Squabble Over Scraps', *International Herald Tribune*, 19 September 2006.
2. Anjali Puri, 'Jaipur's Siamese Twinge', *Outlook*, 14 August 2006.
3. Amelia Gentleman, 'India's Faded Royals Squabble Over Scraps', *International Herald Tribune*, 19 September 2006.
4. Anjali Puri, 'Jaipur's Siamese Twinge', *Outlook*, 14 August 2006.
5. 'Rajmata's Grandchildren Raise Palace Issue', *The Hindu*, 30 July 2006.
6. 'Jaipur Royals in Legal Battle', *Hindustan Times*, 29 July 2006.
7. Prakash Bhandari, 'My Uncles Misled Rajmata, Says Devraj', *The Times of India*, 29 July 2006.
8. Interview, M.R. Priyanandana Rangsit, 16 September 2019.
9. Prakash Bhandari, Step-Uncle Plays Host to Jaipur Scions', *The Times of India*, 30 July 2006.
10. Ibid.
11. Ibid.
12. High Court of Delhi, *Raj Kumar Devraj* vs *Jai Mahal Hotels Pvt. Ltd*, Co App 25 2011, reply on behalf of newly added respondent, being respondent no. 5 Urvashi Devi.
13. Interview, Anjali Puri, 30 October 2019.
14. 'Dubious Wills', *Outlook*, 14 August 2006.
15. Anjali Puri, 'Jaipur's Siamese Twinge', *Outlook*, 14 August 2006.
16. Prakash Bhandari, 'More Bad Blood in Jaipur Royal Feud Over Estate', *The Times of India*, 3 August 2006.

17. Amelia Gentleman, 'India's Faded Royals Squabble Over Scraps', *International Herald Tribune*, 19 September 2006.

18. 'After Children, Mother Joins Fight', *Hindustan Times*, 9 August 2006.

19. 'Jaipur Royal Scion Open to Out-of-Court Settlement', *Press Trust of India*, 13 August 2006.

20. Anjali Puri, 'Jaipur's Siamese Twinge', *Outlook*, 14 August 2006.

21. Amelia Gentleman, 'India's Faded Royals Squabble Over Scraps', *International Herald Tribune*, 19 September 2006.

22. 'On Jaipur battle, Gayatri Devi says: My son made a will, I will stand by it', *The Indian Express*, 7 August 2006.

23. Prakash Bhandari, 'Why This Injustice?', *The Times of India*, 27 August 2006.

24. District Court, Jaipur, *Rajmata Gayatri Devi & others* vs *State of Rajasthan*, reply on behalf of Rajkumar Devraj and Rajkumari Lalitya, case no. 134/1998.

25. Interview, Devraj Singh, 11 January 2020.

26. 'Elderly Fraudsters Jailed for Scam Sale', *The Telegraph*, 17 March 2009.

27. Rakhee Roy Talukdar, 'Royals Won't Tell What Gayatri Will Holds', *The Telegraph*, 16 August 2009.

28. Ibid.

29. Amelia Gentleman, 'India's Faded Royals Squabble Over Scraps', *International Herald Tribune*, 19 September 2006.

30. Interview, Devraj Singh, 11 January 2020.

31. Ibid.

32. Ibid.

33. District Court, Jaipur, *Rajmata Gayatri Devi & others* vs *State of Rajasthan*, reply on behalf of Rajkumar Devraj and Rajkumari Lalitya, case no. 134/1998.

34. Interview, Sudhir Kasliwal, 31 August 2019.

35. Interview, Devraj Singh, 21 January 2020.

36. Interview, Ayub Khan, 19 January 2020.

37. Amit Roy, 'London Friends Remember Ayesha', *The Telegraph*, 28 June 2010.

38. Interview, Momin Latif, 18 January 2020.

39. Richa Shukla, 'Her Grandson Remembers ...', *Daily News & Analysis*, 31 July 2009.

40. Interview, Ayub Khan, 19 January 2020.

41. 'She Wanted to Go Home, Says Doctor', *Daily News & Analysis*, 30 July 2009.

42. Interview Tripti Pandey, 22 January 2019.

43. 'Desert Queen Ends Colourful Journey', *The Times of India*, 30 July 2009.

44. 'Gayatri Devi', *The Times*, 31 July 2009.

45. 'Obituary: Gayatri Devi', *The Economist*, 20 August 2009.

46. 'The Maharani', *The Times of India*, 13 August 2006.

47. Interview, Timmie Kumar, 2 September 2009.

48. Interview, Prem Patnaik, 28 August 2019.

49. Interview, Aman Nath, 15 March 2020.

50. Interview, Kishore Singh, 5 June 2019.

51. In 2004, in a review of a posthumously issued album of Amancio D'Silva's music called *Integration*, the *Guardian* declared: 'Of all the attempts to bring together jazz and Indian music, this must be one of the most successful … [The tunes] strike a perfect balance between the two idioms, and there is none of that phoney "Eastern" flavouring, featuring sitars and such like … the music swings in a completely natural way.' See Naresh Fernandes, 'The Man with the Golden Guitar', http://www.tajmahalfoxtrot.com/?p=189.

52. Ann Morrow, *Highness: The Maharajas of India*, 36.

53. Madhu Trehan, 'Book Review of a Princess Remembers', *India Today*, 30 June 1977.

54. Interview, Akshay Chavan, 5 February 2019.

11. 'A TYPICAL PALACE INTRIGUE'

1. Robert Stern, *The Cat and the Lion: Jaipur State in the British Raj*, 5.

2. 'Rajmata Gayatri Devi Leaves Behind a Bitter Property Feud', *The Times of India*, 5 August 2009.

3. 'Who Will Inherit Rajmata's Wealth?', *The Economic Times*, 6 August 2009.

4. *Press Trust of India*, 9 August 2009.

5. 'Rajmata's Will to be Made Public Today?', *The Economic Times*, 9 August 2009.

6. 'She Left Her Will in Our Favour', *The Hindu*, 20 August 2009.

7. 'Differences Arise Over Rajmata's Will', *Daily News & Analysis*, 20 August 2009.

8. Randeep Ramesh, 'Death of Indian Princess Trigger Rancorous Row Over £200 Billion Estate', *The Guardian*, 1 September 2009.

9. 'Differences Arise Over Rajmata's Will', *Daily News & Analysis*, 20 August 2009.

10. Andrew Buncombe, 'A Battle of Wills', *The Independent*, 19 September 2009.

11. 'Gayatri Devi Was Only Tenant at Lily Pool, Claims her Step-Son', *The Indian Express*, 6 June 2010.

12. Interview, M.R. Priyanandana Rangsit, 16 September 2019.

13. Court of District and Sessions Judge, Jaipur City, suit no. 496/2010.

14. Court of District and Sessions Judge, Jaipur City, suit no. 32/2010.
15. Amit Roy, 'London Friends Remember Ayesha', *The Telegraph*, 28 June 2010.
16. Interview, Devraj Singh, 11 January 2020.
17. Ajay Singh, 'Army Lost a Soldier, Humble Man', *The Times of India*, 18 April 2011.
18. Ibid.
19. Shilpi Batra, 'Remembering a Royal Life', *Daily News & Analysis*, 18 April 2011.
20. Kishore Singh, 'Games ex-Royals Play', *Business Standard*, 14 May 2011.
21. 'Indian Schoolboy, 12, Crowned Maharaja of Jaipur', Agence France Presse, 28 April 2011.
22. Neha S. Bajpai, 'Best of Both Worlds', *The Week*, 16 September 2018.
23. Sudhanshu Mishra, 'Feudal Crown for Jaipur's Boy King', *Mail Today*, 29 April 2011.
24. *The Pioneer*, 4 May 2013.
25. Vishal Baristo, 'Inside Maharani Padmini Devi of Jaipur's 75th Birthday', *Vogue*, 4 October 2018.
26. 'Father's Biggest Mistake Was to Contest on Congress Ticket: Diya Kumari', *Sunday Guardian*, 14 September 2013.
27. Ibid.
28. 'Jaipur Princess Joins BJP', *The Telegraph*, 11 September 2013.
29. Sweta Dutta, 'The Princess Diaries', *The Indian Express*, 10 November 2013.
30. Radhika Ramaseshan, 'Pickle Princess and Bored Rajkumari', *The Telegraph*, 27 November 2013.
31. Rashpal Singh, 'Rajputs Bury Gotra Row, Decide to Back Diya', *Hindustan Times*, 23 November 2013.
32. The court's ruling stated: 'Even if the Will of GD [Gayatri Devi] is not taken into account, for purposes of issue of rectification, the documents clearly entitled the DR [Devraj] Group to have the rectification made.' It also said the CLB had no justification to reject Devraj and Lalitya's claim to their shares in the Jai Mahal Palace Hotel, Rambagh Palace Hotel, Sawai Madhopur Lodge and SMS Investment Corporation. 'The CLB failed to appreciate the scope of its jurisdiction as well as the scope of controversy between the parties. The High Court rightly allowed their appeal.' Supreme Court of India *Jai Mahal Hotels Pvt. Ltd* vs *Rajkumar Devraj & others* on 23 September, 2015. Civil appeal no. 7914 of 2015.
33. Jeerawat Na Thalang, 'Winning the Battle Royal', *Bangkok Post*, 18 October 2015.
34. National Company Law Tribunal, Bench III, New Delhi, C.P. no. 30/2006, 1 August 2018.

35. Ibid. Varadharajan also ordered a chartered accountant to be appointed as an independent auditor to audit the accounts from February 1997 until March 2018 and to examine the siphoning off of funds and their leakage. Any amounts would be recoverable from Pat and Vijit.

36. Rohit Parihar, 'Enemy at the Gates', *India Today*, 17 November 2016.

37. Urvashi Dev Rawal, 'Rajmahal Row', *Hindustan Times*, 31 August 2016.

38. *Press Trust of India*, 1 September 2016.

39. Rohit Parihar, 'Enemy at the Gates', *India Today*, 17 November 2016.

40. Sonia Mishra, 'Diya Kumari: A Princess in the Heat and Dust of Politics', 15 June 2019.

EPILOGUE

1. Interview, Kishore Singh, 17 January 2019.

2. Kera Godfrey, 'Royal Palace that Hosted Princess Diana is Now on Airbnb', *The Sun*, 12 November 2019.

3. Ibid.

4. *Hindustan Times*, 2 November 2019.

5. 'League of Lord Ram's Descendants in Rajasthan Gets Longer', *Outlook*, 15 August 2019.

6. 'Small Talk, The Fresh Prince of Jaipur', *Mumbai Mirror*, 6 September 2015.

7. 'The Millenial: New Muse of India's Luxury Market', *The Week*, 16 September 2018.

8. Interview, Padmanabh Singh, 24 January 2020.

9. Ibid.

10. Interview, Princess Diya Kumari, 24 January 2020.

11. Interview, Padmanabh Singh, 24 January 2020.

12. High Court of Delhi, GTR 2/1981, C.M. APPL. 5764/2013 & 45861/2016, *Commissioner of Income Tax* vs *Bhawani Singh & others*.

13. Interview, H.H. Gaj Singh, Maharaja of Jodhpur, 7 September 2009.

14. Ibid.

15. Interview, Prithviraj Singh, 29 May 2019.

16. Interview, M.R. Priyanandana Rangsit, 16 September 2019.

17. Interview, Ram Pratap Singh Diggi, 5 September 2019.

18. Ibid.

19. James Tod, *Annals and Antiquities of Rajasthan*, vol. 1, 181.

SELECT BIBLIOGRAPHY

Archives

National Archives of India (NAI), New Delhi.

Foreign and Political Department Proceedings, 1883, 1921, 1922, 1928, 1938, 1940, 1942.

Home Political, F-48–4, 1933.

Indian Office Records (IOR), British Library

Cooch Behar: Maharani of Cooch Behar; financial arrangements by the state; proposed curtailment of the allowances of the Cooch Behar family; tutor for Maharaja of Cooch Behar; powers of Maharani as Regent to be curtailed; unsatisfactory behaviour of the Maharani, L/PO/5/ 14 (I).

Cooch Behar: Maharani of Cooch Behar; guardianship and schooling of the minor Maharaja of Cooch Behar L/PO/5/15.

Cooch Behar: Regent and restrictions on her control over the family budget, R/1/1/1786.

Cooch Behar: Succession 1922; Minority Administration, L/PS/11/222.

MSS Eur, F111, vol. 161.

Political Committee Memo, 9 May 1947, 13/1023.

National Archives (NA), UK

India: Abolition of Privy Purses, FCO 37/44, 1967.

Political Situation in India, Confidential, FSE 1/2, Part G, 331– 380,1975.

Political Situation in India, FCO 37/1595, 1975.

Books and journals

Arnold, Edwin, *India Revisited*, Roberts Brothers, London, 1886.

Asher, Catherine B., *Jaipur: City of Tolerance and Progress*, South Asia: Journal of South Asian Studies, 2014, vol. 37, no. 3, pp. 410–30.

SELECT BIBLIOGRAPHY

Banerjee, Anil Chandra, *The Rajput States and the East India Company*, A. Mukherjee & Co., Calcutta, 1951.

Bikaner, Rajyashree Kumari, *Palace of Clouds: A Memoir*, Bloomsbury, New Delhi, 2018.

Bodley, John Edward Cortney, *The Coronation of Edward VII*, Methuen & Co., London, 1903.

Bumiller, Elisabeth, 'Family Feud in the House of Jaipur', *Washington Post*, 3 January 1987.

Butler, Iris, *The Viceroy's Wife: Letters of Alice, Countess of Reading, From India, 1921–25*, Hodder & Stoughton, London, 1969.

Choudhary, Manisha, 'Recruitment, Role and Hierarchy of Khojas-Nadars in the Amber-Jaipur State: A Study of the Rise of Eunuchs,' *Rajasthan History Congress, Proceedings*, vol. xxiii, December 2017, pp. 94–126.

———, The Court Protocol and Social Ordering in Jaipur State', *Journal of History and Cultural Studies*, vol. 1, no. 1, pp. 14–26.

Collins, Larry, and Dominique Lapierre, *Freedom at Midnight*, Collins, London, 1975.

———, *Mountbatten and Independent India*, Vikas, New Delhi, 1984.

Copland, Ian, *The Princes of India in the Endgame of Empire, 1917–1947*, Cambridge University Press, Cambridge, 2009.

———, 'The Princely States, the Muslim League, and the Partition of India in 1947', *The International History Review*, vol. 13, no. 1, February 1991, 38–69.

Crewe, Quentin, *The Last Maharaja*, Michael Joseph, London, 1985.

d'Abo, Ursula, *The Girl with the Widow's Peak: The Memoirs*, ebook, d'Abo Publications, London, 2014.

Devee, Sunity, *The Autobiography of an Indian Princess*, John Murray, London, 1921.

Devi, Gayatri, *A Princess Remembers: The Memoirs of the Maharani of Jaipur*, Rupa, New Delhi, 1995.

———, *A Princess Remembers: The Memoirs of the Maharani of Jaipur*, Vikas, New Delhi, 1982.

Egan, Gina, unpublished manuscript.

Erdman, H. L., *The Swatantra Party and Indian Conservatism*, Cambridge University Press, New York, 1967.

Fenwick, Simon, *Joan: The Remarkable Life of Joan Leigh Fermour*, Macmillan, London, 2017.

Fielding, Daphne, *Mercury Presides*, Eyre & Spottiswoode, London, 1954.

Forbes, Rosita, *India of the Princes*, E. P. Dutton & Company, New York, 1941.

Freitag, Jason, *Serving Empire, Serving Nation: James Tod and the Rajputs of Rajasthan*, Leiden, Brill, 2009.

Gaekwad, Fatesinhrao, *Sayajirao of Baroda, The Prince and the Man*, Popular Prakashan, Mumbai, 1989.

Galbraith, John Kenneth, 'Plain Tales from the Embassy', *American Heritage*, vol. 20, no. 6, 1969.

Gandhi, Sonia (ed.), *Two Alone, Two Together: Letters between Indira Gandhi and Jawaharlal Nehru, 1940–1964*, Hodder & Stoughton, London, 1992.

Gentleman, Amelia, 'India's Faded Royals Squabble Over Scraps', *International Herald Tribune*, 19 September 2006.

Gerhardi, William, *Memoirs of a Polyglot*, Duckworth, London, 1931.

Holt, Richard P.F. (ed.), *The Selected Letters of John Kenneth Galbraith*, Cambridge University Press, New York, 2017.

Hooja, Rima, 'The Garhs of Jaipur', https://www.india-seminar.com/2014/660/660_rima_hooja.htm.

Ismail, Mirza, *My Public Life: Recollections and Reflections*, George Allen & Unwin, London, 1954.

Jain, Kesharlal Ajmeria (ed.), 'Our Present Ruler', *The Jaipur Album*, Rajasthan Directories Publishing House, Jaipur, 1935.

Johnston, James, *Abstract and Analysis of the Report of the Indian Education Commission*, Hamilton, Adams & Co., London, 1884.

Jupp, James, *The Gaiety Stage Door: Thirty Years' Reminiscences of the Theatre*, Jonathan Cape, London, 1923.

Kanwar, Dharmendar, *Rajmata Gayatri Devi*, Roli Books, New Delhi, 2014.

Kapoor, Coomi, *The Emergency: A Personal History*, Penguin, New Delhi, 2018.

Keen, Caroline, 'The Power Behind the Throne: Relations between the British and the Indian States, 1870–1909', PhD thesis, University of London, 2003.

Khan, Muhammad Sher Ali, *The Elite Minority, The Princes of India*, S.M. Mahmud & Co., Lahore, 1989.

Khan, Nasrullah, *The Ruling Chiefs of Western India*, G. Claridge, Bombay, 1904.

Kipling, Rudyard, *From Sea to Sea: Letters of Travel*, Doubleday, New York, 1913.

Knightley, Phillip, and Caroline Kennedy, *An Affair of State: The Profumo Case and the Framing of Stephen Ward*, Jonathan Cape, London, 1987.

Krishnan, Balraj, *Sardar Vallabhbhai Patel: India's Iron Man*, Rupa, New Delhi, 2003.

Lateef, Ahmed Lateef, *Hyderabad to Hollywood*, n.d.

Lord, John, *The Maharajas*, Random House, New York, 1971.

Lownie, Andrew, *The Mountbattens: Their Lives and Loves*, Blink, London, 2019.

Mankekar, D. R., *Mewar Saga: The Sisodias' Role in Indian History*, Vikas, New Delhi, 1976.

——, *Accession to Extinction: The Story of Indian Princes*, Vikas, Delhi, 1974.

Mehra, Sunil, 'Royal Knot', *Outlook*, 25 August 1997.

Menon, V.P., *The Story of the Integration of the Indian States*, Orient Longman, Bombay, 1956.

Moore, Lucy, *Maharanis: The Lives and Times of Three Generations of Indian Princesses*, Viking, London, 2004.

Morrow, Ann, *Highness: The Maharajas of India*, Grafton Books, London, 1986.

Mountbatten, Pamela, *Daughter of Empire*, Simon & Schuster, London, 2013.

Muir, Peter, *This is India*, Doubleday, Doran, New York, 1943.

Nanundar, G.M. (ed.), *Sardar Patel: In Tune with the Millions*, Sardar Vallabhbhai Patel, Ahmedabad, 1976.

Nath, Aman, *Jaipur: The Last Destination*, India Book House, Mumbai, 2005.

Nehru, Jawaharlal, *Selected Works of Jawaharlal Nehru*, Second Series, vol. 23, Jawaharlal Nehru Memorial Fund, New Delhi, 1998.

Nehru, Jawaharlal, *Glimpses of World History*, Lindsay Drummond, London, 1954.

Pachauri, Pankaj, 'Jaipur "Prince" Lt-Colonel Bhawani Singh Set to Join Congress(I)', *India Today*, 31 May 1988.

Panchsheelm Prakashan, Jaipur, 1947.

Pahariya, N.C., *Political, Socio-Economic and Cultural History of Rajasthan*,

Parihar, Rohit, 'Enemy at the Gates' *India Today*, 17 November 2016.

Parika, Nandakisora, *Jaipur that Was: Royal Court and the Seraglio*, Subodh Sahitya Sadan, Jaipur, 2000.

SELECT BIBLIOGRAPHY

Peissel, Michel, *Tiger for Breakfast: The Story of Boris of Kathmandu*, E.P. Dutton, New York, 1966.

Puri, Anjali, 'Jaipur's Siamese Twinge', *Outlook*, 14 August 2006.

Rathore, Sajjan Singh, *A Brave Son of Rajputana*, Ethos Publication, Jaipur, 2015.

Report of the Indian Statutory Commission, vol. 1, H. M. Stationery Office, London, 1930.

Richards, John F., *The Mughal Empire*, part 1, vol. 5, Cambridge University Press, Cambridge, 1993.

Roe, Thomas, and John Fryer, *Travels in India in the Seventeenth Century*, Asian Educational Services, New Delhi, 1973.

Rousselet, Louis, *India and Its Native Princes: Travels in Central India*, Scribner, Armstrong & Co., New York, 1876.

Rubin, Barnett, *Feudal Revolt and State-building: The 1938 Sikar Agitation in Jaipur*, South Asian Publishers, New Delhi, 1983.

Sachdev, Vibhuti, 'Negotiating Modernity in the Princely State', *South Asian Studies*, vol. 8, no. 2, 171–81.

Sarin, Ritu, 'A Royal Soap Opera', *Sunday*, 25–1 January 1987.

Sawnhey, Inder, 'Family Feud,' *The Illustrated Weekly of India*, 1–7 March 1987.

Sengupta, Ananya, 'Classic, Not Cotton, Saris in Tihar Jail,' *The Telegraph*, 29 July 2009.

Seymour, Miranda, *Chaplin's Girl: The Life and Loves of Virginia Cherrill*, Simon & Schuster, London, 2009.

Shah Commission Of Inquiry Interim Report I, 11 March 1978.

Shepherd, Jim, 'India's Modish Maharani Survives Even Armed Robbery in Style', *People*, 24 February 1975.

Singh, Khushwant, *Khushwant Singh's Book of Unforgettable Women*, Penguin, New Delhi, 2000.

————, *Why I Supported the Emergency: Essays and Profiles*, Penguin, New Delhi, 2009.

————, *Not a Nice Man to Know*, Penguin, New Delhi, 2013.

Singh, Kishore, 'Games ex-Royals Play', *Business Standard*, 14 May 2011.

Singh, Nihal, *The King's Indian Allies: The Rajas and Their India*, Sampson, Low, Marsten & Co., London, 1916.

Singh, R.P., and Kanwar Rajpal Singh, *Sawai Man Singh II of Jaipur: Life and Legend*, Roli, New Delhi, 2005.

Stern, Robert, *The Cat and the Lion: Jaipur State in the British Raj*, E.J. Brill, Leiden, 1988.

SELECT BIBLIOGRAPHY

Tennyson, Lionel, *From Verse to Worse*, London, Cassell & Co., 1933.

Thalang, Jeerawat Na, 'Winning the Battle Royal', *Bangkok Post*, 18 October 2015.

Thompson, Douglas, *Stephen Ward: Scapegoat*, ebook, John Blake, London, 2014.

Tillotson, Giles, *Jaipur Nama: Tales from the Pink City*, Penguin, New Delhi, 2006.

Tod, James, *Annals and Antiquities of Rajasthan*, Humphrey Milford, London, 1920, vols. 1 & 2.

Tottenham, Edith, *Highnesses of Hindostan*, Grayson & Grayson, London, 1934.

'Trial by Fire: A Report on Roop Kanwar's Death', Women and Media Committee, Bombay Union of Journalists, n.d., n.p.

Tunzelmann, Alex von, *Indian Summer: The Secret History of the End of an Empire*, Henry Holt, New York, 2007.

Vathyam, Meena, 'The Detours of Boris Lissanevitch: Shanghai, Shashlik and Tigers', cademia.edu/38025433/The_Detours_of_Boris_Shanghai_/shashlik_and_tigers.

Waugh, Evelyn, *A Little Learning: The First Volume of an Autobiography*, Chapman & Hall, London.

'Whistle-Stopping Maharani', *Time*, 10 November 1961.

Wolpert, Stanley, *Shameful Flight: The Last Years of the British Empire in India*, Oxford University Press, Oxford, 2006.

ACKNOWLEDGEMENTS

This book would not have been possible without the help of the Jaipur royal family. I am particularly indebted to Maharaja Padmanabh Singh and his mother, Princess Diya Kumari, for agreeing to be interviewed and to Christopher Miller for facilitating our meeting. I would also like to thank the late Prithviraj Singh (Pat) and his son, Vijit Singh, for sharing their perspective on the House of Jaipur and to Vidya Devi, the wife of Jai Singh (Joey) who was unable to meet me due to health issues. Finally, I am indebted to M.R. Priyanandana Rangsit and her children, Devraj Singh and Lalitya Kumari Singh, for their patience in answering my many queries and for sharing rare and beautiful photographs of Gayatri Devi and Sawai Man Singh II. I would also like to thank His Highness Maharaja Gaj Singh of Jodhpur for taking time out of his busy schedule to impart his invaluable perspectives.

I have been honoured to work with two wonderful publishers. Without the enthusiastic support of Michael Dwyer at Hurst and Chiki Sarkar at Juggernaut in India I would never have had the pleasure of writing such a gripping and important story. When Nandini Mehta and Parth Mehrotra from Juggernaut approached me to write this book, I was taken aback by the scale of the project. Writing on Jaipur seemed superfluous, given the popularity of Gayatri Devi's memoir and the surfeit of coffee-table books on India's princely states. The more I delved into the subject the more I realized there was a paucity of recent historical books on Jaipur aside from Giles Tillotson's *Jaipur Nama* and Aman Nath's *Jaipur: The Last Destination*. Quentin Crewe's biography of Sawai Man Singh II has long been out of print and Robert Stern's excellent monograph *The Cat and the Lion* hardly exists outside a handful of libraries. I hope this book fills a much-needed gap, telling both the social and political history of Jaipur and the extraordinary family that shaped its evolution over the last century. The talented team at Juggernaut, including Arushi Singh and Jaishree Ram Mohan, put on a stellar performance to get this book into shape. My special thanks go out to Lara Weisweiller-Wu, Daisy Leitch and Allison Alexanian at Hurst for their hard work in bringing out the UK edition.

Writing this book entailed several trips to Jaipur, that most magical of Indian cities where I experienced the best of Rajput hospitality. While many people I interviewed asked to remain anonymous, the vast majority of those I approached in India and elsewhere were generous in sharing their contacts, keeping me focused and allowing me to record their thoughts and stories. The following list includes people in many countries and continents who helped make this book happen. My gratitude goes to Aayush Singh Rathore, Adhiraj Singh, Ali Khusru Jung, Aman Rai, Anjali Puri, Anne Wright, Ayub Khan, Belinda Wright, Bronwyn Latif, Chandra Vijay Singh, Chhavi Rajawat, Christine Rai, David Armstrong, Dharmendar Kanwar, Divya Jhala, Durga Singh Mandawa, Elizabeth Lagercrantz de Charmoy, Giles Tillotson, Prem 'Gudu' Patnaik, Gulab Singh, Indira Dhanrajgir, Indranil Halder, Jagat Singh, Jagdeep Singh, Jyotika Pratap Singh, Kishan Sen, Kishore Singh, Kuldeep Singh Garcha, Louis Henry d'Emmerez de Charmoy, Mahiraj Singh, Manisha Choudhary, Manju Kumari Shivraj Singh, Mita Kapur, Momin Latif, Narendra Singh Rajawat (ex-husband of Princess Diya Kumari), Narendra Singh Rajawat (Rajput Sabha), Naresh Fernandes, Nick Spencer, Pia Narayan, Prakash Bhandari, Pramod Kumar, Rajeshwar Singh, Ram Pratap Singh, Rima Hooja, Sajjan Singh Rathore, Samir Kasliwal, Sanjoy Roy, Santi Chowdhury, Shaktik Singh, Sharon Irani, Shivraj Singh, Shivina Kumari, Sidharth Bhatia, Sudhir Kasliwal, Sunil Mehra, Timmie Kumar, Tripti Pandey, Usha Balakrishnan, William Dalrymple, Zafar Hai and Zareer Masani. As always, I must thank the patient and professional librarians and archivists at the National Archives of India in New Delhi and at the British Library in London. Finally, I must mention the great team at the Pearl Palace Hotel, my refuge of choice in Jaipur from the searing heat of summer, the monsoon rains and those chilly winter days.

INDEX

INDEX

INDEX

INDEX

INDEX

INDEX

INDEX